SOUNDING OUR WAY HOME

*Japanese American Musicking
and the Politics of Identity*

SUSAN MIYO ASAI

University Press of Mississippi / Jackson

The University Press of Mississippi is the scholarly publishing agency of
the Mississippi Institutions of Higher Learning: Alcorn State University,
Delta State University, Jackson State University, Mississippi State University,
Mississippi University for Women, Mississippi Valley State University,
University of Mississippi, and University of Southern Mississippi.

www.upress.state.ms.us

DON'T FENCE ME IN (from *Hollywood Canteen*)
Words and Music by COLE PORTER
© 1944 (Renewed) WC MUSIC CORP.
All Rights Reserved
Used by Permission of ALFRED MUSIC

The University Press of Mississippi is a member of the Association of University Presses.

Any discriminatory or derogatory language or hate speech regarding race,
ethnicity, religion, sex, gender, class, national origin, age, or disability
that has been retained or appears in elided form is in no way
an endorsement of the use of such language outside a scholarly context.

Copyright © 2024 by University Press of Mississippi
All rights reserved

∞

Library of Congress Control Number: 2023948590

Hardback ISBN 978-1-4968-4763-8
Paperback ISBN 978-1-4968-4764-5
Epub single ISBN 978-1-4968-4765-2
Epub institutional ISBN 978-1-4968-4766-9
PDF single ISBN 978-1-4968-4767-6
PDF institutional ISBN 978-1-4968-4768-3

British Library Cataloging-in-Publication Data available

This book is dedicated to Glenn Horiuchi (1955–2000)—innovative pianist, shamisen player, and composer. Glenn's music embodied an inventive spirit guided by the history of people's struggle against political and social injustices. Yet his music was also informed by everyday life and abiding artistic integrity. Glenn's wry sense of humor, evident especially in his later pieces, and his practice of Zen Buddhism added complexity to his music, revealing the heterogeneous nature of Asian American creativity.

The following tributes by two musician-composers, posted on the now-inactive website Asian Improv ("Remember Glenn," November 29, 2000, https://www.asianimprov.com/glennstribute.htm), are a testament to Glenn's humanity and musical genius.

> Glenn's loss is a tragedy beyond anything I can express with words. He was a seeker of truth and beauty. He found what he was seeking, and he passed it on to us. That's his legacy. The tragedy lies in the fact that he left us so soon, that he was still unveiling deeper and deeper layers of truth and beauty through his art, and that he leaves a loving wife and son, grieving parents, and countless friends and supporters asking, "Why Glenn?" We have no answers to this question. We can only honor his legacy, his immense contributions, and pull our ranks closer together and appreciate the beauty in each other and in each new day.
> —Art Sato, KPFA

> I just wanted to share my heart's gratitude for his inspired teachings. Beyond the great loss and miss of his profound artistry and personal nature, there will now forever be good lessons to be learned from reflection on the being behind every utterance of his name—Glenn Horiuchi. Now we must prepare, for where creative forces of art stand fearlessly for truth through musical expression, his unbound spirit and thought [are] there, more capable of intimately inhabiting all such endeavors. Now we are drawn closer towards a path he himself helped carve many times through his music: a path of living enlightenment.
> —With heartfelt thanks,
> Hafez Moderizadeh

CONTENTS

ix   **ACKNOWLEDGMENTS**

xiii   **PREFACE**

3   **CHAPTER 1** • The Nexus of Music, Identity, and Politics

21   **CHAPTER 2** • Dual Identities: Japanese Immigrant Community, Identity, and Music

55   **CHAPTER 3** • Caught on the Cultural Cusp: Nisei Politics of Identity and Music

119   **CHAPTER 4** • "Buddhahead Blues": Musical Communities in the US Concentration Camps of World War II

171   **CHAPTER 5** • Sansei: The Political Advocacy of Music and a Turn toward the East

261   **EPILOGUE** • The Promise of Interracial Music Coalitions

269   **GLOSSARY**

275   **NOTES**

303   **BIBLIOGRAPHY**

315   **INDEX**

ACKNOWLEDGMENTS

The journey in writing this book involved many individuals who contributed their insights, knowledge, suggestions, experiences, and hopes along the way. My grandfather Matsujiro Asai, a proud and determined man who boldly sought to become an American citizen at the turn of the twentieth century, is the inspiration for *Sounding Our Way Home*. His remarkable autobiography chronicles not only his family's long lineage in Japan but his modern views and a desire to see the world, which he fulfilled by moving to the United States to start a new life, initially working as a mess attendant in the US Navy, which took him to many parts of the globe. My deep appreciation of Japanese culture began with him. As a child, my exposure to Japanese culture through art objects and artifacts that my grandfather had collected and bequeathed to my extended family left a distinct impression, culminating in my decision as a young adult to live in Japan and explore my cultural roots.

Being socially marginalized as an American of Japanese descent pushed me to interrogate the politics surrounding my Japanese American identity. I want to acknowledge Joyce Nako and other Sansei staff members with whom I worked at the Japanese American Cultural and Community Center, Los Angeles, during the 1980s for raising my political awareness of what it is to be Japanese American. The rise and celebrated success of the mostly Japanese American band Hiroshima opened avenues for me to think about and contribute on the *koto* (thirteen-string zither) to musicking that expressed my Japaneseness. It is for *Yonsei* (fourth generation), *Gosei* (fifth generation), and future generations of Japanese Americans that I write the history of three generations of musicking so they may know the legacy of "artivist" Japanese American musicians as they embark on their own life's journey.

The location of the University of California, Los Angeles (UCLA), where I completed my doctoral studies, prompted my interest in Japanese American musicking as I continued studying and performing Japanese koto. It was serendipitous that my time in Los Angeles in the 1970s and 1980s was a period in which Japanese/Asian Americans were actively building a subculture that highlighted music, the visual arts, literature, dance, and theater. The Asian American band Hiroshima, Visual Communications (media arts), East West Players, *Gidra* (an Asian American community magazine), and Great Leap seeded arts activism, prompting writers, musicians, visual artists, and filmmakers to voice their identities and political struggles.

This book would not have been possible without the many Nisei and Sansei from California that I interviewed. They are too many to enumerate here, but the reader will encounter their spirited accounts within the chapters of this book. Their willingness and candor enlivens the narrative in this volume, providing me with the material I needed to support the framework of this study. It was a joy and honor to have shared their personal stories.

My heartfelt thanks go to family and friends for their love and support as I journeyed to finish this project spanning more than two decades. Special recognition goes to my husband, Thezeus Sarris, whose critical reading and feedback on every word I wrote brought clarity to my ideas. His constant emotional support and encouragement made it possible to bring closure to this volume.

Many thanks to colleagues and friends who took the time to read and comment on the chapters of this book: Robin Chandler, Ann Fleisher, Ann Galligan, Brenda Romero, Adelaide Reyes-Schramm, and Lorraine Sakata. Brilliant was Katherine Lee's suggestion to use Kay Shelemay's musical communities model as I searched for a framework to present the data I had amassed about musicking in the concentration camps of World War II. In regard to the chapter dedicated to musicking in the camps, special thanks go to Prof. Reyes-Schramm who graciously agreed to read about musicking in these unique circumstances, steering me toward a more in-depth analysis of the "musical-communities" model by posing questions shaped by the local circumstances and conditions of the camps. In formulating questions to test the use of Shelemay's musical-communities model against my data, I formed a more substantial conclusion that could be useful in other studies. Recognition also goes to colleagues at Northeastern University: Rei Okamoto for translating titles to Japanese songs and compositions presented in this study and Joshua Jacobson for recommending readings on musicking in the Jewish concentration camps in Germany. I appreciate the support of my friend and fellow faculty member Ronald Smith for forwarding me articles relevant to Japanese/Asian American issues and musicking, enhancing objectivity in my research. I express gratitude to fellow ethnomusicologist Minako Waseda, whose scholarship, similar to my own, aided my retrieval of data from Japanese sources. As well, I acknowledge Christine Oka, librarian at Northeastern University, for her assistance in collecting data and photographs and by alerting me to materials pertinent to my study.

PREFACE

It was my immigrant grandfather's diligence and desire to belong that ultimately planted the idea for this book. This is an immigrant story. A story of America.

A New York City girl by birth, I did not have the typical upbringing of Japanese Americans on the West Coast, where greater numbers formed communities with shared cultural, social, and economic ties. In the 1950s, the community in which I belonged consisted of a small contingent of Japanese Americans in New York City and extended family members. When I turned six, my community narrowed to just family gatherings after moving upstate, following my father's employment at IBM Research Center.

There were always visceral reactions to my "Asianness" while I was living in suburban New York, fifty miles north of the city. Middle school was particularly isolating. My parents imparted to my siblings and I inviolable pride in being Japanese, giving me the strength to defend my heritage whenever necessary. Besides, who would question the unprecedented recovery and growth of postwar Japan as proof of Japanese people's work ethic and determination? The exceptionalism of being the "token Asian" in every school I attended before matriculating at UCLA impelled me to learn more about my cultural origins. As a musician, the most natural way to grasp the ethos of Japanese culture was to play traditional music to comprehend its underlying aesthetic and function.

Visits to my grandparents on 135th Street in Manhattan were a memorable experience. Their apartment was filled with Japanese swords and an array of bronze and cloisonne vases and other Japanese artifacts. By far, the most riveting was a full-length suit of samurai armor with a splendid helmet adorned with a fierce and lifelike warrior's mask; my siblings and I dashed by it in terror and awe. Such were my first encounters with Japanese culture in America, vivid memories that were a spark in claiming my Japanese American identity.

Matsujiro Asai, my paternal grandfather, took a keen interest in Japanese swords as a young man in Japan. As his sword collection grew, he became well known among sword enthusiasts for his knowledge, forming a Japanese sword society in his hometown of Osaka. He later sold his collection of swords to pay for his and my grandmother's passage to the United States. After settling in and raising a family first in Houston, Texas, and then in Ithaca, New York, my grandfather moved to New York City to be near his adult children. His passion for swords rekindled, he started a business buying and selling Japanese and Chinese art objects and antiques, becoming well known for his expertise, and eventually being hired by the Metropolitan Museum of Art in New York as a consultant for their sword collection. My grandfather's sense of tradition and pride in the family's Japanese relics prompted me to own my cultural heritage. As a child, Kabuki theater music resonated with me, and I remember dancing around the living room without restraint to a recording that was part of my parents' collection. From Japanese friends of the family, I also learned that I was the seventeenth generation of the Asai family; a clan that had governed territory near Lake Biwa in central Japan. My deep familial connection and desire to know more about a culture that seemed so distant became my muse.

After completing undergraduate studies in music education at Ithaca College, my muse took me to Japan for a year and a half. Trained as a pianist and oboist, I studied traditional Japanese music while teaching English to support my endeavor. Encouraged to learn the koto as part of my cultivation as a young woman, I quickly found a teacher and began lessons. Learning to play the koto was a tangible way to experience Japanese culture firsthand, and this foreshadowed my decision to earn a degree in ethnomusicology. My study and performance of this instrument throughout my graduate-student days begged certain internal questions: Why am I playing the koto? And what meaning does playing this instrument have for me as a Japanese American?

Being enrolled in the ethnomusicology program at UCLA in the 1970s coincided with the Asian American movement galvanizing Asian American political activity at the national level. I was swayed by Japanese American activists empowered by this movement while working part-time for the Japanese American Cultural and Community Center (JACCC) in Little Tokyo, Los Angeles. My coworkers' political convictions and activism solidified and reinforced my ethnic identity. The Asian American movement led by college students, community activists, and cultural workers, especially on Californian college campuses and in cities, energized my generation and raised our awareness of the inequities we face, emboldening us to take a stand for equal representation, access, and a national voice.

> **U. S. DEPARTMENT OF LABOR**
> **NATURALIZATION SERVICE**
>
> OFFICE OF CHIEF EXAMINER
> WASHINGTON, D.C.
>
> 312 Federal Building,
> San Antonio, Texas.
>
> FILE NUMBER
> 370
>
> Please refer to this number in replying
>
> Fort Worth, Texas, March 21, 1916.
>
> Mr. M. Asai,
>   R. F. D. # 2,
>   Houston, Texas.
>
> Dear Sir:-
>
>   I beg to acknowledge the receipt of your letter of the 17th instant, in which you state that the Clerk of the District Court of the United States at Houston referred you to me for information as to whether, or not, you can become a citizen of the United States.
>
>   You are advised that Section 2169 R. S. U. S. declares that the following persons only can be naturalized:
>
> "Free white persons or persons of African nativity or descent"
>
>   Some Courts have passed on the question as far as Japanese are concerned and have ruled that they cannot.
>
>   Each case stands on its own merits and you have the right to file your petition, upon paying the required fee of $4.00, with your petition you must file a copy of your declaration of intention and have your petition witnessed by two witnesses, both citizens of the United States, who can make affidavit that they have known you for at least five years. The petition will then be posted for hearing at the next term of court and at that time the Judge of the Court will decide the question you have asked.
>
>   As the Court must pass on each and every application you can see that I cannot tell you in advance what the Court will do. I shall be in Houston on April 5 and can be reached at the Clerk's office.
>
>   Very truly yours,
>   *[signature]*
>   Naturalization Examiner.

Figure P.1. Grandfather Asai's rejection letter for US citizenship, 1916. Courtesy of Asai Family Collection.

Awakened politically to the historically unjust treatment of Japanese Americans before, during, and after World War II hit close to home when I learned that my paternal grandfather's request for citizenship had been denied by the Naturalization Service of the US government in Fort Worth, Texas, where he first resided. The rejection letter (figure P.1) he received on March 21, 1916, states:

> You are advised that Section 2169 R.S. [Revised Statutes] US declares that the following persons only can be naturalized:
> "Free white persons or persons of African nativity or descent."

Deep disappointment did not dispel his hopes of creating a niche for his family in the United States. A progressive and curious man who had left Japan at the age of eighteen to see the world, traveling on various US naval ships as a messman, my grandfather mastered the restaurant business and later fruit, vegetable, and dairy farming to support his family. In 1920, he moved his family from Houston, Texas, to Ithaca, New York, to fulfill a dream of educating his nine children at a coed Ivy League institution. Seven of his nine children, including four daughters, attended Cornell University. This story exemplifies the aspirations of immigrant families who have built their lives in the United States. I devote this study to emigrant groups coming to this country with visions of a better life and a desire to belong.

SOUNDING OUR WAY HOME

CHAPTER 1

The Nexus of Music, Identity, and Politics

> *A persistent form of dehumanization against Asian Americans is the erasure of our longstanding involvement in this country, including its music. By looking to the past, and to each other, we might be able to strengthen our collective sense of belonging. We might recognize ourselves anew.*
>
> —Cat Zhang, "What Is Asian American Music Really?"[1]

Nativist national identities are a growing worldwide phenomenon. Populist nationalism in the United States and Europe has shifted the political discourse to the radical right. The crisis of more than 100 million refugees in search of safety and opportunity, surging from 2015 on, continues to send shockwaves throughout the planet, resulting in increased anxiety about national and cultural identity in many Western nation-states considered desirable destinations.

Spiraling anti-immigration sentiments and growing populist nativism in the United States are part of a continuing legacy that narrowly defines who belongs. Former president Donald Trump's blunt, anti-immigration rhetoric whipped up immigration policies aimed at slashing legal immigration in half. Trump's platform and his supporters' beliefs reinforce a long history of white nationalism that strives to "Make [White] America Great Again." The debate about national identity and who is deserving of citizenship is reaching a fever pitch, undercutting the foundational legacy of the United States as a haven for those seeking safety and greater opportunities.

Such nativist sentiments prompted journalists in 1995 to interrogate what an "American" is in a series of articles featured in the July 10 publication of *Newsweek* magazine. In answering this question, journalist Jerry Adler writes about the continual evolution of the American cultural landscape brought on by a dizzying number of popular trends in "fashion, slogans, ideologies, religions, artistic movements, economic theories, therapeutic disciplines, cults and dogmas in fabulous profusion."[2] Intercultural and cross-cultural trends proliferate as we enter the second decade of the twenty-first century. Within this discourse, another question surfaces: Is the United States "too big, too diverse to hold together" as a nation?[3] I advance the ideal that our pluralistic society holds great potential if we can navigate a path toward becoming a nation where people can share and benefit from varying cultural viewpoints.

A new trope is needed to counter the simplistic majority-minority myth[4] that increasingly polarizes Americans. A more inclusive narrative must counter the racist "replacement" theory propagated by the television personality Tucker Carlson, formerly of Fox News, which holds that elites are working to replace the white population with minority immigrants in a "stolen America." The story of America is progressively complex, as witnessed by the rising ethno-racial mixing within a sizable swathe of the population. We must embrace an expanding US demographic and its concomitant sociocultural changes that could transform society for the better.

WHO BELONGS?

As a member of a racial group that historically has been subjected to exclusionist policies, I am impelled to speak to the issue of belonging in US national culture. The idea of belonging is poignantly critiqued in *Time* magazine's November–December 2018 feature essay, "American Like Me," which examines who gets to be an American. Based on his own experience, writer Viet Thanh Nguyen, a Vietnamese American born in Vietnam and raised in southern California, addresses mainstream American society's need for "an Other to define its boundaries and funnel its fears."[5] The subtext to the essay's title, "What It Means to Love My Country, No Matter How It Feels about Me," is a doleful testament to the xenophobic attitude of the United States toward immigrants. Nguyen, while expressing a close connection to his Vietnamese roots, also claims America as his own. He espouses the idea that the American flag and anthem stands for democracy, equality, justice, hope, peace, and freedom, decrying their use as emblematic badges that bar newcomers and create division. The essay closes with Nguyen continuing to question his place in America. By acknowledging the history and contributions of all who have made the United States their home, we can build an ethos that promotes our "interdependence and collective obligation" to defuse racial bigotry and instead build connections.[6]

The present discourse examines the issue of who belongs by interposing Japanese American musicking as a path to forge a more inclusive national identity—an outcome that has ramifications for all immigrants who settle in the United States. The question that arises is, Can musicking inform us of shifting and transformed identities along generational lines within a sociopolitical history of exclusion and dislocation? The expansive definition of musicking is particularly useful in studying early Japanese American communities where musical performances centered on the social relationships of all involved, affirming a sense of self and inventing a place of belonging. In Christopher Small's words, "when we have been present at a good and satisfying musical performance, we feel more fully ourselves, more fully realized, and more in tune with ourselves and with our fellows."[7] I prefer using the term "musicking" for its intentional inclusion of all involved in a musical event. The alternate term "music making" does not readily include an audience or personnel indispensable for the efficacy of a performance. For Japanese immigrants and their offspring, musicking was and continues to be a creative means of survival and *communitas*. Knowing what came before provides a foundation, a direction for future generations. To this end, by chronicling Japanese American musicking, this work aspires to make a modest contribution.

Sounding Our Way Home is a response to calls for greater activism in musical scholarship that interrogates the political agency of musicking.[8] This study examines the interventions of Japanese American music makers in their quest to reconfigure their political and social location and reach for greater acceptance within US society. The political dimension of musicking has become increasingly important with the rise of theoretical frameworks that engage postcolonialism, postmodernism, identity politics, diaspora studies, and transnationalism.[9] Intersecting studies of Japanese American musicking and identity politics underscore the agency Japanese Americans exercise in finding their voice to build political, cultural, and social capital. Throughout the ages, through their art, musicians have served as agents of political change and social transformation. Thus, Sansei—literally "third generation"—constructed alternative identities as part of a politics of resistance. Beginning in the late 1960s and 1970s, the activism of a group of Sansei and other Asian American artists coalesced around building an alternate culture to socially and politically represent themselves. The creation of such cultural sites aligns with Lisa Lowe's assertion, "the question of aesthetic representation is always also a debate about political representation."[10] Such sites serve as models for other minority populations in the United States. In *Immigrant Acts: On Asian American Cultural Politics*, Lowe opens her book with the controversy surrounding the design and representation of the Vietnam War Memorial in Washington, DC, by a young Chinese American architect, Maya Lin.[11] The dispute accentuates the importance of establishing one's social and political representation in a nation and addresses Grace Lee Boggs's belief that "you cannot change any society unless you take responsibility for it, unless you see yourself as belonging to it and responsible for changing it."[12] The continuing sociopolitical challenges Japanese and other Asian Americans face in gaining mainstream acceptance elucidate the ongoing trials of immigrants and their offspring who yearn to make the United States their home, urging greater activism in fostering participation and inclusion.

As a Sansei musician, I turn to musicking to investigate the complexities around identity and an implicit sense of belonging in a population considered beyond the racial and ethnic boundaries of American citizenship. This project discusses identities and additional stances from which one could choose: a diasporic space as experienced by immigrant Issei whose Japanese practices and customs were altered by living in an American cultural milieu; a liminal space as experienced by most Nisei as they attempted to assimilate; a transcultural space developed by Sansei as they disputed whiteness and instead sought to embrace their ethnic heritage; or an intercultural space characterized by an overlapping of two or more cultures to create new identities as illustrated in the collaborations of African American, Latinx, and Asian American musician-composers. My own identity continues to unfold as I constantly negotiate the cultures that define me. I view my own years of musical training, performing European classical piano and oboe, studying Japanese koto and dabbling in jazz, not merely as aesthetic pursuits but a means to belong in the culture at large while acknowledging my ethnic heritage. Throughout my formative years and adult life, a preference for the jazz medium fed my growing awareness of the sociocultural meanings and resistance frequently expressed in African American music. In building a transculturated space, I have participated in a variety of musical worlds: European classical, Japanese, African American, and American popular. The strong aesthetic sensibilities imbued in traditional Japanese music and of African American music fortified my regard for their aesthetic and affective dimension. Music offers us possibilities in transforming our social space, self-expression, and communal sharing and serves as a vehicle for resistance. As an integral component of culture, music embodies aesthetic experience that can operate as a socially, emotionally, and culturally validating force. Central to this study is how Japanese Americans utilize music to establish and mediate their ethnic boundaries and sociopolitical locations as their circumstances shift.

Tracing my Issei grandparents', Nisei parents', and my own Sansei generations' aspirations to *feel* at home in the United States provides an intimate backdrop to studying links between musicking and identity formation of three generations of Japanese Americans. In his study of the South American Japanese diaspora, Dale A. Olsen articulates a similar process to the one that Japanese North Americans share. The construction and negotiation of politicized identities and how they are represented involve multiple layers: the maintaining of ethnic boundaries overlaid with layers of reconciled homeland versus host-land cultural adaptations, further thickened by transcultural-related adjustments to the meaning and practice of musicking.[13] *Sounding Our Way Home* takes us on a journey to reach "home" through musicking and the sense of belonging that reconciling one's identity engenders. In *Cartographies of Diaspora: Contesting Identities*, Avtar Brah distinguishes two conceptions of "home." The first places "home" within the context of a nation's narratives through which racialized or nationalist discourses signify a group's settlement "'in' a place but not 'of' it."[14] This conception chronicles the Issei's—first generation Japanese immigrants—marginalized position, socially, politically, and economically, in the United States in the early twentieth century. The idea of "home" was notably unattainable in California due to policies and laws limiting citizenship and landownership and the other discriminatory sanctions against Japanese Americans in this state. Brah's second account of "home" is "the site of everyday lived experience. It is a discourse of locality, the place where feelings of rootedness ensue from the mundane and the unexpected of daily practice."[15] The first generation to be born on American soil, Nisei, considered themselves "of" the United States, rooted in middle-class life, yet found themselves on the outside, sharing the same disenfranchisement as their Issei parents. Third generation Sansei, although further assimilated, continue to live under the incessant guise of being perpetual foreigners. Thus, as the sociopolitical winds of change dictate strategies to achieve a sense of belonging, the three generations' varying conceptions of "home," reflected in their musicking and their sense of self, differ.

How does cultural practice, in this case music, relate to a discussion of national belonging? Lowe persuasively identifies US national culture as the political force that shapes American citizenry: "The legal and political forms of the nation have required a national culture in the integration of the differentiated people and social spaces that make up 'America,' a national culture, broadly cast yet singularly engaging, that can inspire diverse individuals to identify with the national project."[16] Lowe defines the role of culture as not only a means through which one identifies and connects to a "national collective" but also as a locus to reconcile one's history that, in the case of Asian Americans, breaches universals of the national collective. Although citizenship is commonly equated with meeting official requirements, a more visionary interpretation of American citizenship stems from an ethos created by not only history, narratives, and events but by language, customs, celebrations, and forms of artistic expression that contribute to the social and political fabric of this country. Further, journalist and culture critic Jeff Chang points to culture as an important means of advancing and promoting a national identity. He singles out Canada, New Zealand, South Korea, and Denmark as democratic countries who have subsidized cultural production via cultural sectors established in government ministries.[17] US national culture can play a crucial role in rectifying a history of inequities that economic and political sectors are unable to resolve and in integrating difference when the nation-state is incapable of doing so. Instead of espousing diverse cultural production, US national and mainstream culture functions to gloss over past inequities and promotes an economic agenda that disenfranchises minority populations. Challenging Japanese/Asian American participation in the nation's culture are restrictive immigration laws and policies, social and economic disenfranchisement, and grueling naturalization and citizenship processes.[18] Furthermore, negating Asian American inclusion emanates from a complex and ambivalent relationship of the United States to its Asian immigrants, owing to a history of labor exploitation of this population within the economic sphere of US capitalism and its twentieth-century involvement in three wars in Asia: World War II and the wars in Korea and Vietnam.

WHY CALIFORNIA?

My quest to trace the beginnings of a Japanese/Asian American subculture and its music began more than forty years ago when I moved to Los Angeles for graduate studies. The *San Francisco Examiner* and local Japanese American newspapers in California supplied valuable data about ongoing activities and current developments in Japanese American musicking. I met Sansei musicians in Southern California in the mid-1980s when I worked as an administrator at the Japanese American Culture and Community Center in Los Angeles's Japantown. I was later introduced to musician-composers in the San Francisco Bay Area. My continuing study of koto performance while enrolled in graduate study at the University of California, Los Angeles, drew me to the innovative work of Sansei musician-composers who strove to cross-fertilize traditional Japanese music elements and jazz-based music. For over thirty years, I developed relationships with some of my subjects, allowing me to gain insight into their creative process and to witness its evolution. Discovering the racial and political awareness and musical aspirations of members of my cohort in California set the activist tone for this study and my work going forward.

The concentration of Japanese Americans in California and the highly discriminatory legislation and practices in the American West rendered the Golden State an ideal research site. California is home to the largest settlement of Japanese immigrants, who arrived through the main port of San Francisco, yielding a rich volume of research data. Politically, the Golden State was a historical hotbed of anti-Asian agitation, where the federal and state governments in the region endorsed legislation restricting immigration and the rights of Asian immigrants. Furthermore, California, is a site of displacement, where a total of one hundred and twenty thousand Japanese Americans were removed from the West Coast and incarcerated in bleak camps mostly in the western half of the country during World War II. I have not included Hawaii or the urban centers of Chicago and New York in the present study; these important Japanese American enclaves merit separate studies. Japanese Americans in Hawaii are significant in the larger historical account of this demographic, yet the predominance of Asians (38.6 percent) and multiethnic residents (23.6 percent) formed a dissimilar social and political setting to that on the US mainland. The paucity of documentation of the smaller Japanese American communities in Chicago and New York present challenges worthy of future research.

Studying Okinawan Americans is also beyond the scope of this book since most settled in Hawaii, forming a large portion of the Japanese Hawaiian population. As well, Okinawans have identified themselves as Uchinanchu, forming a distinct ethnic group apart from the Naichi (mainland) Japanese. Like Naichi Japanese, Okinawans emigrated to the continental US beginning in 1899, only in fewer numbers. There is historical precedence for the social, political, and cultural differences between Okinawans and Naichi. In the rise of the modern Japanese state during the Meiji Restoration (1868–1912), Okinawans were regarded as separate colonial subjects. Those who emigrated to the US mainland continue to live in communities separate from Naichi Japanese.[19] A number of studies of Uchinanchu history, musicking, and identity in Hawaii and Los Angeles imports another dimension to the Japanese emigrant story.[20]

The timespan in covering three consecutive generations of Japanese Americans—1882 to the 1980s—necessitated a varied methodological approach. The passing of the Issei generation precluded personal interviews, requiring a historiographical approach. Oral histories and historical data came from archival collections and sources at educational institutions, community organizations, museums, and websites. I am indebted to a number of Nisei who shared their reminiscences of Issei, bringing that generation to life. I further derived meaning of Issei musicking from the diasporic transmission of a variety of Japanese musical traditions that carried cultural and social value for this generation.

Researching Nisei and Sansei musicking was best served by a person-focused ethnographic approach augmented by my own empirical and reflexive insights as a Sansei musician. I formed a network of Nisei and Sansei interviewees during a number of fieldwork trips to the San Francisco and Los Angeles areas over a twenty-year period. Targeting Nisei from varied class and residential backgrounds—mainly in the San Francisco Bay Area, Los Angeles, rural farmlands, and Massachusetts (California transplants)—resulted in an assortment of responses about the role of music in shaping their Japanese American identities. Interviewees ranged from amateur and professional performers of American jazz or traditional Japanese music to enthusiastic dancers and listeners. In San Francisco, I focused on Sansei musicians affiliated with the San Francisco creative-music scene and Asian Improv Records (now Asian Improv Arts), whose experimentation and improvisations most markedly drew from traditional Japanese/Asian music sources. In Southern California, I conferred with members of key Sansei jazz-fusion bands and artists who collaborated with other free-jazz musicians from the Bay Area in musical explorations. Inestimable were interviews with Sansei artist-activist Nobuko Miyamoto, who sang with Chris Iijima and Charley Chin folk songs that captured the spirit of the Asian American movement and became unofficial anthems. Miyamoto's current intercultural and cross-cultural music and dance that is transforming the Obon festival in Los Angeles unfolds in the epilogue.

George Yoshida, my principal Nisei source I interviewed extensively over a period of time, painted a broader picture of Nisei life and musical activities. Captivating were his stories about being lured by big-band jazz sounds as a youngster; his musical endeavors in high school, which he furthered while incarcerated during World War II at Poston, Arizona; his resettlement in Chicago; and his musical pursuits upon returning to the San Francisco Bay Area. Delighting in playing saxophone and drums, Yoshida's love for big-band jazz propelled him to comprehensively document Nisei musicians and bands active over a thirty-five-year span in his 1997 book, *Reminiscing in Swingtime: Japanese Americans in American Popular Music, 1925–1960*. Yoshida's account includes jazz music makers and ensembles in prewar California, the concentration camps of World War II, as well as Nisei musicians and singers who performed in Japan during the 1930s. Forming the J-Town Jazz Ensemble in the 1990s, using jazz arrangements from Poston, and his performance as narrator in Mark Izu and Anthony Brown's *Big Bands behind Barbed Wire* are only two of the many concerts in which Yoshida actively participated.

Questions aimed at interviewees' socialization yielded first-hand information about the social milieu in which my subjects matured and whether musicking was salient in their lives. Participant observation produced field notes taken at music lessons, concerts, festivals, and celebrations, illuminating the contexts and occasions in which musicking was integral. Collecting data from camp newspapers about musicking events and activities, music schools, and ensembles in the ten concentration camps of World War II revealed efforts to normalize daily life amidst deprivation in desolate locations. Far more enriching than academic gain was the emotional impact of mining the stories of Nisei interviewees and uncovering the indomitable spirit of this generation as they persevered through the morass of bigotry and segregation.

CULTURAL POLITICS

Lowe champions Asian American cultural-production sites as counterpoints to political and cultural forms designed to uphold stratification and inequality, attempting to erase a history of discrimination, disenfranchisement, and statelessness in regard to immigrants in the United States. Alternative cultural spaces offer a place to reclaim our lost memories, recover our histories, and reimagine facets of our heritage. Asian American culture, according to Lowe, is a vehicle not only for altering and expanding the national landscape to include the narratives and histories of this demographic but also a means to critically examine the notion of citizenship and the state's function in guaranteeing citizen's rights.[21]

Chang points out that it is artists who have pressed the issue of representation for people of color, for women, for poor people, and for other disadvantaged populations. In challenging the possibility and success of alternative cultural sites, he asks, "Who has access to the means of production?" and "Who has the power to shape culture?"[22] His questions raise the specter of inequity, a culture war in which a people's ability to represent themselves equally is denied. Such inequities prevent a nation's population "from seeing each other in their full humanity. It is to say that the culture does not point us toward a more just society."[23] A lack of access and power make it difficult to advance Asian American inclusion in public life, but we must find a way to generate and interpolate cultural forms and practices that rearticulate our racial and cultural identities.[24] It is exciting to imagine hybrid musical styles as synthesizing strands of one's ethnic heritage with one's American cultural underpinning and the potential for exponentially enriching and expanding the breadth and depth of our national culture.

Cultural politics is a valuable theoretical framework in researching the correlation between music and the politics of identity, framing culture as a resource from which to conceive new subjectivities and practices with the intent of subverting the hegemony of a nation's dominant culture and questioning its governance. Multimedia artist and scholar Coco Fusco argues, "Culture in this country is a critical, if not the most crucial, area of political struggle over identity. Cultural identity and values are politically and historically charged issues for people in this country whose access to exercising political power and controlling their symbolic representations has been limited within mainstream culture."[25] Fusco is referencing the culture wars waged by people of color as they strive to define their own cultural boundaries and determine how they are to be politically represented. Dorinne Kondo concurs, identifying "the world of representation" and "aesthetics" as locations of struggle—places where identities are constructed and interrogated and "hegemonies challenged."[26] It is significant *how* practices, meanings, and aesthetics embedded in Japanese American musicking reflect their cultural heterogeneity and representation. I again turn to Lowe who deconstructs the complex concept of identity into three discrete designations—heterogeneity, hybridity, and multiplicity—to establish a political base for greater inclusion and provide space for shifting and redefined identities as they are shaped by historical and material forces.[27] Heterogeneity, hybridity, and multiplicity capture a spectrum of identities that emerge in the spaces between nativism, assimilationism, and pluralism, averting essentializing identities and instead opening pathways for more complicated and alternate subject positions. The three designations facilitate my comprehension of a complex of practices across three generations that reflect a variety of backgrounds and a broad range of circumstances and sociopolitical and musical experiences.

INTERPLAY OF DIASPORA AND TRANSNATIONALISM

The reciprocity between diaspora theory and transnationalism enriches our reading of Japanese American identities and musical practices. In her influential book, *Claiming Diaspora: Music, Transnationalism, and Cultural Politics in Asian/Chinese America*, Su Zheng asserts that diaspora and its perspectives, operating across national boundaries, have the potential to cogently critique discriminatory nation-based culture and inequities faced by citizens differentiated by race, ethnicity, class, gender, sexual orientation, and nationality.[28] In promoting diaspora as an analytical tool, Zheng elucidates the complexity of a diasporic music's evolution resulting from the migrations of people and the cross-cultural connections that occur.[29] For Japanese Americans, the circular diasporic flow of culture between Japan and its early enclaves in the United States reinforced the cultural and political moorings of Issei and Nisei in their communities. Third generation Sansei musicians embraced premodern Japanese music brought to American shores in the bodies, hearts, and minds of Issei as a source for their newly empowered identities and intercultural musicking. Within the context of cultural politics, the promise of diaspora is its politically oppositional stance that sparks disenfranchised populations and individuals to actively create alternative subcultures. Ethnomusicologist David Rosenberg asserts that diasporic studies shed light on the "processes and experience, roots and routes that enable diasporic consciousness without formulating or holding to any particular paradigm that potentially alienates groups and experiences."[30] My express interest in studying Japanese American musicking through a diasporic lens is the affective and aesthetic connections this population felt toward their homeland traditions and the agency that resulted in neutralizing their hostile environment.

As proposed in Black British cultural studies, the concept of diaspora is politically pertinent in examining and understanding the link between migration and racialization in transnational spaces. Notably, migration and racialization are intertwined processes that can be traced back to the time of the Enlightenment and the Atlantic slave trade.[31] Such processes certainly describe the experience of first-generation Issei who had arrived with hopes of prospering and making a new life in the United States. Instead, they faced racist laws and policies in their struggle to secure their material needs, gain ownership of land, and obtain citizenship.

Coupling diaspora theory with cultural politics highlights the potential of subcultures in pluralizing American cultural identity. Diasporic cultural politics enables Japanese/Asian Americans to raise their visibility and play an important role in establishing a more integrated American identity through their cultural production. The Asian American movement of the late 1960s and early 1970s inspired Japanese/Asian American musician-composers to turn toward the East in developing music that articulated their newly configured identities.

Diasporic music utilizes transnational networks in creating hybrid and cross-fertilized forms that synthesize musical elements taken from one's heritage and host cultures. Transnationalism figures prominently in providing social channels for immigrant populations, constructing a third, in-between space that bridges the homeland and new places of residence through the performance and consumption of music. Japanese Americans over three generations have and continue to use music to connect to their transnational past, often crossing over into hybridity, a place "between past and present, between history and fiction, between art and ritual, between high art and popular culture, and between Western and non-Western influence."[32] Sansei certainly traverse this transnational space in their search for new sounds. Zheng convincingly argues for diasporic transnationalism as an analytical concept in discussions about cultural politics and the "empowering consciousness" it generates for the multiple identities present within immigrant populations.[33] My intent here is to counter the vulnerability of Japanese Americans in the face of the US government's racialized policies and troubling cultural representations. Musicking offers an avenue for Japanese/Asian Americans to dismantle their image of the "perpetual foreigner" and fashion a subculture that seeks to broaden this nation's cultural landscape. In the 1960s and 1970s, Asian American college students and cultural workers involved in the Asian American movement sought to create charged political and cultural identities, transforming their disenfranchisement and shaping a subculture. Zheng maintains that Asian Americans rejected diaspora, claiming America as their "sole legitimate home and its only geographical base for resistance."[34] Daryl J. Maeda offers a more nuanced conception of the Asian American movement, differentiating two distinct ideologies in the construction of Asian American identity: Third World internationalist radicalism and domestic cultural nationalism. He elucidates how Asian American activists in the 1960s and 1970s chose Third World internationalism as their central ideology while the prerogative of Asian American writers and performing artists tilted toward "domestic US nationalism."[35] I suggest that the ideologies outlined by Maeda overlapped in the work of Japanese/Asian American musicians and artists. Being exposed to the independence movements and struggles in Asia and Africa through Third World radicalism, many musician-composers reevaluated their Asian past, excavating musical elements and aesthetic ideas of Japan, China, and the Philippines. Sansei musician-composers were at the forefront of intertwining Japanese musical elements, forms, and aesthetics with jazz-based music to express a cultural identity that integrated their Japanese and American dimensions. Establishing musical ties to Asia enriched their multifaceted identities with the aim of formulating a subculture.

NEXUS OF MUSIC, IDENTITY, AND POLITICS

The intersection of music, identity, and politics offers a vantage point in researching the link between identity formation and musicking among three generations of Japanese Americans in historically specific geographical and political circumstances. The multiplicity of voices that emerge dispel any idea of an essentialized Japanese American identity. In examining music's function, I raise the question of what ways musicking is a performance of social, cultural, and political identification for Japanese Americans in the United States. This inquiry foregrounds musicking as an expression of Japanese American identity in a social and political landscape that continues to challenge their Americanness and the agency exercised by this demographic to shape how they are represented. I sought to ascertain the musical styles they chose to perform and listen to as they negotiated their social standing and hopes for acceptance. The above line of questioning is derived from identity theory in anthropology, which was modeled from literary and postmodern perspectives with an emphasis on narrating and performing identity. In the continual process of "becoming," identity is regarded as something one can perform or enact, with performance regarded as a form of narrative. Along these lines, Deborah Wong asserts, in her study of Asian American performativities, "I treat performance as constructive rather than reflective of social realities. If performance is a site of cultural production, then it is important to look closely at the realities created through performance. . . . When difference of any kind is explored through performance, the result is necessarily performative . . . performing something means making or becoming something."[36] Wong's idea speaks to the intention and power in expressing one's identity through performance. In her work, she focuses on "how performativity is the mechanism for critical newness, which may or may not be oppositional."[37] Performing *music* is the vector chosen here to examine the social location of each generation in this study and their strategic response to a history of marginalization and disempowerment. The cultural and affective meaning attached to Japanese American musicking renders it as a medium to enact a sense of national belonging. Judith Butler is most often cited in discussing performativity, a concept that describes how identities form by enacting or performing ethnicity, race, gender, and sexuality, rather than merely expressing these categories as traits.[38] Inquiring about the link between musical styles, music's emotional function and its assertion of identity within each of the three generations raises questions such as: What social and affective function did Issei musicking have as they endured US exclusionary policies and practices? Were Nisei able to mediate their bicultural identities through musicking? And what musical directions did Sansei take in proclaiming their reconfigured sociopolitical selves? These inquiries entail exploring the sonic, social, and affective dimensions of musicking and the complexities and ambiguities of its role in the lives of Japanese Americans.

Prompted by notions of nation building that Lowe raises, I further inquire how Japanese American ethnic identification and cultural practice relate to a discussion of national belonging and the challenge of nation building in a democratic country.[39] The question proposes integrating and balancing small-group immigrant identities with a national identity in opening eligibility for citizenship and participation in the national polity. Sociologists frame the conception of ethnic identification politically, describing inequality as a product of the forces of domination and subordination. Ethnicity has become a political proposition for disenfranchised populations and a concept of the postmodern world that is tied to the state and to issues of nationhood. Brackette Williams asserts the political necessity of ethnicity in the strategic development of a national identity: "the concept of ethnicity, whether defined in terms of nested segments or horizontal interest groups, is most useful when used as a label for a dimension of the identity formation process in a single political unit, most specifically the nation-state."[40] Consequently, groups that are unable to assert their presence are hindered in their ability to contribute or partake in the building of a nation. This line of thinking follows the notion that ethnicity is "instrumental," i.e., primarily a social construction that serves the political and economic goals of ethnic groups. For racialized immigrant groups, the bar is high for building agency to bring about needed changes. Further, it may take generations to achieve political and economic legitimacy and contribute anything that is lasting. I advance the imperative of expanding national cultural boundaries to include a variety of cultural practices that could transform prevailing racist ideologies of American citizenship and more vigorously promote a firm democratic foundation.

The intersection of music, identity, and politics positions musicking as an inherently political act, particularly because it performs ethnicity and race. Ethnicity and race are prominent markers of Japanese American identity, fueled by a persistent Orientalist discourse that exoticizes and racializes Asian populations in the United States. The hegemonic exposition of race and Orientalism in the United States provides a historically specific context for studying Japanese American musical performance. Of significance is *how* Japanese Americans continue to employ music to construct and mediate their ethnic boundaries in a racist society as their circumstances shift.

Sounding Our Way Home problematizes the discourse of "race" in the United States. Most early twentieth-century American sociologists and political scientists based their research and discussions around two races—white and Black. These narrow racial classifications still held by a majority of Americans promote a binary view of race relations in the United States to the exclusion of Native Americans, Asian Americans, Latinx, and mixed-race populations who fall outside the constricted racial parameters. Claire Jean Kim's article "The Racial Triangulation of Asian Americans" expands the US racial discourse beyond Black and white, introducing the concept of a "field of racial positions" as an alternative to theorizing about the racialization of subordinate populations in the United States. To more accurately represent the interaction among racial groups, Kim's "field of racial positions" graphically describes a plane consisting of two axes, "superior/inferior and insider/foreigner," which she claims are parameters established to uphold white dominance and privilege.[41] The two axes make possible comparisons of divergent racializations experienced by subaltern groups intended to augment white control. Racial positions in the field form from the continual negotiation among interacting racial groups and social classes.

Asian Americans face being "racially triangulated" in their relationship to whites and Blacks in a field of racial positions, according to Kim. She identifies two measures whites apply in preventing nonwhite racial populations from gaining power and influence. One means of racial triangulation is "relative valorization," which Kim describes as a value whites use to maintain their dominant status by pitting Asian Americans against African Americans. Regarding Asian Americans as a model minority exemplifies "relative valorization." "Civic ostracism" is a second tactic that racially triangulates Asian Americans, perpetuating their image as foreigners who are racially and culturally unassimilable. Civically ostracizing this population restricts their participation in the US polity, triggering residual restrictions in social and cultural spheres as well.[42] Further troubling are the economic repercussions of racial triangulation as it becomes part of the public mechanism that governs the disbursement of wealth in the United States.

Relative valorization and civic ostracism are thorny. The two concepts, dating back to the mid-nineteenth century, complement one another in binding Asian Americans in a triangulated state. Additionally, they merge Asian subgroups, failing to acknowledge the cultural heterogeneity of those of Asian descent or to differentiate Asians from Asian Americans. As well, the cultures of Asian Americans and others are misconceived as fixed and stable rather than importantly understood as variable, malleable, and unstable.

Nevertheless, racial triangulation informs us of how Japanese/Asian Americans compared themselves to both Blacks and whites in constructing their multiethnic racial identities.[43] The importance of Japanese/Asian American intercultural collaborations with Black and white artists, resulting in musical hybridity, resists the hegemonic measures of the model. Due to its limited parameters, racial triangulation does not address the intercultural exchanges between Asian Americans and Latinx artists; later, we shall see how Japanese American folk musicians and *taiko* drummers demonstrate strong musical ties to Latinx communities in California.

Musicking in this context illustrates the fluidity and variability of Japanese Americans and presents them in an affirmative and empowering light, transcending their racialized triangulation. Racially triangulating Asian Americans, however, spotlights the difficulty of expanding the American cultural landscape to include the sonic offerings of this population. The prevailing tenacity of "civic ostracism" reveals how Japanese Americans continue to negotiate their racialization in the face of unabated marginalization. My goal is to situate Japanese Americans into the ever-growing complexity and contestation of race relations in the United States and to broaden the discourse and path toward greater inclusion for other groups as well.

MUSIC AND JAPANESE AMERICAN IDENTITY

Under the influence of postcolonial studies, "identity politics" resurfaced from within 1960s politics of identity to become a strategy meant to elicit change in the relationship between dominant and subordinate groups in the United States.[44] Identity politics ideologically serves to support social movements organized around ethnicity, gender, and sexuality—movements that have rallied to bring individuals into collective action by making politics more palpable in their lives. Politics of identity did not emphasize *difference* as a means of leverage for empowering identities; instead, it promoted the goal of *commonality* in a population's desire to participate in the national culture. Discussed in chapter 2 is the failure of Issei leaders to promote common values they believed Japan and the United States shared. Chapter 3 introduces American-born Nisei and their strivings toward whiteness in their assimilative efforts to join mainstream America. In a transformative shift, politicized Sansei chose to underscore difference in formulating an alternative identity that drew from their Japanese heritage yet affirmed America as their "home"; they constructed an intercultural space that allowed them to fashion their own representations.

Ethnicity is central to Japanese Americans' identity. There are many reasons for the reification of ethnicity in postmodernity. Ethnic identity has acquired new meaning in the face of nation-states' increasing diversity and plurality due to widespread economic and political migrations, globalized economies, social and political change, and transnational exchange. Stuart Hall distinguishes new ethnicities from the old—ethnicity now serving as a counterpoint to the cross-fertilization and homogenization of cultures wrought by North American and European popular cultures and a "counterinvention of difference against the global postmodern and capitalism's erasure of difference."[45] Hall describes the new role of ethnicity: "Ethnicity is the necessary place or space from which people speak. It is a very important moment in the birth and development of all the local and marginal movements that have transformed the last twenty years, that moment of the rediscovery of their own ethnicities."[46]

A continuously evolving Japanese American identity aims to counter mainstream society's view of them as Other; as such, ethnicity has come to designate one's political position. Hall frames this politicized form of identity as a "cultural politics of the local." Japanese American musicking in California is a case study of cultural politics of the local population in this state and how the politics of racism in this locale forced them to construct a collective identity against discrimination and rejection. This is significant since Japanese Americans present in small numbers elsewhere in the United States have limited agency. Sansei musicians ignited a transformation that synthesized a recovery of their heritage and history, creating an "imaginary political re-identification and re-territorialization."[47] In the late 1960s to 1970s, the Asian American movement constructed this counterpolitics of "re-identification and re-territorialization" to combat exclusion and marginalization. Emerging as counterpolitics of the local, the movement broadened its efforts to the national level from which to speak, contest, and build their emergent social, cultural, and political subjectivity. The designation "Japanese/Asian American" arose out of the ideological and symbolic struggle of Japanese/Asian American students and cultural workers to replace the Western conceived term "Oriental," connoting a sense of exotic Other. The Asian American movement signaled a *cultural revolution*, bringing about a change in consciousness and agency that enabled Asian Americans to raise their visibility.

Like identity, music has no fixed essence of strict boundaries and meanings. Martin Stokes expansively describes music as "a wide field of practices and meanings with few significant or socially relevant points of intersection. Without understanding local conditions, languages and contexts, it is impossible to know what these practices and meanings are."[48] In analyzing the musical practices of each generation, the localized context and communal relations between musicians and listeners play a role in determining whether or not music signifies a shared identity. Significant is how musical styles performed by each generation affectively expressed the social and political location of its members. Yet for all three generations, music was also a conduit to mainstream society outside their ethnic communities. *Sounding Our Way Home* uncovers a spectrum of intents and identities enacted in musical performance as each generation sought to counter the injustice and inequities they faced to engender a sense of belonging, seek aesthetic fulfillment, match congruities on the path toward citizenship, or create distinct identities that offer alternative cultural practices in hopes of broadening the nation's cultural boundaries.

In this cross generational study, I locate musicking as a cultural practice that expresses not only a complex web of affective responses in each generation's subordinated lives but also a genuine power imbued in their Japanese cultural moorings from which they could draw in coalescing an identity. Musicking in each generation played an affirmative role in the construction of Japanese American racial and ethnic identities, whose attributes shifted as the cultural foundations and sociopolitical circumstances of each generation fluctuated. Several years of grim life in the concentration camps during World War II singularly tested Issei and Nisei, sometimes prompting dramatic shifts in allegiance. Across three generations, heterogeneous identities according to social class, occupational status, gender, geographical location, religion, political orientation, and personal inclination counter the essentializing of Japanese Americans.

"Finding one's way home" is a trope that speaks to all immigrants and their progeny who exist on the margins of US mainstream culture. A feature article published in the *Boston Globe* on September 8, 2011, reveals the ever-present challenge of national inclusion. The title on the front-page story, "Strangers in Their Own Land, as They Came of Age," details the experience of young Muslims growing up in small towns and cities in the United States and the trials they face in confronting fear and discrimination, especially following the tragedy of 9/11. "How can Muslims maintain their religious and cultural identity without isolating themselves?" is an earnest question raised by a young Muslim man interviewed in the article.[49] It is a question pertinent to many whose culture and religion are regarded with suspicion in this country. The article is a reminder of the recurring American narrative of the plight and uncertainty of immigrants who choose to come to the United States as their home but feel unwelcome. Japanese Americans share this narrative with a critical eye toward all that this country could be.

CHAPTER 2

Dual Identities: Japanese Immigrant Community, Identity, and Music

Music, more than anything else is essential. It's almost more important than food. It comes from a Confucian tradition that says the most important department of government is the department of music. And they really meant that because music embodied all the moral and ethical traditions of government. If you knew that and could play it well, it means you embodied all those principles well. For Issei, if you went to a party and didn't contribute a poem, song, or something, that meant you were not quite human, not quite developed—mijuku—meaning "not quite ripened." Their view of performance was very deep.

—Rev. Masao Kodani[1]

First-generation Issei identities emerged as an eclectic and contradictory composite shaped by a strong inclination to retain a Japanese national and cultural identity, a desire to Americanize, and the interstitial social and cultural practices necessary to secure the material conditions for their survival. The oppressive and shifting sociopolitical circumstances that Japanese immigrants endured governed Issei emergent identities, and their Japanese musicking remained a stronghold through these changes.

The expression "between two empires," borrowed from the title of a book by Eiichiro Azuma, best captures the complexity of transnational forces that altered how Issei identified themselves. The boundaries of this generation's cultural and political identity changed numerous times in response to pressure by Issei leaders who navigated and negotiated Japanese emigrants' binational status within the context of the Pacific region's geopolitics and the racist ideology of American citizenship.

The concept of a binational identity was untenable due to racist attitudes in the United States, particularly California, and the growing, tense economic and political competition with Japan beginning in the nineteenth to the twentieth century. Issei attempted to maneuver between the two state ideologies of superiority and expansion by manipulating differences and emphasizing congruities. The resulting native concept of a transculturated identity—*zaibei dōhō* (Japanese in America)[2]—was a compromise that ultimately worked against Japanese immigrants. The growing xenophobia of American racial politics at the turn of the century made the arrival of Issei particularly ill-timed. The Issei leaders' vision of being both frontier Americans and imperial Japanese, coupled with their sense of entitlement in being regarded as "honorary whites," proved to be delusional, considering the growing American fear of Japan's military prowess and imperialistic successes. Issei were doomed to lie outside the boundaries of citizenship and the national culture.

The arts were integral to the Issei's transculturated *zaibei dōhō* identity as a source for aesthetic enjoyment, as a political tool, a symbol of cultural pride, and as a coping mechanism to transcend discrimination and despondency. The affect and emotion expressed in traditional and Japanese popular music enriched Issei lives and provided some sense of affirmation in their unequal relationship with American society. Performing Japanese music subverted their subordination and underscored their ethnic cohesiveness. Western musicking as an acculturative strategy was ineffective, but it did represent the face of progressive and well-educated Issei. Musicking in general created an aesthetic and social space for Japanese immigrants in constituting a place they could call home, but more importantly, it established how they were to be represented—as both Japanese and American—in their effort to become part of the national culture.

The aesthetic and social meaning Issei attached to music is the thread that connected music, identity, and politics in their lives. The epigraph to this chapter underscores music's prominence in the cultivation and refinement of an Issei; being a skillful musician meant you embodied the moral and ethical principles of the nation-state. Music also functioned to establish ethnic boundaries, promoting traditional Japanese music as a stabilizing element within those boundaries. A shared aesthetic experience of music strengthened Issei identities: socially, it sustained their communities; aesthetically, it was a source of pleasure and validation; and politically, it expressed a rearticulated form of Japaneseness, a recalibrated identity, affirming their Japanese national origins yet staking a claim within the United States. The following narrates the specific historical, social, and political circumstances of this immigrant group as it attempted to insert itself, transnationally, into the US national fabric. Issei politics of identity sought to establish common ties to the United States with their patriarchal social structure, musical pursuits, and desire to partake in the economic success of their adopted nation. Musicking gave Issei a voice in demonstrating to Americans the value of their culture, hoping to contribute to the cultural landscape of the United States while expressing deep-felt longings and pride.

ARRIVING ON AMERICAN SHORES

The arrival of Japanese to the continental United States from 1882 to 1924 is a complex story involving a heterogeneous cast of characters comprised of enterprising students, merchants, farmers, and laborers. Waves of immigrants came in response to agricultural displacement and poor wages in Japan, the lure of the West, and expansionist ideas of a newly emerging Japan. Promises of better wages, employment opportunities, and the chance for Japan to establish a political and economic foothold in the States fed the desire of arriving Japanese immigrants.

Starting in 1882, young male students were the first to come in search of a Western education and skills they thought would benefit them upon their return to Japan. They worked primarily as servants in private homes and as dishwashers or "general help" in restaurants, hotels, and bars.[3] My maternal grandfather Kichitaro Taki (b. 1879, Nagoya, Japan) was among the young males who arrived in San Francisco in 1899 with a business degree in hand from Nagoya Commercial College. His uncle, after having lived in the United States and returned to Japan, told my grandfather how one had many opportunities there. Taki worked as a "schoolboy," a servant in private homes, while enrolled in school to learn English and Spanish.[4] Male laborers soon followed, moving to the States in search of economic opportunities and a chance to evade military service as Japan eased its emigration restrictions.[5] By 1890, a population of 2,500 Japanese, mostly student-laborers, settled in San Francisco, forming an early Japanese community. Also, at the vanguard of Japanese settlement in the United States between the years 1891 and 1900 were prostitutes[6] and women laborers, numbering 1,195.

From 1890 on, laborers and farmers came to the United States as sojourners (*dekaseginin*) with the hopes of accumulating wealth and returning to Japan to pay off debts or to serve as capital for business or other endeavors.

Figure 2.1. Logging crew, Snoqualmie Falls Lumber Co., Washington State, ca. 1917. Photo by Kinsey Clark. University of Washington Libraries, Special Collections, UW11554.

During the decade of the 1890s, small Japanese communities emerged, dotting the Pacific Coast, stretching from San Diego north to Vancouver. The 27,440 Japanese who arrived during the period from 1891 to 1900 filled these communities as workers in railroad construction, logging (figure 2.1), canneries, agriculture, mining, domestic service, and the meatpacking, salt, and fishing industries. Others ran small businesses providing goods and services.[7]

A second wave of immigration took place from 1901 to 1907, when 42,457 immigrants from Japan and an additional thirty-eight thousand laborers from Hawaii, whose contracts on plantations ended, disembarked on the West Coast. Agricultural laborers hailed primarily from the prefectures of Wakayama, Hiroshima, and Yamaguchi, all located in the southwestern part of Japan's main island of Honshu (figure 2.2). The Japanese contract laborers in Hawaii were also from these prefectures.

Anti-Japanese sentiment, historically, had its beginnings in anti-Asian agitation against the Chinese, starting in the 1850s. Organized labor, economically motivated to eliminate competition for jobs with Chinese workers, cultivated anti-Asian attitudes in California state politics. Labor's influence nationally resulted in the passing of the Chinese Exclusion Act by Congress in 1882 and subsequent exclusion acts in 1888, 1892, and 1894 legislated to reinforce it. These legislative policies basically cut off further immigration

Figure 2.2. Issei owners of Hara's Fruit Stand in Wapato, Washington. Courtesy of Denshō, the Frank Kubo Collection.

of Chinese to California until the Magnuson Act, which was passed on December 17, 1943. The drive to renew the Chinese Exclusion Act expanded protests and calls for the expulsion of all Asians. Such legislation and actions were the basis for organized labor's anti-Japanese agitation when Japanese immigrants increased in number at the turn of the century. Two decades of agitation made inevitable the federal immigration law of 1924, prohibiting further emigration of any Asian laborers.

Even though Japanese immigration shifted its focus from urban centers to the rural areas in the early 1900s, West Coast cities remained cultural centers of Japanese America; San Francisco was the cultural capital. This city's importance arose in part to its history as the major entry point for Japanese immigrants, and it served as the headquarters for the Japanese consul general and home to the most developed Nihonmachi, or Japantown.

Los Angeles and its surrounding vicinity also experienced tremendous growth. In 1903, more than two thousand Japanese moved to Los Angeles from San Francisco in search of work. These laborers found employment with the Pacific Electric Railway, as well as farms in Moneta (Gardena), the San Gabriel Valley, and elsewhere. Following the 1905 earthquake in San Francisco, more Japanese moved to southern California to rebuild their lives. By the end of 1905, more than ten thousand Japanese made their home in the southern part of the state.[8] Further agricultural expansion of outlying areas by 1910 contributed to Los Angeles being considered an important metropolis of Japanese America.

Exclusionary attitudes toward Japanese were particularly strong in the Golden State, where Japanese farmers played a major role in the ascension of California's burgeoning economy beginning around 1900. In California, the success of Japanese laborers in the agricultural industry and the growing number of land-owning Japanese farmers became a concern for white farmers and organized labor. To arrest the growth of Issei landownership and competitive wholesale and produce markets, especially in central California, anti-Asian agitators created the 1913 California Alien Land Law. The law highlighted the vulnerable political status of Issei as "aliens ineligible for citizenship," stipulating noncitizens be prohibited from purchasing or leasing land for more than three years.[9]

Economic competition in the agricultural sector was not the only source of friction against the Japanese. The white population also based their exclusionary views on what they considered to be the "racial incompatibility and cultural deficiency" of this immigrant population.[10] The rising tide of discrimination resulted in pressuring the Japanese government to ban all labor emigration to the United States and Canada, starting in 1900. Japanese laborers continued coming to the mainland by first acquiring a passport to Hawaii and then migrating to the United States mainland. To plug this loophole, exclusionists pushed for further restrictions, which Theodore Roosevelt formalized in an executive order issued in March 1907, barring any alien from coming to the mainland if they held passports destined to US possessions (including Hawaii), the Canal Zone, or any other country. Euphemistically referred to as the Gentlemen's Agreement between Japan and the United States, the emigration of Japanese laborers to the continental United States ended. The agreement did not terminate the entry of all immigrants, however, and passports continued to be issued to merchants, students, diplomats, tourists, parents, wives, and children of residents, as well as to rice farmers headed for Texas.[11] My paternal grandfather Matsujiro Asai (b. 1874, Osaka, Japan) was one of the rice farmers who settled in Texas, arriving in the United States in 1902. Unfortunately, the land around Houston proved to be unsuitable for rice growing, so farmers turned to cultivating vegetables. In the 1920s, my grandparents moved their nine children and vegetable-farming business to Ithaca, New York, with the goal of having all their offspring attend Cornell University, the only coed Ivy League school at the time.[12]

A crucial development in the promotion of permanent residency was the entry of many women between 1910 and 1920 (figure 2.3). Up until this

Figure 2.3. Picture brides being processed on Angel Island, California, ca. 1910. Courtesy of California State Parks, image 090-544.

time, most Japanese immigrants were male workers who were in their twenties and thirties. With permanent residency as a strategy for assimilating into American society, male émigrés either returned to Japan to marry, bringing back their brides, or sent for their wives. The women who came were "picture brides," so named after the practice of Japanese immigrant men who sent "pictures" of themselves in arranging marriages by proxy in Japan and having their "brides" subsequently sent to the United States to meet them. The newly formed families created a firm foundation for permanent settlements of Japanese immigrants.

Unable to halt the economic advancement of Issei farmers, the Asiatic Exclusion League, a broad alliance representing labor, farmers, and patriotic and fraternal organizations, drafted another Alien Land Law in 1920, which was submitted to voters and passed by a vote of three to one. As an amendment to the 1913 law, it put an end to tenancy of any kind, leaving Japanese farmers completely dependent on white farmers and essentially returning them to the status of laborers with no say or legal recourse. It also prohibited citizens from serving as guardians for any leasing of land, which meant that Issei farmers could no longer lease land through their Nisei children. Such untenable situations, including abuses at the hands of white farmers, forced many Issei farmers in California to give up and head to urban centers or other states to seek opportunities.

All Japanese immigration abruptly ended with the 1924 Immigration Act. The 1924 federal law established the "national origins quota system." The quota for immigrants entering the United States was set at 2 percent of the total number of residents in the country as reported in the 1890 census. A provision in the law made it mandatory for incoming immigrants to be eligible for citizenship. This requirement barred individuals of specific origin from the Asia-Pacific region—Japan, China, the Philippines, Laos, Siam (Thailand), Cambodia, Singapore, Korea, Vietnam, Indonesia, Burma, India, Ceylon (Sri Lanka), Turkey, and Malaysia. Based on the Naturalization Act of 1790, nonwhite immigrants were ineligible for naturalization as well. This discriminatory law was a victory for "the forces of American nativism in general, and for the western (US) anti-Japanese movement in particular."[13] Issei reacted strongly to the completeness of their exclusion with many returning to Japan, taking their Nisei children with them. A central theme that emerges in this tale of Japanese immigrant history is the state of powerlessness that dashed Issei hopes for economic betterment and, for Issei leaders, an opportunity to peacefully expand Japan's influence.

Prior to World War II, white racism subordinated the West Coast Japanese in every aspect of their lives. Politically, they were not allowed to become citizens; economically, discrimination severely curbed their occupational opportunities; socially, they were residentially segregated, ostracized, and denied entry in certain neighborhoods, public facilities, and social institutions; and racially, they were viewed as "base, inassimilable, and objectionable."[14]

Carey McWilliams, journalist and lawyer, introduces what he refers to as the "California-Japanese War (1900–1941)." He describes how first- and second-generation Japanese Americans were victimized in the push for white supremacy in California and Japanese supremacy in the Pacific. White supremacist groups in California, such as the Sons of the Golden West, the State Federation of Labor, the California Grange, and the American Legion, used anti-Japanese sentiment to solidify and unite their membership around the single issue of a common enemy: the Japanese immigrant. The reactionary fear of people who were racially and culturally different manifested in the mantra of "Yellow Peril," cementing anti-Japanese feelings from 1909 on with this pejorative stereotype.[15] The term embodied white people's fear that the influx of Asian immigrants signaled the beginning of an invading horde. This disparaging racial identity formed from the view of Asian bodies as biologically inferior in their Otherness.[16] For over forty years, the continual opposition to Japanese in California created a firm ideological basis for anti-Japanese sentiment, permeating almost all political, social, and economic problems Issei faced.

SOUNDING DUALITY

Issei musical activities from 1893 to 1941 demonstrate a strong identification with Japanese culture. The racial and cultural pride Issei felt grew out of the nationalism Japan enjoyed when it was unified for the first time during the Tokugawa and Meiji periods (1603–1912). In Japan, attitudes were a mix of feeling superior over the West, which had surpassed Japan in material culture, and ambivalence due to an uncertain diplomatic relationship with the United States. A long and rich history fed a sense of preeminence in their spiritual and cultural traditions. In Japan, aesthetic traditions based in Buddhist beliefs held music in high regard: "For the Buddha, the self has two components: one was a distinct, unique element, distinguishing one person from any other person; the other an aesthetically immediate, emotionally moving, indeterminate and hence indescribable 'field' component."[17]

The aesthetic component of the self, considered immutable and everlasting, was believed to exist not only in all people but in all aesthetic objects. If cultivated, the aesthetic self serves as a source of compassion and humanity toward all beings. The primacy of the arts within Shingon Buddhism underscores the importance of cultivating the aesthetic self. Within the Shingon sect, music and literature are included in the four art forms that are a part of its practices. For Kūkai, founder of Shingon Buddhism, beauty was an aspect of the Buddha's nature. The importance of aesthetics within the Shingon sect made it highly appealing to Heian culture (794–1190), a time when Japan was at the height of its cultural development.[18] Issei followed this aesthetic tradition.

Rev. Masao Kodani of the Senshin Buddhist Church in Los Angeles affirmed the vital role of music for Issei:

> Oh, I can't imagine being without music, which third generation Sansei don't understand, and which their Issei grandparents did; that music, more than anything is essential. It comes from a Confucian tradition that says the most important department of government is the department of music. It was important because music embodied all the moral and ethical traditions of government. And if you knew that and could play music well, it meant you embodied all those principles. For Issei, if you went

to a party and didn't contribute a song, poem, or something, that meant you were not quite human, not quite developed—*mijuku*—meaning "not quite ripened." So, the Issei view of performance was very deep.[19]

Issei delighted in performing both traditional and contemporary Japanese music. As an important aesthetic activity, much of the musicking took place in urban centers, where larger concentrations of Japanese resided. Both San Francisco and Los Angeles were major sites for musicking. Social class and upbringing dictated musical preferences, although there is some blurring of these divisions as class distinctions became less important and opportunities to study Japanese music, particularly in urban areas, increased. A variety of musical styles gave voice to the aesthetic impulse of the first generation.

A listing of Japanese music teachers found in community directories and yearbooks, published by Japanese newspapers, corroborates the powerful cultural connection Issei maintained with their homeland. An additional source, *Zaibei Nihonjinshi* (The History of Japanese in America) published in San Francisco in 1940 by the organization Zaibei Nihonjinkai also traces Issei music teachers in following the active transmission of a variety of Japanese musical genres. One of the earliest Japanese musical genres taught in immigrant communities was *gidayū-bushi*—narrative *biwa* (four- or five-string plucked lute) music that became the soundtrack for Bunraku, or puppet plays. *Zaibei Nihonjinshi* recorded information about a professional *gidayū* teacher who offered lessons in San Francisco as early as 1893.[20] In Japan, puppet plays and their accompanying music appealed to urban populations. Originally considered a plebeian form of entertainment, it gradually achieved elevated status as a classical theater form performed nationwide, giving way to *gidayū*'s rise in San Francisco and Los Angeles, centers of Japanese culture in the United States. *Gidayū* clubs formed, offering training and giving performances in both cities. Documentation indicates that Ujikoma-kai was one of the first *gidayū* groups in San Francisco, organized by three Issei women in 1910. Such groups continued to be active until the 1940s. For assistance in the cultivation and training required by this tradition, groups invited *gidayū* teachers from Japan to instruct them. Invited from Japan, *gidayū* artists and teachers toured the American West, advancing the activity of clubs well into the 1940s.[21]

The popular tastes of Issei favored Kabuki theater performances. A Kabuki play presented by the San Francisco Entertainment Club in 1893 was the earliest documented Japanese production in the United States. An Issei impresario, Nishijima Isamu, founded the San Francisco Entertainment Club, staging amateur Kabuki plays, which he choreographed and took part in.[22] A growing

Figure 2.4. Classical Kabuki dance performance. Courtesy of Denshō, the Mamiya Family Collection.

influx of Japanese immigrants to the West Coast through the 1910s stimulated the emergence of Kabuki troupes, one in Sacramento and two in Los Angeles (figure 2.4). Performances given by Kabuki actors and ensembles invited from Japan in Los Angeles in 1916 and 1917 are evidence of the popularity of this music theatrical.[23] It is significant that Kabuki continued to be performed at a number of concentration camps: Poston (Arizona), Gila (Arizona), and Rohwer (Arkansas) from 1942 to 1945.

Nagauta, a narrative shamisen (three-string plucked lute) genre performed as both accompaniment to Kabuki theater and as chamber music, appeared early on in San Francisco, around 1895. Records show that Kineya Yasoyo[24] offered lessons in *nagauta* of the Kineya school and in Japanese dance. Another *nagauta* performer and teacher, Kineya Kimiyo, began teaching in southern California in 1913. Then in 1931, Kineya Yasoyo left San Francisco to live in Los Angeles where she continued to pass on this narrative form. One of her students, Takaie Shōzō, became the first *natori* (professional status) trained in the United States, receiving a professional name from the *nagauta* master Kineya Yajūrō IX in Japan. When Kineya Yasoyo returned to Japan before the war in 1941, her student Kineya Yasokiyo continued her teacher's legacy of transmitting *nagauta*.[25]

The educated Issei elite favored *yōkyoku*, songs from the *nō* theater repertoire. Southern Californians proved to be the most active practitioners of this art form in Japanese communities. Enthusiasts in southern California banded together as early as 1907 in organizing the *yōkyoku* club Ginsei-kai. Because of the small numbers interested in this genre, the separate schools of Kanze and Hōshō that flourished in Japan merged into one group. There is no evidence of *yōkyoku* being performed publicly; it appears that it served as a form of private entertainment and personal cultivation. In 1917, the Ginsei-kai matured into the more formal Yōkyoku Club, which later transformed into the Southern California Yōkyoku Club in 1919. *Yōkyoku* activity picked up during the 1920s, beginning with the arrival of an instructor invited from Japan by the southern Californian Kita Nōgaku-kai in 1925. Thirty members received formal training in the Kita school of *yōkyoku*. Desiring to raise the level of their practice, the Southern California Yōkyoku Group divided itself into two separate groups, aligned according to the two schools mentioned above—Hokubei Kanze-kai and Rafu Hōshō-kai. Both clubs proceeded to contact the head of their respective *yōkyoku* schools in Japan to request that a disciple be sent to come and teach. This heightened interest prompted an increase in membership of the Rafu Hōshō-kai, which grew to thirty members by 1929. This style of singing remained popular during the 1930s with about one hundred people participating.[26]

The Japanese predilection for singing gave rise to the ascent of *shigin*. The vocal genre flourished following the arrival of Buddhist priests in the United States starting in 1898, and it comprises singing Chinese classical poems set to ancient, classical melodies called *koga*. Mr. Seizo Oka, former historian at the Northern California Japanese Cultural and Community Center's history archives in San Francisco, pinpointed the nationalistic sentiments of *shigin* songs: "Russo-Japanese war generals recited these poems and adapted them to say what they wanted to say about Japan. Japanese memorized these poems. *Shigin* contributed to the rise of nationalism in Japan, and it became a source of pride for Japanese. Many Issei embraced these sentiments, and its popularity rose in accordance with Japan's imperialistic successes in Asia."[27] Traditionally, it was practiced as a hobby or a form of personal enrichment, but the continued alienation Issei experienced transformed *shigin* into nationalistic songs.

With the large influx of Issei at the turn of the century, opportunities to study Japanese instrumental music blossomed during the 1910s. The 1914 *Japanese American Yearbook*, published in San Francisco by *Nichibei Shimbun* (Japanese American Newspaper), listed teachers for koto, shamisen, shakuhachi (end-blown bamboo flute), and *biwa*.[28] Of the two major koto schools—Ikuta and Yamada—the Yamada style appears to have been dominant early on in San Francisco and Los Angeles. Nakamura Rakuko spearheaded the first

Yamada school in San Francisco in 1914. San Francisco's *New World Directory*, published in 1922, also listed the availability of two koto teachers, one teaching Yamada style and the other Ikuta. Between the two teachers, almost two hundred students, mostly Nisei, learned to play koto.[29]

Koto training also took root in Los Angeles. Nakajima Chihoko, trained by her koto-master father, began teaching the Ikuta-style technique in 1926. Her collaboration with a shakuhachi player in southern California introduced *sankyoku*, a chamber group consisting of koto, shakuhachi, and shamisen. During the 1930s, the Ikuta school flourished and grew to include about forty students. Performer Wakita Shin'ei and her shakuhachi-player husband formed the Baidō-kai in Los Angeles as well, furthering opportunities to learn and perform both instruments.[30] A listing for one Ikuta teacher and one Yamada instructor appears in the 1941 *Japanese American Directory*.[31] As the consistent listing of teachers show, koto playing in Japanese communities continued to be popular; training in koto performance, along with flower arranging and cooking, traditionally served as part of a young woman's cultivation.

Solo *biwa* music made its way transnationally to California following on the heels of its popularity in Japan. Issei performed two *biwa* traditions: Satsuma *biwa* and Chikuzen *biwa*. Both traditions originated on the southern Japanese island of Kyūshyū and were eventually brought to Tokyo where they flourished during the Meiji period. Each of the schools had a separate repertoire of primarily historical narratives. Singing with *biwa* accompaniment was appealing because of the martial spirit of the heroic songs.[32] Starting in 1914, teachers of both the Satsuma and Chikuzen styles offered lessons in San Francisco. The 1914 *Japanese American Yearbook* registered one Satsuma *biwa* teacher. Records from 1918 show that a Chikuzen *biwa* school opened, and in 1921, the San Francisco Chikuzen-biwa Club opened. The Chikuzen-*biwa* style reached its apex in popularity in 1941 with the listing of three instructors in the *Japanese American Yearbook*.

One could learn narrative *biwa* music in Los Angeles as well, where two *biwa* instructors offered lessons in 1915, one teaching Satsuma *biwa* and the other, Chikuzen style. Four years later, the Chikuzen-biwa Club in southern California gave its first formal concert. In 1925, a branch of the Satsuma *biwa* tradition, the Kinshin school,[33] augmented musical offerings with the addition of two teachers. Great interest in Chikuzen *biwa* music unfolds in the decade between 1928 and 1938, when ten masters of this tradition visited the United States to give performances.[34]

Music of the end-blown bamboo flute, shakuhachi, originally associated with meditative practices of Buddhist monks, was also transmitted and taught in Los Angeles and San Francisco by 1914.[35] The Kinko school of shakuhachi playing flourished in Los Angeles from 1922 on. Then in 1930, enthusiasts of the more martial Tozan style, which developed around 1904 in Japan, initiated the formation of Shūchiku-kai. A variety of Japanese instrumental styles were well represented in Issei urban communities.

Popular entertainment in early Issei communities included music and dance provided by women performers and bands. Hostesses who worked in local Japanese restaurants or were members of traveling troupes of women entertainers from Japan boosted business. They actively sang, played shamisen, and danced, providing a diversion for customers: Issei bachelors who formed most of the Japanese population in the 1910s. Shows by female performing troupes combined classical Japanese dance, singing, and shamisen playing, with the added attraction of acrobatics and magic. An advertisement in the Los Angeles newspaper, *Rafu Shimpo*, for example, publicized the coming of the Miyako Dance Troupe from Japan in October 1915. This troupe and similar ensembles made their rounds in Issei communities on the West Coast.[36]

Japanese immigrant communities also enjoyed listening to popular music from Japan. A 1994 photographic exhibit at the Japanese American Cultural Center of Northern California (JACCNC) in San Francisco featured a snapshot of the Teikoku Band dated 1910. It was the local house band of the Teikoku Hotel located at 1120 Gough Street in San Francisco. JACCNC's historical archivist, Mr. Seize Oka, proposed that members of this band were members of an Issei young men's association.[37] Local bands, such as the Teikoku Band, performed both Western and Japanese popular music for community functions.[38] The Japanese popular music of the day was *ryūkōka*, commercial popular music from Japan, which could also be heard on local radio programs and in Japanese films shown in urban community theaters.[39] Composers and singers of *ryūkōka* enlivened the spirits of Issei and Nisei.

Since many Japanese came to the United States as farmers and laborers, the preferred music of this population is an important part of the Issei musical landscape. Traditionally, farmers played folk music and festival music, marking various stages of the agricultural cycle for Shinto-related observances. Issei farmers and laborers in rural areas and locations on the outskirts of urban centers in California, however, had little time or energy for musical pursuits. Since many Japanese immigrants worked as seasonal laborers, traveling from one farm to the next in search of employment, it was difficult to pursue music. Even when agricultural laborers began to settle in rural areas, musicking continued to be minimal as an activity due to the labor-intensive nature of farming. Itinerant or tenant farmers worked long hours from dawn to dusk, leaving little time to play music, socialize, or learn English. My paternal grandmother is an example of a hardworking wife of an Issei farmer and a mother of nine children. Rising before dawn to begin a full day of cooking, working in the fields, housekeeping, and raising children, her few minutes devoted to studying English at the end of the day only induced much-needed sleep. The koto she brought from Japan, a token of her refined upbringing, remained neglected and unplayed. The neglect pointed to a life of leisure in Japan left behind and a new life of endless work. I imagine my grandmother faced her life without music's beauty and comfort with resignation. Ascetic lives without music and musicking was the fate of other Issei women whose arranged marriages brought them to a new land, often to live an arduous life as a farmer's wife. I wished she had lived long enough to have heard me perform on koto, an instrument from her past.

The annual summer Obon festival, a Buddhist celebration to commemorate the dead, was widely practiced in immigrant communities. Obon rituals existed in many Japanese communities following the arrival of Buddhist missionaries who came to establish congregations in the United States in 1898. The ritual of Obon, based on a Buddhist text meant to express joy, serves as an offering to one's ancestors. Dancing was added as a form of entertainment at Buddhist temple carnivals during Obon to attract audiences and raise money. *Bushi* and *ondo* folk-song genres, both derived from Buddhist chants, served as musical accompaniment for Bon dances along with steady beats played on a *taiko* drum. In later years, if performers were available, *takebue* flute, gong, and shamisen were added to enhance the musical accompaniment.[40]

Regional folk songs made their way to the US mainland in the memories of immigrants coming from different provinces in Japan. Issei emigrated from numerous prefectures *(ken)* in central Japan—Hiroshima, Wakayama, Kumamoto, and Okayama to name a few—bringing their regional music and dance traditions with them. Immigrants from different prefectures formed *kenjinkai*, social and welfare community organizations. *Kenjinkai* picnics in the United States were important events for the performance of regional identities through music and dance as were their New Years' parties, featuring the singing of ancient ballads, traditional dance performances, accompanied by feasting and drinking *saké*. Noteworthy is that divisions among Issei based on regional identities and affiliations existed, and tensions often surfaced around music and dance, particularly folk traditions. Nonetheless, these events benefitted all, creating spaces to unwind and forget pressing cares, however briefly.

Regional folk music is associated with laborers, such as the *hole hole bushi* sung by Japanese plantation workers in Hawaii.[41] For generations, it was

Japanese laborers who disseminated songs from their locales to other regions of Japan as they searched for work. It was natural for Japanese immigrants to draw on the melodies of work songs and folk tunes they knew to express, with fresh lyrics, their new circumstances and environment.

Singing was probably the most prevalent form of musicking among Issei in rural areas. Its appeal is that musical accompaniment is not required, and it is expressive. In her book of short stories, *Songs My Mother Taught Me*, Nisei writer Wakako Yamauchi writes poignantly of the bleak lives of Issei tenant farmers. Her characters express their futility in melancholic Japanese folk and popular songs. The songs convey their longing for Japan and the family members they left behind, the smell of pine forests, or foods desired. In the absence of actual documentation of the tradition of Japanese song in the lives of these immigrants, we have Yamauchi's stories. As a teenager growing up during the war and as an internee at the Poston Relocation Center in Arizona, she sensitively captures the pathos of disillusionment Issei felt by quoting lyrics and referencing pentatonic melodies of prewar Japanese folk and popular songs that evoke what the Japanese American writer Garrett Hongo describes as "aestheticized melancholy."[42] In the short story "Songs My Mother Taught Me," the vernacular song "Mujō no Tsuki" (Transient Moon) figures prominently as a symbol of the mother's longing for Japan. Singing is also the choice of the father when inclement weather dashes his hopes for a good harvest, and he performs the most forlorn Japanese folk songs. Another reference to folk songs in Yamauchi's work is the story entitled "The Boatmen on Toneh River," named after the folk song of the same title. It is a song that expresses a fatalistic view of the transience of life. Sad, plaintive music is central to Yamauchi's descriptions of futility that her characters experience as tenant farmers, and they sing or play wistful Japanese melodies on flutes to express melancholy and longing for their homeland. Her stories convey not only a Japanese emotional attachment to music in voicing sorrow, melancholy, and fatalism, they articulate the Issei's human condition in America shaped by racist policies, disappointment, and a lack of agency to improve their circumstances.

In urban centers, Issei also engaged in Western musicking, ranging from European classical orchestral and chamber music, opera, and art songs to mandolin quartets, hymn singing, and vernacular songs. Issei interest in Western music reflects Japan's exposure to music of the West soon after Japan was forced to open its doors to Commodore Perry and his fleet in 1854. Japan embraced Western music in its efforts to modernize. The mission schools in Japan played an essential role in Western music education, using Protestant hymns as a medium "with their clear melodies, solid harmony, and predictable structure."[43] Christian hymn singing was part of the Issei experience as an activity of *fukuinkai*—Japanese gospel societies—around the turn of the twentieth century. These societies were pro-Western organizations that attracted young intellectuals and encouraged assimilation into American society. The year 1910 is the earliest account of a Western music ensemble formed in Los Angeles. Issei Seiichi Nako created The Mikado Band that performed brass band arrangements of opera excerpts. Seven years later, Nako assembled a Japanese American orchestra. The orchestra played a role in cultivating the interest of a greater number of Issei in Western classical music by inserting Japanese music and drama into musical programs as an enticement to attract Issei audiences.[44]

The formation of the Los Angeles Japanese Symphony Orchestra in 1927 speaks to the ongoing appeal of European classical music. The orchestra performed two concerts annually.[45] For their fifth concert held at the Japanese Union Church on March 2, 1928, the orchestra performed standard pieces of the classical repertoire (figure 2.5). Western classical music appealed to Issei intellectuals and progressives who viewed their participation and patronage of Western music as part of their class status and assimilation. A popular sopranist, Miss Kyo Inouye, regularly sang both European classical and Japanese vernacular songs; "Kojo no Tsuki" was a favorite among audiences. Although there was a paucity of Issei who performed Western music, as parents, they encouraged their Nisei children to master classical music as a possible entry point into American society.

Contexts and venues for music in Japanese enclaves prior to World War II varied. Performances took place in private homes, Buddhist churches, Christian churches, community halls, restaurants, and at picnics, bringing enjoyment and moments to socialize. Talent shows, called *engei-kai*, were common, featuring primarily Japanese music, dance, drama, and comedy in catering to Issei during the 1910s and 1920s. These shows became mainstays of community fundraising events, socials, and birthday celebrations for the Japanese emperor. Audiences soaked in the sounds of the koto, *biwa*, shamisen, and shakuhachi. Performances of classical Japanese dance, Kabuki, and other theatrical sketches drew Issei, evoking "traditional sentimentalism" that emphasized Japanese ideals, such as filial piety, the courage of warriors, and the acceptance of duty.[46] Talent shows occasionally showcased Western classical music along with brass-band music of The Mikado Band and piano or violin solo performances.[47] The variety and mix of musical styles and contexts in Japanese communities point to the rise of biculturalism, a product

SUCCESS OF SPRING CONCERT PLEASES ORCHESTRA MEMBERS

Japanese Union Church Well Filled In Spite of Moist Weather Friday Evening

The uncertain weather last Friday evening, March 2nd, did not bother the several hundred people who were at the Japanese Union Church to listen to the Spring Concert given by the Los Angeles Japanese Symphony Orchestra. Under the capable direction of Mr. S. Nako, the many selections played by the orchestra were presented in a fine manner.

All of the solo numbers were well played. The cello and violin solos by Mr. T. Yagura and Mr. M. Kono, respectively, were well received. But the biggest applause went to Miss Kyo Inouye, talented soprano of the younger generation, who appeared with the Japanese orchestra for the first time

The most popular numbers played by the orchestra proved to be the last two numbers: "Marche Militaire" and "Selections from the Merry Widow." It was a fitting climax to a program composed of many carefully selected numbers.

The following program was given:

PART I
1. Overture to "Norma"—Bellini.
2. Symphony No. 6 in G Major, "Surprise"—Haydn.
   a. Andante.
   b. Menuetto.
3. Romanza—Granados.
   Jota, Opus 5, No. 6—Granados.

PART II
4. Violin Solo—Tomio Yagura.
   Romance in G, Opus 40—Beethoven.
5. Cello Solo—Michiyoshi Kono.
   Allegro from Concerto—Goltermann.
   Nocturne—Goltermann.
6. Soprano Solo—Miss Kyo Inouye.
   Pace, pace, mio Dio—Verdi.
   Kojo no Tsuki—Yamada.

PART III
7. Marche Militaire, Opus 52, No. 1—Schubert.
8. Minuetto—Mozart.
9. Selection from the "Merry Widow"—Lehar.

Figure 2.5. Spring concert performed by Los Angeles Japanese Symphony Orchestra. Mainichi Shimbun, March 5, 1928.

Figure 2.6. Buddhist procession (Japanese court-music ensemble). Courtesy of Denshō and the Seattle Buddhist Temple Archives, the Ishikawa Family Collection.

of Issei attempts to bridge middle-class values of Japanese immigrants with those of white American mainstream society. As Japanese immigrants' dual identity continued to be negotiated, the performance of Western classical music functioned as an acculturative strategy—possibly one path toward mainstream society's acceptance.

With the arrival of Buddhist missionaries in 1898 came transnational music steeped in religious services, ceremonies, and rituals. Issei were divided in their choice in which religious institutions to participate: Should one retain their homeland religion as a source of familiarity and cultural identity or turn to Christianity in one's attempt to assimilate? Nichiren Buddhist services featured traditional chanting and drumming; Japanese court music also accompanied Buddhist rituals and services (figure 2.6). With the passage of time, however, Buddhist temples adapted to their diasporic setting by incorporating congregational singing of Buddhist hymns (*wasan*) in emulating the tradition of hymn singing in Christian churches and employing the designation "church" to attract acculturated Issei and Nisei youth. Also, in noting the popularity of Young Men's Christian Association (YMCA)–sponsored youth groups, Buddhist churches inaugurated Young Men's Buddhist Associations and Young Women's Buddhist Associations. From these social groups, orchestras and smaller ensembles playing Japanese songs and popular music sometimes materialized, such as the Berkeley Young Men's Buddhist Association Orchestra in 1927, which performed for a few social dances.[48]

Live concerts aired on radio in urban centers reveal bicultural programming. One example is KFWM Oakland's one-hour program of Japanese and Western music on January 12, 1930, featuring:

San Francisco Harmonica Band, "Carmen Prelude" (Georges Bizet);
xylophone solo: Tom Tsuji, "Poet and Peasant" (Franz von Suppé);
Japanese monologue: Mrs. Ujigoma Takemoto, "Sankatsu Hanichi at the Saloon";
harmonica solo: Minoru Okamoto, "Dove, Flute, and Drum" and "Barber of Seville";
xylophone: Tom Tsuji, "Serenade" (Franz Schubert) and "Intermezzo Russo" (César Franke);
vocal solo: Tony T. Seki, "Japanese Woodman Song" (Arr. by T. T. Seki) and "Pagan Love Song" (Nacio H. Brown);
violin solo: Tony T. Seki, "The Moon over the Ruined Castle" and "Japanese Cherry Dance" (Arr. by T. T. Seki);
San Francisco Harmonica Band, "Sarashi" (Arr. by T. Fukushima) and "Kappore" (Arr. by T. Fukushima).[49]

The preference for Western instrumentation for all pieces, including arrangements of Japanese songs and what might be either band or orchestral music from Japan ("Sarashi" and "Kappore"), reflect musical tastes of diasporic Japanese in the United States. A proclivity toward Western music in Japan dates to the European fife-and-drum and brass and military bands introduced in the Tokugawa period (1603–1868), the hymn singing of Episcopal, Presbyterian, and Reformed American missionaries, European concert music, and, in the 1880s and 1890s, European and American songs combined with traditional Japanese music (*sesshū*) that Japanese school children learned from music textbooks.[50] Japanese communities in urban areas accessed new music from Japan by tuning into transpacific radio station JZJ, which aired the Japanese national anthem, new Japanese folk songs, and other new Japanese vernacular and popular music performed by musicians in the United States.[51] The predominant use of Western instrumentation in concerts and radio programs points to the growing number of Western-trained Nisei musicians who had reached adulthood by 1930.

Japanese music performances took on new meaning in the 1930s when anti-Japanese sentiments in the United States sharply increased as Americans reacted to the rise of Japanese militarism in Asia. Extensive boycotts, organized pickets, and public demonstrations against Japanese-owned businesses and interests spurred immigrants to conjoin with Japanese consulates in establishing a "campaign-for-education" in promoting Japan-US relations. Traditional music and dance performances became a vehicle in this campaign for advancing positive images of Japanese.[52] Issei elites launched the Japanese Cultural Center of Southern California (JCCSC) as a base for cultural diplomacy. The center pinpointed the culture of Old Japan as a propagandistic medium to present to white audiences. Performances of folk dancing, singing, koto, and shamisen music, tea ceremony, and flower arrangement by immigrant and Nisei women highlighted what the Japanese consul considered the "real worth" of modern Japan.[53] Japanese music and arts strategically used as mediums of cultural diplomacy also expressed Issei elites' nationalist attitudes linked to homeland politics and their resistance to assimilation in a country where they continually faced discrimination and nonacceptance.

Japan's increasing military prowess, starting with the Sino-Japanese War (1894–1895), the Russo-Japanese War (1904–1905), and Japan's advance on Manchuria in the 1930s, stirred nationalism among Issei, and Japanese war songs (*gunka*) served as an effective propaganda tool used to unite this generation and rouse their patriotic fervor. In 1938, the Japanese government promoted the war song *Aikoku Kōshin-kyoku* (Patriotic Marching Song), becoming instantly popular among Japanese immigrants.[54] Soon after, Kiyoshi Nozaki, an Issei from Arroyo Grande, California, composed an American version of *Aikoku Kōshin-kyoku*, turning it into the unofficial song of Issei in southern California. Participants sang both versions of the song at patriotic gatherings.[55] Being denied citizenship and facing ever-increasing anti-Japanese sentiment forced Issei into an ever-more ambivalent relationship with the US nation-state.

The social segregation of Japanese Americans predetermined the audience demographic of most musical performances. Audiences varied depending on who sponsored or organized events, for example, private music teachers, Christian or Buddhist churches, local orchestras and other musical ensembles, or the YMCA, who held dances for young adults. The style of music presented—such as European classical, American popular, Japanese classical, or Japanese folk—also dictated who would come. Performances organized by university Japanese American social clubs or sororities performed on campus, such as Japan Night, would attract a wider demographic. There were also performances specifically targeting white audiences as part of the Issei leadership's "campaign-for-education" programming or other attempts to share Japanese culture with mainstream audiences. Although the composition of audiences was not explicitly described in newspaper reports, talent shows featuring a wide variety of musical genres and styles likely drew entire families that were intergenerational and were enjoyed by both men and women. Musicking in concentrated urban areas doubtlessly attracted broader cross sections of the Japanese American population with more eclectic musical programming.

A TALE OF TWO COUNTRIES

To obtain a fuller picture of the forces preventing Issei assimilation and acceptance as a viable population in California, we must turn to the political arena of the Asia-Pacific region. The United States and Japan vied for political and economic dominance of the Pacific region from the end of the nineteenth century into the twentieth. Western powers advanced their colonialist agendas of expanded political influence and new markets in East Asia and the Pacific Basin.[56] These imperialistic intentions collided with Japan's efforts to establish a foothold in the region in its accelerated move toward nationhood and inclusion into existing global capitalist economies.[57] Japan and the United States were two emerging world powers with Japan's win over China in the first Sino-Japanese War in 1894 and the United States acquiring the Hawaiian Islands, the Philippines, and Guam following the Spanish-American War in 1898.[58] The tension and competition between the two countries accounts for much of the racial prejudice that Japanese immigrants endured.

Recent scholarship about Japanese immigration history underscores the imperialist intentions of both the United States and Japan in the Pacific region and how this set the stage for Japanese arriving in the American West. The competing frontiers of both nations placed Issei in an impossible position of reconciling two nationalities. In his book *Between Two Empires: Race, History, and Transnationalism in Japanese America*, Eiichiro Azuma unravels the ideological strands of Japanese nation building and expansionism that were part of emigration. Japanese leaders of the Meiji era considered emigration as a patriotic act geared toward the expansion of Japan politically, commercially, and territorially. Emigration had a nationalistic cast that the Meiji elite presumed all Japanese shared. This assumption proved false as those who emigrated from rural areas were unconcerned with their duties as "imperial subjects," and their reasons for going abroad were more personally and economically motivated. This discrepancy is indicative of the differences in class, education, and intent of the population that left Japan for American shores.[59]

The two strategies employed by Japan in establishing its foundation for economic dominance, a subtle form of colonialism considered most likely to succeed, included mercantilism and labor. Immigrant leaders in urban areas focused on mercantilism. Entrepreneurial and educated young Japanese came to the States with the simultaneous goal of building a business while expanding Japan's economic reach. Mercantilism was part of Japan's expansionist effort to launch venues in foreign countries for its exported goods. The mass emigration of laborers to foreign countries was also a path toward Japan's "eastward expansionism," thought to be a means to infiltrate and settle "its own frontier" in the Western Hemisphere. In the United States this strategy took form in the agricultural work of laborers who came between 1885 and 1908.[60]

In the late nineteenth and early twentieth centuries, the parallel development of Japanese nation building and imperialism to the United States' international mission of Manifest Destiny and modernization converge in the experience of Japanese immigrants. Social and cultural critic David Palumbo-Liu describes the deep role of the Pacific region in the modernization of America and how "the movement of America into Asia was complemented by the reverse—Asian immigration."[61]

The international scope of the United States' expansion into Asia and the Pacific induced a defensive stance in its national conception, giving way to both a deep-rooted Orientalist discourse and apprehension of a changing world in the throes of modernization. The Pacific region's economic promise sparked an interest in its global prospects, and it became the focus in world fairs and exhibitions prior to World War I. A contradictory and somewhat hypocritical attitude emerged, however. Although Americans favored an "open-door" policy that guaranteed trade between the United States and East Asian countries, their exclusionary views toward Asian immigrants conveyed an anxiety about preserving an American national identity.[62]

THE RACIAL POLITICS OF AMERICAN CITIZENSHIP

There is a precedent for Orientalist racializations early in the ideological development of American national identity and citizenship. Between 1776 and 1815, there was a predisposition toward defining the concept of nationality racially along Anglo-Saxon lines. During this time, American political ideology also formed from "abstract ideals of liberty, equality, and republicanism" drawn from the European Enlightenment. The universalist ideology of American nationality was, in theory, open to anyone without regard to an individual's ethnic, national, linguistic, or religious background. This idea formed within the context of the late eighteenth century when 80 percent of white Americans were British. Such a majority coupled with a "latent predisposition" to defining the concept of nationality from the perspective of ethnicity resulted in a contradictory view that regarded other racial and cultural groups as "falling outside the range of American nationality."[63] Blacks and Indians, therefore, were excluded and only white people were eligible to become citizens without any regard for their national background or native language. After 1830, nativist sentiments grew in intensity when Europeans emigrated en masse to the States. American national identity faced numerous challenges in coming to terms with the different religions, politics, education, and culture of the 4 million people who came to the United States between 1830 and 1855. The American response to this deluge of people who fell outside the Anglo-Saxon mold brought religious and ethnic considerations into the national-identity equation. From the 1890s to the 1920s, debates about restricting immigration marked a reversal of the country's original open-door policy to immigrants. Americans also became intolerant of immigrant groups' perpetuation of native nationalities while living on American soil. For two decades starting in the 1900s, an Americanization movement pushed for all émigrés to conform to mainstream American culture, language, religion, and manners.[64]

It was not until the aftermath of the Civil War that racism evolved into an ideological tenet. Biological racism supported the idea that attributes of superiority or inferiority of people of a given phenotype or genotype can be explained biologically. Racism promoting slavery in the South and discrimination against the Irish did not yet coalesce into an organized defense of Anglo-Saxon nationalism. Historians, political scientists, anthropologists, and eugenicists by the 1880s, however, collaborated in establishing an intellectual foundation for a broad-based racial ideology. The basis for this ideology included the notion that democratic political institutions created by Anglo-Saxon citizens could only succeed within an Anglo-Saxon population, reinforcing a narrow window of who were desirable as Americans. Demonstrated research supposedly proved the superiority of the Anglo-Saxon/Aryan/Teutonic/Nordic race. These ideas became pronounced when the 1890 census showed an increase in the arrival of Italians, Slavs, East European Jews, and Greeks. The changing demographic of the population prompted the formation of the Immigration Restriction League at Harvard University. The league's purpose was to appeal to the politically powerful and campaign for more rigorous immigration policies based on ethnic and racial discrimination. Concerns centered on the "mongrolization of the American population with the intermixing of non-Nordic human types with the Nordic pure race."[65]

White elites applied biological racism as a rationale for subordinating nonwhite racial and cultural groups, establishing it as the norm within US society.

The valorizing of Japanese immigrants by whites triangulated them in a field of racial positions, placing them as superior to Blacks, but remaining perpetually foreign and unassimilable. This made it possible for whites to sustain Japanese immigrants as a source for cheap labor, preventing them and other nonwhite immigrant groups from becoming citizens and playing any role in the US polity. The discriminatory actions of valorizing while simultaneously politically ostracizing Japanese immigrants made them susceptible to belligerent white racism. Japanese and Asian immigrants were the only population in US history to be targeted as "aliens ineligible to citizenship."[66]

Orientalism, a concept of "Otherness" applied to people of Asian descent, is the underlying discourse of the oppressive racism that many Issei experienced. An idea rooted in the European Enlightenment, Orientalism reinforced the dichotomy of submission and dominance: the submission of Asian peoples by dominant European powers.[67] The ideological concept of nationality in the United States, based on Protestantism and an Anglo-Saxon ethnic heritage, shaped the idea of Otherness referred to as "American Orientalism."[68] This form of Orientalism contributed to the social construction of "yellowface," a pejorative racial identity of Asians in the United States, and it explains the deep-seated prejudices toward Asian immigrants today.

Palumbo-Liu talks in detail about the fear of white America toward contact and intermixing with "racial minorities, the poor, and immigrants" in the early twentieth century.[69] Psychological and scientific discourses addressed and fueled white America's fear of the "Other." After 1900, scientific racism's promotion of the superiority of the Anglo-Saxon and Nordic races and the assumption that cultural traits were genetically passed on along with physical attributes fed American xenophobia. The science of eugenics furthered such racialized thinking with the view that "the indiscriminate mixing of races was more likely to result in cultural debasement than cultural improvement."[70] Eugenics argued for extreme measures of exclusion, deportation, imprisonment, commitment to insane asylums, antimiscegenation laws, and forced sterilization in reforming who could become an American. Madison Grant's *The Passing of the Great Race* (1916) extolled Anglo-Saxonism, systematizing and further influencing racializations that played an important role in restrictive laws of the 1920s.[71] The coupling of "Orientalist racializations" of Asians as inassimilable and attitudes of "Anglo-Saxon" or "Nordic" racial superiority gave rise to Asian-immigration exclusion acts and laws against naturalization in 1882, 1917, 1924, and 1934. Repeal of these exclusionary laws between 1943 and 1952 granted Asian immigrants the right to citizenship. However, the almost-one-hundred-year period of racist restrictions politically disenfranchised Asians, and only today do they have a growing political presence.

What also has negated Asian American assimilation into the national culture is the history of labor exploitation of this population within the economic sphere of American capitalism and US victories in three wars in Asia in the twentieth century—the wars in the Philippines, Japan, and Korea. These developments contributed to the schizophrenic stance of the United States, which excluded Asians for citizenship in efforts to maintain the Anglo-Saxon or Nordic national identity while keeping an open door to East Asian countries to bolster economic access and growth.[72]

Racist ideology was pervasive between 1913 and 1924. America's growing fear of Japan's military skill and belligerence and the insistent anti-Japanese propaganda of the exclusionists in California turned American public opinion against the Japanese.[73] This was exacerbated on the local level in California with discriminatory state policies that economically and socially subordinated Japanese immigrants. The Alien Land Acts in 1913 and 1920 in California prevented an increase in Issei ownership of land by enforcing their racialized status as "aliens ineligible for citizenship." Industrious Issei and Nisei farmers proved capable of turning fallow fields into verdant farmland, creating unwanted competition for white farmers. Issei also endured segregation in the form of antimiscegenation laws—Section 69 of the California Civil Code finalized in 1880—forbidding Asians from marrying Caucasian partners. Such social segregation reinforced the untouchable status of Japanese émigrés.

Prejudicial treatment extended to education as well. In 1905, the San Francisco Board of Education proposed sending all Asian children to separate public schools; fortunately, the proposal never passed. Asian children, however, in the towns of Florin, Isleton, Walnut Grove, and Courtland, all in Sacramento County, were segregated and sent to separate public schools. Nisei students living in urban centers fared better, but their social opportunities were clearly restricted.

Most reprehensible of all in the Issei's grim reality was the denial of American citizenship based on race. Their efforts to gain the right of naturalization through the American justice system were thwarted. In a landmark suit of *Takao Ozawa v. United States* in 1922, the Supreme Court confirmed that Japanese and other Asians were not "white" and therefore ineligible for naturalization because of race. This outcome legitimized discrimination against Japanese immigrants as noncitizens with no legal recourse. The defeat of this case along with the 1923 land-law test cases challenging the constitutionality of the California and Washington alien-land laws of 1913 and 1920 brought home for Issei their status as racial undesirables in a land that they had made their home. This realization left many Issei bitter and without much hope for the future. Many Issei chose to return to Japan, joining a continuous stream of immigrants who over the years had gone back to escape the growing racism. In the end, only about *40 percent* of Japanese émigrés permanently settled in the United States. Those who stayed looked toward the future of their American-born children with the intention of rectifying their circumstances.

DUAL IDENTITIES

A fully developed subculture combined with a complex web of social relationships and obligations shaped the immigrants' keen cultural identity. Issei, for the most part, considered themselves Japanese, an identity tied to the roles they held within their native social structure, which was reinforced by the segregated enclaves where they lived and worked and the racial discrimination they endured daily. Living in a new land, however, gradually transformed the way Issei viewed themselves as they negotiated the difficult terrain of simultaneously remaining Japanese citizens while participating in American life.

The transnational context of Japanese immigration elucidates the circumstances in which Issei identity evolved. Azuma adroitly describes the transnational nature of Issei identity:

> Since the consciousness of Japanese immigrants was wedged firmly between the established categories of Japan and the US, the relationships that they developed and maintained in the interstices were ambivalent, unsettled, and elusive. Because they were always faced with the need to reconcile simultaneous national belongings as citizen-subjects of one state [Japan] and yet resident-members (denizens) of another [US], the Issei refused to make a unilateral choice, electing instead to take an eclectic approach to the presumed contradiction between things Japanese and American.[74]

The pull from both sides of the Pacific required a complex negotiation of two very different national identities.

Not all immigrants ascribed to Japan's imperialist intentions of colonizing the American West through agricultural and entrepreneurial enterprise. The average emigrant did not share the vision of elite Meiji leaders of emigration-led expansionism, and their identification with the Japanese state varied, creating tension within their communities. Educated, urbane Issei leaders were the primary purveyors of Japanese expansion. The Japanese Association of America and its corresponding organizations in Los Angeles, San Francisco, and Seattle assisted them in setting goals for the immigrant communities. These associations served as liaisons to Japanese consulates in urban centers through which the Japanese government exercised their influence among Issei. Japan's influence played an important role among the Issei leadership in Japanese communities from 1910 on as it became clear that racial exclusion would continue to restrict immigrants in every aspect of their lives.

Dueling identities surfaced as Issei loyalty and racial pride in the country of their birth vied with the pressure to assimilate into American society. Azuma chronicles the Issei's position as "situational, elastic, and even inconsistent at times, but always dualistic at the core."[75] Maintaining a dual identity was a tenuous and complex racial project. Japanese nationalism among Issei obfuscated their goal to become American citizens. Although they had a strong desire to become citizens of their adopted land, the discrimination and racial bias against Issei placed them in a social and psychological state of reverting back to their Japanese racial and cultural moorings in maintaining their sense of well-being.

Issei community leaders criticized the general Issei population's dismissal of American customs, lifestyle, and culture and organized efforts to socialize them in American ways. The elite leadership coalesced around maintaining a dual identity, promoting cultural assimilation as a strategy to reform immigrants and accelerate their acceptance by mainstream America.[76] The cultural assimilation Issei leaders envisioned involved a "dual process of nationalization" both as a Japanese and an American and was not just to Americanize immigrants.[77] Assimilation efforts promoted congruencies between Japanese and American cultures in an attempt to equalize both nationalities in this dual identity.

Leaders powered the assimilation project by aligning themselves with the white Progressive agenda of the national Americanization movement from 1900 through the 1920s. Two views prevailed in this movement. The dominant view, Americanism, required conformity to the cultural mainstream's language, religion, and manners. This view represented the nationalistic, nativist strain of Americanism based on Anglo-Saxon culture supported by patriotic groups such as the Daughters of the American Revolution and the Boston-based North American Civic League for Immigrants, founded in 1908. Progressivism, a second view, considered the Americanization movement as an opportunity to assist newcomers in acclimating to the changes and difficult situations they faced living in the United States. Supporters of

Progressivism pressed for protective legislation for immigrants based on the potential of the cultural contributions they would bring to American life.[78] The Americanization movement targeted minority populations, including the Japanese, and it added force to Issei reformist efforts to culturally assimilate immigrants in their communities. Community leaders proposed two angles in the assimilation process. A majority favored *gaimenteki dōka*, i.e., assimilation involving only outward appearances such as following American-style clothing, homes, and furnishings, observing American customs and holidays in place of Japanese national celebrations, avoiding use of items conspicuously Japanese, and participating in local American communities to gain recognition.[79] This form of assimilation was superficial and accommodated the resistance of Issei to become 100-percent American. A second form of assimilation conceived by a small minority of Issei leaders was *naimenteki dōka*. This concept embraced more inherent forms of assimilation, such as the adoption of "secular values, such as American democratic principles and practices" and the religious values of Christianity.[80] There was little motivation for Issei to pursue deeper-seated forms of assimilation as they endured racism, alien-land laws, residential restrictions, and were denied naturalization.

The hopes of inculcating *naimenteik dōka* spawned an international program to Christianize Asians as part of the Issei leadership's assimilation reforms. Immigrant organizations and Christian associations arranged activities to culturally assimilate Issei by offering English-language and citizenship classes. Assimilation reforms reached my maternal grandfather, Kichitaro Taki, living in New York City. He became a Christian despite his father being a highly ranked Buddhist priest in Kyoto and adopted a pro-American stance that emphasized American language, customs, and lifestyle. Consequently, my mother and her two sisters never learned to speak Japanese. Instruction for newly arrived immigrant women included lessons in American housekeeping, child rearing, and English.[81] These practical pursuits revolved around culturally assimilating Issei.

A public-relations campaign accompanied reform measures with the intent of focusing public attention on immigrants from the less educated working class to the more refined echelon of Issei.[82] This entailed presenting Japanese cultural events and performances in urban centers and targeting American audiences, desiring to educate them about their highly developed cultural traditions, such as flower arranging, tea ceremony, and koto and shamisen music. Japanese diplomats and immigrant elites felt that racial oppression could be eradicated once Americans learned more about the long history and revered cultural traditions of Japan.

In an eclectic move, immigrant leaders countered white supremacy by considering themselves as "honorary whites" which they equated with the thinking and behavior of a proper Japanese. Their efforts to convince immigrant communities to view themselves as "honorary whites" were generally supported and climaxed with the 1922 *Ozawa v. United States* legal case. This argument was unsuccessful, making it impossible for Japanese to attain naturalized citizenship, one avenue that Issei hoped would advance them.[83] The collective experience of legal discrimination narrowed differences in Japanese communities, intensifying their interdependence and group solidarity.

During the years of World War I on into the 1920s, it became clear that cultural assimilation failed. Much of the failure was due to the inability of the Japanese association network to reach enough immigrants for the reforms to widely take hold. Class differences and weak responses to the reform efforts within Japanese communities challenged efforts to bring Issei into the fold of American society. Japanese farm laborers who continued to receive poor wages and have no job security were left with little time or motivation to culturally assimilate. Governmental legislation barring Issei political and economic rights based on race and citizenship gave them very little recourse in a life they sought to create in a new land.[84]

Forced to concede to their racial disenfranchisement, Issei took on the mantle of *zaibei dōhō*—"the Japanese in America." *Zaibei dōhō* is an identity that emerged out of the Japanese immigrants' collective experience of being "a racial Other in America."[85] For immigrants, *zaibei dōhō* did not evoke an orthodox Japaneseness, but rather a transculturated Japanese identity in which their native heritage was the source of their racially inassimilable status. This identity captured the meaning of what it was to be Japanese in a land where structural racism intensified the dependency of Issei farmers and laborers on white employers and where immigrant landowners and urban residents often faced racial containment in choosing where to live. As a collective identity, *zaibei dōhō* represented an erasure of class, age, social background, gender, occupation, and wealth among immigrants, bringing them together in a shared experience of subordination.

Group solidarity based on ethnicity worked to counter the debilitating effects of institutionalized racism. Historian Ronald Takaki explains, "Japanese ethnic solidarity—a shared identity with countrymen and shared cultural values—contributed to the establishment of the Issei ethnic economy, which in turn provided an economic basis for ethnic cohesiveness."[86] Entrepreneurial activity flourished among Issei as an alternative to employment in the industrial and trade-labor unions from which they were racially barred.

Ie, the most important kinship unit in traditional Japan, broadened in meaning within the United States to refer to entire communities. Sociologist Harry H. L. Kitano emphasizes the importance of solidarity to the Issei: "A system of collectivism and ethical interaction provided mutual assistance for group members and proved effective in protecting the individual from the cultural shocks of both a rapidly changing Japan and, later, of a new land."[87] In the germinal history of Japanese immigration, the community served as a frame for social relationships, economic stability, and a means of deflecting outside hostility.

Increased patriotic zeal developed in tandem with growing ethnic solidarity in immigrant communities during the 1930s. Racial exclusionism in the form of legal discriminatory laws impelled Issei into a defensive stance that reinforced their Japanese ethnicity and self-reliance. The anger and resentment of Issei in their failure to successfully fight racial discrimination rekindled their patriotic identification with Japan.[88] Also fueling Issei nationalism was the rise of militarism in Japan and the aggressive conquest of Manchuria in 1932. Seizo Oka places blame on Issei themselves, whom he felt were partly responsible for the rise of anti-Japanese sentiment. For example, in rural areas, such as the Sacramento Delta area (Sacramento, Florin, Isleton, Walnut Grove, and Cortland), the stifling racism and resultant segregation of Japanese school children from the public schools became hotbeds of Japanese nationalism. Oka claims:

> Everything was getting to be very nationalistic. The leaders in these communities were of Buddhist background. They were not in accord with the leaders of a Christian background and thinking. My father was one of those with a Christian background in the area around Isleton, Walnut Grove, and Cortland. He published a newspaper article saying that the Japanese children born over here, being taken care of by the US, should be educated to be loyal to the US.

Oka's father advocated for the Americanization of Nisei and assisted by assimilating and educating them.[89]

Another identity shift suddenly took place following October 1940, when Japan joined military forces with European Axis powers. In response, the American government ordered an embargo on scrap-metal exports and froze all Japanese assets in the United States. Japanese businessmen in Brazil took up the slack in collecting scrap metal for Japan. My father's difficulty in finding a job in the 1930s led to a position with the Japanese firm Okura and Company in Sao Paulo. His job was to collect scrap metal and cowhide to send to Japan for their war effort. The job placed my father under suspicion by the US government and the FBI maintained a comprehensive file on him. An identity shift away from Japan resulted in immigrant communities quickly ending their partnerships with Japanese consulates and replacing Japanese patriotism with undivided American loyalty. The publication of a bilingual booklet entitled *Americanism* included the Pledge of Allegiance, the Declaration of Independence, the Bill of Rights, and a statement of Issei and Nisei loyalty to the United States.[90] It was sent to Issei households in the entire region, yet a uniform shift did not occur since individual degrees of loyalty to either Japan, the United States, or both varied.

From the very start, both external and internal pressures prevented Issei from successfully forging a national identity. The historical and social forces encompassing geopolitical conflict between Japan and the United States, racialization, exclusion, discrimination, and labor exploitation proved to be insurmountable. Intracommunity class tensions and conflict over Japan's imperialist intentions, assimilation goals, and unequal economic and social capital further destabilized Issei's chances, even as leaders attempted to racially and culturally rearticulate their position. The virulent racial politics and inhospitable social milieu squelched this immigrant population's willingness to forsake their native nationality and culture, locating them outside the boundaries of their adopted nation. "Give me your tired, your poor, your huddled masses yearning to breathe free . . . I lift my lamp beside the golden door!" These are the words of American poet Emma Lazarus, mounted at the foot of the Statue of Liberty, which rang with bitter irony for Japanese immigrants whose racial and cultural differences placed them too far afield from the American mainstream and attaining citizenship.

It was the relationship that Issei had with music that made this expressive cultural form vital for their well-being. Music both powered and stabilized Issei's racial and ethnic identification, which became more fluid as ethnic boundaries shifted, reflecting their changing sociopolitical environment. A shared universe of meanings in the sound, visual imagery, emotions, and ideals generated by music strengthened social bonds in immigrant communities, offsetting the discriminatory laws restricting their assimilation and sense of belonging. Music as a vehicle for compassion and humanity, a Buddhist sentiment presented earlier, perhaps neutralized the bitterness many felt, creating a tranquil space in which they could enjoy beauty and a sense of well-being. As an aesthetic activity, musicking expressed shared tastes while displaying individual musical talents. Musical performances offered an essential source of entertainment that enhanced and brightened Issei lives. Listening to Japanese music triggered symbolic associations of distant Japanese places and hometown life, celebrating its aesthetic display and sense of familiarity, but it was by no means the only music Issei enjoyed. Concert programming, interspersing Japanese and Western performing arts, and Japanese songs crosscut with Western-style musical accompaniment mirrored differentiated forms of *zaibei dōhō* (transculturated identity) that had manifested among Issei. The first generation's enjoyment of Western-inspired Japanese popular music—*kayokyōku*—which had reached diasporic communities in the late 1920s and 1930s, reflected broader and modern ways of how immigrants perceived themselves. Musicking marked the lateral movement of liminal identities between two cultures as individuals sought agency needed to improve their social location. In adjusting to life in the United States, transnational attachments eased, and Issei identities became more variable—transculturated and complex—forged by residential location (urban vs. rural), social class, and individual adaptability.

The racial, economic, and political anxiety that native Californians felt toward Japanese immigrants reverberates today with increasingly restrictive immigration laws being implemented by the US federal government, a product of xenophobic unease that continues to generate suspicious attitudes toward immigrants who are viewed as unassimilable and a source of economic competition. Anti-immigrant legislation and biases have cycled through American history of the nineteenth and twentieth centuries, challenging democratic notions of nation building.

CHAPTER 3

Caught on the Cultural Cusp: Nisei Politics of Identity and Music

> We all wanted to be blond and blue-eyed Americans, hated to be Japanese. We changed our Japanese names into American names. Were criticized for our short hairdos but didn't care. Went to movies, were crazy about Clara Bow and Joan Crawford! Loved jazz... Red Nichols and the Five Pennies, Paul Whiteman "The King of Jazz," and clarinet-playing Ted Lewis; love the vocals of Connie Boswell and Ruth Etting.
>
> —LILY OYAMA SASAKI, Sacramento, 1930[1]

The above quote poignantly expresses Sasaki and her peers' longing for acceptance into American society, but their quest remained wholly unfulfilled. Second-generation Nisei embodied Japanese immigrant parents' hope that their children will finally achieve the American dream of economic opportunity and political legitimacy. Born between 1910 and 1940, Nisei comprised nearly 27 percent (29,672) of the total Japanese American population of 111,055 in the United States by 1920. In 1930, their numbers surged to around 49 percent (68,357) of the total population and, in 1940, close to 63 percent (79,642) of all Japanese Americans in the fifty contiguous states.[2] As the first generation born on American soil, Nisei personified their parents' hopes and dreams, but the social and economic constraints still in place made their task difficult, resulting in little progress toward acceptance. The identity crisis of Nisei during the decades spanning the 1920s to the 1940s was particularly painful since their legal status as American citizens hardly made a difference in how they were viewed and treated. Highlighted in this study is the importance of evolving racial and cultural identities and the politics surrounding these formations. Posing the questions of what historical, political, and social forces from the 1910s to the 1940s shaped Nisei identity and how music served to enact Nisei identity is meant to stir a discussion about the racial ideology inherent in American life and how music connected Nisei to the nation and culture in which they sought acceptance.

Performing, active listening, and dancing to music of the American mainstream enabled Nisei youth to enact what they desired most: national belonging. It is grievous that, at such a crucial stage in constructing their identities, Nisei were treated as outsiders as their two cultural worlds collided. Impeding their quest for validation as Americans was the heterogeneous mix of this population, which included Kibei—meaning "returned to America," a subset of Nisei who were born in the United States but educated in Japan—who strongly identified with Japan, as well as a slightly older cohort, born to early Issei arrivals, whose promotion of Americanism failed to capture the imagination of the Nisei majority. Even more tangled is singer Sue Okabe's argument that the aesthetic and cultural pull of music and culture from both worlds defies any generalization or categorization of Nisei identities and that individuals personally chose a balance that was most agreeable. As the first generation born on American soil, many Nisei felt a natural affinity and inclination toward American customs, culture, and music. While some individuals differentiated themselves by favoring Japanese music and dance, most countered their exclusion by behaving 100-percent American. Performing social dance band music and jazz, classical music, jitterbugging, and popular and vernacular songs or hymns in glee clubs and choirs were Niesei's enculturated responses as Americans. Music most collectively and vividly signified Nisei's shared emotional and social bonds and sense of aesthetics in identifying themselves as either American, Japanese, or bicultural.

Transnationalism surfaced in musical performances of the second generation despite the many who eschewed activities and customs tied to being Japanese, the very source of their social constraints. Some Nisei learned to play koto or shamisen, performed classical or folk dances, or sang Japanese classical, vernacular, or popular songs, maintaining traditions of their heritage but in a *transculturated*, rearticulated form. Signs of transculturation manifested in interpretive performances of Japanese dance, Western arrangements of Japanese vernacular and popular songs, an incorporation of Japanese stylistic features and nuances in Western compositions, combined programming of Western and Japanese music in a single performance, and music taught in a social milieu different from that of Japan, often resulting in subtle shifts in performance practices, aesthetics, or repertoire.

Coping strategies of the second generation gave rise to a subculture shaped by American mainstream culture, creating a false sense of solidarity within the ethnic community. Nisei, unable to participate in the social, political, or economic mainstream of the United States, were forced to share in their parents' disenfranchisement and join in "a highly symbolic struggle to redefine the Japanese American community in a more 'American' style."[3] "American" style referred to dominant white, Euro-American social and cultural patterns. Such redefinition involved neutralizing the racial hostility surrounding them, but it also reflected the demographic shift of rising numbers of Nisei within the ethnic enclave. The collective identity formed in Japanese communities was orthodox and confining, disallowing any views or experiences that differed from the norm.[4] This orthodoxy gave rise to small groups of nonconformists who attempted to rearticulate their identity by criticizing and protesting what they considered the inability of the community for self-determination.[5] The tension between the Issei leadership and nonconformist groups revealed not only generational but also class differences in which the elite leadership dominated those of lower-class status. Wearing the "mask" of their ancestors but having been born an American led to the psychological conflict of "double alienation," a product of wartime racism that forced Nisei to "participate in their own racial and cultural erasure to prove their loyalty and lay claim to an American identity."[6]

Restrictive policies and growing anti-Japanese sentiment posed little possibility of any political change in Nisei's favor. Efforts to establish common ground with mainstream society also failed. Such circumstances led to most Nisei to live apolitical lives. As well, their small numbers and age gap within the Nisei cohort prevented effective coalition building that could support a politically unified voice in countering a deteriorating geopolitical landscape in which Japan's increasing political power in the Pacific was becoming more prominent. Older Nisei formed the Japanese American Citizens League (JACL) and other political advocacy groups but with little success, while younger Nisei filled their days with school, sports, and socializing or working to advance their family's economic survival. Music was one of the few avenues Nisei had to situate themselves socially and culturally. When the United States became enmeshed in World War II, American social dance music, especially, acquired magnitude as Nisei youth more emphatically claimed their status as Americans.

Nisei successfully defining themselves proved to be an insurmountable challenge because of the volatile setting in which national and global racial politics denied them acceptance, and the confining, Issei-controlled communities curbed Nisei development and hampered their efforts to assimilate. A complex endeavor, forming an identity required navigating multiple meanings attached to race, ethnicity, class, age, and upbringing further held back by economic conditions and anti-immigrant politics.[7] Nisei aspirations to belong were thwarted by white America's imposition of race as a marker and Nisei ties to the Japanese community and the strong ethnic bond necessary for their survival as a population. Frustrating for this generation was the quandary of relying on their ethnic bonds within the Japanese community for employment while simultaneously being repudiated by the American public for the close connection. Their desire to find a space where their racialized ethnic identity and status as American citizens could be reconciled never materialized. Mainstream society culturally and socially conflated Issei and Nisei, politically ostracizing both as entities situated outside the US polity. Feeling displaced both within and outside their communities, it is no wonder that sports, dancing, musicking, and socializing took on greater meaning for Nisei. It is in the context of their social and recreational activities that music had the most impact. With its distinct sound and aesthetic, American dance band music not only had a hand in constructing the Nisei's American identity, it also celebrated their youth and good times in a manner typical of teenagers throughout the United States.

LIFE ON THE CULTURAL CUSP

Existing on the cultural cusp between two countries that were geopolitical rivals complicated the formation of Nisei's cultural identity. Nisei's position aptly fit the sociological discourse and concept of the "marginal man," which Robert Park of the University of Chicago conceived in the 1920s as the transitional stage of being suspended between two cultures in the assimilation process and the struggle that may ensue in establishing one's identity. Daniel I. Okimoto, political scientist and author of the book *American in Disguise*, spoke for many Nisei in voicing his marginalization: "Indeed for much of my life, I had struggled with the conviction that I was an American in disguise, a creature part of, yet somehow detached from, the mainstream of American society."[8] The Nisei psychological distress often took the form of self-hate and a denunciation of their Japanese heritage. This generation's struggle to reconcile two contrasting cultures outlines not a single identity, "an authentic self that somehow was either Japanese or American," but rather "fluid, ambiguous, contingent identities"[9] shaped by social class, occupational status, educational background, gender, geographical locale, and varying degrees of Japaneseness and Americanness. Such shifting and unstable identities problematize the binary categorizations of retention and assimilation that simplify and misrepresent the realities of Japanese American identity formation.[10]

Racially, the subjectivities and practices of Nisei in countering their marginalization focused on "whiteness." The notion of whiteness as superior stems from Meiji period officials in Japan who assessed that the West's better military and technological advancements that made it possible for European countries to dominate most of Asia was inextricably connected to whiteness. The sentiment was also a product of the ideological push of the United States to Americanize all immigrants arriving on its shores and a Nisei desire to participate in US white-dominated society. As American youth got swept up in the popular music and dance craze of the 1930s and 1940s, Nisei danced, listened to, and performed popular music in their attempts to become part of white America. In moving toward whiteness, many Nisei suppressed their ethnic and racial identities. During the era in which Nisei matured, they were racially set apart and socially and politically ostracized due to being racially triangulated, a practice continued by whites who essentialized and conflated the race and culture of Chinese and Japanese and ignored the generational distinction between Issei and Nisei. Nisei were kept in limbo between whites, Blacks, and other Asian cultural groups.

Kibei were pariahs who faced an even greater struggle in carving out a social space for themselves. Kibei Nisei were sent to Japan for several reasons. Sojourner Issei, in preparing to return to Japan, would send on ahead their sons or daughters to be educated and learn the language. Other families sent their children to be brought up by grandparents or relatives because working long hours made it difficult to care for them. Yet another reason Issei sent one or two of their children was to mollify their parents in the old country who impatiently waited for their return. The largest percentage of Nisei who moved to Japan did so with their parents, who lost all hope of providing for their families in the United States. By 1941, about half of all Nisei had moved to Japan, approximately fifty thousand, with only one-fifth ever returning. Kibei who received Japanese music training were principal transnational links between Japan and the United States. Upon returning to the United States, they most likely served as significant carriers of musical traditions and advocates in proper performance practices. Musically, Kibei were known to sing *shigin* (recitation of Chinese poems). Kibei returnees, speaking fluent Japanese and knowledgeable about Japanese culture, hoped to assume leadership roles in their communities. Instead, Issei showed little interest in transferring responsibilities and power to Kibei. Adding to their difficulties, Nisei scorned Kibei, considering them to be too conservative and rigid in their Japaneseness. Open hostilities between the two Nisei subgroups prevented Kibei from attaining social normalcy with their peers.[11] Issei parents often found their Kibei offspring unable to move beyond blue-collar jobs, while Nisei children who remained in the United States eventually landed upper-level white-collar employment. Kibei did, however, play an important part in the agricultural economy of their parents as laborers. Issei initiated the Return-to-America campaign as a means to integrate Kibei into the community and facilitate working relationships with Nisei in the continued success of family farms.[12]

NISEI SUBCULTURE

Nisei subculture consisted of two major groups, both American born. One subgroup was raised and educated in the United States; the other consisted of Kibei, already introduced. Nisei living in rural areas led more provincial lives in isolated farm communities, while urbanites had broader social experiences and tended to be more cosmopolitan. "Los Angeles Nisei were said to be 'fast,' casual, interested in a good time while San Francisco Nisei were considered sophisticated, conservative, conscious of the need for good grooming and dressing well. Seattle Nisei had a reputation for being friendly, but naïve and unsophisticated."[13] For most of this generation, sports, dances, fashion, dating, and church life filled their time. The subculture also included noisy and disorderly adolescents who formed gangs. They crashed parties and dances, loitered in pool halls, and spent their time bowling or playing poker—a disaffected bunch, which represented the hopelessness of a generation that wanted to escape either a dissatisfying routine job, unemployment, or an unsure future.[14]

Occupationally, most Nisei relied on Issei enterprises in Japanese enclaves, formed in response to the rather inhospitable socioeconomic environment of the West Coast states. Nisei found employment as commercial fishermen, retail and wholesale managers, sales clerks, craftsmen, chauffeurs, domestic service workers, truck farmers, farm laborers, contract gardeners, and nursery operators and laborers.[15] Many felt confined to their communities but could do little to alter their circumstances since positions in engineering, manufacturing, or education were closed to them and many white businesses either had policies in place against their employment or bowed to employees who refused to work alongside people of Japanese descent.

The socioeconomic class status of Nisei was primarily middle class. Those who practiced law, medicine, or owned large retail businesses in the ethnic economy belonged to the upper-middle class. Nisei proprietors of small retail businesses or wholesale produce operations fell squarely within the middle class. Others employed in domestic service, contract gardening, sales, farming, and other manual service work occupied the lower rungs of the middle class.

Nisei activities were socially segregated affairs held in the ethnic community. Racial barriers denying Japanese Americans access to public facilities, social events, housing, and employment prompted Nisei to stay within their enclaves, which provided a safe but suffocating environment from the hostile society outside its borders. Public schools, churches, both Buddhist and Christian, and Japanese newspapers all served as important institutions within enclaves, playing a central role in shaping Nisei identity and the growth of a rich subculture.[16]

Democratic ideals, individualism, and other socially progressive concepts taught in public schools Americanized Nisei, challenging the formal values and customs of their parents. Public school education exposed Nisei to mainstream American social and cultural norms. Even as Japanese values were cultivated at home, American-born Nisei's most earnestly desired social identity was essentially middle-class American. Young Nisei listened to Bob Hope and Fred Allen, sang the songs of Bing Crosby, and read *Collier's*, the *Saturday Evening Post*, and *American Magazine*.[17]

Buddhist and Christian churches in Japanese enclaves were more than places of worship; they served as community centers offering social services, local networks, and youth activities. Methodist churches and the Council of Churches, an umbrella Protestant organization, were the most active in providing services to Japanese Americans and helping them find employment. Particularly painful for Nisei youth was their social segregation from the rest of society. In easing the social stigma, the YMCA, Young Women's Christian Association (YWCA), Christian churches and Buddhist temples, and youth organizations, such as the Oliver Club,[18] created spaces for Nisei to develop their subculture and organize social activities. Likewise important for Nisei were local and regional conferences sponsored by churches, student organizations, and the JACL, a Nisei-formed civic organization. The gatherings gave members of the second generation a platform to address concerns surrounding their bicultural status, countering the racism around them, and strategizing a course for their future.[19] Questions such as what's wrong with the Nisei and what Nisei's future is were central to most discussions as Nisei wrangled with self-doubt and insecurities in their search for an identity.[20]

More questions than answers were raised at these forums as the second generation strategized ways to cope with another dilemma: an increasingly tense geopolitical conflict between Japan and the United States. Buddhism and Christianity served to mollify Nisei as they struggled to overcome racism and social isolation. By the 1940s, 48.7 percent of Nisei were Buddhist and 35 percent were Christian.[21] The legacy of Christian churches in the Japanese community is traced to the supportive role these institutions played in providing social services and language classes to Japanese immigrants. Buddhist temples in Japan historically functioned as marketplaces and community centers that offered medical treatments and education, thus its expanded social-service role in the enclaves was inevitable.

Newspapers in Japanese communities in the decades leading up to World War II were instrumental as a forum for discussing racial issues their population faced. The English-language sections of this media catered to the second generation, reviewing and analyzing important issues such as antimiscegenation laws and discriminatory policies in employment, housing, and access to public facilities.[22] Reflecting the ideological and political inclinations of the communities' leadership, the press featured articles advising Nisei to counter racism with an impeccable work ethic and a wholesale espousal of American customs and way of life. This optimistic and rather unrealistic approach was meant to appeal to the "egalitarian sensibilities" of Americans and eventually lead to the full acceptance of Japanese Americans.[23] Print media publicized information and opinions that shaped Nisei consciousness and facilitated an emerging subculture.

In addition to their schooling and religious life, Nisei enjoyed recreational activities typical of any young American but only in the company of other Japanese Americans or within the boundaries of their own communities. Although their subculture embraced Americanness, the racist climate that prevailed forced Nisei to create a world of their own.

NISEI MUSIC WORLD

It is striking how vital music was in Nisei life. For many of this generation, listening and dancing to and making music were fundamental to their social, recreational, and religious lives. It expressed a multiplicity of meanings in being an American of Japanese descent.

A variety of music styles and traditions exerted their influence as Nisei traversed between two worlds: that of their Japanese parents and American mainstream society. It is my intention to explore this medium as a source of enjoyment and cultivation and a means to counteract their feelings of inadequacy and alienation.

Musicking was most prevalent in urban centers—San Francisco and Los Angeles—where teachers could be found and where music ensembles and organizations offered many opportunities to study and perform. Urban institutions played a decisive role in creating an active musical environment. Christian and Buddhist churches sponsored concerts, and often their youth groups formed music bands to attract young Nisei while Japanese consulates cultivated direct ties to Japan within communities, asserting their influence and promoting performances of traditional performing arts. Community groups such as the YMCA and YWCA assembled glee clubs and hosted social dances, while the JACL, in their efforts to recruit Nisei, celebrated holidays with dances in addition to other social activities.

Ethnic traditions are effective in maintaining the distinctiveness of a group. Art, music, dance, rituals, folk beliefs, celebrations, and food hold meaning and bind people who share these practices. For Japanese communities in the United States, shared traditions provided a sense of belonging. A fair number of Nisei chose to study and perform traditional Japanese music, following in the footsteps of their parents or using it as a vehicle to learning about their heritage. As children, Nisei heard Japanese music both at home and in school. They learned a variety of Japanese songs while attending Japanese language schools, Buddhist churches, or in segregated public schools in communities such as Florin, Walnut Grove, and other rural towns in California where segregation prevailed. The singing of Japanese folk and popular songs accompanied by piano were common forms of home and community entertainment.

Classical Japanese music and dance continued to hold value as part of a well-bred woman's cultivation and as a symbol of Japan's refined cultural traditions and educated social classes. The Issei leadership considered the Japanese arts as a valuable means to nurture *Nippon seishin* (Japanese spirit) and prepare the next generation to assume their responsibilities as future leaders. Playing European classical music was also an expression and mark of the socially elevated. In her study of Japanese American musicking in Los Angeles, Waseda proposes that Issei encouraged their daughters to pursue these classical traditions as a "dual approach to performance arts," providing both informal entertainment for family and community affairs and serving as an emblem of middle-class gentility.[24] In figure 3.1, the dancers include my aunt Miyo (third from left) and my aunt Hana (sixth from left)—my mother's sisters. My mother's family were members of the Japanese Christian Institute in New York City, immersing young Japanese Americans in their ethnic traditions while practicing Christianity. The dance

Figure 3.1. Young Nisei performing Japanese dance. Christmas 1935, New York City. Courtesy of Asai Family Collection.

performance was part of the Christmas program in 1935, and it illustrates the syncretic aspects of growing up Japanese American.

From the 1910s to the 1940s, young Nisei women studied traditional Japanese music and dance, many at the behest of their Issei parents. *Buyō*—classical dance—flourished more than music since more dance teachers were available for lessons. Nisei girls also studied koto, shamisen (which featured in music of the Kabuki theater and chamber music), *utai* (*nō* drama singing), and *biwa* (the four- or five-string plucked lute along with narrative songs). In the 1930s, some Nisei were serious enough to travel to Japan to continue their training with master artists in dance, drama, and music. A few returned to the United States with their *natori* (certificates of accredited mastery), such as the Los Angeles dance master Fujima Kansuma and shamisen and koto professional Kineya Jyorokusho.[25] By 1940, four out of seven koto teachers in southern California were Nisei, and in 1941, it appears five had received their *natori* in Japanese classical dance.[26]

Issei and Nisei presented a rich assortment of Japanese performing arts in *engeikai* (talent shows). As entertainment, Japanese music could be heard at community benefits, socials, Christmas and New Year's shows, picnics, and traditional celebrations, such as the summer Obon festival and the Japanese emperor's birthday.[27] Programming for *engeikai* included comedy, sword dance (*kenbu*), Japanese *odori* dance, and koto, *biwa*, shamisen, and shakuhachi music. Young Nisei girls mostly performed Japanese dance at these gatherings.[28] One such community social was a two-day program presented under the auspices of the Moneta Mother's Club and the Gardena Young Women's Association in Gardena, California, on November 26 and 27, 1926. The program, consisting mostly of Japanese pieces, included:

Japanese dance;
chorus by the Gardena Young Women's Association;
Biwa music;
sword dance;
jōruri (shamisen music of the puppet theater);
Impossibility—a Japanese comedy;
Bloody Camelia—an operetta;
Konjiki-yasha [Golden Demon]—a Japanese tragedy;
Les Misérables—a tragedy.[29]

A newspaper article in the Los Angeles *Rafu Shimpo* covering the event reported that although the performers were a mix of Issei and Nisei, the audience for this event were mostly Issei. It is not surprising that audiences for traditional Japanese music were primarily first-generation Issei for whom this music expressed an aesthetic close to their heart, conjuring a distant homeland. Chances are Western theatrical pieces were programmed to attract the second generation, many who in all likelihood were also the performers. Westernized Issei would have derived pleasure from the Western offerings as well.

Concerts or recitals sponsored by Japanese music and dance teachers and enthusiasts also engaged Nisei. Music and dance instruction, traditionally organized into schools or clubs (*iemoto*), centered around a head teacher who organized recitals, featuring her students and devotees before audiences comprised of families, friends, and the community.

Radio broadcasts delivered programming for listeners who enjoyed a variety of Japanese music performed by local musicians or visiting artists. Both traditional and popular music could be heard over the airwaves on KRKD, a Los Angeles radio station that hosted a "Japanese Hour," a weekly program on Friday evenings from 8:15 to 9:30 p.m. "Japanese Hour" included a variety of performing arts, as illustrated in the show aired on February 27, 1941:

children's song—"Tondayo Tondayo" (It Flew, It Flew) by Yuko Takahashi;
popular song—"Bakuha Shonen hei" (Explosive Boy Soldier) by Yoshi Tabata;
popular song—"Ano hi kara" (From That Day) by Junko Mikado;
"Kokuminka" (National People's Song) and "Sangyo Senshin no uta" (A Song of Industrial Advances) by June Ono;
the *manzai* (comic dialogue) "Moshimo Oyome ni ittara" (If I Get Married) by Wakaba Tamamatsu;
the *hauta* (short shamisen song) "Tankai bushi" (Tankai Tune), popular song made by comic actor Shiganoya Tankai, performed by Kimiei;
popular song—"Shimeta Hachimaki" (Tied Headband) by Fumiko Yatsuyu;

naniwa-bushi (popular narrative shamisen music)—"Tsuma" (Wife) by Yonewaka Susuki.[30]

The variety programming of mostly popular entertainment genres in this radio broadcast enticed first- and second-generation listeners; the popular songs added to the appeal to younger listeners while also keeping the Issei engaged. Notable are the two nationalist songs, reflecting nationalist sentiments in the community. Radio programming broadcast from Japan kept Japanese Americans current with music trends in the homeland.

The Japanese Broadcasting Society in Los Angeles played a major role in producing Japanese music programs. Radio station KRKD aired programming sponsored by the society on Monday evenings at 9:30 p.m. and on New Year's. Monday-evening offerings featured local performers of both Japanese and European classical music. On March 13, 1933, Madame Yasuyo Kineya, Los Angeles's own *nagauta* master, performed live as part of the program. Additionally, the Broadcasting Society presented special New Year's programming; the New Year's broadcast on January 3, 1941, listed below, was evidently intended to reinforce listener's cultural and political ties to Japan with the exclusive Japanese music programming and greetings by the society's board of directors: Shintaro Fukushima, Consul of Japan; Shungo Abe, president of the Japanese Chamber of Commerce; and Gongoro Nakamura, president of the Central Japanese Association.

"Kimigayo" (His Imperial Majesty's Reign), the Japanese national anthem
"Mikuni Iyaska" (Your Majesty's Kingdom)
"Dai Nippon Koshin Kyoku" (Japanese march)
Yōkyoku (*nō* drama singing)—"Hagoromo" (Celestial Robe)
Greetings by Yaemitsu Sugimachi of the Broadcasting Society
Greetings—"Atarashiki Keshiu" (New Beginnings[?]) by Shungo Abe
Greetings—"Atarashiki Keshiu" by Gongoro Nakamura
Greetings—"Shinnen no Shokan" (My Impressions on the New Year) by Consul Shintaro Fukushima
Vocal solo—(1) "Komori uta" (Lullaby); (2) "Saita Sakurani" (Here's to the Cherry Blossoms)
Sankyoku (chamber music)—"Nebikino Matsu" (Pine Seedlings) with Kuzunai Sokuzan, shakuhachi; Chieko Sakamoto, shamisen; and Tomiko Sakamoto, koto.
Shigin (sung poetry)—"Kokutai Sho" (National Polity)
Biwa solo—"Hōsraizan" (Mount Hōrai)

Operetta *manzai*—"Sensenfukei"
Hauta (short shamisen song)—(1) "Harunimo Ume" (Pine Blossoms in Spring); (2) "Dodoitsu" (Dodoitsu Poem)
Popular song—"Kenko Koshinkyoku" (Healthy March[?])
Nagauta—"Yoi Shojo" (Good Girls[?])
Naniwa-bushi—"Tofu to Konnyaku" (Tofu and Konnyaku)
Naniwa-bushi—"Shamisen Musume" (Shamisen Girls)[31]

The Japanese Broadcasting Society appears to have served as the cultural arm of the Consul of Japan and important business leaders, demonstrating the Japanese political and cultural ties maintained in the community through radio-program design.

Japan Night concerts presented by various community organizations were attempts to bolster Nisei's cultural ties to Japan or introduce Japanese arts to mainstream audiences. It is remarkable that such an endorsement of Japanese culture existed in the years leading into the Second World War when anti-Japanese sentiments in the United States climaxed. The performing arts played a notable role in demonstrating the ethnic community's strong ties to Japan despite the virulent anti-Japanese climate in California. One Japan Night event was planned for the Imperial County Fair programming on March 7, 1941, and sponsored by the Brawley and El Centro Citizens League under the advisement of the Brawley Japanese Association. The program was a mix of traditional Japanese music and dance performed alongside Western musical numbers and martial-arts demonstrations. The moderately nationalistic performance in rural, central California featured:

singing of the Japanese national anthem;
Japanese classical dance by Hakuto Kai (a Japanese dance club);
vocal solo by Akiko Hoshizaki;
accordion solo by Calvin Furukawa;
Japanese folk dances by Brawley and El Centro girls;
Chikuzen biwa by L. A. entertainers;
odori (classical Japanese dance) by Hakuto Kai;
harmonica selections by the Nagata sisters;
odori, "Harusame" (Spring Rain) by Hakuto Kai;
song by El Centro girls' chorus;
Chikuzen biwa;
judo demonstration by Brawley Judo club;
kendo demonstration: matches between El Centro and Coachells.[32]

The event broadly expressed a Japanese spirit with the inclusion of judo and kendo and the national anthem, which were added to attract the participation of Nisei men and express Issei's nationalist ties to their homeland. Diverse organizations presented "Japan" programs: Japan-America Society, Nisei Junior BYPU (Buddhist Young People's Union), St. Mary's Episcopal Church, Rotary Club, Academy of National Culture of the University of Southern California International Relations jointly with Japanese Trojan Students' Club, and Pacific Southwest Exposition at Long Beach. Often generous support from the local Japanese consulate and the Japanese Chamber of Commerce in Los Angeles underwrote the performing arts as a form of cultural diplomacy. Japan Night programs were also promoted for their intrinsic aesthetic value, presenting Japanese culture as a source of pleasure as well as cultural pride.

Singing Japanese songs, both folk and popular, at Japanese-language-school events and graduation ceremonies also instilled a sense of being Japanese. The language schools interspersed singing with recitations and readings of stories and plays in Japanese as part of the curriculum. A typical Japanese-language-school graduation ceremony entailed the singing of the Japanese anthem, "Kimigayo," for the opening, followed by a variety of Japanese children's songs.[33]

JAPANESE MUSIC MAKERS

My interviews with three distinguished Nisei musicians chronicle how performing Japanese music became intrinsic to their identity. These individuals recount how musicking shaped and gave expression to their social, artistic, and/or political selves.

For Kineya Jyorokusho, master of *nagauta*, koto, and classical dance, pursuing Japanese music and dance was initially her mother's idea. In my interview with her on August 30, 1994, she comments:

> It always begins with parents. My mother took lessons in Japan. Odori [dance], koto, shamisen, *o-hana* [flower arrangement] and *o-cha* [tea ceremony] are what ladies learn. So she started me on all of that. Whatever she took—koto, shamisen, odori—I took. So, I have three [professional] names, three degrees.

How Kineya Jyorokusho differed from most Nisei was her continued practice of these art forms throughout her life, transmitting her knowledge and skill as a professional and an instructor to the next two generations. She kept company with seven Nisei masters of classical dance and three Nisei masters of koto, according to the *Teachers of Japanese Cultural Arts in Southern California* directory published in 1994.³⁴ This artist was also unique in having earned *natori* certificates in the three art forms she mastered from famous teachers in Japan—Miyagi Michio for koto and Kineya Jōkan and Kineya Rokushirō for *nagauta* and odori. Kineya Jyorokusho's accomplishments were remarkable. A dedicated artist, she also taught and performed at Gila River Relocation Center in Arizona while incarcerated. Kineya recalled her *nagauta* training: "When I was learning, about eight or ten Nisei were learning from the same teacher. There were also five Nisei girls from Stockton who studied *kiyomoto*.³⁵ *Kiyomoto* is the hardest thing. It is a singing [style] I never could copy."³⁶ As a student, she performed four times a year—New Year's (o-Shōgatsu), spring, summer, and fall—in recitals organized by her teacher in Los Angeles, Kineya Yasoyo. Fulfilling the expectations of her Japanese mother placed Kineya Jyorokusho on a path toward becoming a musician, dancer, and teacher. She strongly identified with her Japanese heritage through music and dance, and the aesthetic demands of her artistry bound her to the Japanese community in shared appreciation. Being a musician specializing in Japanese music set Kineya Jyorokusho apart from most Nisei. Born in Los Angeles but speaking English with a strong Japanese accent identifies her more as a Kibei rather than a Nisei. Her close ties to the Japanese community teaching *nagauta*, koto, and classical dance and being married to a Japanese certainly resulted in her more closely identifying with her Japanese roots.

Rei Kasama's story also narrates the strong influence of Issei parents in her musicking and exposure to several musical traditions. Her absorption into the paired traditions of *shimai* (*nō* drama dancing) and *yōkyoku* (*nō* drama singing) arose from her parent's own interest and instruction in these art forms. As an infant, Rei Kasama listened to her mother practice *yōkyoku*. Her aesthetic tastes further developed as her father honed his skills in *yōkyoku* and had her begin lessons in *shimai* at the age of nine. She describes her father's accomplishments: "He was talented enough to be raised to the level of *jūshokubun*, or associate professional. For lay people, that's the highest level you can attain. As far as I know, he was the only one who studied *yōkyoku* here and in Japan to reach that level."³⁷ With both parents steeped in the *nō*-drama vocal style and Kasama learning *shimai*, Japanese music permeated her early life. Classical European music also became part of her musical world with piano lessons at the age of seven, again at the wishes of her parents. When she and her brothers were older, they also listened to and danced to American popular music: "They went the usual route. I did too. We were into swing music and jitterbugging and all that along with *yōkyoku*." Kasama's bicultural identity was slanted more toward her Japanese heritage. Growing up in Los Angeles's Japantown, attending school with only other Japanese and living in Japan both before and after the war reinforced her Japaneseness. Her imprisonment during World War II interrupted the dance training she received, and after the war, Kasama only occasionally practiced and performed *shimai* with the Los Angeles Kita school of *yōkyoku*. Then in 1987, she began studying *yōkyoku* singing, coming full circle with the music she had heard as a child. Singing *yōkyoku* and dancing *shimai* enact Kasama's strong Japanese identity, which has coexisted with her enculturated American persona on a cultural cusp that she has had to negotiate throughout her life.

The next musician hails from Hawaii. She also resided in Chicago and Seattle before settling in Los Angeles in the 1960s. Lillian Nakano is a Hawaiian Sansei who married a Californian Nisei and participated in Nisei subculture once she moved to the US mainland.[38] For this artist, playing *nagauta* shamisen was more than a cultural and aesthetic choice. Later in life, her playing took on additional meaning to express her political beliefs. Similar to the Nisei presented above, Nakano's parents initiated her musical start on shamisen. Beginning with Japanese dance lessons, her father decided she should also learn shamisen with the intent of knowing music that accompanied dance well. Nakano's first instrument, however, was piano. Having a piano at home gave Nakano a chance to learn to play by ear. She recalls, "I used to play a lot of music by ear just picking up Japanese songs, popular songs, Stephen Foster type songs. I could just listen and learn the song."[39] Nakano's interest in both Japanese and Western music endured. From the age of thirteen, she began studying *nagauta* shamisen, but her incarceration during World War II interfered with her training. Her experience being imprisoned gave rise to the stigma and shame she associated with being Japanese. Nakano recollects, "When the war started and we went into camp, there was this whole stigma about not liking yourself as a Japanese. So, I didn't want to dance or play shamisen."[40] It was a few years after the war that Nakano considered playing again and later earned her *natori*, giving her the credentials to teach in Chicago and later Los Angeles.

A decade after moving to Los Angeles, Nakano and her husband Burt became politically active. In the 1970s, her college-age son challenged them to get involved: "I know you're one of those liberals . . . armchair liberals. You guys always talk about politics but you never do anything. Why don't you guys get out there." Nakano met her son's challenge: "First it was Little Tokyo People's Rights Organization, which was about redevelopment in Little Tokyo . . . the Japanese corporations taking over and rebuilding and dispersing the people that were living in J-Town. So, we got involved." Nakano and her husband also were intensely engaged in the National Coalition for Redress and Reparations (NCRR).[41] She performed little during her politically active years: "I stopped playing and the only time we played music was for NCRR benefits or events." During that time, her nephew Glenn Horiuchi, a composer and pianist who was active in the Asian American creative-music scene centered in San Francisco, started writing music based on Japanese American themes, including the concentration camps. Horiuchi's composition, *Poston Sonata* for shamisen, string trio, flute, percussion, and piano, premiered in 1991 as part of the San Diego Jazz Society's Jazz Masters Series. When Nakano learned that her nephew was planning to write *Poston Sonata*, she approached him: "Gee, I'd sure like to play something like that. Somehow, we got together, but it was like two different worlds meeting because he didn't know too much about shamisen music." Horiuchi collaborated with Nakano, drawing from her traditional *nagauta* repertoire and idiomatic shamisen style in creating *Poston Sonata*, which narrated life in the Poston Relocation Center in Arizona. In 1992, Nakano and Horiuchi recorded *Poston Sonata*, and the compact disc became available through Asian Improv Records in San Francisco. Experimenting on shamisen for the composition was an exciting endeavor for Nakano who had an urge to play new music. The collaboration sparked Horiuchi's desire to play shamisen, and he proceeded to take lessons with his aunt.

Molly Miyako Kimura (1924–2016) is another bright spot among Nisei interested in Japanese music. A budding musician from the rural areas, Kimura was born in Yuba City, California, on March 1, 1924, and grew up in the town of Florin, a once thriving farming community with a large Japanese American population.[42] Florin had endured intense racial and ethnic discrimination, becoming a wellspring of Japanese culture and musical activity. Guided by her mother, Kimura's interest in Japanese culture blossomed at an early age. She learned to speak Japanese at age three, followed by attending Japanese-language school every day, Monday through Friday, and, at the age of ten, commenced lessons on Chikuzen *biwa*—sung narrative with *biwa* accompaniment. She made her debut at a Chikuzen-*biwa* recital held at Marysville Buddhist Church Hall in 1934. Kimura's immersion in Japanese culture included performing a male Kabuki character in a play held at Marysville Community Hall when she was twelve years old and, as an adult, earning teaching certificates in Ikenobo flower arranging, Japanese sandpainting (*suna-e*), and *biwa*. The strong influence of Kimura's parents may have been due to her mother being a devout Jodo Shinshu Buddhist, while the father was a successful businessman who was very influential in the

Figure 3.2. Molly Kimura and her teacher Kyokuso Yamamoto performing *biwa* in the annual Japanese cultural bazaar at the Sacramento Buddhist Church, 1980. Courtesy of Molly Kimura.

Japanese community of Marysville. Kimura recounted the close relationship she had with her *biwa* teacher who encouraged her to pursue practice of the five-stringed lute (figure 3.2). In 1980, Kyokuto Kimura (Molly's professional name) and her teacher Kyokuso Yamamoto performed *biwa* for the annual Japanese cultural Bazaar at the Sacramento Buddhist Church.

Notable is Kimura's activities as an ambassador of Japanese cultural arts in Sacramento. She gave many demonstrations in communities and at schools on flower arranging and sandpainting. Her role as an interpreter and narrator for many visiting Japanese artists, musicians, and dancers and for organizing cultural tours to Japan and China gained her recognition. Kimura's work as a sister-city cultural liaison between Sacramento and Matsuyama, Japan, won her many awards from the city of Sacramento, and the *Sacramento Union* newspaper chose her as a recipient of one of the ten Women of the Year awards in 1971.

While incarcerated at Tule Lake Relocation Center with her family from July 1942 to September 1945, Kimura chose to make the most of her time in camp, actively studying Buddhism, flower arranging (Ikenobo school), tea ceremony, and Chikuzen *biwa*. Regarding Buddhism as a way of life, her acquired spiritual energy paved the way for sustaining her *biwa* playing and later teaching Buddhist Sunday school and eventually becoming an ordained Buddhist minister of the first rank. Kimura's well-defined path bespeaks of her strong identification with Japan.[43]

According to the brief ethnographies above, Issei parents played a major role inculcating Japanese music and culture in their Nisei offspring; there appear to be few cases in which Nisei initiated playing or singing Japanese music on their own. This was inevitable considering their American social and cultural milieu and the pull of popular mainstream culture. The biographies shed light on both sustained and occasional engagement with Japanese music. Jyorokusho and Kimura are examples of Nisei absorbed in Japanese culture and sustained musicking of traditional music and dance. Jyorokusho established a professional career performing and teaching koto and Japanese classical dance. She actively transmitted these performing traditions to two generations of Japanese Americans in southern California. Kimura's inclination blossomed from her family's strong ties to Japan and Buddhist practices. For Nakano and Kasama, music making was an intermittent hobby, a pastime. The disruption of being imprisoned during the war diminished Nakano's and Kasama's Japanese musicking. In contrast, Jyorokusho and Kimura flourished in the camps, regularly performing. Nakano stands out for returning to *nagauta* shamisen practice, purposefully utilizing music to protest unfair redevelopment practices in Los Angeles's Little Tokyo and to support the national redress and reparations for Issei and Nisei who had endured imprisonment.

THE CHANGING MUSICAL LANDSCAPE

Initially, musical events and radio broadcasts for Japanese and European classical music were programmed separately. Later, local newspapers—*Rafu Shimpo* and *Kashū Mainichi* (Japan-California Daily News) in Los Angeles and *Nichibei Mainichi* in San Francisco—reported concerts featuring combined programming of the two musical styles with added vernacular or popular songs, mirroring the cultural intersection of the Nisei's two worlds.

Nisei Week continues to be a highly public event that spotlights the Japanese American population in Los Angeles. It began in 1934 as an affair originally intended by Issei leaders to engage Nisei and prepare them to assume leadership in the community's political economy. It is also a festival that celebrates both Japanese and American aspects of an identity that the Japanese community chose to promote to the public. The Nisei organization JACL took the lead in procuring the success of this community effort in Little Tokyo. "Through spectacles, performances, contests, speeches, essays, advertisements, street decorations, and costumes, the festival heralded the Nisei as a new breed of American citizen who was at home in both Japan and the

United States."⁴⁴ This public-relations promotion of biculturalism, however, shifted to promoting Nisei as 100-percent American when political relations between Japan and the United States deteriorated during the 1930s and early 1940s. Still drawing large crowds, the 2016 Nisei Week program featured visual and cultural arts and music over two weekends in August, with the Nisei Week Grand Parade on the first Sunday and the Ondo/Closing Ceremony on the second Sunday. This celebratory affair exemplifies musicking and dancing as a sustained Japanese American activity.

Ondo, Japanese dance songs, form the centerpiece of a finale parade that closes out the two-week-long programming of Nisei Week. Little Tokyo invites the public to participate in the parade, offering Japanese-folk-dancing lessons in the weeks prior to the festivities. Chiye Nagano, professional dancer and choreographer, recalls, "The idea of the *ondo* was to encourage the community to laugh at the realities of immigrant life and, thus, to release the stresses of its work-a-day world."⁴⁵ The original Nisei Week leaders anticipated that music and dancing would be a focal point for promoting an appreciation of Japanese ethnic traditions and creating an awareness of the Issei's hard work and achievements.

The "Nisei Week Special" broadcast on KRKD in 1935 illustrated music's intrinsic importance. The radio program presented both traditional and popular *ondo*, planned as dance accompaniment in the finale parade of Nisei Week, along with other performing arts:

Popular song, "Tsubaki Saku Shima" (Island Where Camellias Blossom), vocal solo by Yoshie Sato, accompanied by the Wakaba band.
Ha-uta (popular songs in the *niagari*-shamisen tuning of the late Edo period), "Niagari Shinnai" by Miki Mitsu
Radio drama, "Ria Wo" (King Lear[?]) by the Junior Club of Lil' Tokyo
Popular song, "Asa no Makiba" (Morning Ranch) by Taro Shoji
Rōkyoku (another name for *naniwa-bushi*), "Yokyo" (Entertainment) by Aoyagi and Unako Tomoe
Manzai, "Kippari Wakarete" (We Broke Up Completely)
Ondo, "Mawase Haguruma" (Rotate the Gear) and "Rafu Ondo" (Los Angeles Dance Song), vocal by Aiko Magara, Reiko Inouye, Sachiko Hori, Teruko Kiyomura, Rose Tamura, Tsuyuki Matsuura, and Yoshiko Hosoi, accompanied by the Wakaba band
Ko-uta, "Yarisabi" (Rusted Spear) by Ko-Ume
Rakugo (comic story), "Shinken Kyuken" (Real Sword, Old Sword[?]) by Kingoro Yamagiya

Popular song, "Watashiga Oyome Ni Ittara" (If I Get Married), vocal by Yoshie Sato, accompanied by the Wakaba band[46]

Japanese music and dance highlighted during Nisei Week is not solely a statement of the Nisei's heritage but also a cultural *rearticulation* of what it is to be Japanese American: a rearticulation in the sense that traditions are presented in new contexts—on the radio in a mixed program of traditional songs, popular songs, storytelling, drama, and dance, and in *ondo* dancing rendered as a grand finale parade closing out Nisei Week. In addition to these new contexts, future research will likely point out musical differences in arrangements and performances of Japanese music presented due to American music trends and diasporic changes in musical taste. The rearticulation of Japanese music aside, in their intent to have Nisei enact the Japanese part of themselves, Issei leaders secured the inclusion of Japanese music and dance. Nisei Week illustrates Nisei poised on the cultural cusp. On the one hand, music and dancing exoticized the Nisei and the Los Angeles Japanese community, particularly with performers and participants wearing Japanese kimonos; on the other hand, these displays combined with activities such as a beauty contest, fashion show, coronation ball, baby show, speech and essay contests, and talent revue all embodied their life as Americans.

Japanese music and dance programming connected Nisei to a Japanese aesthetic, a cultivated taste that begins to diminish with Nisei's growing propensity for Western music, dance, and popular culture. The inclusion of Japanese popular songs in the Nisei Week concert gave the program a modern spin to broaden its base of listeners and attract Nisei participation.

As a public-relations event, Nisei Week was one of the few functions attended by the Los Angeles public. Audiences for most musical performances were usually insular affairs in Japanese American communities because of the continuing social segregation, but the Nisei Week parade attracted a broad public. The event continues to link successive generations of Japanese Americans in Los Angeles to their Japanese heritage while remaining a commercially based public festivity that draws tourists, boosting Little Tokyo businesses.

Christian churches and Buddhist temples—principal community organizations—supported musicking among Nisei. Christian churches promoted hymn and Japanese song singing, often forming choirs. Social groups, such as the Japanese Student Christian Association or the many Japanese girls' clubs, sparked much musicking with their annual dinners and bazaars, benefit programs, choir festivals, or Japanese celebrations, such as Girl's Day (*Hina Matsuri*), Young People's Night, or Christmas programs. While programming often reflected Nisei's Japanese heritage—Japanese folk, children's, and popular songs and Japanese dance—also featured were an eclectic array of European classical chamber music, Hawaiian music, jazz, and the novelty sounds of musical saw that affirmed their Americanness. One event that stands out is the annual benefit drive of the Japanese Students' Christian Association (JSCA), featuring a "musicale" performed by Nisei students drawn from many colleges in Southern California. The mixed program included:

koto and shakuhachi music presented by Miss Setsuko Miki on koto and Mr. Kurose on shakuhachi;
vocal solo by Miss Yoneko Anderson, Riverside Junior College, "Danny Boy" and "My Lover is a Fisherman";
The Cosmopolitan Male Quartet, Whittier College, the school's alma mater;
piano duet by Miss Julia Suski and Miss Kimi Mukaye, University of Southern California, including a selection from "Martha" by Flotow and "Golliwog's Cakewalk" by Debussy;
mezzo soprano solo by Margaret Hadley, Whittier College, with piano accompaniment by Jeannette Sanders, including "The Raindrop" by Ghiberti (given name unknown) and "The Winds in the South" by Raymond Scott;
piano trio featuring Jimmy Yamamoto, cello; Clara Suski, violin; and Julia Suski, piano, playing "Seville" by Bachmann;
Japanese dance interpretation by a delegation from Riverside Junior High School, "Sakura" (Cherry Blossom);
jazz selections by the Oliver Trio.[47]

While the programming consisted of mostly European, light-classical pieces and Western songs, the inclusion of Japanese chamber music at the opening and toward the end connotes the Nisei's acknowledgement of their community's ethnic ties. An *interpretative* performance of Japanese dance to the well-known Japanese song "Sakura" is also a nod to the Nisei's heritage but in transculturated form suited to the context, age of the dancers, and the teacher's version of the song. Notable is the inclusion of non-Japanese performers in this benefit concert sponsored by youth. The 1928 date of this musicale foreshadows the Nisei's stronger orientation toward Western music.

Buddhist churches[48] supported a wide variety of musicking besides Buddhist chanting for services and rituals, hosting many traditional Japanese music events featuring shamisen music, *shigin* singing, and *utai* singing. Younger Kibei sang *shigin*, which became increasingly nationalistic as Japan's military successes in Asia gained momentum in the 1930s, demonstrating how this subset of Nisei were closer in their sentiments to Issei than their cohorts. Buddhist churches inculcated Nisei with Japanese celebrations, such as Buddha's birthday, which included an elaborate flower festival (Hana Matsuri) held in honor of the Buddha. One such event took place on April 9, 1928, under the auspices of five local Buddhist temples of the Daijo Kai of North America. Sunday-school children combined from a few temples sang Buddhist hymns and Japanese folk songs as part of a program of Japanese plays, dances, stories, games, and speeches by priests and members of the Young Men's Buddhist Association (YMBA).[49] In their attempts to engage the Westernized second generation, Buddhist churches modeled their activities and social clubs to those of Christian churches.

Singing was a popular pastime among Nisei. One event exemplifying this is the third Nisei Choir Festival on May 11, 1941, featuring 125 Nisei from Christian churches in metropolitan Los Angeles in a performance of "Worship Service of Choral Music" at the Wilshire Methodist Church. Leading Nisei musicians participated in the program as soloists: soprano, baritone, piano, violin, and organ. The mass choir performed George Frederick Handel's "Hallelujah Chorus," Wolfgang Amadeus Mozart's "Ave Verum," Schubert's "23rd Psalm" and "Ave Maria," Felix Mendelssohn's "Lift Thine Eyes," as well as music by Johann Sebastian Bach. The Japanese American Christian churches customarily hosted hymn-singing choirs and Japanese singing groups. Songfests and community sings sponsored by both the Japanese Department of YMCA and the Oliver Club in Los Angeles gave Nisei a chance to sing pep songs, popular tunes, and American vernacular songs, expanding the repertoire of choruses in public schools.

Western music was not new to Japanese immigrants educated during the Meiji period. Western-music training became part of the curriculum in Japanese schools in response to Western imperialism and Japan's attempts to modernize. George Yoshida talks about his Issei organist mother, who played church music, and singer father, who performed American songs. Los Angeleno John Miyauchi proudly shared that his Issei father studied opera at the Chicago Conservatory of Music and gave recitals in the Windy City. The highpoint of the father's opera career was his Italian opera performance on an NHK national broadcast in Japan when he was in his eighties. Miyauchi senior also performed in vaudeville shows as a novelty act in which he would sing "Chinatown, My Chinatown," bringing down the house with his baritone voice. Although the father ended up working in produce markets, he managed to pass on his knowledge by teaching European classical voice and piano to others until he was ninety years old.

While some Nisei connected to a Japanese musical aesthetic, it was the sounds of European classical, American popular songs and dance-band music, hymns, American vernacular song, and other Western music genres that resonated most with the second generation in their social and cultural milieu. Western music symbolized modernity and for Nisei an avenue toward assimilating.

As an elite art form, European classical music was not only regarded by Japanese families as a marker of upper-class status to which they endeavored but also as a means for their children to be socially integrated. Issei parents particularly encouraged their daughters to learn an instrument or sing as part of their cultivation. Music lessons were most affordable for middle- and upper-class families. Nisei whose families' primary occupation was tenant farming had little opportunity to pursue music as they often moved from one farm to another and could ill afford such activity. Musical instruction was mostly available in urban centers, making place of residence a factor in whether one had an opportunity to study classical music.

Nisei musicking enlivened many community events; European classical music and Western songs became standard in most programming from the 1920s on. Prior to the predominance of young Nisei women performing classical music, musicians invited from Japan to the United States played a role in building an appreciation of the European classical repertoire. One of the earliest of such performances was a Japan-America friendship concert in 1916, hosted by the Los Angeles Japan-America Association, featuring the Japanese pianist Mitani Shunzō. As a young man, Shunzō moved to the United States to study piano in Indianapolis, New York, and Chicago. He then toured, giving recitals all along the West Coast.[50] Well-known singers also came, including Miura Tamaki, a popular singer who became famous for her role as Cho Cho-san in Giacomo Puccini's *Madame Butterfly* in 1916 and 1917.[51] A decade later, Japan's foremost lyric tenor at the time, Yoshie Fujiwara, toured the West Coast, building further enthusiasm for European classical music. In November and December 1926, Fujiwara traveled to Los Angeles, San Francisco, Portland (Oregon), and Seattle before embarking for Europe to sing with an opera company there and continue his vocal training. In Los Angeles, Fujiwara delighted listeners with his radio-broadcast performance on KHJ, singing "The Volga Boat Song," a Japanese folk song entitled "The Japanese Boat Song," and other pieces.[52] He drew large audiences at two concerts, one at the downtown Japanese Union Church and a second for a benefit at the Methodist Evangelical Church on Normandie Avenue. Fujiwara returned to the United States in 1928, singing not only European classical songs but Japanese new and old folk songs to packed audiences. These musical events paved the way for a flurry of classical-music activity in the 1930s and 1940s.

Musical programming called for light-classical genres performed by string trios, quartets, or other mixed ensembles for recitals, concerts, most talent shows, musicales, and entertainment. Young Nisei women primarily played piano, a string instrument (mostly violin), or sang. The harmonica used to perform a variety of genres was an instrument particularly favored by Nisei men. Another novelty instrument performed by Nisei men was the musical saw occasionally heard in talent shows. Music heard in stores, women's clubs, art-exhibit receptions, prefectural picnics, and the Young People's Salon also afforded concert opportunities for Nisei classical musicians.

Recitals were numerous, and the following performance is an example of a shared program that featured piano soloist Nobuko Suto and baritone George Seno, accompanied on piano by Teruko Hirashiki, at the Assistance League Playhouse in Los Angeles on February 28, 1941(figure 3.3).[53]

There was enough classical-music talent in Los Angeles to form the Los Angeles Japanese Orchestra, established in 1923. Young Nisei women studying music performance at colleges and universities boosted the number of available musicians. The orchestra gave its fifth annual spring concert on March 2, 1928, at the Japanese Union Church. The program that captivated audiences included Vincenzo Bellini's overture to "Norma," Joseph Haydn's "Surprise Symphony," Ludwig von Beethoven's "Romance in G," op. 4 for solo violin, Enrique Granado's "Romanza" and "Jota," and Georg Goltermann's "Concerto in G" and "Nocturne" for solo cello. The two most popular pieces that night were Schubert's "Marche Militaire," op. 52, and selections from Franz Lehar's "The Merry Widow."[54] This event featured Nisei sopranist Kyo Inouye singing Giuseppe Verdi's "Pace, pace, mio Dio" and Rentarō Taki's "Kōjō no tsuki" (The Moon over the Ruined Castle).

Drawn to opera, many Nisei women musically distinguished themselves. As early as 1910, the Opera Reading Club sponsored a concert on January 6 at Grauman's Chinese Theatre. The concert featured Los Angeles sopranist Tomi Kanazawa performing excerpts from Pietro Mascagni's opera *Iris*.[55] Years later, Kanazawa sang the title role in the second act of Puccini's *Madame Butterfly* with other members of Dr. Hugo Strelitzer's opera studio on May 8, 1941. Performances of *Madame Butterfly* engaged Nisei singers in one of the few roles available to them. Full settings, costumes, and lighting delighted audiences with song texts translated into English, making it more comprehensible.[56] Agnes Miyakawa, a popular young soprano from Sacramento, appeared before audiences and on the radio in and around Sacramento, San Francisco,

> **Music**
>
> Selecting a wide variety of numbers, Nobuko Suto, talented young pianist, will be presented in a piano recital by Thilo Becker at the Assistance League Playhouse, 1367 N. St. Andrews pl. this Friday evening, Feb. 28, at 8:15 o'clock. Assisting on the program will be George Seno, lyric baritone, with Teruko Hirashiki at the piano.
>
> The program will be as follows:
>
> I
> Fantasia in C Minor ....Bach
> Variations on a Nursery Theme
> .... Mozart
>   Nobuko Suto
>
> II
> Believe Me If All Those Endearing Young Charms ....
> In the Silence of the Night......
> .... Rachmaninoff
> Kerry Dance ....Malloy
>   George Seno
>
> III
> Pastorale ....Scarlatti-Tausig
> Capriccio ....Scarlatti-Tausig
> Nocturne in G Minor ....Chopin
> Waltz in G Flat ....Chopin
> Fantasie—Impromptu ....Chopin
>   Nobuko Suto
>
> INTERMISSION
>
> IV
> Die Mainacht ....Brahms
> Un Ballo in Maschera ....Verdi
>   George Seno
> Doctor Gradus ad Parnassum..
> .... Debussy
> Serenade for the Doll ......Debussy
> Mouvement Perpetuel ......Poulenc
> Piece en Forme de Habenera ....
> .... Ravel
> The Little White Donkey ......Ibert
> The Night Winds ....Griffes
> Dance of the Gnomes ....Liszt
>   Nobuko Suto

Figure 3.3. Piano and baritone vocalist recital. *Los Angeles Rafu Shimpo*, February 27, 1941.

and Los Angeles. Japanese tenor Yoshie Fujiwara enthusiastically praised Ms. Miyakawa, encouraging her to consider making her debut in Japan. Her performance at the Japanese Union Church in Los Angeles on April 27, 1928, was only one of many, during which she displayed her wide-ranging repertoire. The musical offerings for this event included operatic selections from Puccini's *Madame Butterfly*, *La bohème*, and *Gianni Schicchi*; chamber music for voice, flute, cello, and piano by Bach and other composers; the popular songs "At Dawning" by Charles Wakefield Cadman[57] and "Where My Caravan Has Rested" by Herman Lohr; as well as contemporary Japanese songs.[58]

A few young Nisei men made classical music their careers. Kenshu Wanifuchi, noted Seattle violinist who studied at the Conservatory of Music in Prague, was one. While studying in Europe, Wanifuchi played concerts in Paris, Berlin (under the auspices of the Japan-Duetsch Society), and Prague, as well as being a featured artist on radio broadcasts in Vienna and Budapest. His first recital in Los Angeles took place in 1933 after returning from his training in Prague, followed by a second performance in 1935. Wanifuchi's talent took him to performance tours in New York, Seattle, and Portland.[59]

Many Nisei youth participated in Boy Scout drum and bugle corps. Corps in Los Angeles and San Francisco made their mark in parades, competitions, and other community events. San Francisco's Boy Scout Troop Twelve formed in 1915 was one of the first to organize a drum and bugle corp. Southern California corps also distinguished themselves: the Daishi Mission Boy Scout Troop 379 Drum and Bugle Corps won first place in a contest sponsored by the Beverly Hills American Legion Post, earning them the privilege of appearing in the Memorial Day program of the Southern California Music Fiesta on June 14, 1941. The precision and discipline of Troop 379 did not go unnoticed as they competed with other drum and bugle corps of National Guards, American Legions, universities, high school Reserve Officers' Training Corps (ROTC), and other civic organizations.[60]

A novel instrument piqued the interest of a quartet of Nisei men in San Francisco, who formed a harmonica band, playing classics such as Richard Wagner's "Under the Double Eagle," John Stepan Zamecnik's "Desert Caravan," and Bizet's *Carmen* and "Prelude." One performance was broadcast live on NBC radio on January 24, 1930.[61] In June of that year, a local student's club, the Gakusei Kwai, formed a harmonica band known as the San Francisco Harmonica Society, establishing their headquarters at the Gakusei Kwai office on Sutter Street.[62] The light-classical repertoire of the harmonica bands was the influence of H. Watanuki, visiting from Japan. His successful performance at the Nishi Hongwanji Temple in Los Angeles on August 3, 1928, was the first-ever concert of European classical music performed by a harmonica ensemble in the US. The program featured Jacques Offenbach's overture from *Orpheus*, Daniel Auber's *La muette di Portici*, Vincenzo de Michelis's *Forge in the Forest*, and Bizet's Gypsy song from *Carmen*.[63]

Social and athletic clubs offered many chances for Nisei music makers to ply their talents. Socially ostracized from mainstream American clubs, Nisei created their own groups, filling their social calendars with dinner dances, beach parties, benefits, skate fests, graduation parties, bowling parties, and installation balls. The *Rafu Shimpo* editorial "Why Clubs?" looks at the role of the one hundred active Nisei organizations that existed in Los Angeles in 1940. The clubs played a key role in alleviating the Nisei's sense of dislocation and exclusion from mainstream society and promoted their sense of well-being. Active clubs like the Japanese YMCA and YWCA organized annual New Year's dances for large groups of Nisei. The Southern California Japanese Baseball Club added a musical program highlighting second-generation talent for their booster rally held at the Union Church in Los Angeles. The musical portion of the evening showcased torch-song vocalist Helen Takahashi; banjoist Tib Kamayatsu; and vocalist Grace Sumida, who sang several Japanese songs. The popular Oliver Club Winter Carnaval, coordinated by the Blue Triangle Club, attracted Nisei from all over Los Angeles to hear saxophone and vocal solos with piano accompaniment, ukulele music, and a dance-band quartet composed of piano, trap drums, saxophone, and banjo, which kept couples dancing late into the night.[64]

The busy schedules organized by social groups sponsored a great deal of musicking, active listening, and dancing. Valentine's Day, club anniversaries, New Year's Eve, graduation parties, and sports formals were all occasions for dancing to the latest hits. One such event was an annual ball sponsored by the Silver Echo Club of San Francisco's YWCA, an important social event that drew two hundred Nisei from surrounding cities who showed up to participate in the dance competitions and tag dancing.[65] "Nisei rug-cutters" events in Los Angeles kept youth dancing as they competed in rhumba, la conga, tango, and swing tournaments at the Hollywood Legion Stadium.[66]

There were a handful of Nisei dance bands that provided music for social and community events. The Sho Tokyans,, a southern California combo, animated a sports dance hosted by the Nipponettes, a girls' club of Los Angeles, to celebrate their fourth anniversary on May 30, 1937.[67] The lively music of Tadashi Yamamoto's eleven-piece orchestra generated excitement at the semiformal high-school-graduation dance sponsored by the Santa Barbara Japanese American Citizens League.[68]

Nisei reveled in American popular music as part of their Americanization during the tense years leading up to World War II. Big-band dance music, the popular music of the day, sparked a dance craze during the 1930s and 1940s among Nisei and all young Americans. Because Nisei were coming of age during this time, popular music played a primary role in forming their identities. In my interviews, many of this generation acknowledged the elemental importance of dancing and musicking during their adolescence.

George Yoshida's book *Reminiscing in Swingtime* brings to life the impact of popular music on this generation. The book chronicles the musicking activities of Nisei in the prewar, wartime, and postwar periods. An ardent, amateur jazz musician and aficionado, Yoshida's narrative drives home the active role Nisei musicians played in American popular music from 1920 to 1960. Bringing swing-band[69] recordings in their luggage and forming big bands in assembly centers and concentration camps during World War II disclosed the zeal many Nisei had for this music.

Most Nisei were in their teens and early twenties in the two decades prior to World War II. Music of the big bands of Tommy Dorsey, Glenn Miller, Artie Shaw, Count Basie, and singers such as Frank Sinatra, Jo Stafford, and Bob Eberle filled the dancehalls and living rooms of this generation. American popular music was a way Nisei affirmed their Americanness. In the words of George Yoshida, "We didn't seek to be Americans, we *were* Americans."[70]

From 1935 to 1945, big-band music reached its peak in popularity via radio airwaves. In homes across America, gathering around the radio console became the primary form of home entertainment prior to the advent of television.[71] Families listened to radio programs broadcasting concert music of many styles, ranging from opera to popular music. Two broadcasts that promoted big-band music were *The Camel Caravan* and *Let's Dance*. Both were late-night radio broadcasts that rocketed Benny Goodman's band and other show and dance bands to national renown. These evening programs were on too late for young audiences on the East Coast, but young listeners on the West Coast tuned in, becoming fervent fans of big-band music. *Your Hit Parade*, another program lasting from 1935 to 1958, kept listeners abreast of the latest hits.[72] Avid listeners of these programs, American youth in their teens and twenties, fueled a dance craze in the prewar years.

Nisei enacted their American identity listening to and dancing to big-band music; a few Nisei also performed it. Seattle, Sacramento, San Francisco, and Los Angeles were hubs of American popular music among Nisei in the 1930s and 1940s. Church-fellowship group members or high-school friends formed amateur dance bands sparked by famous big bands and backup bands for popular singers.

Seattle was home to one of the earliest Nisei dance bands on the West Coast. Seattle Japanese Baptist Church youths formed The Nisei Melodians in 1926 (figure 3.4). The band bought and played stock arrangements of "My Blue Heaven," "St. Louis Blues," "Me and My Shadow," "Goodnight Sweetheart," and other popular tunes of the day. The Melodians furnished dance music for Nisei "taxi dances"[73] sponsored by the University Club (University of Washington), the JACL, and church-fellowship groups.[74] A second Seattle group that toured in Oregon and California were The Mikados of Swing, a

Figure 3.4. Nisei Melodians, dance band. Courtesy of Denshō, the Tsubota Family Collection.

group of young Nisei who had originally played together in a Japanese language-school marching band. Following a sharp learning curve, in 1940, The Mikados of Swing advanced enough to catch the ear of Tad Hirota, a producer who arranged a tour for the group in eight cities in Oregon and California hosted by the Young Buddhists Associations (YBA) in each location. Their tour earned them the moniker "Toast of the West Coast," but the bombing of Pearl Harbor and the ensuing incarceration of Japanese Americans ended the band's success.[75]

Musically active Nisei in Los Angeles outplayed their counterparts in Seattle. This occurred because of the migration of Japanese Americans to southern California in search of agricultural jobs, creating fertile ground for the formation of musical groups and events. The Japanese Sandmen, a ten-member band, first heard in the City of Angels on community radio station KGER on July 17, 1933, were so favorably received they began appearing regularly. The group included piano, played by bandleader Charles Izumi, a vocalist, two trumpets, two saxophones, banjo, sousaphone, and guitar.[76] The Japanese Sandmen performed musical arrangements of the professionally established Casa Loma Orchestra[77] and other popular bands. Their performances included playing for UCLA Japanese sorority dances, community events, and at T. C. Talley's Criterion Theater in Los Angeles in 1933 for Japan Night, which was broadcast on KGER. The Los Angeles Melodaires was another Nisei dance band, but the most active and well-known was the Sho Tokyans, derived from the Japanese term for Los Angeles's Japanese district "Little Tokyo." Formed in 1933, the Sho Tokyans didn't make their debut until 1936, at the annually held Nisei Week Festival Talent Show sponsored by the Japanese American Citizens League of Los Angeles. As their reputation spread, they landed many bookings with Nisei social clubs in southern California. A career highlight for Sho Tokyans was a six-month contract to play dance halls in the suburbs of Tokyo, Japan.[78]

Turning to the Bay Area, we discover that San Francisco laid claim to an American popular musician, Kono Takeuchi,[79] perhaps the first professional Japanese American blues singer, who toured extensively in vaudeville and performed as part of the RKO stage circuit during the late 1920s and 1930s. In San Francisco's Japanese community, Li'l Osaka, Willie Ito was a key figure in nurturing Nisei popular music and dance bands. Ito's efforts in the late 1920s resulted in the formation of a jazz combo with members from the Oakland Young Men's and Women's Buddhist Association orchestra, who had played semiclassical and then-popular tunes at church and community events. The Second Generation Orchestra, led by Ito in 1932, was short-lived, as was another offshoot of this group formed in 1934.

Richard's Original Syncopaters Orchestra was Sacramento's premier Nisei dance band. Members of this band were previously high-school friends who played together starting in 1926. Changing their name to Night Hawks, this band supplied dance music for Nisei social dances and community functions not only in Sacramento but also in Florin and rural communities in the Sacramento River Valley. Novel for this time was the group's regular performances at the M Street Café in Sacramento, a popular haunt for Nisei. The Night Hawks also provided music for private parties, senior proms, and New Year's Eve and Christmas holiday dances in the Japanese community.

NISEI TALES

The following personal accounts of Nisei provide a needed perspective in answering how music served to enact Nisei identity. Nisei recollections of music in their youth is meant to complement what we have learned so far. I interviewed ten Nisei: four from San Francisco, one from rural Watsonville (south of San Jose), one from suburban Alameda (north of San Francisco), three from Los Angeles, and lastly, my aunt Hisayo Asai from a rural town in the state of Washington. Four of my interviewees were transplants from

California who settled in New England in pursuit of an education or a job. I met them at an annual o-Shōgatsu (New Year's) celebration in Lexington, Massachusetts, organized by the New England Kenjinkai (New England Provincial Association). I chose interviewees from rural and urban settings to illustrate a range of Nisei experiences. Other considerations included portraying individuals of both genders and varying socio-economic levels. Also represented in this small sampling are varied musical preferences. Learning about the lives of the ten individuals gave me a chance to compare what I gleaned from interviews with data mined for this study to uncover commonalities and differences across the sampling with the hope of teasing out individual anomalies. It was a chance to ask if music was essential or peripheral to them and whether they associated music with their developmental years and how they came to identify themselves. To these means I asked the following questions:

Where were you born and when? Did you grow up in this location? Describe your homelife.
As you matured, was music a part of your life? If music was a part of your life, what kind of music were you interested in? What was the range of musical styles you listened to? Who were your favorite artists? Did you sing or play an instrument? Did you perform with a music ensemble or band?
Was American popular music a part of your life growing up? If so, in what ways did you participate in American popular music? Did you listen to, dance to, or perform American popular music? What style of popular music appealed to you the most? Did you listen to and dance to the music of the big bands of the 1930s and 1940s? Who were your favorite bands? Which popular singers did you like? What radio shows did you listen to? Did you attend live music shows? Where and when? What was the appeal of dance and swing bands to Nisei in general?
- If you listened to, danced to, or played American popular music, how do you perceive the role this music had in your life? Do you think American popular music served as a means for Nisei to express their Americanness, their participation in American mainstream life? If you agree, could you articulate *how* it expressed the Nisei's Americanness? If you disagree, what other aspects or influences shaped Nisei identities?

The passing of most of my Nisei interviewees makes their stories precious. Their narratives portray not only the hardships they faced but also a certain indomitable spirit that enabled them to establish some sense of well-being. I am grateful to them for sharing their personal, sometimes-bitter accounts.

Figure 3.5. George Yoshida, San Francisco, n.d. Courtesy of George Yoshida.

GEORGE YOSHIDA

George Yoshida (1922–2014) endorses the connection between American popular music and the Americanization of Nisei when he states in his book, "Popular American music was an essential, pervasive influence in the Americanization of Nisei."[80] Identifying this correlation proved invaluable to my research. Yoshida embodied jazz hipsters and their devotion to jazz; his warm and spirited character made his passing on May 16, 2014, particularly poignant (figure 3.5).

Born on April 9, 1922, and raised in Seattle, Washington, Yoshida moved to Los Angeles as a junior-high-school student. He stressed that his Americanization took place over time and through a broad range of activities and influences, such as the music to which he listened, danced to, and played, the food he ate, the sports he participated in, and the games he enjoyed. As a mainstream institution, the Protestant church he attended in his East Los Angeles community also contributed to his assimilation. Food, likewise, was a marker of becoming part of mainstream society; Yoshida reminisced, "I brought salami or peanut butter and jelly sandwiches [to school] and learned to eat soup without slurping [acceptable in Japanese culture]. I also drank Coca-Cola and was too embarrassed to bring Japanese rice balls for lunch."[81] Sports were another activity that became a symbol of one's Americanness for Yoshida and other Nisei who participated on teams at school or at the

YMCA. Being a member of the Boy Scouts, along with many of his friends, was another Americanizing activity that reinforced his identity.

Central to Japanese-immigrant communities, Christian churches played a major role in the Americanization of both Nisei and their Issei parents. Yoshida recalled, "The use of English-language hymns, Western harmonies and melodies, English-language Sunday school, and Bible readings in English all Americanized us." This Nisei viewed his Americanization as a comprehensive process of enculturation into middle-class American life.

In strongly identifying himself as American, he harbored a certain reticence toward Japanese culture as he matured: "I didn't enjoy traditional Japanese music, and Buddhism was alien to me; it was more cultural than religious." As was expected, however, he attended Japanese-language school daily after public school: "I learned reading and writing, Japanese songs, and also went to picnics called *undōkai*, where we exercised and played games, and there was food." His connection to Japanese culture was obligatory, but it did not have much impact on the strong identification he felt as an American.

The Yoshida family was musically inclined; his mother played organ in a local Christian church, and his father sang in a male sextet, performing American pop tunes and traditional Japanese songs.[82] Educated in Christian mission schools in Japan and actively participating in the neighborhood congregational church, Yoshida's Issei parents spoke English and adopted Western ways. There were a few recordings of Japanese music in their home, some Japanese folk songs, but none of koto or other classical music. Western musicking prevailed in the Yoshida home.

Yoshida became musically active while in elementary school in Seattle: "I joined the Harmonica Club that played mostly Stephen Foster songs, such as 'Old Folks at Home' and 'Swanee River.' Then, around 1935, I heard Benny Goodman's band on the radio for the first time along with Lionel Hampton, Teddy Wilson, and other African American musicians. This music really appealed to me, and I started lessons on alto saxophone in junior high school." In 1939, while still in high school, he and his friends gathered to listen to the big-band recordings of Artie Shaw and Benny Goodman: "I went to a friend's garage with two other friends, me on sax, and the other two [on] piano and trumpet. We heard Artie Shaw play 'Begin the Beguine'; I bought the record and arrangement, and we tried to play it." During this formative period, Yoshida listened to musicians Duke Ellington and Tommy Dorsey and singers Frank Sinatra, Billy Eckstine, who sang with the Earl Hines band, and Bob Eberly, a singer in Glenn Miller's band. Yoshida's saxophone-playing days continued when he attended Los Angeles City College (LACC) and played in the school swing band. While attending LACC, his most memorable moment was hearing Duke Ellington's band live, performing "Do Nothing till You Hear from Me." In referencing Black musicians, Yoshida comments, "'Race records'[83] kept white and Black bands and their audiences segregated."[84] Although he attended performances by Black bands, the sustained segregation of race records generally inclined Nisei to emulate the music of white bands. A preference for white bands reflects both Issei's and mainstream society's prejudicial attitudes toward Blacks.

Yoshida continued his saxophone playing while imprisoned at Poston, Arizona, from 1942 to 1943; he performed as a member of the camp's eleven-piece dance band, the Poston Music Makers. Dancing was an important part of camp life: "A lot of dances were organized by the social clubs, and the Music Makers provided the music." Yoshida reiterated the importance of music, saying, "Big band was *our* [Nisei] music."[85]

He pursued music listening and dancing when he moved to Chicago in 1943 with other young Nisei from the camps. Yoshida chronicled the coming of age of Nisei living in Chicago away from their families for the first time: "Free at last; free, yellow, and twenty-one!" While working different jobs, Yoshida had a chance to listen to jazz in clubs on Chicago's south side and to dance at the Aragon Ballroom on the north side. His fondest memory of living in this city was seeing Duke Ellington and his band play live at a southside club, sitting directly in front of the stage.

Serving a stint in the army as a trainee in the Military Intelligence Service Language School at Fort Snelling, Minnesota, gave Yoshida another opportunity to play jazz. He played saxophone in the all-Nisei Eager Beavers band until his honorable discharge in 1945.

Acquiring an education, finding a job, and raising a family pushed Yoshida's musicking aside for many years. With music so close to his heart, his desire to play resurfaced, and in 1975, he formed the jazz quartet Sentimental Journey, playing for Japanese American celebrations and social events. Then upon retiring from his teaching career in 1989, Yoshida organized the San Francisco J-Town Jazz Ensemble, a seventeen-piece swing band that was community based, multiethnic, and multigenerational.[86] The band's core members were a mix of Nisei who had played in the concentration camps, Sansei musicians, and an assortment of other interested musicians. For twenty years, the J-Town Jazz Ensemble presented musical entertainment for dancing and social events for Bay Area Japanese American communities.

Yoshida's musical legacy includes initiating the Nikkei Music History Project for the Japanese American Historical Society in 1991. His book

Reminiscing in Swingtime is a product of the research he conducted on Japanese Americans' contributions to American popular music over a period of thirty-five years. The project launched when he was asked about other musicians who played in the camps.

Yoshida's enthusiastic participation in American popular music as both an amateur musician and a jitterbugger is a testimony to many Nisei's ownership of American swing, affirming the importance of this music for the second generation. Also significant is this jazz aficionado's assertion about most Nisei being apolitical, a notion that he felt rested on Issei parents themselves being largely apolitical. Yoshida remarks, "We were very isolated in our minds, culturally and psychologically being Japanese. Besides, at that time we just hung out with our friends and didn't think much about it."

When asked what jazz meant to him, he replied, "It's my passion." He continued, "My favorite thing now is to listen with headphones to hear the great sounds of Johnny Hartman. There's a tune called 'Fools Rush In' and it just knocks me out!" His affinity toward Black jazz musicians positions him even closer to the tradition of this African American art form. George Yoshida's zeal for jazz endured, and it became an integral part of who he was, epitomizing how big-band music embodied his identity as an American.

MAY AND TAKA TAKAYANAGI

Raised in the San Francisco Bay Area but now living in Massachusetts, May (b. 1924) and Taka (1919–2018) Takayanagi were typical Americans in many ways. Both lived in ethnically mixed neighborhoods: Taka in Berkeley and May in Oakland. Their musical interests and activities reflect middle-class American life. May recounted, "We were great radio listeners; there was all this popular music. I couldn't afford to keep buying records, so I used to buy lyrics of different songs, or I'd listen to the radio and try to write the lyrics from the radio. I used to sing in glee clubs. At one point, I learned to play drums—snare drum. We [school band] marched in the county fair."[87] In creating distance with the Japanese part of herself, May rejected the music of her Japanese heritage, remarking, "My mother played the koto very, very well. She tried to teach us [May and her sisters], but we kind of resisted because we felt it made us more Japanese, something that made us different."

European classical music was a staple in many Japanese American families—a musical style that appealed to both Issei and Nisei. May's mother was particularly fond of this music:

I grew up in a household with popular music on the radio, but the records in the house were only classical music. We had one of those big console Victrolas that you cranked. My mother became a Christian because she loved the music and was very knowledgeable about classical music and composers. As a kid, she would tell us the plots of operas. I learned so much about classical music.

Church hymns were also part of May's youth: "We learned all the hymns. We lived in the country at one time and there was a very active Seventh Day Adventist group; they did all the cooking on Friday and met all day Saturday. I thought it was great. My parents didn't go, but they sent us. It was like one big picnic, togetherness."

May was a typical American teen learning to jitterbug while in junior high school during the dance craze of the 1930s and '40s and would sneak into dances: "I was underage, but I used to go to the dances at Cal [University of California, Berkeley] because big bands used to tour [and sometimes play there]." May's husband Taka added, "Once a month there were dances at I-House [International House at Cal]; sometimes bands played, and that's where all the Nisei went. These monthly dances gave Nisei a chance to dance and meet people. It was the Bay Area kids and the Cal Nisei students who were responsible for [organizing] the dances. The San Francisco YMCA would also have Nisei dances."

Taka's musical interests were not unlike many middle-class Americans, ranging from big-band jazz and ballads to European classical music. "Music played a big part in my life," Taka recalled. "As a student and an architect, I would always have music in the background; big-band stuff, ballads—Benny Goodman, Tommy Dorsey, Artie Shaw, Harry James. I also enjoyed listening to classical music, and every Sunday morning, the New York Philharmonic would have a concert [on the radio]." Taka associated classical music with the end of the war:

During the war, I went to the military language school in Minnesota, and after finishing there, we were shipped off to MacArthur's headquarters in Manila, Philippines, and I was attached to the language pool. This one particular day, the Philippine Symphony Orchestra was having a concert, and I happened to go to the concert. Right after the concert, I walked out; all the natives were excited saying, "Japan had surrendered."

Both Taka and May shared their experiences of hearing big bands live. May recalled, "One of the things was that when you were too young, you couldn't go to any club, but the fact that they [commercial movie houses] had the shows [live bands] along with a movie was a great way. That's where I saw some of the great bands." Taka continued, "During intermission, between the reels, they had a stage show, so with the price of one, you could see both; this was ideal." During the war, he enjoyed live performances by Frank Sinatra in a New York movie theater and Kathryn Grayson[88] in Washington, DC. He recounted, "I was stationed in Washington DC, and that's where the big bands used to come through. During the war, what you really wanted was entertainment, and this was ideal. Before, during, and after the war you had ballrooms in your major cities. They had major bands come there, and that's all they did. They would have three shows a day, something like that." While stationed in Minneapolis, Minnesota, Taka had other opportunities to hear live music: "Well, that was a great time too during the war when we were going to language school. They [the army] would throw a dance about once a month in the field house. They would have a big band come in, and as a matter of fact, that's where I met May; she was one of the USO [United Service Organizations] girls."

YUTAKA KOBAYASHI

Still active in his eighties when interviewed, native San Franciscan Yutaka Kobayashi (b. 1924) grew up in Japantown between Laguna and Sutter Streets (figure 3.6). As a youth in the 1930s and 1940s, the activities of a typical American teenager filled his days. Quite athletic, he participated in sports: "Sports was a big part of my growing up. There were baseball teams, football teams, swimming, and track. I was on the track team and won my letter in track."[89] He also enjoyed fishing and going to the movies:

> Movies were a big part of our lives because all we had were radios—no TV. The big thing for us were the Andy Hardy movies, featuring Mickey Rooney, Ann Rutherford, and Judy Garland, where they showed teenage parties and such. We all tried to emulate that; we had our parties. The series, which lasted four or five years, captured everyday life. Everyone emulated the characters and lifestyle in these movies.

Kobayashi's interests and activities reflected those of any young person growing up in middle-class America.

Figure 3.6. Yutaka Kobayashi, Wellesley, Massachusetts, 2009. Photo by author.

The church in his community played an important role in Kobayashi's socialization: "My two older brothers and I were active in our various social clubs, for example, Church Fellowship Club, which was a big thing, Presbyterian, Christ's Church on Post and Octavia. They held Sunday fellowship meetings with people in Berkeley and San Mateo. They used to have these so-called Christian conferences. Fellowship clubs served as a social outlet for Nisei." Annual Christian conferences were organized to discuss social issues—international and evangelical—and included speakers as well as dinners and dances. Japanese American churches functioned as community centers, organizing not only social activities but also assisting families with employment and housing issues.

As mentioned earlier, the local YMCA actively hosted social events for Nisei. Kobayashi attended the YMCA's annual New Year's Eve dances, featuring live music by local Nisei dance bands, whose names he could not recall. He remembered local Nisei social clubs also organizing dances. "These dances were a big deal. Whenever there was a dance planned, it took about a month ahead of time [to organize it]—spring dance, Halloween dance, Thanksgiving dance—whatever a social club could afford." Kobayashi was an avid dancer and loved to jitterbug: "One watched movies, practiced with a chair to learn jitterbug steps and moves. Jitterbug dancing involved a six-beat dance rhythm in half time [two-four meter]." Dances, the primary social activity for teenagers, were central to Nisei living in urban centers.

> American dance music was an integral part of our Americanization. When we became teenagers in high school, we always looked forward to that [dances] because of our restricted homelife. We never invited girls to our house. We only socialized at church, school, or at clubs—that was it, or if you happened to meet in a store. Those were the only social outlets in terms of meeting the opposite sex as a teenager. You could hardly ever invite friends of the opposite sex to your house. You just didn't do that. It was a problem with your parents [who would ask], "Why do you want [her/him] to visit? What's on your mind?" So, dancing became a very important part of our lives, we always looked forward to that. Music was a big part of our lives, because when we were growing up, being the first generation of Americans, we wanted to be Americans and act like Americans, even though we didn't look like Americans. We did everything that the Americans did—the white guys did.

Kobayashi reminisced about the popular commercial bands of the time: Tommy Dorsey, Jimmy Dorsey, Lionel Hampton, and Count Basie. Singers he remembered were Kate Kaiser, Ted Weems, and Sammy Kaye. Radio was the primary purveyor of the latest hit tunes on national programs, such as *Major Bowe's Amateur Hour*, which was one of the most popular programs broadcast in the United States in the 1930s and 1940s. Kobayashi recalled, "All of us knew the top ten hit-parade songs. We knew all the artists. When I was growing up, I thought Bing Crosby was the big guy. Eventually, I changed to Frank Sinatra." He also attended live performances:

> In San Francisco, the Golden Gate Theater, down at Market and Golden Gate Streets, used to have a stage show. I saw a lot of performances; Frank Sinatra used to appear, the Benny Goodman band, and others. In the thirties, people like Sinatra, the big bands all performed in movie theaters. After the movies, they would play a set or two, a juggler would come out, magicians would do card tricks, and someone would do acrobatics. It was expensive [to go to these shows]. In Chicago, they did the same thing, and of course, the Paramount Theater in New York was famous for having Frank Sinatra.

Both listening to music and dancing were requisite activities for this Nisei.

In contrast to the many Americanizing influences in his life, Kobayashi's homelife was traditionally Japanese. Kobayashi's family celebrated o-Shōgatsu (New Year's) every year. O-Shōgatsu lasted a week or longer: "My mother cooked up a ton of food, and then friends would come over and drink *saké* and whatever else. Everyone would eat special foods, such as *omochi* [rice cake]. We looked forward to it because of the food."

Nisei were expected to attend Japanese school, where they learned to read and write Japanese. Japanese school also taught them about customs, morals, and social obligations, creating a bridge to their heritage. Kobayashi and his two older brothers attended, but he rebelled, exclaiming, "I am an American, why do I have to go to Japanese school?" And he never graduated, although his brothers did. Many Nisei grew up biculturally, but when they left home for school or to socialize with their friends, their American persona prevailed.

KIKU UNO

As a young woman, Kiku Uno (1924–2012) enjoyed a busy social life and a comfortable middle-class life made possible by her parents' success as entrepreneurs; her father owned a hardware store, and her mother ran her own seamstress business.[90] Uno was born in Los Angeles in 1924 and raised in this city until the age of seventeen, when she and her family were forced to evacuate and endure incarceration during World War II. Her parents worked in the Japanese ethnic community in Los Angeles: "I lived in the Boyle Heights section. My father at one time ran two hardware stores; one in Little Tokyo and one in the Olympic [Boulevard] section of Los Angeles near St. Mary's Church, where there used to be a Japanese community. My mother had her sewing shop for custom-made clothes on the second floor of my father's hardware store."[91]

Family life for Uno was strongly Japanese: "I spoke Japanese at home as my parents didn't speak English." Her parents considered themselves Japanese nationals since they were not allowed to become US citizens. "I spoke Japanese with my grandmother [who lived with them]. So, I grew up speaking Japanese, learning all the Japanese polite terms and behavior." Japanese food was the standard fare at her home, which included a lot of fish: "My father was a sports fisherman, so he would go deep sea fishing for tuna, albacore." Uno also remembered playing Japanese card games: "We played those Japanese card games—*karuta*—and *karuta* had little sayings on them, and it was like a moral lesson that you learned. It taught you values, Japanese values."

Uno also learned Japanese folk songs: "We had records, and some of them were children's songs—'Karasu' and others." Her parents opened her world. Uno recounted, "Little Tokyo, at that time, had a stage theater called Yamato [Theater]; on the second floor, they had live theater, no movies, but dances and *naniwa-bushi* [Japanese storytelling genre]. There were Japanese dance teachers then, and they put on programs. I also remember watching folk tales there." Exposure to other Japanese performing arts included her father performing *kenbu*, a form of epic storytelling: "There's singing [*shigin*] that goes with it and then dance. He would dance *kenbu* at picnics. My mother played koto, so I heard 'Rokudan' [a touchstone piece] when I was a child."

Although Uno's homelife exhibited strong ties to Japan, both parents came from Christian backgrounds. Consequently, Western and Japanese cultural influences coexisted. Her mother played piano and organ in church. Uno heard European classical music regularly at home and at concerts: "I went to the Philharmonic; they had a special children's program on Saturday mornings." She and her sister studied piano and Uno's sister could play by ear: "My sister was very popular at dances because when the record player broke down, she could sit at the piano and be able to play songs people would call out." Uno remembered purchasing sheet music: "In the dime stores, sheet music was sold. There would be a piano player available to play the music you were interested in, and then you bought it; music was important." Uno's social outings revolved around dancing at clubs that featured live music, such as the Palladium and attending stage shows—Duke Ellington's "Jump for Joy" and the musical *Cabin in the Sky*, featuring Ethel Waters in a downtown theater in Los Angeles. Going to stage shows and dancing to hit tunes reinforced Uno's Americanness.

An important share of her American identity entailed social-club memberships in the Christian Fellowship group and the Girl Reserve Program at the YWCA: "There were different clubs all around in LA, and we would have dances once a week and invite other clubs. Your club would invite two girls' clubs and two boys' clubs; that way, we met people from places other than our immediate neighborhood. There were social clubs in Pasadena, Inglewood, and Boyle Heights." Social clubs scheduled Friday evenings for dance practice in preparation for Saturday-night dances. Uno remembered, "Yeah, it was great. It was a good social life because we had music of the big bands." Busy social calendars for Nisei in Los Angeles also included Sunday-afternoon sports activities—volleyball and softball—and Sunday-night roller-skating.

In answering my question about American popular music being a part of her identity, Uno replied, "It *was* my identity." She grew up considering herself an American, and her parents fostered this idea. In school, she learned American songs, among them Stephen Foster songs, and in church, she sang spirituals. My interview with her concerning music and how she identified as American prompted a discovery she made recently:

> I have a couple of Caucasian friends who have lived all their lives on the East Coast and while visiting with them the subject of music came up. Well . . . we found that we three knew the same songs . . . popular songs, hymns, campfire songs, and songs we learned on the radio. Even commercials . . . like "Cream of Wheat is so good to eat." So . . . this California Nisei and two Massachusetts Yankees grew up singing the same songs. Does this prove that I was Americanized through music?

Music certainly was an aspect of US national culture that Uno absorbed in school, church, social settings, and through the mass media; it played a major role in viewing herself as American.

HISAYO ASAI

My aunt Hisayo Asai's (1920–2014) personal account introduces us to Nisei living in rural areas as a counterpoint to the lives of urbane Nisei interviewees: the Takayanagis, Kobayashi, Uno, and Naka. Asai was born and raised in Yakima Valley, a very small farming area in the central part of the state of Washington (figure 3.7). Yakima Valley was a mixed community where 25 percent of the population was Japanese. Most of the Japanese population were farmers and families who lived in the outlying areas of town. My aunt's family were entrepreneurs: "My father was a very successful businessman who worked with the farmers packing and shipping [produce]. He had a large warehouse and employed many people, so our life was very comfortable."[92]

Hisayo Asai's homelife was essentially American. "We were the only Japanese family in a white neighborhood. Our home was just as nice as the others; it was just that we looked different. Our life was very American because we just went along with everything else in the community. We lived just like our neighbors." Her family conformed to middle-class American customs, such as not taking their shoes off at the entrance of their home, diverging from a common custom in Japanese households. She also mentioned, "Both my mother and my father spoke English because they were living in a white community. I think my mother felt a little more comfortable speaking Japanese, but she spoke both Japanese and English."

Figure 3.7. Hisayo Asai, New York City, n.d. Photo by James J. Kriegsmann Jr. Courtesy of William Asai.

While many aspects of her daily life bespoke middle America, Asai's connection to Japanese culture and the community remained intact. Clearly defined segregation in Yakima Valley forced the creation of a largely separate Japanese community. Her father's success as a businessman made it possible for him to offer financial assistance to many Japanese families in need. On New Year's Day, members of the community visited him at his home to thank him for his past assistance. Asai's father was an important leader in the Japanese community; when Japanese Americans were interned during the war, he was sent to a separate Department of Justice camp exclusively for community leaders. Her family's cuisine reflected their cultural duality too. Although they ate mostly American food, Asai preferred Japanese cuisine:

"Occasionally, my mother would make Japanese food, which I loved more than American food. I was always very happy when New Year's came because my mother cooked all the special dishes for o-Shōgatsu. There was a Japanese store in the community, and they got all the food shipped over." Japanese language use, although not actively practiced at home, was heard daily. Her parents communicated in Japanese with clients, and my aunt attended an after-school, Japanese-language program daily until sixth grade.

Asai gave an account of a social life quite different from that of Nisei urbanites. The intense anti-Japanese sentiment in rural farming areas, stemming from racism and the economic competition between Japanese and white farmers, created a stark social environment for Nisei youth. Racist attitudes severely curbed the social activities of Asai and her age group. When asked about dances and in-school social activities, Hisayo answered, "We didn't go. They must have had dances, but we didn't go. We never went to the prom." The Methodist and Buddhist churches in Yakima Valley had not formed youth fellowship groups since many people lived some distance away; organized social activities for Nisei youth were rare. YMCAs and YWCAs were urban organizations, which meant, in rural settings, there were few, if any, social dances or Nisei sports activities outside of school.

In response to their barren social lives, Nisei youth in Yakima Valley focused on their studies, school sports, or the arts. Asai directed her energies toward playing European classical piano:

> I was given piano lessons ever since I was six years old. I had two younger sisters, and they all had music lessons, but I am the only one that pursued it because I liked it. And so, homelife for me was to go to school, come home, and practice. I did my homework and practiced again. I liked it. We couldn't do a lot of things, so most of the people would just accept it and knew what we could do. I know, in many other communities, people could take part in sports teams, and so, most of the communities had their own Japanese sports teams—I think mostly baseball.

Also, "School was very important. We couldn't go to a lot of things, so the children just studied. We all did very well in school." For Hisayo Asai, playing piano filled her hours and days; it was a way to transcend her proscribed life.

Performing classical music was Asai's primary identification as an American. She was active as an accompanist for the high-school chorus and in the larger Yakima Valley community as a soloist for various ladies' club gatherings. Asai imparted how playing piano was her entrée into mainstream society:

I was in demand in the community. They had women's groups who would have meetings, and they asked me, "Would you play a solo?" They had different clubs; they had garden clubs and different kinds of social clubs. They wanted something to add to their program. I was forever going from one place to another just volunteering. They would ask, and I would go. Through my high-school years, that was very important to me. I enjoyed it. So, I was part of the community, and it softened the racism.

As for American popular music, Asai recalled, "I really liked popular music. I wasn't too aware, but I knew which songs were popular at the time. I was so ingrained with classical music that I liked; I practiced so much that I really didn't have time to listen." Asai's involvement with American popular music was minimal. It wasn't until the war and her move to New York City that this music played a greater role in her life. She danced at social gatherings hosted by the Japanese American Citizens League, where she met and later married my uncle Woodrow Asai.

WALTER MORIYA

Having been born and raised in the small agricultural town of Watsonville, California, did not curb the musicking of amateur tenor saxophonist Walter Moriya (b. 1925) (figure 3.8). Contrary to the usual paucity of musicking activities in rural areas, Watsonville was fortunate to be the home of the Watsonville YBA Orchestra. Assembled in 1940 by Mrs. Helen Iwanaga, musician, composer, and wife of Rev. Iwanaga of the Watsonville Buddhist Temple, the Watsonville YBA Orchestra brought an eclectic array of American dance music and arrangements of traditional Japanese songs to this community and the surrounding towns. Helen Iwanaga, a trained musician, conducted the group and wrote the ensemble's arrangements of Japanese songs. Moriya was one among the "eagerly waiting group of young musicians"[93] who benefitted greatly from the musical leadership of Mrs. Iwanaga. The orchestra included two trumpets, two alto saxes, a tenor sax, clarinet, violin, drums, and piano.[94]

Moriya's interest in music blossomed after hearing big-band music on the radio:

Music came to my attention around 1937 [at the age of twelve] when I first heard Artie Shaw's "Begin the Beguine" on the radio, and I was hooked. All of a sudden, the big band era was upon us with Benny Goodman, Charlie Barnet, Glenn Miller, and many others. The big-band style and

Figure 3.8. Walter Moriya, Los Angeles, 2016. Photo by author.

arrangements had a big impact on me at the beginning of the swing era. Other bands [and musicians] I enjoyed were Count Basie, Les Brown, Coleman Hawkins, Nat King Cole, Stan Kenton, and Stan Getz, and many more. Singers I liked were Frank Sinatra, Billy Eckstine, Johnny Hartman, Ella Fitzgerald, Peggy Lee, Maxine Sullivan, and many others.

Moriya's great interest in big-band music inspired him to pick up an instrument and begin playing in 1939 while a freshman in high school: "My older brother, Art, took up music in school and encouraged me to start. I started with the clarinet but switched to the tenor sax the second year and advanced to marching band later that year." His father bought him a saxophone, and Moriya, then fifteen, began private lessons with the high-school music teacher, himself a reed player.

Performing with the YBA Orchestra fulfilled Moriya's dream to play in a big band. Prior to World War II, the ensemble enlivened YBA social dances, various community get-togethers, and wedding receptions. During the war, his family and four others were fortunate enough to avoid being interned by moving to Brighton, Colorado, in March 1942. When the idea for a farm in Brighton failed, Moriya and his family moved to Denver. There, Walter Moriya joined a Nisei dance band for four years, playing for dances in the local Japanese community. His family's move to Los Angeles in 1953 ended Moriya's band-performing days, although, to this day, he continues to attend live jazz shows regularly and listen to jazz recordings daily. Moriya's musicking and continued active listening to jazz marks his identity as firmly American. His homelife reinforced his Japanese heritage, however; he spoke Japanese, ate Japanese food, and celebrated o-Shōgatsu. Meanwhile, Moriya's parents chose to join the Methodist church with the intent of facilitating their family's assimilation into American society. Both Buddhist and Methodist churches in Watsonville were central to the Japanese American community of eight hundred individuals. Moriya reflected on his performing tenor sax in the YBA Orchestra as an aspect of his Americanization: "As an American art form, big-band music was a part of Nisei American life. In that sense, it was part of the Nisei's Americanization." He continued, "It was good timing for us Nisei who loved the big-band sound, especially during the period when things were difficult for us."

HARUKO AKAMATSU

Haruko Akamatsu's (1916–2007) story gives us a glimpse of Nisei life in suburbia. She was born in Alameda, a suburb northeast of San Francisco. Akamatsu's homelife, modeled on that of families in Meiji-period Japan, required "respectful and obedient behavior of family members." She recollects, "I spoke Japanese at home because of my maternal grandparents who lived with us and could not speak English."[95] Listening to traditional Japanese music at home was part of Akamatsu's Japanese enculturation. Her father and uncle would play shakuhachi together, often inviting a neighbor to play koto. Although Akamatsu was interested in playing koto, she never had a chance to follow up on this desire. She did have an opportunity to experience life in Japan firsthand from 1940–41 when she received a scholarship to study at the School of Language and Culture in Tokyo, where German, Burmese, Korean, and American missionaries were educated.

Akamatsu expressed her cosmopolitan inclinations by joining the French club in high school and pursuing her interest in drama: "I used to do monologues; I was a character actor, playing the roles of old women or old men." While attending high school, Akamatsu drew a connection between the Japanese and American parts of herself: "I gave a speech about the US and Asia. I talked about how, as a Japanese American, I felt responsible to be a bridge between these two." The idea of serving as a cultural bridge was a personal choice of some Nisei who were encouraged by Issei to speak on behalf of Japanese Americans' desire for cooperation between the two countries. Akamatsu's background placed her firmly at the cultural apex of US and Japanese culture.

Akamatsu's social experience mirrors that of Hisayo Asai. Her social opportunities while attending school were very limited; dances and many social activities were off limits for the few Japanese American students. The Buddhist church in Alameda satisfied the youths' recourse for socializing by hosting dances.

Not all Nisei were musically active. Akamatsu did not listen regularly to American popular music on the radio, but when she did, she enjoyed it: "I listened to Italian American musicians, such as Frank Sinatra; I also liked Benny Goodman, and I remember the song 'Red Sails in the Sunset.'" She associates dancing with her interest in American popular music: "The Buddhist church held socials in the big hall for dancing. Dance classes were offered and taught by a Russian woman. While I was at the University of California, Berkeley, I also went to dances on campus." Her move to New York City in 1942 heightened her appreciation of dance music: "My husband, Alfred Akamatsu, learned to dance rumba, tango, and foxtrot at an Arthur Murray Dance Studio." As minister of the Japanese American United Church in New York City, Rev. Akamatsu organized social dances for Nisei as part of fellowship group activities. As an adult, Haruko Akamatsu's interest in music grew, and she decided to take a voice class: "I studied voice with Ruby Yoshino. She was my vocal coach for ten lessons." In closing, I asked about the role of American popular music for her as a Nisei. She responded, "Popular music became a part of my American identity; music expressed my feelings and sentiments as a young, romantic person. I loved to listen to and dance to it."

SUE OKABE

Sue Okabe (1928–2002), originally from Seattle, Washington, was a transplant to southern California. Her upbringing was a mix of East and West. Okabe's parents spoke English and were Western-music trained: "They all played, they all sang. My uncle, after graduating college in Japan, came here to study music, and another uncle, still living in Japan, plays violin very well."[96] During the interview, she remarks how, as Japan opened its doors to the West in the Meiji period, it considered European musical training as broadening, aligning Japan artistically with the Western world. While coming of age, her parents exposed her to the traditional Japanese arts of *utai* and *shimai*—*nō*-style singing and dancing; her father sang, and her mother sang and danced this tradition. The bicultural family enjoyed American theater and classical concert music, as well as Kabuki and local *shibai* theatrical performances.

In this rich environment, Okabe maintained a close connection with her Japanese side. Her family lived in downtown Seattle, where there were very few Japanese. The Japanese American community located within the city limits was a distance away from her home. Despite this, she attended the Buddhist church and Japanese-language school located there. It took walking several miles and taking the bus: "I wanted to be with Japanese." This strong desire was inexplicable to her sister who did not share her feelings, and it accounted for Okabe's pull toward Japanese music and cultural artifacts: "I happen to love Japanese music and Japanese things."

The wide-ranging repertoire of this Nisei vocalist illustrates the multiple musical choices and talents of some Nisei, dispelling any assumption that individuals preferred one tradition or style over another. Her versatility stems from musical parents who performed both Western classical music and Japanese *nō*-style singing and dancing. From the age of six, Okabe learned to sing both *kayokyoku*—Japanese popular songs—and Western classical pieces, which she sang at Buddhist churches, the customary venue for many community events. Okabe regularly sang at the annual talent show at the Buddhist church in Seattle as well as at churches in Tacoma, White River, and Portland, Oregon. She traveled with her sister who accompanied her on piano. Her repertoire included the most current *kayokyoku*, arias from Puccini or Verdi operas, light-classical songs, and Western folk and vernacular songs, such as the Irish ballad "Danny Boy."

Okabe pursued singing while incarcerated at the Minidoka Relocation Center in Idaho during World War II.[97] She recalled, "We had one, big, huge talent revue: Sage Press Revue, I think it was called. A humongous show, a two-hour show outdoors on a stage. We had the Mikados of Swing, a thirteen-piece band, maybe more, and Art Hayashi's band; they played, and Chickie (Ishihara) and I sang."

When the family relocated to Denver during the war, Okabe performed for Japanese American functions, the USO, and war-bond rallies while studying at Lamont School of Music. Her experience singing for war-bond rallies throughout Colorado, Wyoming, and Nebraska epitomizes the thorny settings in which Nisei often found themselves. Okabe acutely remembers having to confront hostile audiences at the rallies: "In the beginning, you have to start singing. Once I started singing, it would quiet down, but they would be pretty noisy, and you could hear people say, 'What's *she* doing here?'" Resilient, she continued to sing at rallies, refusing to change her family name, Takimoto, to a Chinese name, as requested by rally organizers.

Okabe moved to Los Angeles to finish her studies at the Los Angeles Conservatory of Music and University of Southern California. As a single parent, she added to her vocabulary jazz/pop vocal styles and made a living singing professionally in clubs and lounges in southern California. While employed at the Kyoto Club as a piano bar performer, Okabe sang songs in six languages, including Japanese popular songs, expanding her oeuvre to include *enka*—Japanese popular music sung in a traditionally inflected vocal style. This vocalist's vast repertoire included musical theater; she performed as a member of the cast in *Flower Drum Song*, by Richard Rogers and Oscar Hammerstein II, in venues in both Los Angeles and Chicago. When I interviewed her in 1995, she had expanded her repertoire to singing rock music once a month in a club. Teaching piano and singing a variety of vocal styles has been Okabe's steady source of income. Okabe occupies a position in the spectrum of Nisei musicking that bridges her two cultural worlds.

Okabe views her training and interest in both Japanese and Western vocal styles as aesthetic pursuits rather than connected to her identity: "I happen to like all music, and I don't put a restriction on ethnicity [associated with a particular music]." She adamantly believes that the connection between music and one's identity is very individual and cannot be generalized. To illustrate her stance, Okabe cites the difference between her older sister and herself: "We were both brought up quite similarly [including musical training], but I happen to love Japanese music, while my sister hates it. She doesn't like it because she said it has no challenge and it's not musical to her ears. The songs all sound alike." Okabe also opposes the notion that identities shift when comparing one generation to the next: "As far as generations go, it is not clear cut. Music is music." Instead, she argues that people's choice of musicking is based purely on individual preference not necessarily shaped by any social and/or political forces. Okabe cites the example of her grandniece, a fourth-generation (*Yonsei*) Japanese/Chinese American who is about to earn her *natori* professional certificate in Japanese classical dance. An individual's sense of aesthetics and personal preference is at play, she contends: "You have to stop and think of the individual. The reason I teach *enka* and classical Japanese songs is because it's part of music, the world of music." In analyzing how music serves to enact one's identity, this cosmopolitan musician defies any neat categories or generalizations.

Figure 3.9. Bob Naka, Concord, Massachusetts, 2009. Photo by author.

BOB NAKA

Similar to Kiku Uno, Bob Naka (1923–2013) also grew up in the Boyle Heights neighborhood of Los Angeles, which he describes as ethnically diverse and included Italians, Brits, Germans, and Mexicans (figure 3.9). He experienced family life as a middle-class American. "My father elected not to live in a Japanese American enclave; rather, he chose for us to live in what you might call the melting pot of America."[98]

Naka's musical background included some performing:

> When I was in the second grade, I was part of a harmonica band, and I got quite good at it. As a consequence, when we gave a program on the radio, the instructor called me from the back of the room to stand right in front of the microphone when we played. Later, when I was in Boy Scout Troop 197, we had a drum and bugle corps, and I got very good at playing the snare drum. The music director, Mr. Arnold, wrote a special piece for the drummers, and I was the only one who learned how to play it—it was quite tricky and syncopated.

Naka's musical tastes varied:

> I listened to classical and what you might call popular. I used to listen to Glenn Miller on the radio; he was back East playing in some nightclub, but the program was coming in at four or five in the afternoon, and I used to listen to that. I bought a lot of records—Glenn Miller and Tommy Dorsey. I used to go to the Paramount Theater to watch and listen to them play in Los Angeles just before World War II and also to hear Frank Sinatra sing.

Other bands and singers he listened to were Artie Shaw, Duke Ellington, Ray Eberle, and Mary Hunt, who sang with the Glenn Miller Orchestra. During the war, when he attended the University of Missouri, he listened to music in conjunction with dancing: "When I got to the University of Missouri, it turned out that there was a lot of dancing going on; I joined in all of that and jitterbugged. So, all of that was really part of growing up in a culture that was American, and I was a part of it."

Naka agrees with the premise that American popular music was an important measure of Nisei's American identity: "I thought your notion was right on target. I think you are quite right that music was part of the culture and society that made the Japanese American community American." As for music being a part of his own identity, however, Naka answers, "As I sit here and think about looking back, it was a part. But at the time, I didn't think it was a part. It was just what everybody else was doing."

The oral histories provide a fuller and more nuanced picture of how music served to enact Nisei identity. The degree to which music shaped their identity depended on their socialization in line with family customs, residential location, socioeconomic status, and personal choice. The interviewee sampling represented a balanced range of Nisei enculturation, offering a heterogeneous glimpse of the second generation. Yoshida, Kobayashi, Uno, Moriya, and Naka were definitive in their belief about popular music as a marker of their American identity. The Takayanagis didn't state a direct connection in how they identified themselves, but the integral role of Western classical and popular music in their lives tacitly affirms the link. For Asai, performing European classical music was key to her entrée into mainstream America, while Akamatsu's association with music was that of a "young, romantic person" and not necessarily tied to her cultural identity. Further, Okabe viewed the correlation between music and identity as highly individual; for her, musicking was an aesthetic pursuit and not a requisite emblem of her identity. Music played a significant role in most of the interviewees' lives; half the members of this cohort—Yoshida, Okabe, Naka, Moriya, and Asai—were performers, mostly amateurs; the remainder were solely active listeners and social dancers. Akamatsu's interface with music was minimal until later in life when she moved to New York City, studied voice, and attended Nisei social dances hosted by her husband, Rev. Akamatsu, at United Union Methodist Church.

Contagious was the exuberance of some of the interviewees in recalling the heady days of musicking, dancing, socializing, and dating. The accent on music and socializing functioned to anchor Nisei as they countered their social segregation and liminal space of statelessness. Moriya affirmed that the popularity of big-band music was well timed, serving as a panacea for his generation when life was grim. Learning about Issei parents who were either trained performers or active listeners of European classical or Christian music in the families of Yoshida, Okabe, Uno, and May Takayanagi expanded my understanding of Issei musicking. Such activity took place more in families living in urban centers compared to farming families with less free time and financial means. In some cases, Issei parents reinforced their offspring's American identity, as illustrated by Yoshida's father, who sang American songs, and mother, who played organ in church. May Takayanagi shared with me about how European classical music was a staple in many Japanese American families—a musical style that appealed to both Issei and Nisei.

The interviewees raised in urban centers had by far the most socially active lives because of the proximity of Japanese American communities, which maintained institutions that hosted social activities. Swing music naturally played a much larger role in the social lives of these urbanites. The association of swing music with dancing and socializing gave popular music its power and appeal. In rural communities, where social activities were scarce or nonexistent and tenant farming families moved frequently to secure agricultural employment, popular music had less of an impact on Nisei. European classical music practiced among those who could afford lessons was also limited in its reach. Taking into account a wide variety of styles is a fuller measure of music's influence in Americanizing Nisei. Several Nisei I interviewed recalled singing Stephen Foster and other vernacular songs in school, hymns in church, campfire songs, and spirituals in a variety of social contexts. Together with other related activities, songs played an important role in Nisei enculturation.

Valuable was the interview with vocalist Sue Okabe, who broadened my view about how music fashioned Nisei identity. This interviewee challenged the idea that Nisei were culturally conflicted as she enthusiastically pursued both Western and Japanese music throughout her life. The singer singularly opposed the notion that identities shift from one generation to the next, citing the Japanese cultural continuum running through four generations of her own family. To Okabe, an individual's sense of aesthetics and personal preference is at play, not cultural patterns and assumptions.

Interviewees further reflected on why Nisei were, in general, apolitical. Notable were two viewpoints offered by Yoshida: first, many Issei parents themselves were apolitical; second, Yoshida felt that in those distant times he and his cohort weren't inclined to deep analysis, instead desiring only to congregate with peers. One is prompted to also speculate that an absence of a political stance among Nisei resulted from despair and resignation in the face of growing anti-Japanese sentiments restricting their social, political, and economic circumstances—sentiments that in broader terms denied Nisei their very humanity.

Importantly, Nisei accounts point to music as only one facet of a more comprehensive assimilation process into middle-class American life. Going to the movies, playing games and sports, attending church services, keeping an American diet, and immersion in school were all significant. Here too, the degree of enculturation varied according to the individual. Nisei lived culturally bifurcated lives, and not all families were equally assimilated. Yoshida, Naka, Uno, and Takashi Takayanagi, for example, far from being raised in a Japanese enclave, grew up in ethnically mixed neighborhoods in Los Angeles, broadening their contact with mainstream society. Further, attending mandatory Japanese-language school had little influence on a generation more comfortable with their American identity, feeling little or no affinity or loyalty to the "mother country." Yet, the retention of Japanese language and customs at home and living on the cultural cusp of two contrasting cultures, although at times problematic, was ultimately enriching, imparting greater depth to Nisei lives.

Anomalies I found salient were the different experiences of Asai and Moriya, both raised in rural farming communities. Settled rural areas were known to be wellsprings of Japanese culture and musical activity by necessity because of the virile discrimination Japanese farmers and their families faced. In the case of Asai, performing Western classical music on piano, enabled by her family's upper-middle-class status, differentiated her experience. Not only was her family able to afford piano lessons for their daughter but performing piano for women's social clubs and providing accompaniment for the high school chorus served as her entrée into white, mainstream society. Classical music became integral to her identity, granting her a degree of acceptance. Moriya was fortunate to live in the small agricultural town of Watsonville, California, where the Young Buddhist Association Orchestra, led by Mrs.

Helen Iwanaga, blossomed. The ensemble performed American dance music and Japanese songs in Watsonville as well as the surrounding towns. Active musicking in rural areas was rare, and Moriya benefitted greatly from his unique experience, instilling a strong affinity to a variety of jazz styles.

Racially, Nisei considered "whiteness" as ideal. One needs to look no further than the opening epigraph to this chapter in support of this premise. There was no inclination to look to Blackness as African Americans continued to be denigrated by mainstream society in the prewar period. Yoshida aptly remarks that the music industry's category of "race records" intentionally formed a musical boundary that separated white and Black bands and their audiences. A preference for white bands reflected both the Issei's and mainstream society's bigoted views toward this segment of the population. Despite racial segregation, Yoshida, Kobayashi, and Moriya crossed over and enthusiastically listened to Black singers, instrumentalists, and bands such as Billy Eckstine, Lionel Hampton, Coleman Hawkins, and the bands of Duke Ellington, Count Basie, and Earl Hines. It must be noted that Nisei appreciation of Black music is not a reliable marker of their racial position toward Blacks. It is conceivable that, too busy navigating their own racial predicament, brought on by the hegemonic policy of whiteness within Americanism propagated at the beginning of the twentieth century, the Nisei stance was at best ambivalent.[99] Not until almost three decades later, when the Asian American movement emerged, did Americans of Japanese ancestry seek to embrace their Black American counterparts in a quest to secure their place in the American landscape.

POLITICS OF IDENTITY

I examine additional historical, political, and social forces that shaped Nisei identity from the 1910s to the 1940s. Historically, a legacy of race and the perpetuation of Asians as unassimilable in the United States were fundamental to the development of Nisei identities. The American Orientalist view held that the Asian body was "biologically different and inferior" to the Protestant, Anglo-Saxon ideal. Eugenics and other pseudoscientific theories "proved" that "Mongoloids" and "Malays" were situated halfway between Caucasians above and Negroes below in a "scale of human development,"[100] graphically illustrating the racial triangulation of Asian and Japanese Americans. Popular culture reinforced such characterizations, as in circuses where Asians were often featured as exotic or grotesque beings distant from the norm. Films, cartoons, media publications, recordings, and Tin Pan Alley sheet music also had a hand in mimicking and distorting aspects of the Asian body, mannerisms, and behavior.[101] The proliferation of these stereotypes ignited "immigration and civil laws, court cases, foreign policies, and ultimately segregated work and residential landscapes."[102] It is little wonder that Nisei suffered from the notion that their bodies were perceived as Other and inferior, yet knowing their true selves—Americans who happened to be of Japanese descent. As the second generation matured, their bifurcated existence created an identity conflict acutely expressed by this young Nisei woman:

> We belong to two groups, the Japanese and the American. In ancestry and in physical appearance we are Japanese, while in birth, in education, in ideals, and in ways of thinking we are American. Nevertheless, the older Japanese will not accept us into their group because, as they see us, we are too independent, too pert, and too self-confident, and the Americans bar us from their group because we retain the yellow skin and flat nose of the oriental. Thus, we stand on the borderline that separates Orient from Occident.
>
> Though on either side of us flow the streams of two great civilizations—the old Japanese culture with its formal traditions and customs and the new American civilization with its freedom and individualism—the chance to perceive and to imbibe the best things from each has been withheld from us.[103]

This bitter account poignantly describes the dilemma Nisei faced.

Politically, the Nisei's positioning was assimilationist; socially and racially, they strove toward whiteness, mainstream society's hegemonic Euro-American standard of Americanness. A politics of identity frames the exigencies Nisei faced in attempting to assimilate into US mainstream culture and attain full rights as citizens prior to and during World War II. It is a framework useful for narrating Nisei experiences of racial discrimination and political exclusion in the United States from the 1910s through the 1930s, climaxing in the imprisonment of Japanese Americans primarily from the West Coast in the 1940s. Nisei, in emphasizing commonalities and positioning themselves as Americans, became embroiled in a politics of identity, historically rooted in whiteness and how the United States viewed itself economically and politically as a nation and an evolving world power. The growing political enmity in US-Japan relations in the 1930s, resulting from Japan's aggression in the Sino-Japanese War and the Manchurian Incident, intensified negative public perceptions of Japanese Americans. This state of affairs fed the racist view Americans held toward Japanese immigrants and their offspring, further distancing the Nisei in their attempts to establish themselves as American citizens.

Sociologist Jere Takahashi expounds on the political response of Nisei to their disenfranchisement in his article "Japanese American Responses to Race Relations: The Formation of Nisei Perspectives" (1982) and book *Nisei/Sansei: Shifting Japanese American Identities and Politics* (1997). He describes the difficult period of the 1920s and 1930s as a time when maturing Nisei failed in their attempts to gain acceptance despite their status as American citizens.

Passage of racist legislation—the federal Immigration Act of 1924 and five anti-Japanese bills in California—an anti-alien corporation bill, anti-alien fishing bill, anti-alien language-school bill and the 1913 and 1920 Alien Land Acts—created a political crisis for both Issei and Nisei. Takahashi delineates the Nisei's reaction to this growing crisis in terms of four political styles or responses to their racial subjugation: (1) serve as a cultural bridge between America and Japan; (2) identify with American life; (3) concern for progressive social change; (4) alienation from American society.[104]

Dawning in the 1920s through the 1930s, eminent American and Japanese intellectuals conceived the "cultural-bridge" notion, proposing that Japanese American students serve as "cultural ambassadors" to bridge the cultural divide between the United States and Japan. This concept naively presupposed that the exclusion movement was not just about racism, economic competition, or political machinations, but a consequence of knowing little about Japan and Japanese immigrants. The hope was to defuse the exclusion movement and nurture mutual understanding between the United States and Japan in the coming Pacific era, a time in which the two countries could partner.[105] Ambassadorial duties of the Nisei involved serving as interpreters of the East and West with the goal of establishing common ground between the two nations to facilitate peace and cooperation. The cultural-bridge concept, representing the perspective of older Nisei intellectuals and businessmen, *did not* diminish in any way the racist circumstances that could improve one's social acceptance or attempts to find employment. Hence, the majority of Nisei maturing in the late 1930s did not embrace the "intellectual character" of the bridge premise.[106]

The Nisei's second political reply favored the "ideal of Americanism," entailing loyalty and full assimilation into American life. In rejecting the Issei strategy of passive accommodation to their socially, economically, and politically circumscribed lives, some Nisei sought to take a more active approach.[107] Nisei college students promoted Americanism and established civic clubs between 1918 and 1920 to collectively strategize ways to unblock their career opportunities and respond to political criticism of their dual Japan/United

States citizenship. Nisei college graduates founded the American Loyalty League in San Francisco and the Progressive Citizens League in Seattle. Commencing in 1923, leaders of the second generation assembled California chapters of the American Loyalty League (ALL) with financial support of the Japanese Association, an Issei organization that provided financial and leadership assistance. The goal of ALL was to emphasize Japanese American loyalty rather than focus on ethnicity in the cultural-bridge approach. Rural communities where anti-Japanese agitation was the most vitriolic were the most supportive of ALL chapters. The American Loyalty League lost its impetus due to a lack of proactive strategies, the loss of financial support from the Japanese Association, and the inexperience of Nisei leaders.[108]

Continuing efforts to express loyalty and assert an American identity led to the founding of the JACL in Seattle in April 1929. The JACL was one of the most important Nisei organizations of the 1930s not only as a clearinghouse for political, educational, and social welfare issues but also for socializing. The membership included Nisei in their late twenties or early thirties who were already established in professional fields or business. At its height, between 1930 and 1940, the JACL boasted fifty affiliate chapters on the West Coast with a membership of about 5,600 members.[109]

Politically, the JACL held views that were aligned along two fronts. While the organization defended Japan's political moves in Asia, it also advocated for legal and legislative reforms, such as the repeal of the Cable Act, denying US citizenship to Nisei women who married alien Japanese, and the Nye-Lea Bill granting citizenship to Asian men born abroad who had served in the US armed forces.[110] Other political activities of the JACL included creating lawsuits to assess the constitutionality of different state and federal statutes and utilizing the right of franchise in order to elect officials considered sympathetic to their interests. JACL public relations also promoted business for the ethnic economy, propagating the conception that Japanese Americans were loyal citizens. Efforts to inculcate in its members democratic principles and an emphasis on good citizenship were a part of the organization's agenda.[111] Politically, the JACL advocated a nonpartisan approach rather than traditional party lines as they voted in local, state, and national elections. In general, the JACL promoted full assimilation into American life and advocated strategies of cooperation and conciliation.[112]

The conciliatory approach of the JACL did little to address the racist political ideology of white supremacy that prevailed on the West Coast. The mainstream's view of Japanese immigrants as perpetual foreigners thwarted the Nisei's struggle to establish their identity as Americans, regardless of their generational status.

Nisei Progressives were another political faction whose liberal politics and affinity with the organized Left suggests a class differentiation of its members from the strongly republican JACL and its ideal of Americanism. Unable to find employment in professional fields outside Japanese communities, Nisei Progressives were primarily workers who plied their trade as gardeners, produce workers, and clerks. Their social lives and job opportunities restricted, Progressives turned toward more liberal politics and the Democratic Party, focusing on labor issues and improving their political mobility.[113]

Leftist-leaning college students also played a political role. One example is Kazu Iijima, an undergraduate at the University of California at Berkeley in the 1940s, who joined the Young Communist League (YCL), an affiliate of the Communist Party of the United States of America (CPUSA). Iijima's awakening to poverty and racism in this country based on her own experience spurred her to become politically active. Her activist sister, Nori, who at the time was president of the UC Berkeley campus YWCA, involved Iijima in picketing the YMCA for its racist practices. Kazu became disillusioned, however, when the CPUSA, in support of the war effort and the Soviet Union, expelled all Japanese American members.[114] Moving to New York City, she continued to be politically active and later joined other leftist Nisei and third-generation Sansei in founding Asian Americans for Action (AAA). In the next chapter, we shall see how Iijima's son, Chris, a musician and member of AAA, was instrumental in politically organizing Sansei in the 1970s.

Progressives also took a political stance on international affairs, concerning themselves with "racism and fascism" not only at home but also in Germany, Italy, and Asia. They clearly opposed the rising militarism in Japan and the ripple effect it would have on anti-Japanese agitation in the United States. Liberal Nisei attempted to draw a clear distinction between taking pride in one's Japanese ancestry and taking a cultural, nationalist stance in supporting Japanese militarism. Their critical view of Japan's incursion into China was in line with their opposition to fascists in Germany and Italy.[115]

Instead of accepting their disenfranchisement and making the best of their marginalization, Progressives strove for greater egalitarianism, starting in their own communities. Their goal was to increase their political mobility in hopes of creating greater opportunities. But as the tension between Japan and the United States reached crisis proportions, Progressives realized the importance of generational and racial unity, and many joined the JACL with the intent of liberalizing the views of its members. The potential of joining forces with the JACL to achieve that unity meant the league was considered the primary force in mobilizing the second generation during this time.[116]

A fourth political stance was unique to Kibei Nisei. Having lived and received an education in Japan fostered a Japanese nationalist view among this subgroup. The Kibei's loss of English-language fluency combined with their predominantly Japanese worldview made it difficult for them to relate to their American-raised siblings and cohort. This group clearly felt alienated from American society, increasing their sense of isolation since they were not considered "true" Japanese while living in Japan either. Kibei social clubs and civic groups catered to this population; some joined JACL in their attempts to create ties with American-born Nisei.

Such were the avenues Nisei followed in politically responding to their subjugation. The difficulty in making their voice heard, however, was due to the small size of their voting population and their inability to coordinate and organize political agendas, especially those contrary to Issei ethnic orthodoxy and leadership in their communities. Contributing to this generation's political impotency was the simple fact that most Nisei were apolitical and more interested in absorbing the social and cultural practices of American mainstream society to prove their assimilability. What mattered most to a majority of Nisei during the 1930s and 1940s were the interests and preoccupations of young people across the United States, such as dating and the latest music, movies, hairstyle, and dress.

Social and cultural forces that Nisei confronted in establishing their American identities included generational pressure from within their families and communities. Heightening the Nisei's dilemma and resistance to Japanese culture was the Issei's push for their children to attend Japanese schools, which taught Japanese language, history, and geography in fostering a positive Japanese identity. *Shushin*—moral education—was taught in connection with these subjects. Issei hoped Nisei would improve their Japanese to ease the communication gap that created friction between the two generations and learn social obligations, such as filial piety, respect for elders, and a sense of group rather than individual decision-making. Japanese schools functioned to foster *Nippon seishin*—Japanese spirit—meant to fortify Nisei. The immigrants' postulation of *Nippon seishin* was a transculturated version that differed from that of militarists and right-wing intellectuals in Japan. It was not meant to instill patriotic fanaticism as an ideology that would serve Japan's imperialist cause; instead, the concept was a milder interpretation, "a set of moral precepts and behavioral norms that they felt would help their children grow, first and foremost, into good citizen-subjects of the American state."[117] Sei Fujii, publisher of the newspaper *Kashū Mainichi*, justified the transmission of *Nippon seishin* by equating it with American moral precepts that he identified as "Americanism."[118]

A political subtext for the Japanese-language schools, however, is evident. A moral education meant instilling ethical codes of behavior in an effort to affirm the Nisei's blood ties to Japan. An eclectic reading of *Nippon seishin* advanced a biculturalism that was untenable and a source of suspicion by white racists who interpreted the objectives of the Japanese schools as Japanese nationalist. It was also unrealistic to expect Nisei to walk a fine line between two contrasting nationalities whose racial, political, and cultural boundaries differed.[119]

Class antagonism and criticism within the ethnic community generated social tension endured by Nisei in establishing a coherent identity. Many of the second generation's educated elite disapproved of their fellow Nisei for their clannish social behavior, sense of insecurity, lack of initiative, and superficiality in adopting American customs and behavior without achieving what they considered the cultural and class refinement of Americans. Elite Nisei leaders sought to shift the average Nisei's interest from sports and dancing to that of high art and society with the hopes of raising their generation's acceptability in mainstream America.[120] Such ideas were misconceived considering the growing racist fears toward Japan and its émigrés.

Despite Issei attempts to shape them, most Nisei were more comfortable with their American identity and felt little or no affinity or loyalty to Japan. A Nisei, Daisuke Kitagawa, describes the attitude of many in his generation:

> The Nisei in his adolescence in fact and in practice was in every way a member of the Japanese community, except that his language was English. This irked him not a little; and to counteract it, he turned to an extreme form of Americanism, rejecting everything, with the possible exception of food, which in any way identified him as a Japanese.[121]

Rebellion against Issei parents and their Japaneseness sometimes manifested in a form of self-hate. Others took on a more conciliatory attitude and made it their goal to improve themselves and work twice as hard to gain respectability as they sought to be a part of mainstream society. Unfortunately, because of the little social contact Nisei had with white Americans, these responsible efforts went unnoticed. Another tact taken by some Nisei in response to their complicated circumstances was to reconcile their Japanese and American backgrounds. George Muramoto of the San Francisco YMBA called for a "balanced identity," an "integrated identity" in which American and Japanese cultural orientations complemented rather than replaced each other.[122] Such an approach proved insurmountable without American society's acceptance and support of Nisei's American half of the "integrated identity" equation.

Most Nisei found it difficult to maintain the protocol and customs of their Japanese parents. Observing specific social obligations and maintaining deferential attitudes important in Japanese culture were the most challenging for Nisei to follow. According to Japanese tradition, life-cycle events—birth, marriage, and death—require a prescribed social behavior of individuals, families, and the community. On these social occasions, one is expected to present gifts or money to the appropriate individual(s) or families. Gift giving is reciprocal, necessitating remembering or keeping a log of people one has received gifts from to ensure that one fulfills their obligation to repay the favor on some future occasion. A person who did not observe these obligations was considered irresponsible and consequently became socially ostracized. Further, on New Year's Day, one was expected to visit people to acknowledge one's gratitude for past favors, such as assistance in procuring a job, or to wish them well for the coming year. If a Nisei did not take his obligations seriously, they often were marked as too Americanized.

Nisei identities evolved as a transculturated mixture of Japaneseness and Americanness. There were factors that determined which culture one leaned toward more heavily. One factor was how much Japanese was spoken at home and the level of communication Nisei had with their parents, many of whom spoke little English. Life in an urban or rural milieu made a difference; virile racial discrimination in rural areas generated tight-knit communities with strong Japanese cultural bearings in contrast to the mitigated Japanese demeanor of Nisei urbanites. Membership in either a Christian or Buddhist church was another factor; those belonging to a Christian church were more Americanized, while Buddhist members tended to be markedly Japanese. Despite the strong American identification of a majority of the second generation, by 1940, Buddhist churches had greater Nisei membership—48.7 percent—compared to 35 percent Nisei membership in Christian churches—an anomaly that requires more research. The amount of social contact Nisei had with white children as they developed also contributed to whether they leaned toward being Japanese or American.[123] Nisei daily life was a mediation of two worlds and the liminal spaces in between, creating multiple identities that shifted, depending on the individual's level of enculturation or life circumstances.

Focusing on the lives and musicking of Nisei up until World War II sets the stage for the next chapter, which details musical activities in the wartime concentration camps. The abrupt incarceration of all Japanese Americans on the West Coast violated Nisei's civil rights as American citizens, destabilizing this generation's identity.

It is the travails of the Nisei that pushed the next generation of Japanese Americans toward an identity politics that call for greater acknowledgement of their Japanese heritage as a source of political agency and a leftward move toward the rights of all people considered Other. The repudiation Nisei endured pointed the way for third-generation Sansei to seek alternatives and choose separatist politics in forming the Asian American political movement in the late 1960s and 1970s. Today, Asian Americans continue to be culturally and racially situated outside the boundaries of the nation. This continuing legacy of racialization and the enduring anti-immigrant sentiment in the United States speaks to the need for a more inclusive and just society that recognizes merit and worth over skin color and heritage.

CHAPTER 4

"Buddhahead Blues"
Musical Communities in the US
Concentration Camps of World War II

"Buddhahead Blues"

Going to sprout my wings and fly right over that fence,
Going to sprout my wings and fly right over that fence,
'Cause staying in here don't make no sense.

Buddhahead boy, what makes you so yellow?
Buddhahead boy, what makes you so yellow?
You seem like an ordinary fellow.

Dream every night of a big roast and candied yam,
Dream every night of a big roast and candied yam,
The food they give me here is a no-good sham.

Beat down, sun; blow wind, through my hair,
Beat down, sun; blow wind, through my hair,
Who said life's any kind of fair?

Searchlights shining in my face always give me a start,
Searchlights shining in my face always give me a start,
Makes me feel like Cagney or a Humphrey Bogart.

Call me a taxi, call me a limousine,
Call me a taxi, call me a limousine,

I want to go riding—out where the grass is green.

Oh, big, red sun, you going away tonight,
Oh, big, red sun, you going away tonight,
When you come back tomorrow, I'll be clean out of sight!

Want to ask Jimmy Rushing to sing these blues,
Ask the Count and Jimmy to wail these blues,
Dream on baby; ain't nothing left to lose.
Oh, I don't know why
I want to cry,
I want to die.
I'd sure get tight
If there were gin in sight
for me.

—Ernest Michio Masunaga, Santa Anita Assembly Center, 1942[1]

"Buddhahead Blues" is an ironically whimsical entreaty of a people denied their dignity and right to belong. The song's significance arises out of its creation in a detention center where American citizens were unlawfully imprisoned, and its irony is a counterpoint to the euphemistic language used by the US government to describe the removal of Japanese Americans from their homes on the West Coast and Hawaii as "relocation" instead of "enforced incarceration."

Blues as the chosen music genre along with the lyrics to this song reveal the Nisei's identification as Americans, yet the context in which they were composed displaced their American identity beyond the reach of Masunaga and his fellow inmates during World War II. The term "buddhahead" references Japanese Americans in Hawaii, of whom about one thousand were confined on the mainland. The pairing of "buddhahead" with the word "blues" in the title of the song accents the disenfranchised state of Japanese Americans in the camps. The verses give voice to a full spectrum of Japanese American youths' responses to their incarceration: desire for freedom, interrogation of their racial phenotype, access to desired and decent food, commentary on the harsh environment, enduring prison-like conditions, reveries of escape, and the blues wail ending, accenting their predicament. A twelve-bar blues was an apt musical style used to express the sentiments of Japanese Americans in 1942 as they were rounded up and placed in temporary holding cells, euphemistically called "assembly" centers. The context in which Masunaga

Figure 4.1. World War II US assembly centers and concentration camps. Public Domain. National Parks Service Map, Wikimedia Commons.

composed "Buddhahead Blues" nullified this generation's American identity, symbolically linking it to the origin of the blues as an expression of African American personal, social, economic, and political disenfranchisement. One can imagine Nisei musicians playfully emulating bluesmen to voice their plight and desires in "Buddhahead Blues," standing as a form of resistance by resentful youth with time on their hands.

The imprisonment of 120,313 Japanese Americans came on the heels of the bombing of Pearl Harbor naval base in Hawaii by the Japanese military and the official entry of the United States in World War II. In 1942, the federal government rounded up Japanese Americans from the states of California, Oregon, Washington, and Hawaii,[2] placing them in temporary holding centers. Soon after, this displaced population found themselves in ten concentration camps and six Justice Department camps located in desolate areas of Arizona, Arkansas, California, Colorado, Idaho, Montana, New Mexico, North Dakota, Texas, Utah, and Wyoming (figure 4.1).

Musical activity in Japanese prewar communities carried over into the camps, serving to generate a sense of normalcy and stability. Musicking was an emotional outlet for coping with increasing tensions caused by deplorable living conditions and unreasonable demands by the War Relocation Authority (WRA).[3] A broad purview of musical activity in the camps reveals both tacit and deliberate choices and a touch of irony as art making became possible for many sequestered Japanese Americans for the first time in their lives.

Nisei George Yoshida's declaration conveys the importance of music for an American teenager as he heads into a life behind barbed wire:

> The sign on the telephone pole ordered us to assemble nearby on Saturday with just our bedding and clothes . . . just stuff we could carry. I could not leave my records . . . put about fifty of my favorites—Tommy Dorsey, Artie Shaw, Duke Ellington—into a case. Clutching my lifeblood I sighed a heavy-hearted "good-bye" to East LA.[4]

The resignation expressed by Yoshida captures the rush and desperate decisions made by this Nisei in preparation for his unlawful incarceration. Certainly not singular in his response, Yoshida's anguished unwillingness to leave behind his beloved recordings reveals the unwarranted and grievous disruption of Japanese American lives. For Yoshida and a majority of second-generation Nisei, the dance-band music of the 1930s and 1940s captured their hearts and minds as they sought to prove their Americanness. "Dance bands proliferated for a while during our wartime incarceration. One can imagine Nisei youth performing with abandon to rebuff their imprisonment for the moment, encouraging dancers to do the same. It was a matter of survival and a subconscious affirmation of self—a way to express through music: 'I am an American!'"[5] Such statements were endemic among American-born Japanese American youths who struggled to be accepted within US society and instead were rejected because of their race and ethnicity.

CULTURAL POLITICS OF MUSIC IN THE CAMPS

The evacuation and incarceration of Japanese Americans during World War II offer a chance to research musicking in adverse and politically charged circumstances. The heart of this chapter narrates inmates' agency in performing their retained or shifting cultural and political identities through music. Identities began to shift in response to the authoritarian policies of the WRA administration. The untenable and insensitive demands for loyalty to the state and the US Army's attempts to recruit young inmates fueled Japanese Americans' indignation and loathing.

Sixteen assembly centers, ten concentration camps, and six Justice Department camps became sites for myriad performances. For a population forced to live in isolation from mainstream society in substandard living conditions, musical activities entertained, soothed, and healed as well as channeled anger, resentment, and discontent. Responsible for administering the camps, the WRA encouraged musicking to pacify their charges. The activity functioned to piece together inmates' lives, bringing pleasure, affirming a preferred aesthetic, or serving a political purpose.

The United States' war with Japan during World War II intensified racial discrimination toward Japanese Americans. Yasutaro Soga, author of *Life behind Barbed Wire: The World War II Concentration Memoirs of a Hawaiian Issei*, pinpoints racism as the basis for the clamor raised against Japanese: "Regardless of the reasons the politicians and community leaders gave for wanting the Japanese removed," writes Soga, "there was one reason that underlay them all. Racism."[6] Chinese and Filipino immigrants also suffered racial discrimination and barriers to citizenship, but the vulnerability felt by Americans at the bombing of Pearl Harbor intensified the racial hatred of Japanese in America. The passing of federal Executive Order 9066 pacified the feverish racist sentiments of the West Coast community and its organizations. The racial tension exacerbated by the impulse to retaliate in response to the bombing of Pearl Harbor sets the stage for how race and music intersect in the musicking of the evacuees.

The coupling of race and music considers the intensely racialized experience of the incarcerated that affected the aesthetic and political choices some Japanese Americans made either in steering more sharply toward their Japanese heritage or toward their Americanness. I seek to elucidate how camp life amplified race consciousness and how music reflected cultural identities of this new consciousness. In *Music and the Racial Imagination*, Ronald Radano and Philip V. Bohlman comment how "race contributes fundamentally to the issues of belonging and ownership that music articulates."[7] The intent here is to explore the correspondence between political and cultural identities and the music inmates chose to perform, either to give voice to a Japanese heritage and racial difference or to express their rightful membership in the American mainstream. The range of musicking in the camps paints a complex picture of the various ways Japanese Americans dealt with their imprisonment and how they chose to be culturally and politically represented.

The political nature of the Japanese American incarceration draws attention to cultural politics within the camps. At the center of this bleak chapter in American history is how Japanese Americans were positioned politically and socially outside the nation. Considered "the enemy," alien, a population too far afield from the Anglo-Saxon or Nordic ideal, Issei and Nisei were never given the opportunity to establish legitimate national representation for themselves. The bombing of Pearl Harbor only intensified the wariness and doubt about the assimilability of Japanese Americans, and the backlash was swift with concentration camps set in place. Probing the connection between music and politics within the context of the camps actively tests the artist and writer Coco Fusco's notion about people of color's ideological battle over symbolic representation and culture as central to the political struggle over identity.[8]

To illustrate cultural politics as practiced by Issei in the camps, the narrative of a banquet held on January 5, 1943, at the Canal Camp of the Gila River Relocation Center in Arizona proves instructive. Disempowered by their incarceration, a group of Issei, attempting to gain leverage, reverted to hosting a banquet for administration officials.[9] Historian and Asian American studies scholar Arthur A. Hansen frames the Issei hosting of the banquet as strategic in its use of cultural politics, asserting that his narration of the event is an example of resistance historiography, a perspective that emerged in scholarship of the early 1970s.[10]

Hansen unfolds the banquet as a sociopolitical drama whose aim was to restore the imprisoned community's traditional cultural and social order, i.e., the revitalization of Japanese customs and cultural practices with Issei placed in decision-making positions within the Canal Camp.[11] It is important contextually to know that the banquet took place in the aftermath of the sentencing of Chota Hirokane, a Kibei accused of assaulting Takao Tada, a Nisei who was considered an accommodationist aligned with camp authorities. Hirokane was imprisoned in a nearby county jail for approximately one month. The banquet held in Hirokane's honor was supposedly a gesture of goodwill and a fresh start between camp administrators and their appointed inmate leaders, the *kenkyū-kai* (a study society), and other Issei and Kibei clubs and organizations at the Canal Camp.

Understanding the conservative background of the banquet hosts sheds light on the political intent of the event in reaching a détente with camp administrators and influencing them to side with Issei. Evacuees residing in the Canal Camp came primarily from farming areas in California's Sacramento delta and San Joaquin Valley—strongholds of Japanese culture and behavior among not only Issei and Kibei but also Nisei. The relative social and cultural uniformity among Canal Camp inmates facilitated the *kenkyū-kai*'s culturally hegemonic hold on the camp population, enabling them to influence people across lines of class, gender, and generation.[12]

The plot of this drama unfolds in the sharing of a meal of Japanese and Western fare, served with bourbon and followed by Japanese cultural entertainment. It was a formal event created by Kiyoshi Tani, a savvy and charismatic Issei poised to socially engineer a sense of community among prisoners that resisted being deprived of their "cultural dignity and self-determination."[13] Several subversive features of the banquet reinforced the revitalization of Japanese culture. Tani, in his welcome address to all the guests, spoke in Japanese, a defiant act that countered the administration's attempts to present the use of Japanese as a source of shame. The serving of bourbon, derisively referred to by Tani as "Japanese tea," was also a bold move in the face of the administration's campaign against the possession of alcoholic beverages, which was considered a federal offense. The Japanese cultural performance[14] functioned to promote a Japanese aesthetic, and, lastly, the attendance by members of pro-Japanese clubs and organizations was meant to demonstrate the communal solidarity of a group that would rise against and resist any policies or actions on the part of the administration that were not acceptable or interfered with their strategies for rejuvenating Japanese culture.

The actors invited to the banquet included four administrators of Canal Camp's WRA, four representatives of the Japanese American inmates, and one hundred formally dressed inmates of the *kenkyū-kai*, the Engeibu (a dramatic society), and the Sumo Club. Members of these organizations included nationalistic Kibei and Issei who promoted Japanese cultural renewal, coercing reluctant inmates to bend to their wishes.[15] These individuals focused on Japanese traditions and the performing arts both as a means of resistance against Americanization and as sources for bringing about the "transformation of identity" among internees. Their goal was to refashion the camp community around the Japanese notion of collectivism, or *wa* (social harmony), over and above personal elevation.[16] The transformation they sought was to unite inmates by healing the psychological divisions between the various factions in the Canal Camp and building solidarity within the community. A key point is the role of Japanese culture in the Issei realization that collectivism could be achieved more readily by appealing to evacuees' innate "cultural impulses" rather than to any specific ideology.[17] The *kenkyū-kai* was particularly forceful in politically pressuring Nisei in positions of power, and any individuals who did not share their objectives were placed on blacklists of people to be "dealt with." The subtle show of force by Issei and Kibei participants at the banquet enabled them to hold sway over WRA administrators and thereby control the Community Activities Committee and organize cultural activities that advanced their pro-Japanese agenda.

Pertinent to the subject at hand is Emily Roxworthy's study of the "spectacle of Japanese American trauma," bringing into play the psychological and political underpinnings of the incarceration. Roxworthy's research on racialization and racial performativity in the camps supports the link between the racial and the musical. In her analysis of theatrical performances held at Manzanar Relocation Center, she argues that most of the cultural performances at Manzanar politically subverted the colonialist policy of the War Relocation Authority and that this intent was not acknowledged in the recent commemoration of the performances by the US National Park Service at the Manzanar National Historic Site. She decries how this performed resistance exists only in the memories of Issei and Nisei who have since passed and is convinced that the meanings attached to the performances were more than just a form of "spiritual resistance" aiming "to make the best of things."[18]

Roxworthy identifies the existence of what she calls "the myth of performative citizenship" during World War II, which specifically includes the recitation of the oath of citizenship in a special ceremony for new citizens, participation in patriotic parades and events, and enlisting in the armed services.[19] The "myth of citizenship," as defined by Roxworthy, serves opposing purposes: the first is presenting US citizenship as being racially inclusive based on one's patriotic acts; and the second, within the context of war, is denying Japanese immigrants official citizenship and rejecting Nisei as part of the national culture. The myth functioned to shore up national unity during the war and rationalize incarceration as a necessary step to counter alleged Japanese American sabotage and treachery.

Later in the chapter, we will note how some musical, theatrical, and a myriad of performing arts chronicled in the incarceration camps counter "the myth of performative citizenship"; some were intentionally subversive and oppositional.

ART IN THE CAMPS

Each concentration camp was a self-sustaining town with populations ranging from 6,386 to 17,107 people. Many worked in canteens, hospitals, schools, fire stations, WRA administrative offices, and mess halls while others filled coal-delivery and garbage-removal jobs. As prisoners, their movements were restricted so everyone had time on their hands, making way for the rise of various clubs, classes, and activities organized by the inmates themselves.

Art flourished in the hands of the inmates, particularly Issei, who, for the first time since coming to the United States, had moments of repose from the hardships they endured. The surge in artistic activity could be described as "a huge renaissance in art" for Japanese Americans.[20] Artistic activity not only fed individual inspiration, but it also served to restore a sense of dignity and a chance for inmates to fulfill their aesthetic inclinations and create beauty in their desolate environment.

Many art ventures began with those who had prior experience in some art form and were willing to teach others. Visual art was wide-ranging, and each camp specialized in forms that were often dictated by the materials available to them in the natural environment surrounding a given camp. The Japanese proclivity toward nature was in full expression when natural materials found, such as *kobu*—gnarled cypress tree roots and trunks in the Rohwer and Jerome Camps in Arkansas—were polished and admired as sculpture. Shells abundant in the dry lake beds of Topaz and Tule Lake found form in decorative flowers or jewelry. Women filled their time attending classes in embroidery, decorative needlework, artificial flower making, weaving, painting, drawing, and ceramics. Instruction in the Japanese art traditions of ikebana (flower arranging), *shodō* (calligraphy), and *bon-kei* (miniature landscape on a tray) were also often offered under the auspices of the Recreation Department in each camp. Issei followed their creative impulses by painting, drawing, carving wood reliefs of Japanese birds and pine trees, and fashioning three-dimensional bird and animal wood figures. The desire to enhance their barren camps inspired inmates to create rock, water, and other decorative gardens. Japanese painting skills and calligraphy combined with the ability to make papier-mâché theater costumes and stage props enhanced Kabuki performances in the camps.[21]

Professionally trained painters and visual artists among the inmates often took on the responsibility of offering and organizing art classes for anyone interested. In many of the camps, administration officials encouraged and financially supported such classes. Small and large arts and crafts exhibitions, both in the assembly centers and the concentration camps, added a spark of excitement and appreciation, countering the drabness of life and low morale of the population. The exhibitions put on full display latent individual talents that had been waiting to be tapped.[22]

An artist who played a crucial role in the uplift of Japanese American inmates was Chiura Obata, a venerated art professor at the University of California, Berkeley, who opened art schools in the Tanforan Assembly Center and later Topaz Prison Camp. Renowned for his California coastal landscapes—often sumi-e black and white brush paintings—Obata designed art classes for all levels and ages, offering twenty-three courses subdivided into fine art, commercial art, and techniques. Concerted artistic activity at the Tanforan Art School culminated in three art exhibits in July, August, and September of 1942, prior to all prisoners being transferred to the Topaz Camp in Millard County, Utah. The expanded curriculum in Topaz mirrored that of the California School of Fine Arts, providing "eighty-eight class sessions per week for six-hundred thirty-six students from ages five to seventy-eight."[23] Sixteen instructors taught classes from eight in the morning until eight at night, with art supplies obtained from the personal caches of inmates, churches, friends, and activist organizations, like the American Friends Service Committee. In Chiura Obata's papers, housed in the Archives of American Art, Smithsonian Institution, he succinctly summarizes his reason for generating artistic pursuits during this distressing time: "We feel that art is one of the most constructive forms of education. Sincere creative endeavoring, especially in these stressing times I strongly believe will aid in developing a sense of calmness and appreciation which is so desirable and following it comes sound judgment and a spirit of cooperation."[24] Obata articulates art making as a stabilizing force for inmates as they sought to create beauty at a time and place that denied them their humanity. The idealism articulated by this art educator exemplifies the strength of character needed to endure unjust imprisonment with quiet tenacity.

MUSICKING IN THE CAMPS

Music played an integral role in transforming depressing camp life into some semblance of the community people left behind. Musical activities contributed greatly toward reconstructing a "sense of place," i.e., a familiar place, a frame of reference, a social space where collective memories served to ease the humiliation and hardship. The performing arts offered sustenance and joy to many Issei and Nisei inmates during their unjust imprisonment.

The Recreation Department in each detention center scheduled musical activities, lessons, and events. One of the programs they sponsored was the *Music Listening Hour*, a radio show variably named depending on the camp. Inmates gathered at designated locations to collectively listen to programs of either popular American music (such as the swing-band music of Tommy Dorsey, Glenn Miller, Artie Shaw, and Bunny Berigan), European classical, or traditional Japanese music. The programs featured a commentator who organized the playlist. Weekly newspapers advertised the dates and times of the gatherings. Various musical communities formed and met separately based on the type of music offered.

The role of musicking was one of spiritual and cultural renewal and, in some instances, resistance. For performers and audiences alike, music ostensibly was a source of *jouissance*, delight in the remembrance of former days, or plausibly a passage for escaping a dismal reality. Writings about life in Nazi concentration camps describe musicking, and by extension all art making, as "a life-affirming survival mechanism through which they [victims] asserted solidarity in the face of persecution, the will to live, and the power of the human spirit."[25] Music made by inmates in the German camps was an active form of "spiritual resistance" performed to counter oppression and fear.

Forced imprisonment begs questions about its impact on Japanese American identities and the meanings attached to cultural performances in such a setting. In finding answers, it is important to delineate the varied political positioning and cultural orientation among inmates. Shifting identities and attitudes of social groups in response to their incarceration, hostile treatment by War Relocation Authority staff, and rabid racism on the outside are important factors in reconstructing the musical lives of the prisoners. Significant is the range of attitudes and intents in the pursuit of musical and cultural activities in the camps.

Within the concentration camps, collectivities formed around various genres of musicking. A suitable framework for describing these collectivities is one based on Kay Shelemay's approach to thinking about musical communities.[26] Shelemay writes:

> Rethinking the notion of community opens opportunities first and foremost to explore musical transmission and performance not just as expressions or symbols of a given social grouping, but as an integral part of processes that can at different moments help generate, shape, and sustain new collectivities. This discussion therefore seeks both to reappraise community studies in musical scholarship and to shift the focus to music's role in community formation.[27]

In defining "musical community," Shelemay frees the concept of "community" from conventions of structure, place, or time, although she recognizes that "both structural and local elements" may be significant in the development of a community. Her emphasis is on the process of musical performance and transmission; she proposes that "a musical community is a social entity, an outcome of a combination of social and musical processes, rendering those who participate in making or listening to music aware of a connection among themselves."[28]

Shelemay identifies three social processes as integral to the creation of musical collectivities: (1) descent, (2) dissent, and (3) affinity. Applying these distinctions clearly differentiates the clusters of musicking in the camps. The three categories of musical collectivities pinpoint social orientations that accommodate a range of identities differing in generation, class, geography, and political leanings. The communities provide a structure that brings to light a variety of meanings attached to music. The three designations serve as guidelines in proposing correlations between social and musical processes that evolved in the repressive circumstances of the camps over a three-year period. My aim is to analyze how well this model describes correspondences between musicking and the social groups formed. How does the model respond to what actually took place in the camps? Does it account for all the significant variables in how inmates viewed themselves? And is the model adequate in considering the active role of all participants—inmates, the War Relocation Authority, the larger society—in the formation of musical communities?[29] These inquiries interrogate the efficacy of this model in analyzing the impact of musicking in the camps. We shall see how the social processes accommodate the separate collectivities created around performances of traditional Japanese music, Western classical music, and American vernacular and popular music.

An important feature of this model is the capability of placing the three social categories—descent, dissent, and affinity—on a continuum within the larger framework of the camps, a continuum that allows for the horizontal movement of members from one group to another in the context of shifting loyalties, attitudes, and/or political and cultural leanings and the corresponding effect it had on their musicking. This flexibility is particularly important because of the fluid, unstable, and temporary conditions of the incarceration. As well, a continuum makes it possible to conduct translational research in comparing musical communities in other musical and social spheres.[30]

MUSICAL COMMUNITIES OF DESCENT

Broadly construed, musical communities of descent focus on socialization generated by shared identities based on ethnicity, kinship, religion, and/or nationality, which are either historically constructed, newly conceived, or the result of a combination of circumstance and subsequent alteration, such as the concentration camps. Descent communities are tied to specific locations or regions, but the widespread migration of peoples and cultures together with emerging technologies, which facilitate the construction of virtual and symbolic communities globally, transform traditional notions of this social unit. Within communities based on descent, the act of performing or listening enacts one's identity while also serving to clearly demarcate boundaries of a collective identity.[31] I customized this category's broad definition to accommodate what I have identified as a musical collectivity based on the Japanese descent of its members whose performances expressed their collective ethnic and cultural identity.

The racial composition of the concentration camps makes it possible to define communities of descent in a straightforward manner since its members were of the same ethnicity and nationality (Nisei had dual citizenship both in Japan and the United States) and, in many cases, shared kinship ties and religious practices. Musical communities formed around Japanese musicking echo the groups in prewar Japanese communities. There were cases where traditional Japanese music and dance teachers and their students registered together to be placed in the same camp. Communing by descent easily explains the active involvement of Issei in performing traditions of their homeland; it also frames the draw some Nisei felt toward the Japanese arts. There were also deliberate efforts, on the part of Issei, to cultivate all prisoners' interest in Japanese performing arts. The first generation gained control of descent communities in the camps by underscoring Japanese tradition and language in the performances of traditional music and dance. Not known is the size of this collective in each of the camps; the paucity of data on Japanese music performances point to more intimate settings and less advertised announcements of such events, as well as the WRA's greater support of Western/American music in their goal to Americanize their charges.

Issei artists generated activity around the sharing and teaching of Japanese traditional arts, drawing in inmates eager to learn. Nisei Kayoko Wakita recalls how arts such as origami, tea ceremony, flower arranging, as well as Japanese games were the first to surface in Manzanar War Relocation Center, where she and her family lived. Gradually, teachers of koto, *buyō*, and shamisen music began to instruct others despite the lack of instruments and supplies. Wakita recounted people's inventiveness in constructing crude kotos from blocks of wood, nails, and string or wire from mattress springs. Both her shakuhachi-playing father and her koto-performer mother taught anyone in the camps interested in learning. It was the spirit of sharing and teaching among inmates and the unjust constraints imposed by their incarceration that reignited or stimulated new interest in Japanese traditional arts among participants in Manzanar, cultivating an appreciation that might not have taken root otherwise. Wakita's musical activities as a koto and shamisen performer and teacher after the war were a continuation of her interest spawned in the camps. She observes that Nisei exposure to and participation in traditional musicking continued long after they left camp.[32] Sustained practice in the camps kept Japanese music and dance vital, facilitating the resumption of these arts in rebuilt lives and communities after the war, successfully transmitting them to coming generations.

The WRA, despite their agenda of Americanism, tolerated Japanese cultural activities, recognizing their importance in achieving equanimity among the inmates. As the imprisoned communities came under the control of Issei leaders, this generation's efforts to build communal and cultural solidarity in the camps revitalized traditional Japanese culture and arts. Promoting *Nippon seishin* coincided well with Japanese music, dance, and drama activities. Men and women of the educated class practiced *utai* singing—the intoning of classical poetry—in classes organized in the camps. *Utai* singing was a favorite pastime for social gatherings.[33] Waseda's article on music in American concentration camps narrates the variety of musical genres heard in the musical landscape of these sites. She writes about the continuation of Japanese classical dance and music along with a revival of the narrative genres *nagauta, gidayū,* and *naniwa-bushi,* following their decline in prewar communities in the 1930s due to the popularity of modern Japanese entertainment via radio, recordings, and the cinema. Recitals of the older *yōkyoku* style of singing heard in *nō* drama also were periodically held, as in the Central Utah Detention Center in Topaz. Limited access to Japanese films and entertainment in the camps also fueled the rejuvenation of narrative genres. In her research, Waseda identified names of teachers who founded music and drama groups while imprisoned. Among the twenty-six music instructors she names, a majority taught narrative genres: *nagauta, gidayū,* and *yōkyoku.* Her list also includes teachers for Kabuki (see figure 4.1), dramatic plays (*shibai* and *shinpa*), comic drama, *naniwa-bushi,* Japanese classical dance (*buyō*), koto, and shakuhachi.[34] Koto performer Shirley Muramoto Wong, in her years of investigating teachers of Japanese traditional arts in the camps, uncovered an additional twenty-six teachers specializing in *buyō,* Bon odori (dances to celebrate Obon), koto, *nagauta* shamisen, and *biwa.* This incomplete list of fifty-two Japanese performing-arts teachers demonstrates continuity in the transmission and practice of a variety of genres. It is only through word of mouth and the individual efforts of researchers that these names have come to light.[35] Photos or records of Japanese music performances are rare because of the WRA's policies and lack of support. The WRA policed the types of musical activities they sponsored. Community Activities Division official Alex Nielson states that the

Japanese music policy at Manzanar in northern California was as follows: "The WRA does not intend to promote ideals and cultures of nations with which we are at war. So long as patriotic music is not played, Japanese music may be played in the center, but it will not be sponsored by the government. Paid teachers or special rooms or quarters cannot be provided for them."[36] It was meant to hinder Japanese musicking; it might have hardened the determination of individuals in pursuit of maintaining traditional music instead. Exceptions to this policy, though, existed, as in the case of Japanese dance teacher Bando Mitsusa at Tule Lake, who, because of high demand for her instruction and the large number of students under her tutelage, was paid the highest level of wages allowed in the camps at nineteen dollars per month through the auspices of the Recreation Department.[37]

The shared ethnicity of the population in the prison camps facilitated the formation of collectivities based on descent and expressions of a Japanese heritage. Traditional-arts teachers and their students performed their Japanese collective identity with cultural forms that demonstrated a shared diasporic consciousness. Playing Japanese music or dancing *buyō* was more than just an enactment of a social process of descent. Having interviewed Nisei who had taught, studied, and performed Japanese music in the camps, Shirley Muramoto Wong learned that these individuals sought "to exercise their 'cultural citizenship'"—the right as American citizens to express and maintain the cultural practices of their Japanese heritage—in response to the repressive conditions of the camps that, as a rule, discouraged anything Japanese. According to Renato Rosaldo: "Cultural citizenship refers to the right to be different and to belong in a participatory democratic sense. It claims that, in a democracy, social justice calls for equity among all citizens, even when such differences as race, religion, class, gender, or sexual orientation potentially could be used to make certain people less equal or inferior to others."[38] Inmates' intention to express *cultural citizenship* in their musical performances is remarkable, and it represents a tacit form of resistance on the part of musicians who pressed for a sense of cultural belonging despite their incarceration. Cultural citizenship can be viewed as inmates "talking back" in response to the violation of their civil rights. This idea also represents well the bicultural identity of Nisei choosing to culturally belong to both Japan and the United States.

There is no documentation of the number of Nisei who chose to study or perform Japanese music on their own or at the urging of their parents. There are only singular anecdotes, such as how music lessons offered at Manzanar concentration camp afforded Shirley Nagatomi Okabe and her

Figure 4.2. Kabuki: A group of actors from a scene in a play depicting a legendary incident of old Japan, Heart Mountain Concentration Camp, Wyoming. September 19, 1942. Courtesy of University of California, Berkeley, Bancroft Library, WRA no. E-102.

older sister a chance to learn koto. She recalled: "My father had my sister and I take koto lessons and calligraphy lessons. After a while people could bring things in to camp other than what we initially brought. So, someone brought in two kotos. Our teacher had us go to her place; we played one and she played the other."[39]

Being incarcerated did not dampen Issei parents' desire to have their children receive training in the Japanese arts. It is similar to what prevailed in prewar communities, when, at the urging of Issei parents, Nisei studied traditional Japanese music. Even in the extraordinary circumstances of the camps, some Nisei did choose to partake in music of their heritage as we shall see in Madame Molly Kimura's example.

Those who performed Japanese music conceivably enacted their "cultural citizenship." One instance of a Nisei choosing to do the "unpopular thing" was Molly Kimura, introduced earlier, who decided to study Japanese cultural arts—flower arranging, tea ceremony, and *biwa*. While imprisoned at Tule Lake, Kimura found that playing *biwa* was popular among Issei as an accompaniment to singing *shigin* or epic songs (figure 4.2). This discovery spurred opportunities for her to perform with other *biwa* players in weekly

Figure 4.3. *Biwa no Yuube* (Evening of Biwa Music). Minidoka concentration camp, Idaho, March 4, 1945. Courtesy of Japanese American National Museum, the Shohei Arase Family Collection, 94.113.

programs with both Japanese and Western music sponsored by the Recreation Department.[40] Having studied *biwa* from an early age in Marysville, California, Madame Kimura's affinity toward playing the instrument illustrates well the aesthetic appeal of Japanese art forms to some Nisei.

Among Issei inmates, singing *shigin* was widespread. Muramoto Wong suggests that the popularity of *shigin* rests in its expressiveness—perhaps serving as an emotional outlet for Issei in adverse circumstances. The nationalistic cast to *shigin* songs, stemming from the time of the Russo-Japanese War (1904–1905) and its popularity in prewar Japanese communities, added to this vocal tradition's appeal. *Shigin* performance was a testament to Issei attachment to homeland politics and their resistance to assimilation in the host country that discriminated against them.

Another musically active Nisei was Kineya Jyorokusho, introduced earlier, who mastered koto, shamisen, and *buyō* in the years prior to the war. Imprisoned with her family at Gila River War Relocation Center, Arizona, Jyorokusho taught *nagauta* shamisen, koto, and classical *buyō*. Inmate demand required her to teach in two locations within the Gila Camp even though she was not certified to provide instruction in these arts. The absence of music books was not an issue since Jyorokusho had memorized all the music, as well as movements of the dances.[41] Her mother greatly facilitated her daughter's efforts by sewing kimonos and obtaining instruments and supplies that she needed. Other performers joined this artist in presenting full-length performances of classical music and drama for entertainment, sustaining the vibrancy of these performing traditions.

The Japanese classical dancer Hanayagi Reimichi is yet another example of a Nisei drawn to the performing arts of her heritage while incarcerated. She first received *buyō* lessons in Granada Relocation Center in Amache. Initially learning from the *buyō* teacher Bando Miharu in camp, she trained until her imprisonment ended and then proceeded to study in Japan for three years to obtain her professional certificate (*natori*). In the 1970s and 1980s, Reimichi served as an assistant to Madame Michiya Hanayagi in her San Jose dance studio.[42]

Personal photos and biographies collected from Nisei Japanese music and dance teachers who taught in the camps appear in a program booklet of an event entitled Hidden Legacy: Tribute to Teachers of Japanese Traditional Arts in the War Relocation Authority Camps. The concert took place on April 24, 2010, at the Koyasan Buddhist Temple in Little Tokyo, Los Angeles. Currently available is a film of the same name as the concert, and it wonderfully features some of the traditional music and dance teachers who performed in 2010. In the program booklet, images documented in the camps display elegant kimonos and robes worn by musicians, dancers, and Kabuki actors together with beautifully painted backdrops, props, and other stage construction. The photographs are a testament to the richness of performances given for camp audiences. It is plausible that these performances momentarily transported inmate audiences from the desolate environs of the camps to the communities they were forced to leave and, for Issei, nostalgic memories of their homeland.[43] *Hidden Legacy* documents a counternarrative to the wholesale Americanization of inmates promoted by the War Relocation Administration governing the camps. The film contributes significantly to diaspora studies; the treasured photos and actual film footage of Japanese music and dance in the camps imbue the stories being told with the strength and beauty of diasporic traditions transmitted to America by Issei immigrants. The viewer is directed toward Japanese diasporic culture and performing arts, which brought pleasure and pride to many Issei and Nisei during their imprisonment.

The stories captured in *Hidden Legacy* also describe transculturated modifications of Japanese performing arts. Traditionally, music genres in Japan are gender and class specific, although adherence to such tradition is gradually diminishing, resulting in greater social mobility. As the division between classes in the camps became blurred, camp life became more egalitarian. The availability of teachers in the camps spurred opportunities to learn and perform, making it possible for anyone to partake in genres typically reserved for the upper class. Training in Kabuki, traditionally performed by men, became accessible to women in the unique setting of the incarceration (figure 4.3). Kabuki productions featured women singing, playing *nagauta* shamisen, and dancing, some specializing in men's roles. Another adaptation by a dance teacher was choreographing dances for *kouta* (short lyrical songs) since they were especially popular with camp audiences. The anomalous circumstances of the camps combined with training Americanized younger generations engendered slight modifications of Japanese performing arts, resulting in Japanese American nuances of these traditions.[44]

Engei-kai—musical and dramatic performances—served to both entertain inmates and distract them from the drudgery of camp life. The following program headlined Japanese instrumental and vocal music and dramatic plays at the Gila River War Relocation Center in southern Arizona:

"ISSEI NIGHT"

1. Vocal solo—Yoshiko Iwashika
2. Ha-uta—Ms. Yamada, accompanied by Kiyoka
3. Gidayu—Mr. Fujii
4. Vocal solo—Takao
5. Shakuhachi—Sami
6. Japanese dance—Kiyoka and her students
7. Drama (Tragedy)—"Namida no Imonshi"—Biwa Group
8. Vocal solo—M. Nishino
9. Japanese dance—Kiyoka and her students
10. Drama (Comedy)—Drama Group[45]

Audiences for these events were primarily Issei, but Nisei did participate as dancers and protégés of master performing artists. Increased leisure time for Issei spurred them to revive the traditional performing arts and to enjoy a renewed sense of the aesthetic value of their music and agency in being Japanese.

Japanese Obon, the well-known Buddhist festival commemorating deceased ancestors, also reinforced the inmates' sense of community and cultural heritage. Celebrating Obon sustained regional folk-dance songs (*ondo*) associated with this festival. The sounds of *taiko*, singing, and sometimes shamisen set the rhythm and pace for dancers performing in a circle surrounding the musicians. Rehearsals for Bon dance were held at many of the camps in the weeks before the festival to ensure coordination among dancers. Bon dancing promoted intergenerational mixing and socialization and soon came to be performed on Fourth of July, Labor Day, and other summer events besides Obon, reinforcing a cultural expression of a musical community based on descent.[46]

MUSICAL COMMUNITIES OF DISSENT

"Fuchusei" (Disloyal)

"Fuchusei" to	"Disloyal"
kokuin osare	With papers so stamped
Tule Lake ni	I am relocated to Tule Lake.
okurareshi mizo	But for myself,
kuyuru koto naku	A clear conscience.

—Otokichi Muin Ozaki[47]

Within the politicized context of the concentration camps, musicking was an important avenue of resistance; levels of dissent ranged from tacit to overt. Performing Japanese music to express one's cultural citizenship was a tacit form of resistance that better suited Japanese inclinations toward indirect and less overt responses. Choosing such music subverted the WRA's policies of "coerced assimilation."[48] An affective field sonically created by the performance of music or visually constructed by the shaping of an object of beauty gave inmates a chance to claim their identities and establish positions of agency. Their participation could be interpreted as engaging in a covert performance of difference. At the other end of the resistance scale were Japanese ultranationalists who used the cultural arts to reinforce a Japanese orthodoxy in building communal solidarity and preparing people to expatriate and repatriate to Japan. The coercive, radical clique at Tule Lake, in their push to Japanize the entire population of prisoners, promoted the cultural arts for direct political purposes. The political slant of artistic pursuits functioned to construct how inmates were to be politically represented, coupled with a deliberate aesthetic choice that challenged the dominant culture that oppressed them.

Issei's and Kibei's push to inculcate Japanese culture among inmates strategically countered American society's racist war hysteria at its most feverish pitch. Revitalizing Japanese culture was the foundation of Issei's efforts to restore a sense of collectivism based on Japanese values of *wa* (social harmony) and *amae* (roughly meaning "dependency"). The form of Japanese culture cultivated in the camps by this musical community was a rearticulation of the customs, beliefs, and values attached to music that Issei initially brought with them, modified by the extraordinary circumstances of their incarceration. Japanese music in this context functioned as a political tool to subvert Issei and Nisei subordination.

Traditional Japanese musicking in many of the camps evolved into a medium of dissent that pro-Japanese groups promoted to revitalize their culture amidst growing tensions and heightened conflicts. Before exploring the performing arts' political role, it is important to first describe the sociopolitical dynamics in this highly politicized setting. Such dynamics among inmates and distrust of the US government became particularly heated because of two major crises that occurred in all ten concentration camps. In February 1943, the War Department and the War Relocation Authority's goal of reintegrating all inmates into mainstream society soon had politicians in Washington devising a questionnaire that would provide information needed for the clearance and testing of inmates' loyalty. The US Army's use of the questionnaire to filter and recruit individuals for an all-Nisei combat team doubly aggravated the offense felt by all prisoners. Highly scurrilous are how Washington officials chose not to acknowledge the cruel irony of the questionnaire and, particularly, two questions:

Question #27: Are you willing to serve in the armed forces of the United States on combat duty, wherever ordered?
Question #28: Will you swear unqualified allegiance to the United States of America and faithfully defend the United States from any and all attack by foreign or domestic forces, and foreswear any form of allegiance or obedience to the Japanese Emperor, or any other foreign government, power, or organization?[49]

A furor arose over the preposterous nature of the questions. Misinformation and a lack of information concerning the purpose for registering were widespread. Nisei reacted to the absurdity of question twenty-seven after many had volunteered and been rejected for military service. Many resisted, refusing to complete the questionnaire since their civil rights as citizens were violated when imprisoned. The authorities' response was that volunteering to join the army was the only way for Nisei to regain their citizenship. Utter confusion prevailed among Issei who were being asked about their loyalty because they were never allowed to become citizens! Alarming to Issei, in question twenty-eight, was being asked to "forswear" allegiance to the country where they held citizenship. If they answered "yes" to this question, they would become nonentities—subjects without a country. Issei were also agitated and apprehensive about being permanently resettled in a society where anti-Japanese sentiment continued to be strong.[50] The gross insensitivity of the registration process further fueled the crisis when the WRA mandated noncompliance as punishable by segregation, deportation, or both. Authorities further declared that noncooperation was a violation of the Espionage Act of 1917, punishable by twenty years in prison, a $10,000 fine, or both.

The lack of transparency on the part of the War Department and the WRA concerning the purpose of the registration created turmoil and great distress for families whose members disagreed on how to answer questions twenty-seven and twenty-eight. The coercion that authorities applied worsened the dilemma for family members in deciding what was best for all or how to reconcile opposite stances among them. Nisei found it particularly difficult in weighing which was more important: duty to their parents or to their country. The irony of possibly sacrificing their lives in war for a country that denied their parents citizenship and obliterated all that they had achieved put terrible pressure on the second generation. Many internees avoiding the draft or attempting to keep the family intact made extreme decisions to expatriate. It is little wonder that many Nisei answered negatively to both questions to voice their protest and commit to familial piety and solidarity. With more than twenty thousand Nisei eligible for the draft, 25 percent—five thousand—either answered "no," qualified their answers, or resisted answering at all.[51]

In the fall of 1943, yet another divisive event affecting people in all ten concentration camps was the government's decision to segregate the supposed "disloyals" from the "loyals," following the registration catastrophe. The authorities chose Tule Lake Segregation Center as the site for housing those who answered "no" or else declined to answer. It is significant that 42 percent of Tule Lake internees seventeen years and older either answered the loyalty questions in the negative or failed to register at all. Segregating the disloyals and loyals involved a massive migration of all disloyals in all ten camps to Tule Lake and resettling loyals to the other nine centers. This governmental action created great turmoil among families whose members were divided on the loyalty question. Tule Lake Segregation Center swelled beyond its capacity; eighteen thousand people were crammed into a camp built for fifteen thousand, creating unstable conditions and increasing tensions between inmates and the camp administration.

In the meantime, malicious propaganda whipped up by the media, especially in California, about the "faithless disloyals" residing in Tule Lake fueled the radical inmates' militancy and extremism.[52] Such radical dissent widened and accelerated the revival of Japanese culture at Tule Lake. The small but forceful group of radicals in each block promoted Japanese customs, games, dances, and entertainment not for relaxation, but as part of their "Back to Japan" mission. The cultivation of *Nippon seishin* became a priority in preparing families for repatriation and expatriation to Japan. Identification with Japan's ancient legacy and achievements neutralized inmates' sense of inferiority and degradation. Efforts to educate themselves about Japan sparked the formation of lectures on Japanese history, customs, ideals, and current affairs updated from Radio Tokyo reports. Cultural activities expanded with classes on Japanese etiquette, cooking, and other domestic training complemented by the teaching of classical odori dance and music. *Senryū* poetry clubs, *utai* singing, and classical drama clubs for the more educated prisoners multiplied. Many Nisei realized the need to improve their Japanese fluency and learn proper manners to avoid bringing shame on their family once they moved to Japan. Widespread pressure to speak Japanese prevailed as Kibei youth bullied reluctant Nisei to attend Japanese-language schools in the center. The same youth would break up Nisei dances to discourage American social and cultural practices. The activities described above outline acts of resistance on the part of inmates in responding to their circumscribed lives at that specific moment in time. Performing music in this politicized context was a form of agency for Japanese Americans if not to overtly express their discontent, to at least exercise their cultural citizenship and engage in racial and cultural difference.

MUSICAL COMMUNITIES OF AFFINITY

An affinity community materialized as a third musical group in each camp. Its members included some Issei and most Nisei who embraced Western/American music—classical, popular, and vernacular—as their social, cultural, and aesthetic personal preference. Members of this community shared a strong affinity with performing, dancing, and listening to Western/American music, linking them to American mainstream society and bolstering their identity as middle-class Americans. This affinity community transferred to the camps musical practices that were in place in their enclaves prior to the war. Age was another source of affinity shared by most members of this musical community, many of whom were teenagers or college students. Yoshida, who was interned at Poston War Relocation Center in Arizona, talks about the social affinity shared among Nisei: "There was a great bonding [that formed] being in camp for many years. Especially for those in high school, seeing each other every day, all day long for three years. And that was good in the sense that when we got out of camp, there was that bond still in the Japanese community. [We shared] the same frame of mind. Today that's gone. Although the memories linger."[53]

Social affinity among youth softened their circumstances, spotlighting the joys of socializing and the attempts to normalize daily life in the camps. Shared musical activities propelled Nisei in the direction of their desired assimilation. The racial and political reasons for their incarceration intensified the worth of American popular music for Nisei, more strongly stamping their American identity.

Affinity communities in all ten camps organized a wide range of musicking activities. The most common were social dances, talent shows, variety shows, piano recitals, songfests, community sings, benefits, chamber-music recitals, and Christmas concerts. Other occasions, although infrequent, were Fourth of July celebrations, Memorial Day parades, symphonic-orchestra concerts, sacred-music recitals, opera performances, and Summer Follies programs. Figure 4.4 captures a Girl Scout drum and bugle corps, followed by Boy Scouts, in a Fourth of July parade in Rivers, Arizona (Gila), in 1944. A more eclectic mix of performances and musical styles filled the program of a variety show held at Tule Lake in March 1944:

1. Orchestra [dance band]: "Downbeats" with accompanist F. Nagata
2. Tap [dance]: Reiko Kumesaka, Keiko Onouye, and Kaz Izumi
3. Acrobat[ics]: Toshiko Ikeda
4. Baton [whirling]: Sumi Suguro
5. Ballet: Reiko Kumesaka
6. Vocal: Masako Sofye, Aiko Sofye, and Howard Takeo
7. Drum Solo: Sam Maeda
8. Saxophone Duet: Hisao Kataoka and George Nakao
9. Vocal [Japanese]: Ruby Kumasaka, Roy Tajiri, Joe Yamada, and Yoshiharu Tani
10. Harmonica: Masaru Doi and Noboru Doi
11. Manzai [comic dialogue]: Mitsuharu Matsudo, John Kono, and Frank Furuya
12. Odori [Japanese dance]: Mitsuko Suyekawa, Ayako Suyekawa, Yoshiharu Tani, and Alice Takeda
13. Shig Tamai's Hawaiian Strings[54]

Figure 4.4. Girl Scout drum and bugle corps marching in the Fourth of July parade, concentration camp at Gila River, Arizona, July 4, 1944. University of California, Berkeley, Bancroft Library.

The lineup of variety acts illustrates the overlap of descent and affinity musical communities in catering to performers and audiences young and old. Shig Tamai's Hawaiian Strings informs us about Hawaiians of Japanese descent who were incarcerated in camps on the mainland. Their music could be considered within the affinity group as American vernacular music, but the fact that Hawaii did not become a state until 1959 problematizes its inclusion as such.

Opportunities to study music were plentiful. Classical music lessons on piano, violin, and voice were the most prevalent, although lessons on a broad range of instruments were also taught. Instrumental and vocal solos and chamber music could be heard regularly at music school or music-department recitals and community talent shows and revues. Orchestra, concert band, harmonica band, and Boy Scout drum and bugle corps persisted as popular instrumental ensembles. The following is an example of a lineup at a European-classical-music concert performed by the Starlight Symphony at Gila River War Relocation Center on July 14, 1943:

"Invitation to the Dance" by C. M. von Weber
"On the Trail" from Grand Canyon Suite by Ferde Grofé
"One Fine Day" by Piccine Darbin
"Night on Bald Mountain" by Modest Mussorgsky
"Moonlight Sonata" by Beethoven
"Spring in My Heart" by Johann Strauss
"Intermezzo" for violin by Johannes Brahms
"Song to the Evening Star" from Tannhauser by Wagner[55]

One can imagine that the Starlight Symphony's performance attracted an audience of all ages and generations as a welcome distraction. It is one example that complicates categorizing this event as that of an affinity group and not that of descent or dissent community, considering the appeal of entertainment of any kind in the dreary circumstances of the camps.

Ironically, camp life offered Nisei opportunities to learn and play music they might not have had in their communities back home due to lack of time, resources, or teachers. All camps had some semblance of a music program, some even organized a music department, often in association with school activities. Many camps had active music programs. Nisei in Manzanar, for example, had a dynamic music department and a separate music hall designated for lessons and rehearsals. Yoshindo Shibuya, a Nisei interviewed as part of the Manzanar Historical Site Collection, recalls, "Well, they had practice rooms and rooms for the instructors to give you lessons, and then at one end of the barracks it was open because that's where the band would practice, you know the concert band or the marching band." Shibuya bought a tenor saxophone secondhand through a Los Angeles music supplier who supplied the needs of the music program. He remarks, "They had two reed instructors. One was a Nisei fella, Mr. Konishi. My instructor was Mr. Kodama; I think he was first generation and must have learned to play clarinet and saxophone back in Japan." After playing in a marching band, Shibuya and other younger players formed a swing band, prior to the well-known Manzanar Jive Bombers: "So we played for a few dances back there in the camp." Shibuya's siblings also studied; his sister played in a mandolin band, and his brother studied shakuhachi: "It must have been [with] a group of Isseis. I never remember them holding concerts or anything like that." He remembered, however, "when you did have an event where they had a stage, a program, the koto and shamisen, [you did perform]."[56]

Nisei revealed how important musicking was in bringing a sense of normalcy to their lives in the camps. Music teachers and programs provided a fount of activity and recreation in their dismal circumstances. Manzanar had a particularly enthusiastic music teacher, Louis Frizzell, who was a UCLA graduate. Mary Kageyama Nomura, the "Songbird of Manzanar," benefitted greatly studying with Mr. Frizzell: "I thought we had a terrific teacher. He came to Manzanar to teach kids about music. So, he taught band and orchestra and singing and drama. He was my mentor; he just took me under his wing. He supported me and [even] went to Los Angeles to buy sheet music for me so I could learn new songs, and every time there was a program he would accompany me. We all survived and functioned like normal people because of him."[57]

In continuing her musical studies at Manzanar, she recounts, "Yes, I was able to join the *a capella* choir. I was able to take music appreciation and partake in the different functions that the Music Department put on, at a school program or a camp program. I even sang at a funeral. Later on, as I got to know the [music] faculty, they asked me to sing at graduations, different events."[58]

Cornetist and trumpeter Bruce T. Kaji also had the privilege to learn from Mr. Frizzell when he performed in the school orchestra under this talented teacher's direction: "Thanks to his [Mr. Frizzell's] efforts, we had musical instruments donated to us, and we were able to have a full orchestra with strings, brass, woodwinds, and piano."[59] Kaji further depicts the energetic music teacher:

> At Christmas we performed with various choirs that he directed, and I even got to perform a solo piece called "Toy Trumpet." I remember the 1944 Christmas performance of an original cantata written by Mr. Frizzell—"And Mary Wept"—performed by the talented Nisei singer Mary Kageyama [now Nomura]. The Christmas spirit was with us, even as we played and sang behind barbed wire. Mr. Frizzell also wrote an original musical, *Loud and Clear*, which we performed with the choir in June. It was as if God sent Mr. Frizzell to help keep our spirits and morale up. I will never forget the joy that the camp music experience brought me.[60]

In their recollections, Shibuya, Nomura, and Kaji expressed gratitude for the dedicated teachers and the musical opportunities that enriched Nisei, keeping them busy and elevating a sense of normalcy.

In acknowledging the meaningful role of individuals who took a lead in structuring life in the assembly centers and camps, we must also mention the efforts of Ruth Watanabe, an older cohort of Nisei. Launching music theory, music appreciation, and advanced piano classes at the Santa Anita detention center in Los Angeles was central to Watanabe's vision to create order in the chaos and indignity of the center. She perceived the need to cultivate inmates' self-esteem and purpose through her educational offerings. Watanabe's advanced training in piano, musicology, and literature positioned her to share her love of music and impart beauty to those around her. Her Music Hour appreciation concerts attracted large audiences—two thousand participants seated in the Santa Anita racetrack grandstand every Sunday evening. Watanabe presented a broad array of European classical composers and compositions, even specific works requested by the audience. Alecia D.

Barbour argues for Watanabe's music-appreciation concerts as not only a form of entertainment but also as "a tool for a kind of 'cultural acclimation'" aimed at Issei audience members with a propinquity for traditional Japanese musical styles and expressive mediums.[61] What motivated Watanabe was her desire to express her unshakable sense of belonging in America despite the government illegally imprisoning her community, marking them as undesirable. She firmly believed in the "good that is in music," its ability to soften the harsh living conditions.[62]

Among the religious institutions established in camps—Shinto, Buddhist, and Christian—the Methodist church presented Nisei with the most musicking opportunities. Nisei singer Mamie Noda from Livingston, California, organized various musical pursuits in Amache detention center where she and her family were imprisoned in November 1942. While there, she formed a large choir at the Methodist church, serving as choir director before leaving the camp in January 1943 to continue her music studies at St. Olaf College, a Lutheran liberal arts college in Minnesota. The choir sang mostly Methodist hymns in four-part harmony; Noda added, "We didn't have any music, so we used the hymnal."[63]

The affinity music communities were the most active in the camps partly due to the steady support of the WRA, which was eager to promote Western/American cultural arts to assimilate their wards. Music makers of American popular music were integral to the affinity community, brightening the lives of youth by supporting a schedule of social activities and dating opportunities.

RUG CUTTERS

> [T]he Down Beats will open the local Dance Week tonight at Barrack #1020 from 7:30 pm with a Swing Concert. The Down Beats band leader, Riki Matsufuji, claims he will have the audience "cuttin' the rug" before the evening is over.[64]

The Nisei's strong affinity for American swing music of the 1930s and 1940s played an essential role in stabilizing life in the camps. American popular music was a panacea for the humiliation and sense of isolation young people endured during their three-year imprisonment. Entertaining their peers with big-band music helped Nisei to transcend the bonds of incarceration. Dance-band music was an outlet for this generation in channeling angry responses to their imprisonment, and bands in nine out of the ten camps created a flurry of musicking that enlivened social dances and other events. The number of dance bands was unprecedented, giving Americanized Nisei opportunities to express their cultural, social, and aesthetic preferences. Dancing to swing music was a way to assert themselves as American.[65] According to George Yoshida, the dance bands proved to be a novelty: "I think we Music Makers at Poston were a big hit because kids from the farm country, seeing all Japanese American faces—that was really something out of sight! We felt good too. For the first time in my life, to play music that I really loved, it was great, it was great, so enjoyable."[66]

The joy of performing in a dance band was a rare opportunity to which Nisei youth eagerly signed on, filling the ensembles. It is ironic that the camps offered Nisei the opportunities many never had to learn an instrument or sing. For most, it was the only time in their lives to fulfill their musical aspirations. Their musical abilities ranged from complete neophyte to accomplished musicians who were members of musicians' unions. Experienced musicians taught beginners and those with little experience. Prior to the war, Nisei commonly started their musical training on harmonica, playing for their own pleasure. This often was followed by participating in Boy Scout drum and bugle corps, and later performing on other instruments as part of high-school concert bands.

Vocalist Chickie White of the Harmonaires, who was interned at Minidoka detention center, was among those who had some experience:

> At thirteen, I did sing in a band in Seattle, and this was the Mikados of Swing. Then later, when we went into the assembly center, the same band got together, and they asked me to sing with them regularly while we were in the assembly center. Of course, I have to tell you they did change the name of the band. They were no longer Mikados of Swing. They changed their name to Harmonaires because our camp [Puyallup Assembly Center] was called "Camp Harmony," whoopee! [sardonically declared].[67]

Irrepressible youth made the most of their detention by the light-hearted sarcasm evident in the above quote.

Joe Shiro, member of the Music Makers in Amache detention center, shed light on the less experienced: "It took a while before we got to sounding like a band. It was fun learning. It was fun getting together. It was fun performing for all the dances that we played to a point where the military guards who guarded the camp invited us out to play for them. Unfortunately, I guess, somehow, we never did play the type of music they liked. They liked the real fast jitterbug type of music that's not the kind we played. We played the soft, 1940s-style string music."⁶⁸

Another neophyte was Joy Takeshita Teraoka, vocalist in the George Igawa band at the camp at Heart Mountain. She states: "I became involved in the George Igawa Orchestra. When they announced they were looking for a vocalist, my girlfriend said, 'Why don't you try out?' Having more guts than brains, [I said,] 'Oh, I will.' And so, I did and got the position. It was like a dream come true, and I know it could never have happened outside of camp. If I had still been living in Los Angeles, first of all, my parents wouldn't have allowed me to go singing in nightclubs there."⁶⁹ For this young Nisei woman, being chosen to sing in the George Igawa Orchestra was liberating—a unique opportunity that she would not have had living in Los Angeles.

Among the ones with some musical training was Yoneichi Fukui, member of the George Igawa band at Heart Mountain detention center, who had played trumpet in junior high school.⁷⁰ He describes his desire to play but lacked an instrument:

> Then, when George Igawa posted that notice about recruiting musicians for a dance band, I said, "Gee, I'd like to audition for that, but I don't have a horn." So, I asked around, and fortunately, I ran into some kid who bought a trumpet in a pawn shop for ten dollars. The instrument wasn't contraband, so I took it and auditioned for the band using my mouthpiece on that trumpet. George Igawa said, "Play this tune." He puts up this music. It was "Stardust"; I had played that in junior high school. I wouldn't tell him though. I took the horn and played a take on it, and they said, "Oh, that's great! You're hired!" Now, I didn't have a horn, and it turned out a lot of the other kids who auditioned didn't have an instrument either. I went to my Dad and said I want to buy this instrument, so I bought my first instrument for sixty-five dollars.⁷¹

Being detained ironically advanced Fukui's chance to play in an all-Nisei dance band; it was a dream come true!

Experienced or not, the visceral joy of performing dance-band music is captured by Noboru Nakamura, who had played with the Rhythmaires at Poston detention camp in Arizona: "You're playing with a lot of emotion and a lot of jump to it because of the crowd. The crowd is jumping and this makes you feel good too. You pick it up; you pick up the tempo and everything else. It's a great feeling. The only regret that I had was not dancing with the girls."⁷²

George Hirano, member of the Music Makers at Amache detention center, describes the preparations for social dances:

> Well, at least you had dances at the mess halls in many of the blocks [structural housing units used in the detention centers]. And when we started to play, then they thought we'll have one dance at our mess hall, so we'd send the bids out and let everyone know that we're going to have a dance on a certain Saturday night. We would take the tables and stack them on the outside of the mess hall. Then we'd sweep up all the concrete area, and then we'd take cream of wheat; we'd get boxes of it and spread it all over the concrete [floor] to make it nice and slippery so people could dance.[73]

Maintaining prewar practices of organizing social dances and adapting the mess hall into a workable venue kept Nisei youth busy and actively socializing.

Playing and dancing to American popular dance tunes was a "slice of paradise" for Nisei youth. Paradoxically, during their imprisonment, their musical lives peaked, and most were never able to repeat the thrill. Besides the recreational and social appeal, the dances and music served as soothing agents, as Chickie White shares: "That was a time to forget you're incarcerated. It was a time to relax and enjoy the hour or two we had listening to the music and dancing. It was a very good thing for everyone. I loved it; I love it. I loved the music. I loved the atmosphere, the camaraderie with the musicians. That was my whole life."[74]

"Sox" Kitashima, an inmate in Topaz detention center for three years, expresses similar feelings: "For some of us who enjoyed jazz and all, it was the music that helped to pass that day, to face the next day."[75]

George Yoshida's sentiments are personal, alerting us to the psychological and emotional toll on youth in the camps: "For me, it [music] was certainly a matter of healing my self-image and healing my frustration about being put into camps, being labeled an alien, a Jap. It was about us having fun. We got more psychologically [sic] too, I suppose. At that time, I didn't think about it. I just liked to play. Without it, it would have been pretty bad."[76]

Chicagoan Art Hayashi speaks about how "the music got our minds off the war and what was happening to us." Hayashi led the Harmonaires, formerly the Mikados of Swing, one of the most active Nisei bands on the West Coast. The summer of 1941 proved to be their busiest tour that included stops in nine cities and towns: Gresham, Oregon, and, in California, Sacramento, Pismo Beach, San Jose, Watsonville, Oakland, San Francisco, Los Angeles, and

Fresno. Hayashi paints a picture of the Harmonaires' activity in Minidoka: "We would try to convert almost all of our arrangements to the Glenn Miller sound, which was so beautiful. We would be in there, in the camp, working up these [musical] scores, then we'd test them out during our rehearsals. And because we were so concerned about the music, it took our minds off the bad things."77 He adds:

> Under our new name, the Harmonaires, we played in Areas A-B-C-D almost every night and really banded together. I would walk away from the band to listen to them over the loudspeakers and proudly realized that we actually did sound like Glenn Miller! In those worrisome days, I wonder if anyone noticed. Remember, here we were isolated with only our music to carry us. If we weren't playing for a camp dance, we'd be rehearsing. It's too bad that we couldn't make a recording. Then my boast would be more believable.78

Yoshida's participation in the Music Makers in Poston gives us an idea of the coordination involved in forming a band: "We did a lot of rehearsing. We didn't play too many gigs. We used to sit together. First of all, we had to round up ten or fifteen people, or if that many—maybe seven people. We'd have to have instruments, music, some kind of leader, a place to rehearse."79 He mentioned that some people had brought their instruments to camp. Others had white friends who would send them musical instruments through the post, while others received them by mail order from Sears and Roebuck Co. Additionally, some high-school music departments, funded by the government, provided instruments and band and choral music. The Music Maker's band arrangements were by mail order or procured by the Music Department and paid for by the WRA. It was the first time Yoshida had played in a dance band, performing the music that he had heard all throughout high school. While suggesting that the music produced by some of these bands was substandard, Yoshida emphasized, "It didn't matter how good it was. We were young kids and we enjoyed what we were doing. That's the most important part."80

Bruce T. Kaji also narrated his exuberant musical experience in Manzanar detention center:

> A highlight of my life in camp was joining the Jive Bombers orchestra. Bill Wakatsuki, an older Nisei who played trumpet and who also had a powerful baritone voice, organized the dance band and invited me to join. We had musical scores to popular songs such as "Blues on Parade,"

"In the Mood," "String of Pearls," "Woodchoppers Ball," "Moonlight Serenade," and "Stardust," to name just a few. Being confined to camp, we had a lot of time to practice. We played at outdoor concerts and dances; Block 24 was converted into a music hall, and we eventually soundproofed individual rooms so that we had private practice rooms. Dances were a big part of the social scene in camp, and we enjoyed our part in them, playing and swinging to the popular tunes of the day.[81]

Swing-dance bands flourished in the camps. Each camp, except Rohwer, had at least one band: the Jive Bombers in Manzanar; the Downbeats and Starlighters in Tule Lake; the Music Makers and Rhythmaires in Poston; the Harmonaires in Minidoka; the Starlight Serenaders and Music Makers in Gila; the George Igawa Orchestra in Heart Mountain; the Jivesters, Savoy 5, Topaz Tooters, and Rhythm Kings in Topaz; the Densoneers in Jerome; and the Music Makers in Granada. Dance-band music was a part of entertainment in the camps for a variety of occasions: talent revues, graduation celebrations, President's Ball, New Year's dance, socials of various groups, such as the Girl Reserves, Winter Carnival, and junior and senior proms. Some ensembles even played outside the camps for benefits and events due to the paucity of local bands. The Topaz Tooters, led by Tom Tsuji, had a few successful engagements in Salt Lake City. The George Igawa Orchestra performed outside the Heart Mountain camp for a Mormon church reunion dance in Lovell and, later, for the town of Powell's Shoshone Chapter Red Cross fund drive.

Swing music in the detention centers was more than just entertainment; it embodied being American. Yoshida argues, "It was an unconscious assertion that we were Americans. We literally grew up with this music, we absorbed American culture very quickly. We certainly did not dig the Japanese music that our parents brought over with them."[82] Todd Yamamoto articulates the meaning of swing music this way: "We were brought up in the American style for everything. We might eat some Japanese food, but we still liked American food, American movies, American music, American everything. What people forgot was that we *were* Americans, and we *are* Americans."[83] Larry Nobori recalls playing in a dance band at Minidoka detention center as liberating: "When they [swing bands] were performing at camp, they provided entertainment, but there was a sense of becoming free of the boundaries of being interned, for one, being Japanese, for another."[84]

Swing music reinforced Nisei's sense of national belonging despite their public rejection. A performance held at the Japanese American Cultural and Community Center in Los Angeles from February 18 to 19, 1995, entitled

"Music to Remember: A Tribute to Japanese American Musicians and Singers of the '40s," recalls this sense of belonging, and the welcome message in the program booklet reinforced the sentiment:

> These artists, most of whom made their marks during the turbulence of World War II, must be recognized not only for their musical contributions but for the social statement made by their works. Their renditions of popular hits of the '40s served as a vital link between the more than 110,000 Americans of Japanese ancestry interned during the War, and Americans of every other ethnic background. And as their voices rang out during those infamous years, their message was a resounding affirmation of something most of America seemed to forget: We were Americans too.[85]

All bands played stock dance-band arrangements obtained from camp music departments or from organizations such as musicians' unions. The music of Glenn Miller, Tommy Dorsey, Artie Shaw, Count Basie, Harry James, and Woody Herman filled camp mess halls for numerous events. The Glenn Miller Orchestra's arrangement of "Moonlight Serenade" was a popular tune that served as the theme song for many of the camp dance bands. Other requested songs included Miller's "String of Pearls," Dorsey's "Song of India," and Shaw's "Begin the Beguine." Other popular tunes were "Tuxedo Junction" and "Jumping at the Woodside." In addition to playing standard tunes, bands played original compositions, such as "Buddhahead Blues," composed by Ernest Michio Masunaga while he was incarcerated at the Santa Anita assembly center in 1942.

Musicians even organized dance bands at assembly centers, where the average stay was only three months. The Santa Anita Racetrack, in Los Angeles, was an assembly center that housed 18,527 inmates from Los Angeles, San Diego, Santa Clara, and San Jose. This center featured a thirteen-piece band, the Starlight Serenaders, whose instrumentation included four saxophones, two trumpets, two trombones, guitar, drums, piano, and two vocalists. At the Pomona Assembly Center, south of Los Angeles, saxophonist George Igawa formed The Pomonans, a seven-member band showcasing three saxophonists, two trumpeters, guitar, piano, and occasionally featuring vocalists. A high-school age trombonist, Paul Higaki, formed the band The Stardusters at the Merced Assembly Center in central California. The Stardusters boasted five saxophonists, two trumpeters, one trombonist, two female violin players, a female pianist, and a female drummer. On occasion, they also featured vocalists. Tom Tsuji, a xylophonist, was one of the many volunteers to organize musical

Figure 4.5. Music Makers at Poston War Relocation Center, camp #1, performing for the Fourth of July dance in 1943, Arizona. Courtesy of George Yoshida.

activities at the Tanforan Assembly Center, south of San Francisco. Tsuji formed The Tanforan Tooters to play standard band pieces for social dances.

The largest concentration camp was the Poston War Relocation Center, which, because of its size, was divided into three separate sites. Seventeen-year-old Hideo Kawano headed up the Music Makers (figure 4.5), an eleven-piece band at Poston camp #1 with a population of 9,483 inmates. Kawano was an experienced jazz drummer, who, prior to the war, played in talent shows in Little Tokyo, Los Angeles. He switched to trumpet when he formed the Music Makers, which featured three trumpets, one trombone, two tenor saxes, two alto saxes, guitar, piano, and drums. The band's playlist was a mix of dance-band standards of sentimental, slow ballads, such as "Dream" and "Blues on Parade," and up-tempo pieces for jitterbugs.

Helen Iwanaga formed a dance band at Poston camp #2. She had experience as a bandleader in Watsonville, California, where she led a group that played dance-band music for community events. Members of the band from Poston camp #2 included three saxophonists, one trumpeter, one trombonist, one violinist, a pianist, and a drummer.

The Rhythmaires supplied music for dance and entertainment at Poston camp #3. The camp's Recreation Department sponsored this nine-member band; each member was paid sixteen dollars per month to rehearse during the week and perform on weekends.

The Harmonaires at Minidoka detention camp in Idaho had sharpened their musical skills and talent in prewar Seattle, Washington, as a local band.

Unexpectedly, the Harmonaires were in demand outside the camp in two local towns—Twin Falls and Filer, where they were invited to play for local high school proms.

The Gila River War Relocation Center in Arizona was divided into two sites. The Starlight Serenaders, an eight-member band, including trumpets, saxophones, violin, and a singer, all resided at the Gila River Canal detention site. Even though the band didn't have a piano, bass, or guitar, dancers enjoyed their live music, which was a step up from recordings. Inmates at the other Gila River site, Butte Camp, enjoyed the sounds of the Music Makers, an ensemble of saxophones, trumpets, and trombones also with no rhythm section (string bass, guitar, drums, piano). Despite the incomplete instrumentation of the bands, dances at these two sites were spoken of as lively events.

Instead of a dance band, Rohwer detention center in Arkansas had deejays who played seventy-eight-rpm records on phonographs for social dances. Zany characters in Rohwer were Los Angeleno "hepcats" (hipsters), who brought the "pachuco" (young urban Mexican American) zoot-suit style to this desert outpost.

The Densoneers at Jerome detention camp, also in Arkansas, kept the place hopping. Also known as the D-Elevens, this lively band consisted of three saxophones, two trumpets, one trombone, guitar, vocalist, piano, and drums.

As an experienced bandleader, George Igawa pulled together a dance band under his name at the Heart Mountain detention center in Wyoming. Igawa was formerly the leader of the Sho Tokyans, an all–Japanese American band from Los Angeles who toured the West Coast and had the opportunity to perform at dance halls in Japan in 1937 and 1938. At the height of its success at Heart Mountain, the George Igawa band was a nineteen-piece ensemble of six saxophones, five trumpets, three trombones, piano, guitar, string bass, drums, and a vocalist. To build cordial relations with the local population near the camp, the WRA volunteered the band to perform for War Bond Drives(!), local lodge gatherings, high-school dances, and other social dances and fundraising affairs. The group was in demand, being the only big band in all of Wyoming.

The Jive Bombers enlivened life at the Manzanar detention center in California. The camp was home to a conservatory of music, which organized harmony classes, a glee club, a concert band, an orchestra, and a swing band. Lessons on almost any musical instrument were offered. The Jive Bombers were the size of a standard big band with four saxophones, two trombones, four trumpets, guitar, piano, drums, and string bass. Three female vocalists also performed, singing in the style of the famous Andrew Sisters, a professional swing vocal group. A favorite tune was "Don't Fence Me In":

Oh, give me land, lots of land under starry skies above,
Don't fence me in.
Let me ride through the wide-open country that I love,
Don't fence me in.
Let me be by myself in the evenin' breeze,
And listen to the murmur of the cottonwood trees,
Send me off forever but I ask you please,
Don't fence me in.
Just turn me loose, let me straddle my old saddle
Underneath the western skies.
On my Cayuse, let me wander over yonder
Till I see the mountains rise.

I want to ride to the ridge where the west commences
And gaze at the moon till I lose my senses
And I can't look at hobbles and I can't stand fences
Don't fence me in.

Oh, give me land, lots of land under starry skies,
Don't fence me in.
Let me ride through the wide-open country that I love,
Don't fence me in.
Let me be by myself in the evenin' breeze
And listen to the murmur of the cottonwood trees
Send me off forever but I ask you please,
Don't fence me in

Just turn me loose, let me straddle my old saddle
Underneath the western skies
On my Cayuse, let me wander over yonder
Till I see the mountains rise.
Ba boo ba ba boo.

I want to ride to the ridge where the west commences
And gaze at the moon till I lose my senses
And I can't look at hobbles and I can't stand fences
Don't fence me in.
No.
Poppa, don't you fence me in.[86]

Directing their instruments toward armed guards in the towers at Manzanar gave members of the Jive Bombers a chance to playfully "talk back" to the isolation and unlawfulness of their incarceration. It was a call to freedom—freedom to be themselves and live their lives as American citizens.

The Amache detention center in Granada, Colorado, exemplifies musicking activities at a high level. The Amache center's School Music Program employed three teachers, all of whom taught fifty-five classes a week. The music school had a beginner band, an advanced band, and a ten-piece dance band. The Music Makers dance band consisted of three trumpets, two trombones three saxophones, and a rhythm section that included piano, string bass, guitar, and drums. "As Time Goes By," "I'll Be Seeing You," and "Pennsylvania 6-5000" (phone number of a famous hotel in New York City) were favorites in the Music Makers' repertoire. The band also had outside opportunities to perform; one of their engagements involved playing dance music at the US Army Post social hall for the very GIs who worked as sentries in the Amache concentration camp!

Two dance bands graced the ears of Tule Lake inmates in northern California. The Starlighters and the Down Beats competed for dancers and swing-band enthusiasts. Band personnel of the Starlighters included five saxophonists, three trumpeters, two trombonists, a pianist, guitarist, drummer, and vocalist, half of whom were high-school students. This band attracted a great following in the camp. The playlist of the Down Beats, a band that named itself after the popular jazz magazine, consisted of up-tempo, swing-band pieces of the Count Basie, Tommy Dorsey, Woody Herman, and Jimmie Lunceford bands that were popular among jitterbug dancers. Three trumpeters, three saxophonists, a trombonist, and a full rhythm section rounded out the sound of the Down Beats. The band was often featured with a variety of vocal ensembles in musical revues. They also participated in programs highlighting an assortment of vocal and instrumental arrangements of American standards that were popular in the 1930s and 1940s.

The Topaz detention center in Utah boasted a bevy of swing bands: the Topaz Tooters, the Jivesters, the Savoy Four, and the Rhythm Kings. The Topaz Tooters made a smooth transition from the Tanforan Assembly Center where they were known by the same name. After being detained for a few months, many Nisei inmates had opportunities to leave the camps to attend college or work, making it difficult to keep dance-band personnel. Late in 1943, a new band called the Jivesters succeeded the Topaz Tooters. The seven-piece Jivesters was led by a tenor saxophonist who played alongside an alto saxophonist, three trumpeters, a pianist, and a drummer. The Jivesters were lively musicians who offered diverse music for a variety of social occasions, including the Topaz High School's

Musical Fun-tasia, a variety show that presented dancers, comedy skits, singers, and dance-band music. The Savoy Four made their debut at Topaz detention camp by challenging the Jivesters to a battle of the bands. The Savoy Four was a jazz combo rather than a dance band, with a pianist, Mabel Sugiyama, who played in the style of Count Basie and a tenor saxophonist, who fashioned his playing after the well-known jazz saxophonist Ben Webster. The Savoy Four favored music that allowed for jazz improvisation, such as "Basie Blues," "Tuxedo Junction," "Jive at Five," "The Man I Love," and others. At one point, the drummer for the Jivesters decided to form his own band called the Rhythm Kings, an eight-member band with Ich Sasaki, the bandleader, on rhythm and solo on the Spanish electric guitar. The power of swing-dance music prevailed, softening the harshness of the bleak regions where Japanese Americans were imprisoned, keeping alive the hope for a better future.

Additional musical ensembles that enhanced life in the camps were Hawaiian-string bands comprised of mostly guitars and ukuleles performing Hawaiian pop songs of the time. From the early 1900s on, many Japanese immigrants from Hawaii left plantation work for the West Coast where there were more opportunities for employment and business. Also, at the beginning of World War II, more than one thousand Japanese Hawaiians were sent as inmates to the mainland camps. The US government assembled individuals from the islands considered potentially dangerous because of their leadership roles in Buddhist churches and other community organizations that had ties to Japan.

Eddie Tanaka's Sierra Stars diversified musical offerings, entertaining audiences at Manzanar and Tule Lake incarceration centers with old-time country music and delighting listeners with songs accompanied by guitars, gutbucket bass, and percussive washboard (figure 4.6).

Social life did not mask the reality in the camps for all Nisei. Imprisoned at the Tanforan Assembly Center in 1942, Charles Kikuchi reflects:

> And yet the social activities are meaningless—they seem so unreal. Somehow, it seems that nothing matters any more except the war and the future. I resent this unreal environment and the people who look like they accept it. I'm trying to escape reality at the same time I face it. It doesn't make sense. Sometimes I get such an awful empty feeling; my nerves are so jangled. Waves of resentment come over me at the funniest times. Outwardly, I try to pass off as adjusted to this setup, but things happen or I read something, which brings almost a violent reaction. The only stabilizing thing in this whole mess is the family.[87]

Figure 4.6. Eddie Tanaka's Sierra Stars. Manzanar and Tule Lake concentration camps. Japanese American National Museum, Jack and Peggy Iwata Collection, no. 93.102.138.

The bitterness and resentment expressed by Kikuchi was widespread, especially among older Nisei whose professional lives were interrupted. It was the Issei, however, who suffered the most, having lost everything they had built from scratch upon their arrival, followed by restoring their lives after the Great Depression.

The sonic and affective appeal of swing music combined with the desire to consort with other American-born Nisei youth naturally formed affinity communities. Although social activities were the primary context for musical participation, keeping the heartbeat of American music steady, this music was also the Nisei's source of cultural capital that they believed validated their status as American citizens.

What distinguished the affinity community in the camps is the age cohort and generation it represented: predominantly Nisei youth bent on emphasizing their American self-image. In asserting their Americanness through music, they demonstrated greater affinity with mainstream America in general.

The boundaries between the three musical communities in the detention centers blurred as individuals partook in more than one community and as music styles blended from one into another. One example is how some individuals in the communities of descent and dissent intersected in their focus on Japanese music, although the two communities differed in intent and attitude. Musical communities of descent consisted of members in pursuit of their aesthetic and musical preference for Japanese music. It is true, however, some performed this music to express their cultural citizenship as a tacit form of resistance to the American identity imposed upon them. Communities of dissent led by Issei or Kibei, in contrast, overtly politicized Japanese music and arts as a counterpoint to racist war hysteria and the hegemony of Americanism exercised by the WRA.

A striking example of musicking that intersected two musical communities—dissent and affinity—was the performance of "Ballad for Americans" at the commencement for graduating high-school seniors at Manzanar War Relocation Center in 1943. Conducted by music educator Louis Frizzell, the Manzanar High School chorus, with a singing narrator, presented "Ballad for Americans," a patriotic cantata composed in 1939 by Earl Robinson and John Latouche.[88] In her article, "Ballad for Incarcerated Americans: Second Generation Japanese American Musicking in World War II Camps," Marta Robertson details how the piece was originally composed in support of the Popular Front social movement and it's view of a pluralistic America, which wove ethnic heritage and identity into the ideologies of Americanism and popular internationalism. Frizzell, sympathetic to the plight of Japanese Americans and their unjust imprisonment, chose "Ballad for Americans" after reading about it in a volume of the *Music Educators Journal*. Robertson purports that Frizzell's choice offered Nisei at Manzanar a chance to "construct hybrid identities that simultaneously resisted the injustice of incarceration and envisioned belonging in a pluralistic America that welcomed their cultural heritage."[89] It is remarkable that Frizzell chose this piece in what appears to be his own opposition to imprisoning American citizens unlawfully and not only to provide Nisei a chance to dissent. Japanese American affinity with "Ballad for Americans" can be attributed to the lyrics that narrate America's struggle for unity as a nation ideally based on liberty and equality, as penned in the US Declaration of Independence and built by unsung Americans from all occupations, ethnicities, races, and religions. The pluralistic nature of America claimed in the piece appealed to not only Nisei youth but also to the entire audience whose standing ovation embodied a collective desire to be counted. The programmatic and upbeat music of "Ballad for Americans" climaxes with a rousing march "of the people" in a spirited declamation of their belief in America.[90]

Instances of overlap also existed between communities of descent and affinity, as in the case of Americanized Nisei inclined toward the singing of Japanese pop songs in talent shows and revues while primarily performing or dancing to the latest American swing music, singing vernacular songs,

Figure 4.7. Norakuro Harmonica Band, Minidoka concentration camp, Idaho. Wing Luke Museum, the Hatate Collection, no. 1992-4-4 U.

or playing European classical styles. Illustrative is the Norakuro Harmonica Band at Minidoka detention center in Idaho whose members included Kibei, performing both American and Japanese popular music (figure 4.7). I would categorize Norakuro as part of the affinity community because of the younger generation to which they belonged and their performance of swing-band tunes. Yet, the band's inclusion of Japanese popular songs and American songs sung in Japanese reveal the cross-cultural repertoire maintained by its Kibei members. Nisei George Nakata comments on the band's musical abilities: "They could do their renditions of Artie Shaw and Glenn Miller and Harry James and all the rest of them. I mention my sister, Mary, because together with her best friend, Betty Nakashimada, they became the two singers for the band. And I remember hours and hours where Mary and Betty were practicing in our little apartment singing 'Shina no yoru' [China Nights] and 'This Hour' for the eighteenth time." He reflected on how the harmonica band transpired: "If you can imagine Niseis who had to pack one bag only, go to the assembly center and then on to Minidoka; you can't exactly carry a tuba or some huge instrument, and so most of them were able to bring their harmonica. And some of them were extremely talented; a couple of them had small clarinets, and there was one used piano [added later]."[91]

The Norakuro Harmonica Band granted Kibei members a chance to highlight Japanese music with which they most closely identified. Performing for camp dances and other musical events that filled the inmates' social calendars marked Minidoka as a musically active site, hosting a broad variety of entertainment, including singing contests because of all the good singers.

SOCIOPOLITICAL DYNAMICS IN THE CAMPS

Analysis of the complex sociopolitical makeup of life in the ten concentration camps sheds light on the various meanings and intent attached to musical participation in this setting. The forced removal and imprisonment initially muffled generational and class differences that existed in communities before World War II.[92] At the beginning, egalitarianism reigned in the assembly centers and concentration camps as people were stripped of their previous status and wealth. Kikuchi notes, "Social barriers have also broken down and people are on a much more equal footing. Money and former position do not mean so much as they did on the outside."[93] As time passed, however, Issei leaders were able to reestablish their power, no longer based on their economic capital, but on their prior experience as community leaders and the strength of their cultural capital.[94]

Following the initial shock of being forcibly removed and imprisoned, feelings of anger, resentment, and bitterness set in. Losses suffered by inmates in underselling or abandoning their businesses, property, and homes, and the restrictive and repressive conditions set by the War Relocation Authority in the camps all contributed to rising tensions and animus. Life in the camps required constant adjustments to changing circumstances, causing a flux in cultural identities and power relationships as the months and years passed and events and crises unfolded.

Generational, cultural, and class differences that existed in prewar communities gradually became stark in the camps as discord and disunity increased among inmates attempting to resolve the many issues they faced in creating some semblance of a normal life. In the words of anthropologist Robert F. Spencer, "Disunity was striking; unity was not." In the Gila detention center, he observed complex divisions between generations complicated by the rise of clubs or organizations formed according to age or interest, shifting social dynamics away from traditional loyalties and family ties. Issei tenaciously maintained close ties to Japanese culture and customs. The strength of their primordial ties correlated with the racial and political statutes that barred them from gaining citizenship and owning land. The denial of both citizenship and landownership in tandem with their forced incarceration pushed Issei closer to their heritage as a source of strength, stability, and belonging. The first generation was the most disenfranchised population in the camps. Issei bachelors, who had worked as migrant workers before the war, identified most with Japan and were the least assimilated since, in not raising a family, they were minimally socialized within American society.[95] They tended to be the most nationalistic with strong ties to their homeland and openly expressed their hopes for Japan's victory in the war.[96]

As aliens ineligible for citizenship, official decision-making positions in the concentration camps were denied Issei because their loyalty to the United States was in question.[97] The disempowerment of Issei tipped the balance of power toward younger Nisei during the early years of incarceration. This sharpened the generational conflict between the two groups, which had manifested before the war when Nisei began to strike out on their own instead of subordinately taking part in the ethnic economy controlled by Issei.

The WRA's plan to have prisoners better govern themselves generated policies that were insensitive to the generational and cultural conflicts among their charges. The authorities set up Community Councils in each camp to serve as the central self-governing units with members elected from each block. The Community Council functioned as an advisory group to the administration and an enforcer of WRA policies and rules. The administration required council members to be American citizens of at least twenty-five years of age, disallowing Issei from playing any role.[98] The WRA's reliance on Nisei for decision making in the camps further fueled the generational conflict since it was Issei who held such posts in prewar communities. The incarceration curtailed the political and economic dominance of these elders, although the scope and depth of the many problems and issues inmates faced, such as crowded living conditions, the shortage and poor quality of meals, and serious concerns about health and medical care, required the experience and acumen of the first generation.[99] Issei leaders who effectively addressed these problems eventually shifted the balance of power back to their generation. In Tule Lake, the generational clash was resolved. Nisei appointments to the Community Council made by the WRA were counterbalanced by a practice of submitting issues back to the Block Council, a unit Issei dominated, consisting of one representative from each block (a unit of eight or ten barracks).[100] Issei also formed a Planning Board at Tule Lake with representatives from each block.[101] In the fall and winter of 1943, the release and transfer of Issei leaders originally incarcerated in Justice Department camps to the detention camps to join their families helped to bolster the Issei's authority due to their increased numbers.

Nisei, nonetheless, played an important role in the camps, holding key positions and exercising their newfound leadership, operating detention-camp newspapers, farms, and hospitals, and teaching in schools. Because most of this population ranged in age from teenagers to adults in their early twenties, social activities, such as weekly dances, movies, church services, ping-pong contests, baseball leagues, and beauty contests were all important as a tacit expression of their Americanness.

As citizens who eventually cooperated with the federal government in the forced removal and incarceration of their communities, Nisei leaders of the Japanese American Citizens League filled liaison positions between the Japanese community and the military. Holding these positions gave the JACL a chance to continue their campaign of Americanism in the camps. This focal point aligned well with the WRA's goal of instilling American ideals through governance, educational curriculum, and various programs. Although the JACL raised objections to the incarceration, the federal government persuaded the organization to accept it as a military necessity. The JACL's push for "constructive cooperation" was a strategy to stave off growing negativity toward Japanese Americans by promoting Nisei as loyal American citizens and urging all Japanese Americans to cooperate with the US government by complying with the directives of Executive Order 9066. Sociologist Art Sakamoto suggests that the decision to comply points to a certain Japanese attitude based on the idea of cooperating to the point of shaming one's oppressor.[102] Because of the legislated racial and legal actions taken against Japanese Americans for three decades prior to the war, the JACL realized they had limited options. By cooperating with the government, Nisei hoped to prove to mainstream society that Japanese Americans were law-abiding citizens who were willing to comply and help with the war effort.[103]

The JACL's stance of loyalty, Americanism, and constructive cooperation exemplified the social and economic status and ideology of older Nisei who were already established as professionals and entrepreneurs before the war. The organization's firm belief in cultivating an American identity was generally embraced among Nisei, a majority who were still in their teens and early twenties. But the social divisions among the second generation exhibited a diverse and complex demographic. Conservative Nisei tended to more closely associate with the culture of their parents. They spoke fluent Japanese and were most likely Buddhist. American-born Kibei, raised and educated in Japan, were particularly set apart because of their poor English-language skills and strong Japanese cultural orientation.[104] They were the most maladjusted with limited social acceptance among their Americanized peers.

There was also a more rebellious and boisterous Nisei cohort that included Hawaiian Nisei or Kibei. More affluent Nisei socialites, Progressive Nisei, and radical liberals were other divisions that made it difficult for this generation to organize a unified front.[105]

Other challenges to unity among Nisei in their drive to assert their authority included the exodus of this population in a resettlement program promoted by the WRA between March 1943 and December 1944. The resettlement program, coined the "salvage" by social demographer Dorothy Swaine Thomas,[106] made it possible for approximately thirty-six thousand individuals to resettle in urban centers and locations in the Midwest and East that were amenable to Japanese Americans. Most of the resettlers were Nisei who were dispersed to Chicago, Cleveland, Des Moines, Minneapolis, Milwaukee, and New York to find work and enter the American mainstream. The National Japanese American Student Relocation Council,[107] under the leadership of the American Friends Service Committee, enrolled Nisei in colleges that had agreed to accept them. In total, about one-third of all inmates took advantage of the resettlement program.

Two starkly contrasting views prevailed among inmates during the first two years that it took to stabilize camp life. For those remaining in the camps, growing unrest and the increasing influence of Issei gave way to stronger anti-JACL sentiments and the hope for community solidarity. The JACL became the scapegoat for all the problems and difficulties inmates faced. JACL leaders were blamed for deferring too much to the government, failing to take a stronger stand opposing the forced evacuation. Considered "collaborators" with the US government, JACL leaders became "symbols of betrayal" as rumors spread of their collusion in identifying Issei community leaders who were detained and brutally treated by FBI agents following the bombing of Pearl Harbor. Opposition to JACL members and supporters grew more trenchant when Manzanar JACL leaders petitioned Washington politicians to reopen the armed services to Nisei[108] and advocated for the government's resettlement program. For many JACL opponents, the notion of drafting Nisei to fight in the war pushed the loyalty issue too far; it was considered the "ultimate injustice" that would dismantle the last remnants of security and unity in the camps: the family.[109]

Issei, in their effort to create communal solidarity, promoted the idea that the camps were a safe, peaceful refuge until the war ended. A resigned acceptance of their circumstances included acquiescence to administration orders, but they carefully protected their rights as enemy aliens in accordance with the Geneva Convention, prohibiting the administration to force them to do any work that supported the war effort against Japan—their country of legal citizenship.

Issei hoped to create a more positive relationship with Nisei in crafting a united front against poorly thought-out social-welfare policies of the WRA and insufferable living conditions in general. Issei repeated the phrase "We are all Japanese together" to bring Nisei into their fold.[110] The sense of abandonment by the US government that Nisei felt following the initial jolt of being incarcerated led many of them to gradually accept the Issei's notion of communal and cultural solidarity. This shift was accompanied by their increased Japanization and social pressure to act in the spirit of the Japanese—*seishin* or *yamato damashii*. Invoking *seishin* advanced Japanese pride as a line of defense against further injustices and provided an impetus for protests and strikes.

Edward H. Spicer et al. insightfully describe the sense of Japaneseness felt by Issei:

> Being Japanese . . . a meaning not to be explained in the simple concepts of loyalty and disloyalty used by nations at war. In the first place there was the feeling of being Japanese, which had nothing whatever to do with Japan's place in international affairs. Pride in being Japanese was something every Issei had. It was a feeling embedded in each, permanent and unchanging, independent of distance from Japan or rises or falls in the fortunes of the Japanese nation. It was the sense of pride of being some sort of human being, the sort of human being that one was. It was a simple and basic fact for Issei, but it was also one of the most difficult spots in the relations between Issei and Nisei. Few Issei had escaped the sharp disappointment and dismay of finding that their sons did not have a simple pride in being Japanese.[111]

Spicer et al. articulate well Issei's self-identification as Japanese, which they fundamentally equated with being human. Their confinement also fortified their self-conception as *zaibei dōhō* (Japanese in America)—being Japanese *in* America, but not *of* America. Strong adherents of the Issei's outlook tended to be agricultural workers who were less educated and were more culturally Japanese.[112]

A second view harbored by a minority of Nisei opposed the Issei's ascendant influence in viewing their imprisonment as a neutral interim period and an opportunity to revitalize a Japanese spirit and its attendant culture. Nisei supporters of the JACL stood by the organization's Americanist stance and advocated efforts to make American society aware of the error of incarcerating citizens by cooperating with the WRA administration and supporting Americanization and the war effort. Supporters of this stance were college-educated Nisei, mostly from urban centers, who were established entrepreneurs and professionals.[113] Although a small number of Nisei men and women held these views, their pro-American position boosted the WRA's Americanization program. With the push to Americanize, issues of the inmates' ethnic identity became subsumed in efforts to prove one's loyalty to the United States.[114]

Important avenues for promoting themes of Americanism and loyalty were camp newspapers, literary works, and educational curricula. Literary works by second-generation authors affirmed an American way of life rather than express bitter disappointment and loss of faith in their country. The administration offered Americanization propaganda through adult-education programs, featuring speakers who lectured on American law, American history, American foreign policy, and the American West. English-language classes designed for the first generation were a particular draw for Issei women who wanted to be able to communicate with their Nisei children. Primary and secondary schools in the camps offered educational curricula designed by Stanford University, featuring core classes that taught the tenets of democratic citizenship, as well as vocational classes and college preparatory courses. WRA educational objectives were to prepare students to socially integrate into mainstream society once they were released.[115] Perversely ironic was the continued indoctrination of students about the ideals and principles of American democracy, freedom, and forbearance while they remained incarcerated in detention centers in isolated wastelands as American citizens held against their will.

The racialized treatment of Japanese Americans by the federal government, the larger society, and the WRA generated conflict within the camps, creating a political undertow in every aspect of the inmates' lives, including musicking. The War Relocation Authority's disciplining and Americanizing policies created a fraught and traumatizing experience for Japanese American inmates, forcing them to choose sides socially, culturally, and politically.

CONCLUDING THOUGHTS

Oppositional culture and consciousness spread amongst inmates as they endured political oppression and social isolation in barren regions of the United States. Mass demonstrations, draft resistance, labor strikes, legal challenges to detention, and other organized resistance not detailed here transformed the normative character of Japanese American acquiescence to one of activism as they sought to take control of their environment and sufficiently govern their restricted communities.[116] A heightened awareness of the social injustice responsible for their confinement led to, in the words of Nisei activist Yuri Kochiyama, "that set of insurgent ideas and beliefs constructed and developed by an oppressed group for the purpose of guiding its struggle to undermine, reform, or overthrow a system of domination."[117] Oppositional consciousness matured during the camp years, laying the foundation for the next generation's political strategy and agenda for the Asian American movement.

Shelemay's tripartite musical-communities model draws attention to the major divisions of the inmate population and the amplified race consciousness that reverberated in the formation of political and cultural identities arising from extreme circumstances. The model separates three distinct social groups engaged in cultural or racial reification, power struggles, and resistance against unreasonable demands, and reiteration of citizenship and belonging through musicking. The three types of musical collectivities—descent, dissent, and affinity—do not capture all the permutations of individual identities in the camps and their corresponding musical expression. Neither do they account for individuals caught between two prevailing views in camp: Americanness or Japaneseness. One might speculate that the liminal state experienced by some prevented them from finding their place in any of the three musical communities. The location of the three musical communities on a horizontal continuum of musicking, however, accommodated individuals who participated in more than one collectivity. The ability to traverse the continuum accommodates inmates whose identities overlapped or were in flux, but the three-community model does not provide a complete range of inmates' identities and how their identities correlated to their musical activity. It does describe music practices in the camps, suggesting, paradoxically, a certain freedom exercised by individuals in choosing what music to play and enacting cultural and political identities that matched their inclinations and adaptation to the setting. Assessing whether inmates consciously or tacitly formed the three distinct musical communities proposed is difficult, but the acute conditions in the camps support their proposed existence.

Artistic activity took on greater meaning, providing inmates a medium through which to assert their identity and forge a sense of agency against the racism and fear that resulted in their imprisonment and the WRA's prohibitive regulations. Some inmates advocated using artistic expression to advance a sense of freedom from within and to foster aesthetic inspiration. Aesthetics, a culturally implicit aspiration for many Issei, provided an outlet for their emotional release and self-expression. Musical participation was not only an act of collective identity, but one of spiritual and cultural renewal and simple pleasure as people sought ways to transcend the inhumanity they were experiencing.

The enduring aesthetics of Japanese music sounded its difference and voiced inmates' cultural citizenship and ties to their heritage. On the other end of the spectrum, many Nisei stranded in the camps played music to reinforce ever more strongly their cultural identities as Americans. A small minority of Nisei embittered by their imprisonment stamped out their former identification as 100-percent American, turning to their Japanese roots. Shifting identities and correlative musicking transpired due to tensions created by the WRA's Americanization campaign and its insulting demand for loyalty and the wrongful and coercive recruitment of inmates by the US Army and the pro-Americanization stance of the JACL. The forceful influence and nationalism of Issei and Kibei and the power struggles between the Issei and Nisei for control in decision making were also contributing factors. The driving impact of these forces reveals the dynamic of cultural politics within the camps and how music enacted the cultural orientation of differentiated groups.

Shown in sharp relief are incarcerated Japanese Americans' performance of social, cultural, and political identification. The concentration-camp experience generated extremes in cultural and political choices for inmates; driven to despair, some were compelled to prove their Americanness in extreme ways (e.g., enlisting in the US Army), while others prepared to expatriate or repatriate to Japan. The imprisonment of innocent US citizens and residents challenged democracy itself. The ruined lives and psyches of the inmates are the unfortunate consequence of a country's failure to transform destructive racial ideologies, which have hindered the forging of a nation of great potential and squandered the resources and generative capacity of a racially and culturally diverse society. The unconstitutional detention was the culmination of civic ostracism, a process of racial triangulation that had denied Issei citizenship and marginalized their American-born offspring, leading to the arrest and imprisonment of Japanese Americans. Current, twenty-first-century anti-immigration sentiments are part of this legacy of US racial and cultural intolerance and an underestimation of the important economic role of immigrants who come to contribute and pursue opportunities in starting their lives anew.

Japanese American concentration-camp experiences epitomize the complete failure of democracy in a powerful nation. Yet, as Japanese Americans mediated their ethnic boundaries in such extreme circumstances, they claimed agency, which empowered them to resist their incarceration and move toward strengthening their Japanese roots or asserting their American identity. Music offered inmates the means to choose and enact cultural identities that voiced their aesthetic inclinations and sociopolitical stance. Musicking in talent shows, concerts, social dances, and community events brought a sense of normalcy, stability, and joy that neutralized the rage, frustration, and humiliation of inmates' confined lives. The story of injustice and suffering told here underscores how cultural identity is a socially and politically stirring issue for the powerless, accenting the need for a more welcoming trope that opposes nativism and a national landscape that is open to the richness engendered by a spectrum of races and identities that are emergent and adaptable.

CHAPTER 5

Sansei: The Political Advocacy of Music and a Turn toward the East

The jigoku club inside
j town, bold rebels jamming
Cross from black town, udon,
Grits, barbecue
—QUINCY TROUPE[1]

The poetic excerpt identifies the shared space—the intersection of Japantown and the Fillmore District in San Francisco at Post Street—of Japanese American and African American musician-composers in the 1970s. The shared space is emblematic of the musical alliances that fed and ignited innovative musicking by Asian American artists. Active clubs and nightlife surged during the 1940s and 1950s in the Fillmore District, making it an obvious spawning ground for musical creativity and experimentation.

The first wave of Sansei musician-composers, featured in the following pages, articulate contemporary heterogeneous subjectivities that celebrate their ethnic heritage and, through interracial and intercultural collaborations, generated fresh sounds. I introduce the first wave of musician-composers in San Francisco and Los Angeles, who, in the 1970s, pioneered new musical directions, giving rise to incipient Asian American music scenes. The intention here is to uncover the early, most politically active years of Sansei musicking that elevated sociopolitical consciousness and a bold stance. This is a history I feel compelled to narrate for subsequent generations so they may learn of the fortitude of Sansei artists in their struggle to be visible, proactive, and creative.

When focusing on pan-Asian activism at its height within the Asian American movement in the 1980s, it is difficult to separate the intertwined work of Japanese American and other Asian American musicians who recorded under the auspices of Asian Improv Records. The contributions of Sansei musician-composers stand out, however, because of the radical direction some took in exploring their identity and the singular history of Japanese American rejection and incarceration during World War II in the United States. The rise of *taiko* ensembles in California, whose sound and movement became emblematic of a Japanese American identity, also distinguishes the creative musicking of this population. Equally pronounced is the commercial success of southern California's jazz-pop fusion band Hiroshima, which pioneered a Japanese/Asian American sound, raising the visibility of this demographic nationally. This study elucidates in detail the confluence of social, cultural, and political ideologies and the Afro-Asian connection underlying the evolution of Japanese/Asian American musicking and the advent of Asian American jazz-based music.[2]

The question of how Sansei express themselves musically in ways that articulate a contemporary heterogeneous Japanese American subjectivity considers the racial border crossings and intercultural influences in their work and the culture of resistance that colored it. Sansei engage in intercultural collaborations with African American and Latinx musician-composers and their diasporic music practices, expanding the sonic palette of their musical excursions. Shared sonic spaces and subjectivities arise in cross-fertilized musical tapestries created from individual reinterpretations of stylistic and aesthetic features of Japanese music woven into African American music styles. The resulting hybridity counters essentializing music generated by Japanese Americans,[3] transforming it onto an American soundscape. Latinx musical influences that catalyzed hybridity in the work of Asian American musician-composers are evident in the songs of folksingers Nobuko Miyamoto, Chris Iijima, and Charlie Chin and in contemporary *taiko* compositions. Such composite music sonically parallels the activist alliance of African Americans, Asian Americans, and Chicanos in the Third World Liberation Front (TWLF) responsible for leading the student strike that successfully instituted the College of Ethnic Studies at San Francisco State University.

Sansei musicking practices follow divergent paths that reveal varied upbringing, regional orientations, individual self-expression, musical inclinations, and political leanings. The Asian American movement and sociopolitical milieu of the 1960s to the 1980s served as a catalyst for many Sansei in reframing their citizenship and sense of self—a departure from the former generation's efforts to fully assimilate. Integral to the re-formation of Japanese/ Asian American racial and cultural identity were the ideology and performance practices of creative musician-improvisors and the Black Arts movement allied with the Black liberation movement. African American music emboldened Japanese/Asian Americans musicians to construct alternative identities as part of a politics of resistance to their continuing marginalization in US society and the music industry. As a site of cultural production, Sansei musicking rises out of a history of struggle, claiming its Japanese heritage and sensibilities as a wellspring to draw from in creating multiple narratives of who we are and how we want to be portrayed. Musicking enables us to exercise agency as we strive to integrate our creative spaces into a pluralistic mainstream with the aim of expanding its borders and engendering a sense of belonging for not only ourselves but also for other subordinated and immigrant groups to come.

As a Sansei musician, the sound of the koto resonated with me; I found it to be an ideal medium to express my Japanese sensibilities. I had the opportunity to learn this iconic instrument while residing in Japan for eighteen months (1983–1984), an exploratory time that allowed me to absorb the aesthetics and culture of this island country. Studying koto symbolized my desire to recover and strengthen diasporic cultural ties to the birthplace of my grandparents. Raised in New York, Sansei in my circle were busy building professional careers and attempting to become part of American mainstream society; few were interested in their Japanese past. Moving to Los Angeles for graduate study at UCLA placed me in a city and its surrounding environs with the highest concentration of Japanese Americans on the US mainland. It was serendipitous that I was able to secure an internship working at the Japanese American Cultural and Community Center in J-Town, Los Angeles, where my association with coworkers, Japanese American activists, opened my eyes to the politics of being Japanese American. This political awakening transformed how I viewed myself as a Japanese American within the national context. My experience working at the JACCC prompted the following narrative, which speaks to the solidarity I share with Japanese/Asian Americans striving to build political capital and utilize music to express emergent identities that evoke our heritage in challenging hegemonic US discourses on race and Orientalism.

The rise of Sansei musicians is best viewed through the lens of the broad social and political milieu in the San Francisco Bay Area, a site that provided fertile ground for artists, activists, and students. In his book detailing the musical renaissance and social revolution in San Francisco from 1965 to 1975, author, activist, and musician Mat Callahan paints the legacy of revolutionary politics in San Francisco with broad strokes, stretching back to the growing prominence of this city's seaport from the time of the Gold Rush of 1849 to the 1960s. He describes the transformation of a small Spanish-speaking, agricultural community into a world-class seaport where manufactured goods were imported and gold reserves were exported to British and US banks. The civil rights, farmworkers, and antiwar movements united the local population of all backgrounds, spurring political and artistic activity in reforming discriminatory employment and housing practices along with poor wages and working conditions. Close ties between artists and labor organizers developed as they worked collaboratively to address work-reform issues. The local culture flourished with the elite class's support and funding for the arts and sciences, drawing poets, artists, intellectuals, and revolutionaries to San Francisco, creating a radical and vibrant community. The burgeoning art community's coffeehouses and nightclubs set the stage for the ascent of music and theater, which became a nexus for "different art scenes, political perspectives, and social conflicts," culminating in the growth of audiences with eclectic tastes.[4] The confluence of politicized and creative individuals and the cross-fertilization of ideas and forms foreshadow the intercultural activity primarily between Asian American and African American musicians in the 1970s and 1980s.

NASCENT SANSEI MUSICKING

Activist Sansei musician-composers were at the forefront of musical explorations in the nascent period of experimental Asian American musicking. Searching for their own voice, Sansei musicians merged Japanese and other Asian musical elements and aesthetic sensibilities into free jazz, jazz fusion, or rock to express their reimagined identity and political consciousness. They emulated what Dorinne Kondo envisioned: "the world of representation and of aesthetics is a site of struggle where identities are created, where subjects are interpellated, and where hegemonies can be challenged."[5] This challenge matched their reconstructed social identities and boundaries in a racist society. The continuous unfolding of their music decenters and stirs Japanese American musicking, engendering complex meanings in its sounding. For those drawn to jazz-based music, there is also an ascendant and spiritual desire for a united humanity, which could ideally be expressed through collective improvisation.

Japanese American musician-composers lured by experimental and improvised music looked to creative-music collectives formed by Black musicians in the 1960s and 1970s. Sarita Gregory documents the activities of several music collectives, referring to them as a "creative music movement," a designation that embodied musicians' initiative to address intertwined artistic and sociopolitical struggles.[6] Located in major cities, active music collectives included the Association for the Advancement of Creative Musicians (AACM) in Chicago, the Black Artists Group (BAG) in St. Louis, the Creative Arts Collective in Detroit, Horace Tapscott's Union of God's Musicians and Artists Ascension (UGMAA) in Los Angeles, and the Collective Black Artists in New York.[7] Creative Music Studio (CMS) in Woodstock, New York, invited San Francisco Bay Area's multi-instrumentalist and experimental improvisor Gerald Oshita to work with composer-improvisors from varied backgrounds and practices. Oshita also conjoined with AACM members, introducing them to young Japanese American musician-composers for mentoring. In his article, "Asian Americans and Creative Music Legacies," Michael Dessen insightfully points out that creative-music improvisors in the 1960s "did not simply use conventional musical practices as vehicles for espousing oppositional politics, but instead saw artistic experimentation as a means to interrogate changing social realities in their full complexity."[8]

Sansei musician-composers interfaced with other ethnic groups in their multiethnic neighborhoods, yielding a broader sonic palette from which to compose. Black cultural nationalists inspired Sansei to embrace their Japanese heritage and aesthetic as a means of creative political resistance. The AACM posited a political and aesthetic direction for many Asian American musicians, encompassing the idea of a cultural continuum in which music of the past links with that of the present. The musical affinity Asian Americans shared with African Americans centered on jazz-based music as a genre of choice, particularly free jazz, and the collective nature of improvising. Cultural historian, Daryl J. Maeda, underscores the performance of Blackness as key to understanding the development of Asian American identity. What is significant about Asian American performance of Blackness is "the power of mimesis to produce new subjectivities and identifications across ideological boundaries."[9] Emulating Black political and performative power enables Asian Americans to rearticulate their racial identity and expand music's subversive potential, which they intertwine with their own histories and experiences in authorizing a distinct identity.[10] Music continues to be a meeting ground; it provides a space where musicians can not only say something about their social and political location but also express a shared humanity with their fellow artists.

Diasporic transnationalism is captured in sounds composed by Sansei through the incorporation of Japanese music genres and practices: court music, koto and shakuhachi instrumental music, folk songs, and folk festival music. Japanese American musician-composers who answered the call for cultural forms aimed at supporting their newly conceived cultural and political identities rearticulated Asian musical elements in innovative ways. Aesthetic concepts, idiomatic playing styles of instruments, musical forms, melodic style, and rhythms of premodern Japanese music continue to stretch artistic boundaries and create new sensibilities. One can view these efforts as a continuum of Japanese music retained in the concentration camps of World War II by incarcerated Japanese Americans as remnants of their prewar communities. As well, the more than one thousand *taiko* ensembles in the United States and Canada today demonstrate a transnationalized Japanese folk drumming tradition that has captured the hearts and minds of not only Japanese/Asian Americans but members young and old from multiple races and ethnicities. Spread globally to all continents except Antarctica and performed by diasporic Japanese and non-Japanese, Japanese American *taiko* is now an international phenomenon.

There is no singular Sansei sound one can speak of. Sansei musicians capture a certain Japanese or Asian sensibility in their work but in reimagined form, reflecting their experiences and participation in multiethnic America. What is important to many musicians is the affective quality of their work in sounding their participation in mainstream culture yet asserting resistance to cultural hegemony in shaping their own voice.

ASIAN AMERICAN IDENTITY POLITICS

Today, the term "Asian American" may not sound particularly revolutionary, but it *did* signal a sea change for Americans of Asian descent. Usage of this term first occurred in the Asian American Experience in America—Yellow Identity conference on January 11, 1969, at the University of California, Berkeley. The conference focused on identity and the Asian American experience and was attended by nine hundred students active in the civil rights and anti–Vietnam War movements. Participating Asian Americans addressed the need to reconfigure their cultural identities, requiring that they reject assimilation and instead reflect their experiences as Asians living in America. They realized that constructing a separate identity and culture would be the only way to build self-esteem and begin forming a collective consciousness required for shared action in reforming society's structural racism against Asian Americans. In forging an Asian American identity, visionaries understood that they had to dismantle racialized stereotypes that belittle them, recoup their heritage and history in the United States, and recreate an identity

Figure 5.1. Leaders of the UC Berkeley Third World Liberation Front; from left to right: Richard Aoki (Asian American Political Alliance), Charles Brown (African American Students Union), and Manuel Delgado (Mexican American Students Union). *Muhammad Speaks*, February 7, 1969.

and culture that mirrored their experiences.[11] In recognizing that music and art had the advantage of voicing resistance and creating anew an alternative site, Japanese/Asian American youth harnessed music to instantiate their social and political empowerment.[12]

To properly understand the musical relationship between Asian American, African American, and Latinx artists, one must gain a solid grasp of the sociopolitical interdependence between these groups. Coalitional politics of the TWLF's strikes and Asian American movement in tandem with cultural nationalism promoted by the Black Arts movement—cultural arm of the Black liberation movement—propelled Sansei identity politics and musicking. The multiracial alliance of Black, Chicano, Native American, and Asian American students involved in the TWLF and their strikes moved to inaugurate courses that represented their histories and contributions to the nation as an integral part of university curricula (figure 5.1). Political activism spurred by the 1968–1969 TWLF strike at San Francisco State University and the University of California, Berkeley, raised student awareness of the social and economic inequalities not only in their communities caused by discrimination in education, employment, and housing but also, by extension, in Third World countries as well, victims of capitalist industrial policies. Such incitement along with protests opposing the Vietnam War prompted Asian

American students and community workers to coalesce, forming the Asian American movement (AAM), a panethnic Asian coalition needed to address and effect change. The AAM sought to strengthen the political position and participation of individuals and their communities in overcoming the civic ostracism imposed on earlier generations.

Social scientist Diane Fujino singles out a Japanese American political lineage, linking the radicalism of premovement activists—Yuri Kochiyama, Richard Aoki, and Mo Nishida—to the founding of the Asian American movement.[13] She narrates how Japanese American radicalism grew out of these activists' connection to Black communities and Black resistance in the mid-1960s. The Black liberation movement nourished Kochiyama's, Aoki's, and Nishida's oppositional consciousness, which had its origins in Japanese Americans' resistance to their incarceration in the concentration camps of World War II. The three were incarcerated as adolescents. The emotional residue of that damaging lived experience compounded by the "economic barriers and residential segregation" that families endured following the war all contributed to the revolutionary nationalist or socialist leanings of the three Japanese American politicos.[14]

Richard Aoki directly navigated the Asian American movement, initially forming the Asian American Political Alliance in 1968 and, in the following year, serving as the Asian American spokesperson of the TWLF strike in its call for ethnic-studies curricula at San Francisco State University (SFSU) and UC Berkeley. Aoki grew up in the Black ghetto, West Oakland, home of the Black Panther Party (BPP), which he joined and eventually became political adviser for, instructing Huey Newton and Bobby Seale in Marxist, Leninist, and Maoist thought. Aoki's political experience and background in the Black Power movement provided a solid base for the success of the TWLF strike and the AAM.

Nisei Yuri Kochiyama's radicalization in New York City took ideological form that combined cultural nationalism, civil rights, and socialism.[15] Attending Malcolm X's Organization of Afro-American Unity's Liberation School, Kochiyama understood the importance of moving beyond integrationism and reform and instead push for racial autonomy and equal rights.[16] The breadth of her activities included promoting social justice for African Americans, Puerto Ricans, and Asian Americans, taking part in anti-imperialist and anti–Vietnam War protests, and labor organizing. It was her Black separatist views and interest in the use of art and culture in social movements that played an influential role in the rise of the AAM.

The following chronicles the Asian American movement's role in mobilizing a political agenda and catalyzing an emergent identity and hybrid music.

The movement embodied what Coco Fusco considers "two interrelated but seemingly contradictory struggles over identity."[17] The first falls within the public sphere of political representation and the need for people of color to be able to govern how they are to be characterized, defining for themselves their cultural boundaries as a step toward dismantling inequality. This requires engaging power relations involved in symbolic representation and negotiating control. A second struggle over identity emphasizes promoting cross-cultural and cross-racial hybridity as a strategy to unify communities of color in building a power base. Fusco asserts that "artistic and musical hybridity, irreverence, and exuberance create conditions for spiritual and cultural renewal, as well as critical reinterpretations of the world in which we live."[18] The seeming contradiction of these two approaches is that while the first calls for delineating one's identity and cultural boundaries (a danger in becoming essentialist and separate), the second prescribes blurring those boundaries in hybridity. I view the two approaches as processual. Before one can contribute to cross-cultural projects, one must have cultivated an intrinsic sense of self and have an idea of how to represent that self. The Asian American movement made it possible for Asian Americans to initiate control over their representation. The appellation "Asian American" revitalized Americans claiming their Asian heritage, making it possible to shed "Oriental," a term that cast Asian Americans as foreign and inassimilable. The confluence of cultures in the work of Japanese/Asian American musician-composers point to the hybrid nature of their compositions. Musicians could now "move back and forth between past and present, between history and fiction, between art and ritual, between high art and popular culture, and between Western and non-Western influences. In doing so, they participate in multiple communities."[19] Although the AAM was salient to the rise of Asian American musical explorations, many musicians were at cross purposes with radical political colleagues who favored the creation of "simpler songs with straightforward lyrics emphasizing the party line."[20] Simple songs could serve as a tool for social change at protest rallies, uniting participants in a common cause. Many musicians were interested in developing an aesthetic that would recast their identity and image according to their own vision, while others—Jon Jang, Frances Wong, Fred Ho (New York)—proactively composed music ideologically linked to the Asian American movement.[21] Artists did not limit themselves to creating only politically charged music; they utilized music, particularly improvisation, as a means for cross-cultural communication to support their universalist ideals.

One song that could be considered an anthem of the AAM is "We Are the Children" (1970), composed by Chris Iijima and Nobuko Miyamoto, folk singers

Figure 5.2. Joanne Nobuko Miyamoto, Chris Iijima, and Charlie Chin, n.d. Photo by Bob Hsiang

who performed this and other politically inspired songs at college rallies, conferences, and political gatherings as they toured nationally (figure 5.2). "We Are the Children" promotes coalition not only among Asian Americans but alongside US Indigenous people and freedom fighters around the globe. The final verse demands unity and making "our" mark in working toward greater equality and inclusion. The chorus is self-affirming and a call to action. A blues-inflected melody, lyrics recounting the history and marginalization of Asians in America, and the accompaniment of conga rhythms sonically represent a partnership between African Americans, Asian Americans, and Latinx. The catchy melody and singable lyrics invited audiences to participate, reinforcing their resolve.

The lyrics of "We Are the Children" is as follows:

We are the children of the migrant worker
We are the offspring of the concentration camp
Sons and daughters of the railroad builder
Who leave their stamp on Amerika.

[chorus]
Sing a song for ourselves.
What have we got to lose?
Sing a song for ourselves.
We got the right to choose.

We are the children of the Chinese waiter,
Born and raised in the laundry room.
We are the offspring of the Japanese gardener,
Who leave their stamp on Amerika.

[chorus]

Foster children of the Pepsi Generation,
Cowboys and Indians—ride, red-man, ride!
Watching war movies with the next-door neighbor,
Secretly rooting for the other side.

[chorus]

We are the cousins of the freedom fighter,
Brothers and sisters all around the world.
We are a part of the Third World people
Who will leave their stamp on Amerika.
Who will leave our stamp on Amerika.

[chorus].[22]

Attaining power and a voice in the social, economic, and political landscape requires an identity and culture that stands for itself in the culturally pluralist United States. This prerequisite made identity and its concomitant culture a central aim of the Asian American movement in advancing its ability to act politically.[23] Groundbreaking in the AAM's process of building an Asian American identity was the "multiethnic racial formation" that altered Asian Americans' notions about their race and national belonging in reconfiguring a new Asian American identity.[24]

Anti–Vietnam War activism paired with Third World struggles further raised Asian American racial and political consciousness. The evolving Asian American coalition mobilized high-school youth, tenants, small-business owners, workers, senior citizens, and new immigrants to build an extensive network of grassroots organizations that provided community social services and spaces for emerging Asian American artists and cultural workers. The Asian American Political Alliance (AAPA) was one of the driving forces of the movement, and they skillfully linked Asian American activists in different parts of the United States by organizing AAPA chapters that kept members informed of political goals and activities. Although individuals and organizations represented competing ideologies—of reformers, revolutionary nationalists, cultural nationalists, and mixtures in between—they agreed on the major assertion that the most cogent means for battling racism and imperialism is forging "multiethnic, racially-based" alliances.[25]

Constructing an Asian American identity has been and continues to be a complex racial project. In his study of the shifting identities and politics of Nisei and Sansei, sociologist Jere Takahashi refers to racial formation as both "a social and historical process," "an unstable and 'decentered' complex of social meanings constantly being transformed by political struggle."[26] The TWLF strike brought into contact white, Black, Asian, Chicano, and Native American activists, representing, in microcosm, race relations that need to be negotiated if we are to disassemble racial and cultural classifications built to separate us. Japanese/Asian American musician-composers blazed a path as they traversed the bifurcated racial and national space between whiteness and Blackness in their search for a sociopolitical identity. In light of Asian Americans' racial development from the 1960s on, Maeda characterizes Claire Jean Kim's notion of racial triangulation as "a social construct that enables us to understand how Asian Americans exist not simply as intermediaries between black and white but instead as a racial group formed through constant comparisons to both blacks and whites."[27] Racial triangulation frames the interracial connection and boundary crossings with Blacks and whites experienced by Asian Americans in the formation of their racial identity.[28] While racial triangulation clarifies the connectivity between the three groups, there is still much to discover in terms of the degree to which such encounters with whites and Blacks influenced or shaped Asian American racial identity.[29] In the dawning of Asian American cultural production, it is true that interaction with Black musicians far outweighed any connection to whiteness; in fact, they tended to resist whiteness in a strategic move away from assimilation. The performance of Blackness racially located Asian American musicians alongside a racial group to whose history and artistry they felt a stronger affinity.[30] Black performance style sparked a musical direction for Asian American artists as they set out to forge an aesthetic of their own.

BREAKING NEW GROUND

Asian American art exhibiting social and political veracity already existed. Artist and writer Lucia Enriquez attributes the beginnings of Asian American art in the early part of the twentieth century to isolated individual artists of Asian descent and their efforts to express the exigencies of being Asian American. She writes: "At this point in its evolution, what represents the movement is not any particular artistic style but rather conditions and messages describing the social and political reality of Asian America. Although many Asian American artists derive influences from variously linked Asian and American traditions, a sense of diversity, independence, and resiliency rather than the propagation of tradition propels the movement."[31] The multiplicity of voices in Asian American art is evident early on. This quote infers the social and political intent of fracturing the national culture of the United States by intermingling both Asian and American elements in very individual ways. Enriquez's insight brings attention to the Asian diasporic interpretations of artists' work in expressing their independence and reaction to the social and political conditions of living in America.

In fashioning art that was both politically and aesthetically dynamic, Asian American artists turned to Black cultural nationalists who actively generated poetry, literature, and visual arts, as well as theater, dance, and music performances as avenues to achieve their political liberation. Art functioned as a vehicle for nationalists to express the richness of their African heritage and "notions of a Black identity."[32] A central concept of the Black Arts movement (BAM) was their assertion of a "Black aesthetic" that was pan-African in scope. A Black aesthetic celebrated core African traditions and forms and their African diasporic interpretations, improvisation, and innovative and experimental approaches to the arts.[33]

The creative force of artists in the BAM spawned Asian American literary and visual art collectives in San Francisco and New York, building a cultural base for Asian American musicking. Determined to change their powerless and invisible sociopolitical status as the silent minority, Asian Americans reached for cultural forms that liberated them and voiced their new political viability. Black cultural nationalists embodied the idea of culture as a form of resistance, a concept advanced by the African revolutionary Amilcar Cabral, who prescribed a "return to the source" (one's ethnic, ancestral roots) for artists and activists as a fundamental principle of national liberation.[34] Such ideas fueled the newly imagined political identity of being "Asian" American and not "Oriental."[35] The BAM offered a site of resistance, a subversive potential, and a strategy for Asian American artists as they sought new subjectivities to express an emboldened political stance.

The TWLF strikes reinforced cultural nationalism. In their demands to institute ethnic studies programs, the Third World Liberation Front required that each student organization be given the freedom to design their own curriculum. Integral were courses that taught the cultural histories and struggles against colonialism and oppression tailored for each student demographic.[36] The idea of constructing a cultural identity was central to the activities of Asian American artists taking part in the strikes. Poets Janice Mirikitani and Francis Oka sparked the formation of the Third World Communications Collective, the Third World Women's Collective, and the publication of the first Asian American journal, *Aion*. The radical newspaper *Gidra* provided exposure for artists by publishing graphic art, photography, fiction, and poetry. Both publications laid the groundwork for the rise of the Asian American arts movement.[37]

Spurred by artistic collaborations among artists in the Black Arts movement, revolutionary nationalist artists within the AAM initiated community arts organizations and media that encompassed Visual Communications, Japantown Art and Media, Kearny Street Workshop, Asian Cinevision, Community Asian American Mural Project (Oakland/Bay Area), *Bridge Magazine*, *East Wind Magazine*, Basement Workshop (New York), Ating Tao, Kalayan, and Dragon Thunder Arts Forum.[38] Activists housed these organizations in the International Hotel in Chinatown, a residential hotel for Asian immigrant workers, mostly Filipino bachelors, with the purpose of embedding themselves in the community. The proximity of the art groups and the community promoted creative collaborations, cultivating a fertile milieu for Asian American artists and musicians. These cultural workers made a conscious effort to forge an Asian American aesthetic with loosely created parameters, allowing for individual interpretations and style but evoking an Asian sensibility.

Many Asian American musician-composers intentionally chose Black music as a starting point in developing their own voice—looking to Black musicians who had already started their journey toward experimentation, self-determination, and community building. Artists drew inspiration from politically minded musicians, such as Max Roach, Archie Shepp, and Charles Mingus, and from "the symbolically charged fervor of John Coltrane, the far-reaching representational and compositional ambitions of Duke Ellington, and the resistance strategies of the '60s jazz avant-garde."[39] Others actually had the opportunity to perform with or be mentored by artists James Newton, Roscoe Mitchell, Muhal Richard Abrams, or George Lewis; the latter three were influential members of the Association for the Advancement of Creative Music based in Chicago. Some musicians, however, interrogate Asian Americans' move toward Blackness. Pianist, kotoist, composer, and activist Miya Masaoka considers the issue of Asian American artists utilizing African American music forms as problematic; she feels that Asian Americans need to define themselves in their own ethnic and cultural terms first. Masaoka asks, "How many of us can speak our mother tongue, or sing even one song from our cultural heritage? As Asian Americans, we need to self-examine how we relate to our own culture. Only then can we look to other cultures."[40] This statement echoes Fusco's interconnected but seemingly contradictory struggles over identity and cultural boundaries. Although other Asian American artists have expressed a similar self-consciousness in regard to engaging African American music genres for their own work, they nevertheless feel strongly about their rapport with Black musicians and the bold, creative impulse they are able to capture in their work as a result of interacting with these musicians.

In formulating a creative musical style that addressed their newly emerging sense of self, Asian American musicians drew inspiration from central features of African American music's Black aesthetic, rooted in African music and culture. The Black aesthetic encompasses call and response, polyrhythmic layering, syncopation, improvisation, and interplay between soloist and ensemble. Improvisation, soulfulness, innovation, and experimentation directed musicians along a cultural continuum that elicited new ways of playing and *feeling* music, intended to connect one's past, present, and future.[41] For Asian American artists, that meant connecting their Asian past to their Asian American present through improvisation and experimentation, creating an aesthetic and affect that suggested a cultural link to Asia.

Paul Yamazaki, formerly a bass clarinetist and early organizer of San Francisco's Asian American Jazz Festival, draws a connection between Asian American artists and the Asian American Political Alliance established by students at the University of California, Berkeley, and San Francisco State University. He recollects:

> I think for a lot of us a really important person in the AAPA was Francis Oka, who was an important poet. He and Janice Mirikitani put together one of the first Asian American cultural magazines, called *Aion*. So, through these activities, at the same time, people were setting up cultural centers in the various communities. In the Asian community, the Kearny Street Workshop was a direct result of that. All the work that had been done at San Francisco State University and other places was brought back to communities in a cultural context.[42]

Artistic activity intertwined with political activity in the hands of poets, writers, visual artists, and musicians. Asian American artists aspired to express their political beliefs through art forms and established cultural centers as a means to support their communities. Performing artists were active in the early stages of emerging Asian American art forms. Yamazaki continues:

> The San Jose group was particularly important. G [Gerald Oshita] was down there at that time. Russel Baba also was down at San Jose State. Founding members of theater groups came out of San Jose. So, there was this kind of huge spectrum throughout the whole Bay Area of cultural and political activity from '68 to the early seventies. Organizations were being formed rapidly in developing community work. And then, out of these efforts, people continued their further individual expression.[43]

San Jose, just south of San Francisco, played an active role in the emergence of new music by Japanese American musicians. The musical innovators Gerald Oshita and Russel Baba pushed for new sounds and musical routes. The founding of San Jose Taiko in the 1970s by J. P. and Roy Hirabayashi further placed San Jose as an important site for Japanese American musicking. Their vision and dedication led to forming a *taiko* ensemble that could speak for newly empowered Japanese American students and cultural workers involved in or bolstered by the Asian American movement.

THE QUEST FOR FREEDOM

The Asian American creative music scene in San Francisco coalesced around musician-composers searching for new avenues in music. The 1970s mark the efforts of groundbreaking musician-improvisors: Gerald Oshita (saxophone), Paul Yamazaki (clarinet), Russel Hisashi Baba (saxophone), and Mark Izu (bass). All hailed from the Bay Area and formed bands with African American musicians originally from music collectives in the Midwest. The African American transplants who partnered with Bay Area musicians were saxophonist Lewis Jordan, trumpeter George Sams, saxophonist Ray Collins, and drummer Eddie Moore. The bands they formed set a precedent for future collaborations. Four groups emerged: Lewis Jordan's Liberation at Large Orchestra and three Afro-Asian bands—Eddie Moore and Russell Baba's Space Shuttle Omnibus, Mark Izu and Lewis Jordan's group Marron, and United Front, the most active band, whose members included Mark Izu, Anthony Brown (drums), Lewis Jordan, and George Sams.[44]

Many Japanese/Asian American musicians were members of the Asian Improv Records collective of performing artists, including dancers and actors, all whose individual approaches to composition and presentation exhibited multiple streams of influences in a primarily jazz-based music. Asian Improv Records (AIR) began as a San Francisco–based recording company in 1987 not only to promote Asian American musician-composers who wanted to record and to market their music but also to exhort artists to be active in assisting the development of their communities. Many musicians drew their inspiration from the political drive of the Asian American movement. When the movement's activities subsided, AIR filled the vacuum, providing a space for musician-composers to persist in honing their professionalism and maintaining an active music scene.[45] Activist founders of this independent record label, Francis Wong and Jon Jang, had resolved that the time to end the exclusion of Asian American artists from educational and cultural institutions, as well as the American entertainment industry, had come. Some of AIR's recording artists—Wong, Jang, Fred Ho, and Glenn Horiuchi—had been members of the League of Revolutionary Struggle (LRS). The LRS affiliation of these artists point to the initial revolutionary nationalist stance and mission of AIR, which was considered an achievement for the artists involved and for the Asian American movement. Saxophonist Fred Ho defined the approach taken by this organization: "By developing close working relationships with progressive and supportive music critics, presenters, musical organizations and Asian community groups, AIR is contributing to an effort for a real alternative, multicultural new American music movement."[46] AIR promoted the notion that the success of Asian American artists is linked to the political empowerment of Asian American communities.

Seminal recordings produced by AIR—Jon Jang's *The Ballad or the Bullet*,[47] saxophonist Fred Ho's *A Song for Manong*, and pianist Glenn Horiuchi's *Next Step*—all feature music about the struggle of Asians and other oppressed people in America. AIR's artistic goals challenged artists to know their Asian American history and to develop a distinct musical voice by incorporating traditional Asian music elements into their work.[48] Other musicians in this collective throughout the 1980s and 1990s included bassist Mark Izu, percussionist Anthony Brown, kotoist and pianist Miya Masaoka, saxophonist and multi-instrumentalist Hafez Modirzadeh, percussionist and *taiko* drummer Kenny Endo, bassist Tatsu Aoki, pianist and violinist Vijay Iyer, bassist Jeff Song, Kulintang Arts, and many more; all collaborated and performed on one another's AIR recordings. Musician-composers wrote for both small and large ensembles, either composing collectively or creating more formal concert-style pieces with full scores. With the waning influence of the Asian American movement, artists today have gone in different directions with performance practices, sonic worlds, and approaches, varying greatly within the collective.

In the San Francisco Bay Area, we find that free jazz[49] had a strong pull on musicians in their quest for freedom of expression. The idea of returning to one's cultural source and the improvisational freedom offered in free jazz is central to the cues Asian Americans took from African American musicians. Free jazz was revolutionary in moving beyond a predetermined harmonic structure or a fixed number of bar lines; opening a space to explore atonality; boldly applying and interpreting musical sound into the realm of noise;[50] "thematically developing melodies rather than harmonies; highlighting collective improvisation; using drums to add color and texture; utilizing pedal points and ostinatos in creating static harmonic environments; performing angular, jagged intervals to express abstraction; and employing modal scales and polyrhythms."[51] These innovative approaches enriched the jazz vocabulary of the day, propelling Asian American musician-composers to create their own musical landscape. The appeal of jazz was its spirit of openness to musical ideas.

Free jazz was an expressive medium of the African American "avant-garde" starting in the second half of the 1950s. Activist musician, composer, author, and producer Fred Ho asserts that revolutionary nationalism of the Black avant-garde served as a framework for deconstructing "white-supremacist" national culture based on "Eurocentric patriarchal capitalism" and inspiring new forms of music, poetry, theater, and other arts for a "new society that promoted equality and justice for all."[52] Ho proposes that the Black avant-garde begins with the jazz maker Sun Ra in the 1950s, followed by the musical experimentation and innovations of the Art Ensemble of Chicago, a performing unit affiliated with the Association for the Advancement of Creative Musicians. The intent of these artists was to "return to the source" and borrow, reinterpret, and rework musical elements from their African past within the broad parameters of the avant-garde.[53] Some historians attribute the inauguration of the free-jazz movement in 1959 to Ornette Coleman and his innovative concept of "harmolodics."[54] Coleman firmly rooted his music in African American folk and blues traditions. Although the music was harmonically abstract, one could discern the blues and gospel influence. More abstract variations of free jazz and its aggressive collective improvisations were associated with the radical Black Power movement.[55]

Percussionist and composer Anthony Brown traces the trajectory of free jazz's connection to politics and social protest:

What spoke to the early pioneers [of free/progressive jazz] was the fact that jazz has been a vehicle of protest, and it's a megaphone, at least a grapevine for the African American community for spreading and continuing ideas of protest and addressing issues of social equality or inequality. Of course, this history goes all the way back in African American jazz to 1939 with the recording of Billy Holiday's "Strange Fruit." So, that legacy of jazz serving as a vehicle for social protest was something I'm sure resonated among Asian American musicians because they saw African Americans not only playing the music but using the music to address inequality. What I think was most attractive about progressive jazz, or avant-garde jazz, or free jazz was that you could hear the independence in the music. The zeitgeist, or the original idea behind the original movement in the late fifties, was to break away from the conventions of jazz that were felt to be restrictive at the time and to limit individual expression. So, in the late fifties and early sixties free jazz musicians started to really express themselves in an aesthetic that was mirroring the civil rights movement and a new consciousness of the black community. And even though free jazz never enjoyed a great deal of commercial popularity among musicians and artists, it served primarily as a vehicle for social protest and a vehicle for social expression, allowing for a new identity through music. And that identity was one of independence and a very progressive outlook on a new social order.[56]

An established musical style by the 1960s, free jazz was a cultural nationalist art form of the Black Arts movement, and musicians Archie Shepp, Pharaoh Sanders, Sun Ra, the Art Ensemble of Chicago, Eric Dolphy, Albert Ayler, Ornette Coleman, John Coltrane, and others served as musical spokesmen for the Black community. Using the term "free jazz" coincides with the spirit of breaking away from or resisting conventional ways of approaching and developing musical ideas; for Asian Americans, it symbolized freeing themselves from their state of inequality. As well, a more introspective approach toward one's artistry is what first attracted Asian American musician-composers to this improvisational music. Paul Yamazaki articulated the sentiment this way: "What inspired many Asian American musicians was that in African American improvisational music, to really become a good improviser you have to explore the self. For the Asian American, part of that self is . . . taking a deeper look into Asian American culture and what informed that."[57] Appealing to Asian American music makers was the collective aspect of African American improvisational music. Musicians from a variety of cultural backgrounds, composing and performing together and moving between and across musical parameters, continue to experience that cooperative spirit. In free jazz, the egalitarian participation of band members is critical in collectively exploring new musical horizons.

The importance of improvisation for cross-cultural and intercultural communication as an expression of one's humanity is a widely held notion among musicians. Trombonist, composer, and teacher George Lewis, a guiding figure for many Asian American jazz makers, instilled this idea. Lewis's influence as a composer-improvisor had to do with his innovative approaches to composition and improvisation shaped by his training with Muhal Richard Abrams of the AACM school. A protégé of Lewis, saxophonist, composer, and violinist Francis Wong speaks about Lewis's notion of improvisation as an effective means to interact with other musicians. Because improvisation is not defined by an a priori musical structure, it allows dialogue between musicians, a space in which people can speak their own language yet communicate with one another:

> Improvisation is a very organic way to develop language. So, one looks at music as a language. A major part of the way we develop language is by talking to each other. Also, it's the different personalities. So, improvisation just means you're having this ongoing conversation with musicians who are going through their lives. Like me and Hafez [Modirzadeh], we kind of have this ongoing dialogue playing our instruments, but also talking to each other. That's how our relationship develops. In a lot of ways, that's what improvisation allows for, to get closer to that kind of intimate conversation that people have with speech. In some ways, it could be more intimate when you're getting beyond words. More down to spiritual and emotional communication. It humanizes the music.[58]

Improvisational exchanges create meaning for those making music together; Asian American musicians found the shared experience exciting.

Yamazaki's perspective on improvisation broadens the idea of dialogue and communication and the potential for coalition through music: "Improvisation was key: it was all within the context of what was happening in the group and that dialogue back and forth. So many of us thought of it as a social metaphor, the embodiment of a larger, possible ideal of how people can work together without expressing the individual and enhancing the collective." The leading figure who helped musicians to develop the practice was Gerald Oshita, nicknamed "G." Yamazaki recalls:

G was one of those people able to articulate it most clearly to a lot of us. He would help us with our thinking; as well, he was a musical and individual example. G had been out there by himself, playing the music that even jazz people thought was contemptuous. There was a lot of controversy about what people called free jazz, and [G] was right out there in the forefront of all that development and had thought a lot about it; he was able to articulate it and it came through his music and his relationship to a huge variety of instruments that he was conversant with. I think all of these things tie into the [TWLF] liberation movement, along with Amiri Baraka, Max Roach, and Archie Shepp and all of those people who were earlier. These were all part of the influences that helped shape creative Asian American music at that time. I think the major thing that people should take away is that the African American musical experience has been this incredible gift to the entire world. The core of it, in a certain way, is that it is the little spark in the center of how an individual can function with full freedom within a group context. The great thing that African American music has given us is a really concrete way of expressing our humanity, an example of how that can be a more ideal world. So, when we see people improvising, you see a glimpse of what a possible world could be with that sort of cooperation and interaction.[59]

According to Yamazaki, the combined forces of improvisation, liberatory politics of the Third World Liberation Front movement, and African American political activism and art played a part in shaping Asian American creative music. Further, improvisation opened a space to express one's humanity with others in a spirit of collaboration and utopian possibilities.

Improvisation enabled many Asian American musicians to grow and express themselves freely within a collective. Koto performer Miya Masaoka, whose work has been a part of San Francisco's Asian American creative-music scene since the 1980s, views improvisation as a critical ingredient that informs her artistic insight:

I think that is a big part of what I do and a big part of what the role of improvisation is in this whole notion and construct of free jazz. Thinking about different ways of improvising is the very critical thing I was always honing in on. There's thinking of ways of improvising as a soloist, thinking of ways of improvising as a duo, which is very, very different, and ways of improvising as a trio, and then as a whole orchestra.

> So, that's been the crux of a lot of my work when I put together the Masaoka Orchestra for the album called *What's the Difference between Stripping and Playing the Violin?* So, this notion of improvising is very deep in the sense that it's a lifelong kind of study, and just learning about what improvisation is from Cecil Taylor and Ornette Coleman, whom I was also able to work with in the 90s. I've been step-by-step going on this road, learning more about improvisation, what it means in different contexts with different musicians and different species because I've done performances with different insects, and now I'm doing performances with plants. So, it's improvising and interacting with plants and thinking about improvisation as an interactive activity that occurs and what that means. It's something that could be considered the free jazz part of things [and], in the older sense, can go in and out of styles to a certain extent in terms of ways of playing, which definitely are related to the times and to people.[60]

Masaoka's improvisational artistry continues to expand as she integrates computer and laser technology to broaden her sonic palette and enhance the visual impact of her work.

An active and innovative member in San Francisco's music scene is saxophonist and composer Hafez Modirzadeh. When he began his musical collaborations with Francis Wong, Mark Izu, Miya Masaoka, Anthony Brown, and many others in the 1980s, he discovered that musicians were looking toward a variety of Asian musical systems and sources for their sonic explorations. His Persian musical heritage was his source of inspiration for composing and improvising.

> As I look into my Persian musical heritage, I find that it relates best to a free jazz kind of mindset. When my Asian brothers and sisters look towards Korea, Japan, and China, and all the way down to the Southeast, they found several systems that were open and accommodated approaches that were very closely related to Ornette Coleman's music. Because if you listen to Ornette's melodies, I relate them very closely to Burmese, to Myanmar, to *saung* [arched harp] melodies.

Modirzadeh notes the contributions made toward the rise of free jazz in Ornette Coleman's harmolodics, George Russell's Lydian chromatic concepts, and Coltrane's use of the suspended sound of quartal harmonies combined with African-based rhythms in expanding the then-existing harmonic landscape and its improvisational possibilities. Modirzadeh gives tribute to those that came before him in providing a platform for greater freedom in musical composition and performance: "I think, also, we can't ignore or deny the fact that John Cage, Lou Harrison, and others who had a Buddhist understanding were creating a lot of music by the forties and early fifties, along with Cecil Taylor. I'm assuming, but I can say that certainly with the so-called avant-garde movement, there was a comfortable grey area between so-called jazz and so-called twentieth-century experimental music."[61] Noting the congruency between free or avant-garde jazz and twentieth-century experimental music, the saxophonist suggests yet another possible impulse in the evolution of Asian American musicking and the search for a sound that could represent them.

Asian American musician-composers experiment with applying musical systems and practices in their work. In devising a method that combines Persian music and jazz, for example, Modirzadeh created a cross-cultural musical practice: chromodal discourse. Here is his definition:

> Chromodal Discourse is a unifying approach which superimposes various parameters between two or more musical idioms in order for both to flourish simultaneously beyond their traditional boundaries. And yet, instead of blurring these boundary lines, cultures' musical distinctions are continually enhanced, this by reinforcing, rather than dissolving, their traditional acoustical and rhythmical characteristics within a single performance context. So, *how* can distinctness of style be exposed when universals are concentrated upon, indeed, *how* can such perceptions of particularity and universality be compatible? Furthermore, how can a musical perspective *in itself be both* inclusive as well as exclusive?
>
> These questions really involve the larger scope of Chromodal Discourse, linked to an understanding sympathetic to those common sensitivities that reach beyond cultural barriers, sensitivities shared by humanity as a whole, such as separation, community, faith, love or passion—conditions of life related here through storytelling and music.[62]

Within this approach, Modirzadeh clarifies his impetus:

> I've been in this place so far with my latest CD, wanting to work within accessible formats as a way to get into the eye of the storm, into the lion's den, subverted, changed, and transformed from within. I've been wanting, from inside, to stretch and change, and . . . also my chromodal

concept focuses a lot on using limitations. It focuses on complementary opposites: Sufi and Dao concepts of complementary opposites. So, expanding by contraction, the idea that by mastering limitations, looking at limitations in limited situations, you squeeze or find your freedom. This is also an important concept that African Americans have lived through: through limited situations finding an incredible and creative potential and realizing it. I look for parameters, that's what I am always dealing with, where are the structures, so I can work through them. I'm looking for liberation. I'm looking for a spiritual, . . . I'm looking for a connectedness, not a liberation necessarily from a condition.[63]

Other musicians I interviewed echo the same sentiment; for them, improvisation offers a transcendent path in bridging to others, a perspective gleaned from the struggle, resilience, and innovation of African Americans. Modirzadeh adds his perspective on music as a unifying practice:

The great thing that we've been given from our African American legacy is the ability to transform anger into love. Because music has transformative powers. Sadness into celebration: it's a type of mystic alchemy. So, there's a universalism that can be played out when you talk about freedom in that regard. But now we're in a time in the world where we need to look at our commonalities as a humanity.

With the events in the world, it seems that what's more important for us is improvisation: anything that can go across cultures to help us see what our common humanity is. That, to me, would be our mission.[64]

Cofounder of Asian Improv Records Francis Wong offers what he considers the overall context for the rise of Asian American music. He describes the evolution of Asian American art and music as an organic outgrowth of people affirming their humanity, their culture, and themselves. Here too, Wong sought inspiration from African American musicians, testifying how they had "a way of being . . . carrying yourself as a human being. If the society says you're less than human, what are your practices that affirm your humanity? And a lot of that music was an affirmation of the humanity of the African American people. That's what was inspiring to everybody in the world!"[65]

Artists who took part in the Third World Liberation Front strike formed an artistic community of poets, actors, dancers, writers, visual artists, and musicians, who desired to find their place, their creative voice. Artists formed relationships and spent time together, often meeting for drinks to exchange ideas at Red's Bar in Chinatown. Collaborative projects resulted, such as the publication of an anthology called *Time Degrees*, and organizations were formed, like the Jackson Street Gallery, the Kearny Street Workshop, the Kalian Collective, and other cultural organizations established and run by student activists in the basement of the I-Hotel, a residential hotel located at Jackson Street and Kearny Street in San Francisco's Manilatown. The one-block square of gallery space for artists, poets, dancers, muralists, and social workers in the I-Hotel merged and interacted with leftist college students and the tenants, mostly *manongs*—bachelor Filipino workers. For Wong, this coalition of artists, social workers, and the I-Hotel community was the heart of the movement. Activities and events at the I-Hotel molded the cultural and social milieu from which Asian American music emerged. Wong asserts that this self-consciously Asian American idea about playing music came about after the TWLF strike. Music was associated with integrating the political, social, cultural, and artistic. In addition to discovering one's own creative voice, it was through the arts that many musicians connected to their communities.[66] Wong calls attention to the community-driven impetus of Asian American art and music in the Bay Area. He speaks for artists whose work comes out of their participation in and relationship to their communities, pointing out that Japantown, Chinatown, and Manilatown served as important sites for Asian American creative musicking. Notably, Wong singles out Japanese American musician-composers as primary influences in the embryonic stages of Asian American creative music. Trailblazing musicians stimulated a great deal of musical activity and experimentation. Russel Baba, Makoto Horiuchi (guitar), Mark Izu, Anthony Brown, Glenn Horiuchi, Hafez Modirzadeh, P. J. and Roy Hirabayashi (*taiko*), Joanne Nobuko Miyamoto, George Abe (shakuhachi), and Hiroshima (jazz fusion) band members all created a sound that was impactful but, most importantly, an aesthetic that captured a certain Japanese sensibility shaped by local tastes and personal inclinations.

In rearticulating their heritage through music, Sansei turned to a number of sources from which to evoke a Japanese sensibility and aesthetic in their work. Sansei exposure to Japanese music took place in numerous contexts: home (recordings, radio, live), especially if they were living with Issei grandparents; cultural festivals (e.g., Obon festival); varied performances in the community; and Buddhist services. Japanese folk songs (*minyō*), Buddhist chanting (*shōmyō*), chamber music of the koto, shamisen, and shakuhachi, *shigin*, and music of the Kabuki theater were all part of the soundscape in Japanese American homes and communities in California. Folk music was frequently heard in rural communities, at festivals, and in urban centers at concerts by local musicians and visiting folk ensembles from Japan. Sansei musicians developed their aesthetic palette through direct instruction of the musical traditions of *gagaku* (ancient court music), koto, shamisen, shakuhachi, and *taiko*. Immersion in these genres introduced Sansei to Japanese instrumental and vocal techniques and repertoire, pentatonic scales and traditional melodies, musical phrasing and form, rhythmic timing, aesthetic concepts, and timbres inherent in Japanese music.

Learning traditional Japanese music was vital for musicians in attempting to capture Japanese musical subtleties in their work. Bay Area musicians had a rare opportunity to study *gagaku* in a class taught by Master Suenobu Togi—a trained musician and dancer of the Japanese imperial court—at the Buddhist Studies Institute in Berkeley.[67] The class played a decisive role in connecting pathfinding–Asian American musician-composers in their search for musical inspiration. The years of 1976–1977 mark a fertile time, when everyone in the *gagaku* group was actively composing. After rehearsals, they would head to Chinatown to share a meal and ideas. Their interactions buoyed collaborations on various projects as they performed in different bands together. *Gagaku* group participants included Russel Baba, Paul Yamazaki, Mark Izu, Bob Hsiang, Kenny Endo, Robert Kikuchi-Yngojo, Gordie Watanabe, Makoto Horiuchi, Miya Masaoka (later), and others. Many musicians came and went, departing with a changed musical perspective. Phrases shaped by breath length, the tripartite form *jo-ha-kyū*, and the aesthetic importance of *ma*—silences between notes, carrying as much weight as the sounding of notes—expanded musical parameters for these artists. Learning a twelve-hundred-year-old Japanese tradition was a particularly rich experience for Japanese American musicians. Among the musician-composers whom Master Togi taught, bassist Mark Izu was the most profoundly influenced. *Gagaku* remains an important sonic orientation in much of Izu's work, arising from lessons with Togi Sensei for more than forty years.

GERALD OSHITA: BOLD INNOVATOR

A Sansei musician-improvisor and multi-instrumentalist with a widely divergent background, including R&B, pop, rock, jazz, avant-garde, and traditional Japanese music, Gerald Oshita (nicknamed "G") emerged as a key figure in the Asian American creative-music scene. Oshita launched his R&B musical foundation as a teen, when he would furtively slip into San Francisco's Western Addition jazz clubs: Jimbo's, Bop City, Plantation Club, and other places along Divisadero Street.[68] His relationships with Black musicians ignited Afro-Asian interactions among Bay Area musicians. Saxophonist and flutist James Moody, whom Oshita considered his "musical father," gave the young musician a solid start. By the time Oshita performed solo saxophone at the Asian American Jazz Festival debut in San Francisco in 1981, he had already recorded and performed with Janis Joplin, Taj Mahal, and Michael Bloomfield. Due to his growing reputation, the Creative Music Foundation in Woodstock, New York, selected Oshita as an artist in residence to teach New Concepts in Composition jointly with Anthony Braxton, Joseph Jarman, and George Lewis.[69] G was also one of the first Sansei to travel to Japan to study shakuhachi and other bamboo flutes prior to the rise of the Asian American movement. While living in Japan, he performed music for avant-garde *butoh* (dance theater) performances and was introduced to the Japanese jazz scene by well-known saxophonist Sadao Watanabe. Both experiences enriched his sonic palette and expanded his musical inventiveness.[70] Well versed in the tradition of the blues, Oshita collaborated with Black musicians in his pursuit of more improvisational and unconventional music. In the 1980s, he collaborated with saxophonist and clarinetist Roscoe Mitchell of the Art Ensemble of Chicago and Tom Buckner, singer and musical director of the Arch Ensemble, in the ensemble Space, a free-music trio. The trio recorded an album in 1981, entitled *New Music for Woodwinds and Voice*. Using old, obscure instruments for new music, Oshita composed pieces for and improvised on sarrusophone, baritone sax, and Conn-o-sax on the album: "It was during a period in the creative music area when everybody was searching for new colors and textures, and these instruments gave that."[71]

In 1983, a cycle of compositions called the "Extinct Series" showcased the rare instruments Oshita revived. His oeuvre also included "Solo Piece for Alto," a composition rooted in the blues similar to Ornette Coleman's style in its "sustained notes, variations in pitch and volume, and performed mostly in the middle register at medium tempo."[72] G served as a conduit to innovative ideas and extended musical boundaries. One example is the "Piece for Eb Saxophone and Gong" in which he experimented with the sound of the saxophone to generate certain harmonics from the hanging gong with the intent of forming a dialogue between the two instruments. Interested in a scientific view of music, Oshita also explored theories of consonance and dissonance, chaos, and space expressed in musical textures and layers in his compositions, swaying musicians to think conceptually about music. The kernel of his influence on younger musicians is captured in the saxophonist's musings about the underpinnings of his work: "My music is an organic statement, doing naturally without the use of electronic devices. For instance, my use of circular breathing in the dance piece . . . I wanted to take that piece out of the realms of normality, to make a supernatural effort and hopefully inspire others to make such an effort themselves."[73]

Oshita's compositions exemplify a hybrid synthesis of traditional Asian music, European new music, and African American new music. As a Japanese American musician-composer at the forefront of the Bay Area's new music scene in the late 1960s, Oshita encouraged younger Asian American musicians eager to embark on sonic explorations of their own. Yamazaki details Oshita's inventiveness:

> G and Oliver Johnson in the early mid-sixties were doing parallel things as the AACM in Chicago or BAG in St. Louis.[74] My understanding was that it was a parallel development [among these groups], and they were experimenting with group collaboration and handing out noise makers to audiences and having them participate. I've talked to various musicians. All of them acknowledge G as a direct inspiration, both musically and as an individual. He was a role model of how to be an Asian American artist . . . Oshita also collaborated with dancers; G was working with Sachiko Nakamura who went on to found the Asian American Dance Collective in San Jose. And they were doing both movement and sound performances together.[75]

Oshita's innovative vigor, multi-instrumental facility, and capacity to bridge his creative spirit across artistic mediums, racial lines, and national borders qualify him as one of the principal Asian American musical figures particularly conversant in "where the music has been and where it might be going."[76]

RUSSEL BABA: INTUITIVE EXPLORER

Russel Baba followed Oshita's musical direction, teaching himself saxophone, flute, and percussion. Baba's intuitive musical approach influenced the direction of the Asian American music vanguard (figure 5.3). In following his muse, Baba broadened his musical boundaries while searching for his Japanese roots:

> Politically, it was just that time period. It was the sixties, early seventies, the Vietnam War and people discovering their own roots, self-esteem issues, those kinds of things. That's why I started playing *taiko*. I first started out playing jazz, and I always felt a little uncomfortable—that it was another world that I was a part of, but it wasn't part of my heritage. So, when I saw Tanaka Sensei play *taiko*, it hit me, and I wanted to study it.[77]

Figure 5.3. Russel Baba playing alto saxophone, 1996. Photo by James Adams.

Learning *taiko* and Japanese court music expanded his musical palette in sounding his cultural heritage:

> I was looking for ways to become closer to Japanese music and these things came up [*taiko* and *gagaku*]. So spiritually I felt I was finding what I was looking for. I got to a point where yeah, I'm playing black music, but I'm not black. I have to check out something about myself, so that's why I started *taiko*, *gagaku*, and that gave me a foundation.[78]

Baba echoes Paul Yamazaki's notion that one must know oneself before exploring and creating music that expresses one's perception and one's message.

> If you're sure of who you are, then you can . . . do anything. And that's why I feel if I never play *taiko* again and I play saxophone, I know the *taiko*'s there, and I'm sure about my culture. Other people wouldn't recognize maybe the Japanese or the *taiko* in my playing, but at least

I know it's there. And so, I feel much better about myself. I'm not just playing a Black person's music; I at least have my own foundation.[79]

The great appeal of *taiko* for Baba was the tradition's roots in Japanese culture together with the physicality and body awareness of drumming that contrasted greatly to playing woodwinds. Moving from Alaska to San Francisco in 1968, Baba narrates his entrance into the *taiko* world:

I started playing *taiko* in 1972. It was after I moved to San Francisco from Alaska and seeing the Cherry Blossom Festival for a couple of years in a row. I was very attracted to the *taiko*. I had never seen anything like it. To me, Japanese arts, musical arts, the koto are very refined kinds of music. So, when I saw *taiko*, it blew me away, especially to see women playing *taiko*! Growing up in Alaska, I didn't have much experience with an Asian community because it was basically my family, and that was it. I had no Asian identity really, so that was another factor that interested me in *taiko*—it was something Japanese.[80]

Following a ten-year stint playing with San Francisco Taiko Dojo, trained by Seiichi Tanaka, Baba and his wife, Jeanne Mercer, formed Mount Shasta Taiko in 1985; the group has become an important fixture in the Mount Shasta area, where they organize an annual ShastaYama Taiko Festival in Shastice Park. A full view of the Shasta twin mountain peaks creates a magnificent setting for a Japanese American rearticulation of a folk *taiko* tradition.

The variety of musical instruments Baba plays is indicative of his search for a musical voice that speaks to being Japanese American. When learning Japanese court music under the tutelage of Suenobu Togi in San Francisco, he chose one of the melody instruments:

I played *hichiriki* [double-reed pipe]. I picked that because it was sort of close to saxophone; it was also Togi Sensei's family's instrument. The way you play it, it's just like a voice. It's just incredible. So, I had a nice balance, from *taiko* to this court music; it was really wonderful to study under Togi. And that music is not improvised. It's all written out. I think it's one of the world's oldest written orchestral forms of music, and it's so complete, you can't add anything else to it, in my mind.[81]

Today, Baba continues to play both jazz and *taiko*. His approach to each genre is contrasting but complementary; *taiko* is formal—it requires a prescribed protocol and respectful behavior, while playing jazz is less circumscribed and freer, more individual. A feature of Baba's oeuvre is its embodiment and intertwining of Japanese music elements and jazz, giving meaning to his artistic output, thus fulfilling his sense of self. There's a certain flow and intensity in his music. His eponymous 1979 album, *Russel Hisashi Baba* (Ruba Music–BMI), pointed Asian American musicians toward a freer musical style and more experimental sounds:

> I've always been interested in more of a freer expression. It was my search for liberation in my own way because, as a human being, I'm still trapped on this Earth, I still have issues I have to deal with. But playing music gives me this freedom. I like the liberation and freedom of that style [free jazz]; I've listened to artists: John Coltrane, Ornette Coleman, Cecil Taylor, Eric Dolphy, and others.[82]

The music of Ornette Coleman and Eric Dolphy particularly inspired Baba and governed his musical approach. He drew insight from both artists when performing with drummer Eddie Moore's Space Shuttle Omnibus band. The group often played at the Jigoku (meaning "Hell," alluding to its basement location) club in San Francisco's Japantown; performing with this band gave him the improvisational training that helped launch his work. Baba collaborated with an array of Asian American musicians in San Francisco who later coalesced as a stable of musicians affiliated with Asian Improv Records. Paul Yamazaki recalls the community of artists whose numbers made it possible to launch the first Asian American jazz festival in 1981:

> Baba performed with Makoto Horiuchi and a lot of other people who were playing around with various people, and collaborations became more pronounced. Kenny Endo came up from Los Angeles and Mark Izu, from San Jose. Anthony Brown came into town. More and more people were coming around. And George Leong, who thought that a critical mass had been reached, was quite frankly tired of hearing musicians complain that there was a lack of venues and a lack of organization. So, he pretty bluntly stated that he would put together [an Asian American jazz festival] the first time because he had been excited about the music. He was one of the ones who really began making connections to prior generations of musicians, and he was very aware of the talented group of Filipino piano players coming out of Stockton. Anyway, he put together two days of music of several generations.[83]

The jazz festival coalesced the talent of Asian American musician-composers, catalyzed musical partnerships, provided a base for the evolving Asian American creative-music scene, and linked the prior generations' Filipino musicians with upcoming artists. It was an effervescent time.

Baba regarded jazz improvisation as fundamental to his musical development and Japanese American identity. He maintains that free forms allow musicians to explore and be open to new sounds and ways of playing. Baba took on the challenge to combine a jazz-saxophone style with *taiko* music and technique. In the long process of mastering both instruments, he has become more intuitive in fusing Japanese music into his jazz compositions. The synthesis does not always come easy: "Sometimes I don't accomplish what's inside my head, but it comes out in my heart somehow, and I listen to it later on, the recording, and I'm very pleased with how it comes out. This doesn't always happen. To play free, you have to accept what happens. You take risks and accept what comes out. That's the beauty of it too."[84] Baba's comment hones in on the process involved in his improvisatory explorations and the beauty and risk of expressing oneself freely.

The music on *Russel Hisashi Baba* spearheaded Japanese American musicking. "Ancestral Space," the second piece on the album, conjures the music of *nō* theater in its sparseness and sense of mystery, with accented high-pitched *nōkan* (transverse flute) notes projected in breath-length phrases and sustained notes suspended above rhythmic punctuations of a *shimé daiko* (a tunable shallow drum) accompanied by a bassline that alternates between meandering lines and short rhythmic motives. The interweaving of a second flute line thickens the texture accompanied by rhythmic figures played by a bowed-string bass to create tension and a sense of urgency. The music gives way to improvised passages that gradually build on the sounds of *gagaku*-inspired, accelerating drum rolls of the *kakko* (hour-glass-shaped drum) with steady rhythms of a second drum. The improvisational lines of the three instrumentalists flow freely in a minimalistic texture. Two flutists play modified *nōkan* melodic lines, using sustained notes juxtaposed with short motives, building tension. The musical form loosely suggests that of the Japanese tripartite—*jo-ha-kyū*—form in which the tempo and thickening texture gradually increases to a climax, followed by a diminuendo. The piece nears its end with a steady, repeated rhythm performed on Tibetan drum and concludes with a single ringing of a Tibetan bell. The timbre and stylized melodic lines of the flute and idiomatic drum rhythms heard in *nō* are modified in a spirit of adventure and experimentation. Pushing the boundaries of a strict musical tradition to create a new sound, Baba turned toward Japan in his fascination with breath-length phrases, high-pitched, accented flute sounds, sustained melodic tones, and the momentum produced by gradually accelerating drum rolls, taking him into unchartered waters. The insertion of Tibetan drum and bell added an intercultural dimension that enhanced the overall musical synthesis.

NASCENT AFRO-ASIAN COLLABORATIONS

The ethnic enclave of San Francisco's Japantown played a critical role in the rise of Sansei musicians within the Asian American creative-music scene. Japantown shared a border with the Fillmore District, an historically important jazz hub in the Bay Area.[85] This geographical proximity connected African American and Japanese American musicians. Musical offerings at the entertainment club Jigoku featured African American and Asian American musicians who rotated in and out of groups or partook in jam sessions. Eddie Moore's Space Shuttle Omnibus, besides Russel Baba on alto saxophone, included Michael White on violin and others. Sansei guitarist Makoto Horiuchi performed with bands booked regularly at the clubs Jigoku and Nishiki, both located in the same building. For the Japanese clientele at the Nishiki club, Horiuchi and Sansei drummer Kenny Endo learned Japanese pop and folk songs from keyboardist Eiji Tsuchiya. Horiuchi and Endo also played regularly at Club Dan for a period of two to three years. The racial and ethnic mix of musicians who jammed at Jigoku became the face of the jazz scene at the time.

> The jigoku club inside
> j town, bold rebels jamming
> Cross from black town, udon,
> Grits, barbecue
>
> Cherry blossoms blooming
> in lady day's hair, greens & fat back,
> sashimi staining kimonos
> you, walking fillmore.[86]

Verses three and four of Quincy Troupe's poem "Shades of Blue for a Blue Bridge" distill the intercultural synergies between Japanese American and African American musicians as they formed bands to play in clubs in Japantown and the Fillmore District, situated on its western border. The mention of food in the poem conjures images of musicians, Americans of

Japanese and African descent, sharing a late-night meal and, by extension, savoring communion following gigs in these contiguous neighborhoods. It was at the Blue Dolphin Club on Fillmore Street, a venue known for alternative music, including music set to poetry, that Sansei bassist and composer Mark Izu joined forces with saxophonist, composer, and poet Lewis Jordan and drummer Ray Collins. In 1977, Izu and Jordan formed Marrón, a primarily African American and Asian American band, featuring Ray Collins, bass clarinetist Paul Yamazaki, drummer Kenny Endo, *conguero* Duke Santos, and guitarist Gordie Watanabe. The group grew to be an eight-, at times, nine-piece band that was too large, prompting the band's dispersal.

Although Marrón's Asian American and African American alliance of musicians came to an end, another group surfaced on the San Francisco scene in 1979. United Front—a pioneering band in the 1970s and early 1980s—coalesced when Izu and Jordan recruited trumpeter George Sams from St. Louis and Bay Area–drummer Anthony Brown.[87] The Bay Area attracted jazz musicians from cities as far flung as Chicago and St. Louis—many of them members of either Chicago's AACM or an analogous organization in St. Louis, the BAG. United Front musically, racially, and politically mirrored the alliances and coalitions among people of color brought together by the TWLF strike in the 1970s. Members included two African Americans, Jordan and Sams, one Japanese American, Izu, and Brown, half Japanese American and half African American, in an ensemble that relied heavily on collectively composing pieces that gave the band its signature sound. The quartet composed music with "a sense of empowerment and self-sufficiency."[88] One perceives this empowered and determined sensibility in their piece "I Will Be Free," a track from their *Ohm: Unit of Resistance* album (RPM Records, 1981). The piece crackles with energy as it heralds a call to stand and declare one's freedom, socially, politically, and artistically. The collective improvisation performed in the middle of the composition typified the group's free-jazz-inspired approach. The track "Nothing Is More Precious than Independence and Freedom" highlights spoken word, performed by Lewis Jordan, alternating with the band's free-form sections that sonically narrate the text. The remainder of the composition is a series of either collectively improvised segments, jazz vamping, or free-flowing passages that allow players to explore musical ideas, giving the music a fresh and liberatory feel.

United Front experienced their greatest success in Europe. They toured Europe three times, performing at jazz festivals, and recorded five albums. Regretfully, the group never reached a point of which members could support themselves solely through their music. Izu reflects on how the band's music

Figure 5.4. Mark Izu holding a Chinese *sheng*, n.d. Photo by Kaz Tsuruta.

was ahead of its time in explaining their low record sales and a shortage of bookings in the United States.

The band's vision of combining original compositions with poetry and theatrical elements forged a new direction for Asian American musician-composers. The synthesis of music with theater, poetry, dance, and storytelling is prominent in the work of First Voice, a collaborative team comprised of Izu and his playwright, actor, storytelling wife, Brenda Wong Aoki; Ethno-tec, a husband-and-wife duo (San Francisco); East West Players (Los Angeles); and Grateful Crane Ensemble (southern California).

MARK IZU: ARBITER OF SOUNDS FROM THE EAST

Mark Izu was not only a driving force as the bassist in the pioneering United Front, his accomplishments as an Emmy-award-winning composer, bandleader, music curator, and arts advocate identify him as a central figure who helped to power Asian American arts (figure 5.4).[89] For fourteen seasons, he produced the Asian American Jazz Festival, sponsored by the Kearny Street Workshop, and his success in attracting and retaining new audiences had a decisive impact. As resident bassist for Asian Improv Records for many years, Izu's innovative and prolific activity prompts a more in-depth exposition.

Mark Izu's oeuvre as a composer includes works for small and large jazz ensembles, symphony orchestra, numerous large-scale theater pieces and spoken-word plays, soundtracks to several documentaries, and other incidental music. Izu's formal training as a bassist in classical music at SFSU equipped him for a professional career as a performer and composer. As a recording artist, he has credits spanning four albums as a leader and over forty albums as a featured artist or sideman. A 2009 Emmy for his soundtrack to *Bolinao 52* (a documentary about Vietnamese boat people); credits for writing the soundtrack to the Academy Award–winning film *Days of Waiting*, about Japanese American incarceration; a Dramalogue Award for composing the score to Brenda Wong Aoki's *Queen's Garden*; two INDIE awards for composition; a Tokyo Critic's Choice for top ten jazz releases in 2008 for his *Threading Time* album; and other numerous awards all acknowledge the originality and high caliber of Izu's artistry. Much of his current work involves composing scores for his wife's monodramas, based on traditional Asian legends and tales or original stories often conveying universal themes or contemporary issues.

Izu's musical inventiveness continues to evolve, and his musical vocabulary features a mature and subtle synthesis of many musical styles. As a composer, he reflects on early influences that shaped his music. Izu speaks about music's ability to express his Japanese heritage as one of the reasons for becoming a musician, inspiring him to keenly reinterpret a Japanese aesthetic and affect in many of his compositions. He recalls the smell of incense accompanying the sound of chanting and gongs during Buddhist funeral services that he and his family attended. Izu also listened to his parent's Japanese music collection and was particularly struck by *gagaku*, a genre that continues to play an important role in his work. Studying court music and specializing in *shō* (Japanese mouth organ) expanded Izu's musical vocabulary, introducing him to new timbres, chord structures, musical textures, forms, and ways of phrasing music. Under the apprenticeship of Suenobu Togi,[90] he learned *gagaku*, recasting his musical and aesthetic sensibilities in creating a transculturated music with a certain ineffability that captures Japanese nuances within a jazz-based idiom. The perceived Japanese sensibility in much of Izu's music is possible because of his training in Japanese musical aesthetics. In Izu's words, "It is not so much about different scales, pitches, or melodic and harmonic structures. Rather, the cultural essence of the music is based in its emotion and feeling." He talks about the underlying concept of musical phrasing: "The sense of space is very important in Asian music. The beauty of the music is in how it breathes. The time between every breath you take isn't exact. It's the same idea at work in Asian music."[91] Prominent in many of his compositions is the Japanese aesthetic concept of *ma*, translated as "space," which Izu roughly defines as "the place in a wave's movement immediately before it breaks." He describes *ma* in the following way: "It's the space around the notes that defines what the note is and how the note sounds and feels."[92] *Ma* creates affect in music; it supports the feelings Izu expresses in connecting with audiences. He strives to create an affective response, a shared musical experience that reinforces a listener's humanity. The use of *ma* can be found in "Scattered Scars," a piece about his parent's internment experience, and "The Shadow," both works that appear on Izu's *Circle of Fire* album.

The 2007 *Threading Time* recording is the culmination of more than thirty years of Izu developing Japanese musical and aesthetic concepts in his work. For this musician-composer, the fourteen-hundred-year-old *gagaku* tradition provides the grounding for most of the album's compositions. *Threading Time* is a companion CD to *Circle of Fire*, recorded in 1993. "Circle of fire" refers to the volcanic chain that rings the Pacific and "the circle of creation and perception that occurs when like minds collaborate";[93] it is symbolic of the cross-cultural mix of music heard on the companion album. The title piece, "Threading Time," sonically embodies the *nō*-drama concept of past, present, and future existing simultaneously, which Izu achieves by presenting ancient musical material in new contexts, an example of artists repeatedly traversing past and present, as Coco Fusco observes and which Fred Ho calls creating a cultural continuum. "Threading Time" incorporates ancient *kagura* songs (Shinto ceremonial music) and a gradual building of musical texture with a quickening tempo, followed by a deceleration at the end, emulating *jo-ha-kyū* musical form. The timbre and tonality of *hichiriki* and *shō* playing *gagaku*-inspired melodic lines create a stately, ritualized Japanese aesthetic, as interpreted by Izu in his understanding of ancient court music. Inviting master *gagaku* musician and teacher Suenobu Togi to perform *hichiriki* and sing on the album imparts weight to the music in its aesthetic reach and intention. New treatment of this ancient music in "Threading Time" and other compositions on the album engages a panoply of sounds with master *tabla* player Zakir Hussain, providing rhythmic and timbral inventions; improvisations on the *neh* (Persian end-blown flute), saxophone, and alto clarinet by Hafez Modirzadeh; and changing textures and sound combinations of instrumental and vocal lines all contribute to a new sound echoing ancient music in a new framework. Togi Sensei expressed high hope in Izu's ability to bring *gagaku* into the twenty-first century by contemporizing and diversifying its form and features. He experienced great satisfaction in contributing to "Threading Time," dispelling his fear of *gagaku*'s demise. The recognition and award the album received in Japan holds promise for the continued evolution of this tradition.

As an instrumentalist, Izu's approach to playing bass is unconventional in its use, at times, as a melody instrument, enabling him to better interpret and more intuitively navigate through a piece to enhance its affect. Izu's attention to melody is governed by this musical feature's primacy in Asian music. The improvisational approach of the Chicago Art Ensemble, Archie Shepp, Albert Ayler, and others guided his move away from merely playing notes to outlining chords. As a result, we see Izu's music evolving from both his study of Asian music and the improvisational practices of innovative African American musicians.

A prominent feature of Izu's musical style is his use of a variety of Asian instruments, creating a pan-Asian hue to his jazz-based music. The unique timbral qualities of Japanese *gagaku* instruments—*shō*, *hichiriki* (double-reed pipe), and *taiko* (barrel drum)—together with the differentiated sounds of Chinese *sheng* (mouth organ) and *erhu* (two-stringed bowed lute) woven into jazz-based melodies, harmonies, and rhythms produce an ambient sound that conjures an Asian sensibility. In referring to their use, Izu remarks, "My philosophy of fusing different cultural instruments is that you don't just add them to music that already exists; you build it from the ground up."[94] Writing for specific musical instruments from the outset of the compositional process ensures their integral role in realizing the intended outcome.

Izu's compositions evoke a variety of instrumental music traditions and musical styles he has absorbed, weaving their sonic features into his work. In addition to his strong affinity for Japanese court music, he also received training in Cantonese folk music and salsa. Joining the Chinese music group Flowing Stream Ensemble offered Izu a chance to study *erhu* and *sheng* with a master Chinese musician. The Flowing Stream Ensemble was a semiprofessional music group that performed Cantonese folk music in the San Francisco Chinatown community. Izu internalized some of their repertoire and gained some fluency on the *sheng* and *erhu* by attending informal rehearsals that functioned primarily as social gatherings. He experimented with and innovated upon the idiomatic style of these instruments forging his own sound. Izu's desire to learn different music styles while an undergraduate music student took him to the Mission area to study salsa in workshops given by Carlos Frederico.

Izu does not view himself as overtly political, one example of the varied activist stances among Sansei musicians. Although he was a student at SFSU from 1968 to 1969 during the TWLF strike, his work, rather than serving as a vehicle for direct action, seeks to inspire people and reinforce their humanity:

> I feel the role of music is not so much to educate someone and convince them of a certain political point of view, but to inspire people. And for myself, if I felt like I've inspired someone, that goes much farther for me because I realize everyone has their own ways of thinking. And if you can inspire someone to think more clearly about what's going on, they could come up with a solution that I never thought of. And that's my role. I don't think I have answers to political questions. Hopefully, we're all in this room together. What I'm doing will help inspire people to kind of move on and do different things. Yeah, it is about humanity. Over the years, this has become more important to me. After the Third World [TWLF] strike, trying to organize around ethnicity and culture is more about humanity. That's what the arts are all about.[95]

An event that affirms Izu's pledge to humanity is the Ghost Festival[96] performance he and Brenda Wong Aoki organized in the week following the death and destruction of the 9/11 attack on the World Trade Center. Although the performance was due to be cancelled out of deference for those who lost their lives, the need to bring people together was stronger, and the musicians involved in the Ghost Festival managed to reinstate it at the Yerba Buena Museum of Modern Art, drawing in six hundred attendees. The event began with a blessing by Rev. Masato Kawahatsu, followed by prayerful musical performances, ending with the Hawaiian anthem about the sovereignty of its people, the land, and of healing. As the audience rose to sing the anthem from printed lyrics, everyone held hands, swaying and crying. It was a cathartic moment of expressing sorrow and restoration. The blessing, performances, and singing of the anthem united all attendees in a moment of shared humanity, inspiring feelings of hope and healing.

Izu enacts his political conscience in two compositions—*Last Dance* and *HIBAKUSHA! (Survivors)*—exposing the inhumanity of World War II against both Japanese Americans and Japanese. His multimedia composition *Last Dance* is a tribute from Sansei to Issei and Nisei as it upholds the stories of Japanese Americans imprisoned during World War II—a story Izu felt was too important to be forgotten. It is a piece that uses music and narrative to situate the incarceration of Japanese Americans within the context of the broader Japanese American experience, highlighting the continuing struggle for justice. Izu's performance of *Last Dance* (which is the name of both the composition and the album) appeared on the program of Jazz & Justice: Contemporary Works on February 21, 1998, at Yerba Buena Center for the Arts in San Francisco in observance of the 1998 Day of Remembrance, the first nationally observed anniversary of Executive Order 9066. Anthony Brown's Asian American Jazz Orchestra (AAJO) and members of San Jose Taiko were crucial in the enactment of *Last Dance*. The story is told in three parts: part 1, The Pioneers, honors Issei who ventured to the United States in hopes of a new life, surviving racial prejudice and discriminatory laws with fortitude and resilience. Through spoken word, poetry, and music, the story of The Camps in part 2 narrates the circumstances of the internment and the uplifting effect of music and dance in bleak camp environments. This section comes alive in the words of George Yoshida, a Nisei jazz maker, author, and educator who was incarcerated at Poston concentration camp in Arizona with his family. Painting a picture of life in the camps and the nourishing power of music, Yoshida chronicles the adaptability of prisoners in their efforts to normalize life amidst trauma. The third part of *Last Dance* celebrates the courage and indomitable spirit of Issei and Nisei from which Sansei and succeeding generations will draw upon in raising families and building their communities.[97] The concluding piece, "Kiryoku" (Focusing Chi), is rousing music reminiscent of a Japanese Obon dance, a fast-paced, rhythmically rambunctious version performed by members of San Jose Taiko, sounding the resolute spirit of the Japanese American people—a spirit that helped them endure the dark days of incarceration. *Last Dance*, a collage of impressionistic musical vignettes, dance-band jazz pieces, and mood-setting music weaves personal stories and poetry intended to reveal the outcomes of prejudice and injustice with the hope that they never repeat.

Asian Improv Records expanded, becoming Asian Improv aRts, an Asian American umbrella organization that supports artistic activity in the Bay Area and Chicago. Izu wrote *HIBAKUSHA! (Survivors)* in 1995 as a commission for Asian Improv aRts. It is a composition that addresses the consequences suffered by Japanese in the aftermath of the atomic bombing of Hiroshima and Nagasaki for generations to come. At the 1995 Asian American Jazz Festival, Izu performed *HIBAKUSHA! (Survivors)* as the closing piece for the Concert of a Thousand Cranes Festival.[98] He resolved to write about *hibakusha*—atomic-bomb survivors—after reading about the offspring of these radiation victims, expressing, "I realized that the most damage done by radiation to the human race is on the genetic level, the altering of our DNA. This literally changes one's past, present, and future."⁹⁹ The fact that Izu's father served in the acclaimed all-Japanese American 442nd Battalion and that his mother's relations are from Hiroshima further reinforced his decision to compose on this somber theme. Izu notes that many *hibakusha* were Japanese Americans visiting Japan to connect with relatives or study when the war broke out. He conveyed the moving experience of listening to *hibakusha* tell tales of lives changed forever and how, to this day, they are struggling to be recognized by the US government for financial reparations.

HIBAKUSHA! (Survivors) is a five-movement composition outlined below. Izu's idea of incorporating native Karuk chants occurred to him after he was invited to attend a healing-the-Earth ceremony.¹⁰⁰ Every year the Karuk perform ceremonies to heal the Earth; they fast, pray, chant, and dance for two weeks at their sacred grounds. Very few non-Karuk people are invited, making Izu's attendance a rare honor. Touched by the experience, he summoned his Karuk friend Julian and his family to perform a healing chant at the end of *HIBAKUSHA! (Survivors)*. The intercultural sonic mix created by the inclusion of the Karuk chant underscored the composition's intent of uniting people in a process of healing.

HIBAKUSHA! (Survivors) is scored for a mixed ensemble of Asian and European instruments. The Asian instruments employed are Japanese *shō*, shamisen, koto, *hichiriki*, and Chinese *sheng* and *suona* (double-reed wind instrument). Filling out the ensemble are non-Asian instruments: a string quartet, trombone, tenor saxophone, Eb clarinet, bassoon, electric bass, drum kit, and West African pressure drum. The score consists of a basic outline, indicating entrances of different instruments and providing some motivic ideas and rhythms for the musicians to improvise on in realizing and interpreting the subtext provided. Izu's identification with the spiritual, emotional journey *hibakusha* experienced melded with the affective response to the Karuk healing ceremony he had attended forms the soul of the composition. The piece proceeds from the horrific destruction of life to sonically narrating such an experience, followed by healing and renewal. The use of a *saibara* melody from the Japanese court-music repertoire brings suspension, resolved by transcendence from chaos and darkness and followed by the recuperative power of the Karuk chant. It is an intercultural collage of sounds that express Izu's vision of the *hibakusha*'s anguish and the repercussions of such an assault on future generations, sonically represented by the ripples of a drop of water in a still pond in movement III. The ripples convey a close tie to nature, a common motif expressed in traditional Japanese arts. The structure and subtext of the composition is as follows:

Movement I subtext: numbness, shock, self-awareness, starts after the bombing
Movement II subtext: confusion, anger, realization (the most dense and atonal portion of the composition)
Movement III subtext: questions, the unborn, past, present, future (beginning with strings and evolving into echoing motifs initiated by the trombone), with an image of a drop of water creating ripples on a still pond
Movement IV subtext: understanding, coping, telling the story (based on a Japanese *saibara* song, a vocal piece from court-music repertoire, about a fleeting moment of the ocean at Ise)
Movement V subtext: healing, ritual (a Karuk Native American chant to the accompaniment of the Japanese court instrument *shō* and the Chinese equivalent, *sheng*).

The unaccompanied sound of the Karuk healing chant at the end of the piece instills tranquility and reconciliation. The healing that is meant to take place in *HIBAKUSHA! (Survivors)* attests to Izu's musical credo to reinforce and enrich our connection to one another and to cultivate one's aesthetic self, serving as a source of compassion and humanity toward all beings.

Izu, as an arts advocate and producer, supports the tenet of art as a vehicle for effecting social change. From 1989 on, he played a major role in serving as the artistic director of San Francisco's Kearny Street Workshop, an artists' collective, which started out as an Asian American grassroots organization. The workshop was an outgrowth of the Asian American movement and its push for young Asian Americans to connect with and assist their communities. As the oldest multidisciplinary Asian Pacific American arts organization in the United States, it continues to offer classes, exhibitions, screenings, and readings, including a host of intergenerational and cross-cultural activities. The workshop promoted musicians by sponsoring the Asian American Jazz Festival, its main performance event, lasting three decades from 1981 to 2011. While serving as artistic director of the Asian American Jazz Festival for fourteen years, Izu focused on increasing turnout for the event. Izu was open to myriad musical genres in his quest to engage audiences. Thus, his advocacy of music and arts sustained a flourishing landscape for Asian American musicians, aiding them to develop their unique voices.

The most recent incarnation of Izu as a composer-musician are story dramas in which he and his nationally renowned Asian/Pacific storyteller and writer wife, Brenda Wong Aoki, actively combine their talents. Their highly original story dramas are rooted in *gagaku, nōgaku*, contemporary theater, personal story, history, and legend. The duo incorporates world music, spoken word, jazz, and dance in their adaptations of non-Western theatrical, musical, and spoken-word traditions that are combined in new work. Izu and Wong Aoki joined forces in 1995, founding First Voice as a nonprofit organization. First Voice served as the principal producer of the Asian American Jazz Festival in San Francisco for many years. The organization has its roots in the social, political, and cultural activism in San Francisco's Japantown and Chinatown, and it is connected to the *hapa* (mixed-race) community in the Bay Area. The appeal of Izu's and Wong Aoki's interdisciplinary work in interpreting the "pluralistic nature of the American experience from a unique Asian American cultural perspective" has drawn a loyal following locally, regionally, and internationally in Japan.[101] Izu's instruction in *gagaku* and Wong Aoki's traditional training in Japanese theater forms, *nō* and *kyōgen*, equip them to approach contemporary issues from an Asian-inflected perspective Americanized by jazz-based music and contemporary urban choreography that all come to life in wonderfully imaginative and innovative ways in their theater productions. Add the avant-garde music and theater experience of Izu and Wong Aoki and Wong Aoki's mixed ancestry of Japanese, Chinese, Spanish, and Scots into the cross-cultural mélange, and you have a blueprint for intercultural and intergenerational performances. Dancer, actor, and son Kai Kāne (known as K. K.) has been an integral part of their productions, linking generations with his contemporary urban choreography and acting. Recognition of Izu's and Wong Aoki's bold work is evident in the multitude of awards bestowed on them—Hollywood-Dramalogue awards, National Education Association (NEA) fellowships, Critic Circle awards, INDIE awards, Dramatist Guild, American Society of Composers, Authors, and Publishers (ASCAP) awards, and an Emmy. The rich medium of theater had its roots early on in the genesis of Asian American arts, and it continues to appeal to diverse audiences. Theater provides a coalitional creative space for increasing numbers of racially and culturally mixed Americans.

ANTHONY BROWN: MUSICALLY MELDING CULTURAL IDENTITIES

Yet another important link in the lineage of pioneering Japanese/Asian American musician-composers is percussionist, composer, educator, and ethnomusicologist Anthony Brown. He embodies the interracial and intercultural collaborations among Bay Area Asian American and African American jazz artists and easily traverses two worlds: that of diasporic Japan and African America. Brown is a progeny of a Japanese mother and African American, Choctaw, and Cherokee father. The father's military career mandated the

Brown family's move from San Francisco to Okinawa, Japan, where Brown spent four impressionable years of his childhood. Listening to his mother sing Japanese lullabies and popular songs, witnessing live Okinawan folk and festival music, and hearing Japanese classical and folk music as well as *gagaku* on the radio immersed Brown in Japanese music culture and instilled in him an appreciation of its aesthetic and affect. His daily exposure to Japanese radio and television further deepened an awareness of his cultural heritage.

Facing racial discrimination upon his return to the United States as a teen, Brown promptly identified more closely with his African American roots. He channeled his creative impulses into performing as a way to ameliorate his bitterness. Brown's politically astute father reinforced his son's racial identification by engendering pride in being African American and exposing him to the ethos of the civil rights movement. His father's blues collection forged Brown's music of choice as a youth, blues, pop, rock, and soul—styles he performed with various bands while living in San Francisco and then Germany where his family relocated. In Germany, Brown received Western classical-music training while attending high school. As an American student on the military base, he was recruited to play drums in military club bands with a repertoire consisting of American and British popular music. Brown performed a wide range of music expected by the broad clientele at the service clubs, including tunes from famous bands of the day, such as Yes, King Crimson, ELP, Sly and the Family Stone, Crosby, Stills, & Nash, James Brown, Sex Machine, and Cold Blood.

Upon returning to the United States, Brown's musical activities proliferated, starting with his formal musical training in orchestral percussion, arranging and composing at the University of Oregon. He further expanded his musical palette performing jazz in big bands and small combos. The music of Duke Ellington, John Coltrane, Miles Davis, Pharoah Sanders, Thelonius Monk, as well as Mahavishnu Orchestra and Tower of Power exemplify influences that shaped Brown's growing musical oeuvre. Fulfilling his ROTC commitments took this artist to Athens, Greece, where he heard music of the Romany people and Greek celebratory music. Exposure to such sounds piqued Brown's interest in world music traditions and led to his eventual doctoral degree in ethnomusicology. During his three years of military service, Brown played pop music in service bands, sat in as house drummer in an Athens jazz club, and conducted the US Army Chorus, during which time he also became immersed in gospel music.

In 1980, Brown moved back to the Bay Area at a musically fertile time, a moment when Japanese/Asian American musician-composers, writers, theater and visual artists, and poets generated artistic momentum. It is at this juncture that he met his future jazz partner Mark Izu, along with Paul Yamazaki, Gerald Oshita, Russel Baba, Jon Jang, Francis Wong, Miya Masaoka, and other musicians active in the Asian American creative-music scene. Brown was invited to play drums for the interracial and free-jazz group United Front. The primary aesthetic of this band was grounded in African American creative jazz—music stemming from Charles Mingus, Rahsaan Roland Kirk, Eric Dolphy, Albert Ayler, and the Art Ensemble of Chicago.[102] His burgeoning musical partnership with Mark Izu in United Front sparked Brown's interest in synthesizing Asian stylistic elements to create a jazz piece. In the liner notes to his album *Family*, he writes:

> I could see how he [Izu] was integrating and blending the two musics. He was not just adding the sound of Asian instruments, but he was bringing concepts of how to write music influenced by Asian concepts. Like instead of thinking in terms of metric time, thinking in terms of breath length. That's unheard of in Western music, most everything is metrical. Those kind of concepts and thinking of cyclical structures opened my eyes and ears to Asian music and sent me off on a path to study it formally in the academic institution.[103]

Brown acknowledges Izu's influence as he forged new directions in his thinking, drumming, and composing. The two musicians collaborated for over three decades, following their stint in the pioneering band United Front. Their close relationship is presented in the short documentary film, *Don't Lose Your Soul*, including footage of the thirtieth anniversary of the Asian American Jazz Festival in Oakland, California, that honored Nisei George Yoshida.

In 1987, after studying jazz history at Rutgers, performing with bands in New York, and touring five times in Europe, Brown decided to return to the Bay Area. That year, Jon Jang and Francis Wong formed Asian Improv Records and its satellite presenting organization, generating a burst of activity during which Brown learned the Japanese koto, shakuhachi, *gagaku*, and the Indian *tabla* (pair of tuned drums). Brown's growing role as a major player working with Jon Jang's Pan Asian Arkestra, Middle Passage, and other bands influenced him to musically identify with his Japanese heritage. He thrived in the local scene of Asian American activity, performing, studying Asian music, and in general sounding his way home and discovering what it is to also be Japanese American.

Among his contemporaries, Brown formulated a musical niche, owing to his strong inclination to write compositionally based pieces—as opposed to music that was less structured and more improvisational—in tandem with his interest in synthesizing the Western concert tradition with musical structures, timbres, rhythms, and phrasing he absorbed in studying Japanese *gagaku*, koto, shakuhachi, and *taiko* and other forms of percussion. Brown composed multimovement works for large ensembles as well as pieces for small groups. The twentieth-century Japanese composer Toru Takemitsu, who deftly used the Western orchestra to convey and reinterpret Japanese sensibilities in his compositions, inspired Brown to interlace Japanese musical elements and aesthetics into his own work. He combined this approach with ideas gleaned from groundbreaking musicians Gerald Oshita, Russel Baba, Mark Izu, Jon Jang, and Francis Wong among others.

Collective work with Asian American musicians awakened Brown's political consciousness and a desire to add his voice in condemning the Japanese American incarceration during World War II. Two compositions—"E. O. 9066 (Truth Be Told)" and "Never Again! (Mo, Shimasen!)"—arose from Brown's observance of the fiftieth anniversary of the closing of the incarceration camps. "E. O. 9066" references President Franklin Delano Roosevelt's executive order during World War II, authorizing the unconstitutional removal and imprisonment of all Japanese Americans from Washington State south to California and inland into southern Arizona. The piece came to life as a four-way collaboration between Brown, San Jose Taiko, Marco Lienhard (shakuhachi), and Liu Chi Chao (*suona* and *sheng*). A recording of "E. O. 9066 (Truth Be Told)" on Brown's 1997 album, *Family*, featured liner notes with the following description:

> "E. O. 9066 (Truth Be Told)" commemorates the courageous spirit of Japanese Americans unjustly imprisoned during World War II. The Prelude creates an ambiance of timelessness, transporting the listener through the musical themes of the work. Ichikotsu-cho is an arrangement of the original 11th-century *gagaku* composition and is dedicated to Issei, the first generation of Japanese in America. The abrupt "Entry of General's Order," a traditional Chinese composition, heralds the upheaval and incarceration of Japanese Americans precipitated by Executive Order 9066. "Rhymes (for Children)" celebrates hope for a future that will not see the imprisonment of children.[104]

In this semiprogrammatic composition, the use of traditional Japanese and Chinese instruments transports the listener to a sonic world that introduces the protagonists: Japanese immigrants, their offspring, and bombed citizens of Nagasaki. The idiomatic playing styles of *fue* (Japanese transverse flute), koto, and shakuhachi are threaded throughout the work as a symbolic motif of the indomitable spirit of the Japanese people. By altering the voicings and nuances in the *gagaku* composition, "*ichikotsu-cho*," Brown reinterprets the piece to fit into a new context. The assertive sounds of *taiko* punctuate the music, symbolizing Japanese American ties to their homeland, while the jazz-based closing movement claims the American identity of Japanese Americans. The 1998 Day of Remembrance concert—Jazz and Justice: Contemporary Works—was the perfect setting for the presentation of "E. O. 9066 (Truth Be Told)." The concert held at the Yerba Buena Center for the Arts in San Francisco is significant in that it marked the first nationally observed anniversary of the incarceration order.

In 1995, the Asian Heritage Council commissioned Brown to write "Never Again! (Mo Shimasen!)" to commemorate the fiftieth anniversary of the bombings of Hiroshima and Nagasaki during World War II. Also featured on the *Family* album, the composition was his response to the devastation and death caused by the atomic bombs dropped on the two civilian centers. The premiere performance of "Never Again!" demonstrated Brown's collaborative talent as the celebrated poet Janice Mirikitani and San Jose Taiko headlined the event. Brown unites his two cultural identities by centralizing the role of drums, as he reveals in his liner notes:

> The work combines musical influences from Japan and West Africa, cultures in which drums play a central role. The piece was written to represent basic life forces, with the drums signifying the heartbeat and the wind instruments the breath of life. The title expresses the plea for successive generations of children that they never experience the horror of nuclear war. The finale is an anthem in celebration of the indomitable human spirit rising from the ashes of ruin in rebirth and rejuvenation.[105]

Partnerships with other musicians spurred Brown's artistic output. In 1997, he was the musical director of the Asian American Jazz Orchestra, an ensemble formed as part of a San Francisco–based Civil Liberties Public Education Fund multimedia project. The intent of the fund is to educate audiences about the Japanese American internment during World War II. The AAJO made its debut performing excerpts from extended works by pioneering composers Izu, Jang, and Brown. The pieces involving AAJO partnering with San Jose Taiko were curated and toured as part of AAJO's recording *Big Bands behind Barbed Wire*. The performance spotlighted Izu's composition *Last Dance* and Brown's "E. O. 9066 (Truth

Be Told)." The focus on the incarceration in these works gave Japanese Americans and their communities a voice in expressing the injustice they endured.

The AAJO sowed the seed for an expanded ensemble, renamed Anthony Brown's Asian American Orchestra (AAO), which was constituted to perform new settings that Brown arranged for Duke Ellington and Billy Strayhorn's *Far East Suite* to mark Ellington's centennial in 1999 and, at a later date, Ellington's suite *Afro-Asian Eclipse*.

In the year 2000, Asian American jazz-based music made its mark in mainstream society when Brown's interpretation of Duke Ellington and Billy Strayhorn's *Far East Suite* (1964) received a Grammy nomination for Best Large Jazz Ensemble Performance. Brown's recognition established Asian American music as a legitimate expressive form. The original version of *Far East Suite* is an impressionistic piece inspired by Ellington's tours of the Middle East and Asia for the State Department. In reconceptualizing *Far East Suite*, Brown achieved a more Asian cast both in terms of timbre and conceptually through the use of Asian musical instruments and scales used in Persia (Iran), China, and Japan. The reinterpreted version incorporates *taiko* to represent an Asian American sound.

In fulfilling the social justice mission of the Asian American Orchestra, Brown composed a soundtrack to commemorate former Japanese American inmates in *After the War* (2007), a play by Phillip Gotanda about internees released from the camps and returning to San Francisco. Jon Osaki's notable documentary *Alternative Facts: The Lies of Executive Order 9066* (2018) also featured a soundtrack written by Brown. *Alternative Facts* outlines the fictionalized findings of a US government investigation regarding acts of espionage by Japanese Americans that served as the rationale for evacuating and imprisoning them on the West Coast.[106] More recently, Brown was commissioned to compose the soundtrack to *Go for Broke! A Salute to Nisei Veterans*, featuring the original poetry and spoken-word recitations by former internee and activist poet Janice Mirikitani. "Go for Broke" was originally the motto of the all–Japanese American 442nd Regimental Combat Team during World War II. The album evinces the all-out risks the infantry took in battling for the United States. The 2017 commission, which marked the seventy-fifth anniversary of the signing of E. O. 9066 ordered by General DeWitt in 1942, is an ironic testament to a policy that imprisoned Japanese American families at the same moment their sons laid their lives on the line for their country's cause in war-torn Europe.

Anthony Brown's Fifth Stream Music, a San Francisco–based nonprofit arts organization, is the venue through which he continues to compose, collaborate, and provide exposure for racially and ethnically diverse artists. Fifth Stream

Music's mission is to promote the art of jazz through intercultural music exchange in the form of concerts and educational events that reflect America's cultural diversity.[107] In 2015, under the auspices of Fifth Stream Music, the Asian American Orchestra and Voices of a Dream, a cappella vocal group specializing in freedom and protest songs, gospel music, and spirituals, joined forces with poet and playwright Genny Lim and the Ojala Bata ensemble to premiere *1945: A Year of Infamy* in San Francisco's Japantown in commemoration of the seventieth anniversary of the atomic bombing devastation of Hiroshima and Nagasaki. In both *1945: A Year of Infamy* and a second work, *We Insist! Freedom Now Suite (2016)*, Brown again celebrates his African American and Japanese American facets, using the same ensemble of musicians. He reinterpreted and recorded *We Insist! Freedom Now Suite*—originally written by the jazz drummer Max Roach in partnership with Oscar Brown Jr., Abbey Lincoln, and master drummer Michael Babatunde Olatunji. Brown's reworking of *We Insist!* speaks to the Black Lives Matter movement and the spike in anti-Muslim violence in America today, continuing the legacy of the original Max Roach recording sold in 1960 to critical acclaim.[108] Dr. Brown's ongoing collaborations with artists within the past few years include working and performing with Miami-based Dimensions Dance Theater in *Cross Currents* (2007) and San Francisco–based Zaccho Dance Theater in *Port of Embarkation* (2016).

Brown advocates building a vocabulary of different musical languages to convey ideas and promote working in association with other musicians to express diverse experiences. Asian American musician-composers, he asserts, "aspire to be able to express one's experiences or one's sense of values. We strive to be able to render tangible that which we feel inside. That's our greatest desire."[109] As well, Brown regards improvisation as a key element to building an Asian sensibility in Asian American jazz: "We are still evolving; we're still coming up with our own criteria for what works and what doesn't. But the influences are clear. We're all influenced by jazz, and it's how you mix the parts. We're not only coming from a jazz tradition, we're presenting and reinterpreting it in a new suit. We want to do something different."[110] Today, Anthony Brown continues to compose, arrange, and perform from the wellspring of his Asian American and African American cultural heritages.

SAN FRANCISCO MUSIC AUDIENCES

During the 1970s and 1980s, Asian American jazz bands and rock ensembles drew diverse audiences in San Francisco. Musicians relied on Asian American students, community, and cultural workers as well as jazz or rock aficionados to fill music venues. The Bay Area, known for its eclectic music scene, attracted audiences to local concerts. I witnessed a racially and culturally mixed crowd for a live performance by Mark Izu and Lewis Jordan, whose performance intertwined spoken word and music in a San Francisco church-turned-concert venue. Clubs, particularly in the Fillmore neighborhood, sharing a border with Japantown, cultivated interracial audiences, while jazz and rock listeners at community venues mostly reflected a blend of the local demographic. The Jigoku Club in Japantown stands out in featuring bands in which Black and Asian American musicians collaborated; audiences were mostly Japanese and Japanese American. Artists experimenting with free jazz drew a more specific crowd, yet less discerning racially and culturally mixed audiences also attended in supporting and encouraging musicians in their quest to explore and push boundaries.

GLENN HORIUCHI: AN ECLECTIC MAVERICK

Although a more commercial jazz-fusion sound prevailed in the Los Angeles area, this metropolitan hub did have its free-jazz artists. Pianist, composer, and shamisen player Glenn Horiuchi had a dynamic sound that contributed greatly to the Asian American creative-music scene. His untimely passing in 2000 is a bitter loss.

Horiuchi, a central figure in the development of the Asian American jazz movement, showed promise as a youngster, starting piano lessons at age six. From high school on, he played jazz piano on his own. When he matriculated at the University of California, Riverside, hoping to be a music major, Horiuchi received training in the European classical repertoire. Jazz was not considered serious music by the music department at his university (and at a number of other schools); instead, he set out to earn two degrees in mathematics before succumbing to his passion as a pianist and composer. Musically inclined family members instilled his love for music:

> My grandfather was a musician. In fact, he was the first Japanese American I know of to get on the radio in the US when he played the shakuhachi on Hawaiian radio in the 1930s. He was also a pretty well-known singer. In Heart Mountain [camp,] he wrote and sang a long narrative song about camp. He would actually tour the barracks and sing that song and people would cry. It was pretty heavy.[111]

His grandfather also played ukulele and violin and performed *naniwa-bushi* dramatic storytelling. Horiuchi was brought up hearing and singing Japanese folk songs; his mother sang *hole hole bushi*—folk songs sung by sugarcane workers in Hawaii—while an aunt exposed him to Beethoven and Stravinsky. Horiuchi further honed his musical tastes in garage rock bands, listening to the blues, performing as a sideman in a Latinx band, and eventually becoming ardent about bebop and free jazz.

Horiuchi began to incorporate Japanese music influences into his compositions, recalling, "When I became more politically conscious, the folk dances and songs from Japanese American festivals, such as Obon and Nisei Week, became a major source of my writing."[112] His composition *Next Step* is based on *dongo*, a rhythmic pattern widely used by Asian American *taiko* performers, who describe the pattern as a bright, triplet feel. The narrative included on Horiuchi's artist statement speaks to the importance of music in his identification as a Japanese American, and he strove to express this in his work:

> Horiuchi's music is an expression of his Japanese American identity, and of his struggle to create an organic synthesis of the sounds which have shaped his aesthetic—Japanese folk rhythms, the African American jazz tradition, and Western art music. He sings the exuberance of Japanese and Mexican laborers in the historic 1904 Oxnard strike, and whispers the silent strokes of his grandmother's portrait. He captures the desert heat of an Arizona concentration camp, or the infectious rhythms of a contemporary *mochitsuki* festival. In sharing a personal voice which is both moving and provocative, Horiuchi provides us with insight into the forces which are redefining the fabric of US society.[113]

Horiuchi shared stories of Japanese American struggle and history with young audiences. In his educational project—Finding the Groove—he dramatizes his search for a Japanese American identity in music by performing on piano while relating anecdotes based on personal experience and Asian American history. The piece was a forty-five-minute lecture-demonstration intended to reach audiences as young as thirteen, exhibiting the humility of this consummate artist and his desire to effect social change.

The music and politics of this composer aligned closely with fellow artists in the Bay Area, where he became a member of the Asian Improv collective and a fixture in its music scene. The complex chord clusters and kinetic energy of Horiuchi's percussive-piano sound brings to mind the music of Cecil Taylor, but there is a singularity in Horiuchi's music that speaks to his experience as a Japanese American, an aesthetic response of a marginalized human being. The comparison to Taylor's music is inscribed in the liner notes to Horiuchi's debut album, *Next Step*. Fellow musician Jon Jang characterizes the musician-composer's percussive style as "eighty-eight tuned *taiko* drums," a twist on "eighty-eight tuned drums," a phrase used to describe Cecil Taylor's piano performance.[114]

Horiuchi's individual style evolved from different political, social, and musical streams. Black Panther Party ideology and *The Autobiography of Malcolm X* exposed Horiuchi to the civil rights struggles of African Americans. He equated their battle with that of Asian Americans, compelling him to join the Asian Pacific Student Union in California in 1979 and the League for Revolutionary Struggle for nine years, starting in 1980. Horiuchi underscored the connection between his political consciousness and his music, noting the affinity he felt toward the free jazz of the Black Arts movement:

> In the music that I'm doing I'm trying to capture some of the strength, some of the sense of spirit—of struggle and determination and fighting the Issei had and, at the same time link that with, as much as a Japanese American can, the music that came out of the Black Liberation Movement. To me it's the most natural kind of connection. I don't know if it works in the music, but that's what I'm trying to do.[115]

Horiuchi denoted the musicians' role in responding to their sociopolitical milieu: "A musician can't help but be moved by the political climate, because he is an active person living in a society."[116] He cited John Coltrane's reaction to political upheavals in the 1960s[117] and the connection between the saxophonist's *Love Supreme* album with the Black nationalist movement as interpreted by Amiri Baraka in his poem "Trane."

Critical musical influences—Horace Tapscott, John Coltrane, Thelonious Monk, Cecil Taylor, Ornette Coleman, and AACM members Andrew Hill and Muhal Richards Abrams—informed Horiuchi's compositions and the liberation he found in free jazz. His classical-piano training equipped him with the technical mastery to build on the music of these artists and blaze his own musical trail. The abstract quality of Horiuchi's compositions manifests in his use of unusual meters, repeated motives, spare, atonal phrases, disconnected chords, and jagged contours, as heard in the solo piano piece "Saburo" on his second album *Issei Spirit* (1989).

Horiuchi imbued in his oeuvre traces of traditional Japanese music and avoided "conventional bebop harmony," which the pianist considered antithetical to a Japanese aesthetic.[118] He used pentatonic scales to evoke an Asian tonality, and rather than employing the scales in a melody, which would affect a clichéd Asian sound, the composer often placed pentatonic scales in the bassline. Such a bassline alters the harmonic structure away from conventional chord changes and opens the sound while retaining a pentatonic feel.[119] The application of scales in this manner is heard in his solo piano performance of *Issei Spirit* the title track of his second album. The Japanese pentatonic scale, *hirajoshi*,[120] is deployed in the melodic opening motif played on piano and outlined in the bowed-bass melody; both lines are accompanied by impressionistic flourishes on trap drums before a Japanese flute (*fue*) sketches out an improvised folk melody. The piece shifts into double time, and Horiuchi plays an extended piano solo reminiscent of what Cecil Taylor might render. Also notable in this recording is an expressive effect on piano that Horiuchi developed from Japanese flute music, a concept Anthony Braxton calls "dimensionality": rapid shifts in volume that give the listener the illusion of the sound originating from different places in a sonic field. Horiuchi expressed it this way: "I always try to include a solo piano piece on my recordings, to experiment with dynamics in a way that's hard to do effectively in a group. I love having that freedom of dynamics and space."[121]

An extended work based on Japanese pentatonic scales, rhythms, and idiomatic elements of *nagauta* shamisen music is the 1992 recording *Little Tokyo Suite* performed by the Glenn Horiuchi Octet. The six-movement composition is Horiuchi's most intentional nod to his Japanese roots as he weaves shamisen musical lines into flute, clarinet, bass clarinet, string bass, piano, and percussion parts. The pianist dedicated separate movements of the piece to Los Angeles Japantown with references to First Street (heart of J-Town) and the annual Nisei Week parade, along with a musical statement of the arrest of Japanese Americans on Terminal Island sent to incarceration camps.

The following speaks to Horiuchi's direct political action as a musician. In memory of the injustice Issei and Nisei endured, the pianist temporarily ceased any musical activity in 1981 to help found the national Coalition for Redress/Reparations and serve as chair for the San Diego Redress/Reparations Committee from 1979 to 1983. This flurry of activity led to Redress and Reparations Committee hearings followed by a passage of the Civil Liberties Act of 1988.[122] Hearings that Horiuchi attended in Los Angeles had a powerful and lasting impact on him, especially upon witnessing his father and others testify to their hardship in the concentration camps, touching a deep nerve in Horiuchi's consciousness.[123] He recalled his response to the hearings:

> Every time someone testified you could feel that everyone in the room felt it was their story; there was such a sense of unity. One guy was separated

from his father in camp and had not seen him since. Stories like that just tore your heart out. Some people said they had never even told these stories to their kids. But they felt they had to share these experiences or else it might happen again. My dad and grandfather testified. It was the highlight of my life, just being there. It was a very emotional experience.[124]

The fortitude it took for former inmates to share their painful stories of oppressive life in the camps and the unity required to demand justice provoked the pianist-composer to create several works that captured his experience at the hearings; three albums resulted—*Next Step* (1988), *Issei Spirit* (1989), and *Manzanar Voices* (1989), which were all released by Asian Improv Records.[125] Horiuchi's work as a community activist in southern California continued following the hearings, but his need for an emotional outlet grew, pushing him to restart his music career.

In 1990, the San Diego Community Foundation commissioned Horiuchi to compose *Poston Sonata*. The piece commemorates the San Diego Japanese American community for sharing their experiences in the Poston concentration camp; it showcases transculturated Japanese melodies, rhythms, and abstract, impressionistic flourishes. *Poston Sonata* solemnizes the site of a World War II concentration camp that housed twenty thousand Japanese Americans, including most of San Diego's Japanese American community. Incorporating shamisen as a solo instrument and interpolating Japanese-inspired melodies and *taiko*-inspired rhythms give this modern jazz-based composition a unique sensibility meant to claim a space for Japanese American history. In the score, Horiuchi weaves idiomatic phrases of *nagauta* shamisen with jazz instrumental parts on alto sax, tenor sax, bass clarinet, bass, percussion, and piano.

The composition's four movements—"Remembrance," "Internment," "Camp Scenes," and "Celebration"—acknowledge the composer's debt to community spirit. The first movement is written in song form, the second in sonata form with two themes, featuring Lillian Nakano on shamisen, the third is a theme and six variations, while Japanese folk dance with *taiko* breaks inspired the last movement. Horiuchi was fortunate to collaborate with his aunt Lillian Nakano, a master of *nagauta* shamisen.[126] Nakano's incarceration at Heart Mountain and Jerome concentration camps heightened the meaning of her participation in this work. The fourth movement, "Celebration," for example, highlights a melody created from the *nagauta* shamisen's patterned music supported by a jazz-based harmonic and rhythmic framework. Shamisen music featured in the opening and middle sections, the first three choruses in the solo section, and the final section serve to unify the movement. The plucked lute's main theme is accompanied by *taiko*-inspired rhythms written into tenor sax, bass clarinet, bass, and percussion parts. Scalar material for this movement draws on G-Phrygian, a musical scale embodied in the Japanese pentatonic scale, *kumoi-joshi*, containing a flatted second degree. Use of this scale facilitates inclusion of the shamisen and lends a Japanese tonal and timbral aesthetic to the movement and entire piece.

A unifying element in Horiuchi's music is rhythm, an influence of the groove Horace Tapscott captured in his playing, evident in the composition "Mochi Groove." *Taiko* drum rhythms heard in Japanese folk dances at Obon festivals provided the inspiration for Horiuchi's socialist gaze in creating music for the people, the community. As an example, his piece *Next Step* evokes a Japanese American transculturated sound, synthesizing the *dongo taiko* rhythm[127] into a jazz idiom, which pianist Jon Jang whimsically describes as a "bright, triplet feel—a sort of a Japanese American swing."[128]

The fifteen albums Horiuchi recorded over a period of eleven years display a rich outpouring of musical ideas and the versatility of a highly gifted composer. Horiuchi's compositional concepts up to 1992 were largely driven by his political convictions and exploration of a Japanese American sensibility, as exemplified by his pieces *Oxnard Beet* and "In Movement." *Oxnard Beet* is a solo piano work and album dedicated to the 1903 sugar-beet strike by Japanese and Mexican farmworkers in Oxnard, California. Horiuchi revealed the musical inspiration behind his first two albums, reflecting his socialist inclinations that spotlight folk music as "music of the people": "When I became politically conscious, the folk dances and songs from Japanese American festivals, such as Obon and Nisei Week, became a major source of my writing."[129]

Compositions on the two albums—*Next Step* (1988) and *Issei Spirit* (1989)—firmly establish an air of freedom inspired by the expanded boundaries of free jazz and explore approaches to synthesizing Japanese music influences. Horiuchi presented another side of his musical personality in his extended compositions "Little Tokyo Suite" (1992) and *Poston Sonata* (1992)— more melodic, lyrical works that rearticulate Japanese musical elements in a jazz-based idiom. These pieces are more structured and arranged as works for larger ensembles. The album *Calling Is It and Now* (1995) marks a transition in Horiuchi's music, following a shift from Asian Improv Records as his producer to Soul Note, an Italian jazz label founded in 1979. The album debuts his new quartet: tenor saxophonist Francis Wong, bassist Anders Swanson, and drummer Jeanette Wrate. Music journalist Brian Phillips writes about the music on *Calling Is It and Now* as "an unsettling blend of influences and at times, it almost seems that there is a battle to see which side wins. At this point the quartet are still feeling each other out, but it is a fascinating process."[130] After 1992, Horiuchi's change in residence from San Diego to the Los Angeles area along with the arrival of the CD as a recording media seem to signal his departure from intentionally relying on a Japanese American sound and taking on a more spontaneous, eclectic character that gave him free reign. Subsequent albums exhibit continuing development of Horiuchi's musical language that synthesizes jazz, Japanese musical elements, and atonality in unchartered territory that was uniquely his own. The shamisen becomes more prominent after learning the traditional repertoire from his aunt Lillian, facilitating his understanding of the instrument's musical potential. Horiuchi constantly explored new sources for musical ideas whether from newly born son Kenzo's gestures and expressions when asleep or his meditation on the beauty of a single drop of dew in "Dew Drop." The latter composition reveals Horiuchi's Zen practice of the Kwan Um School. A dew drop symbolizes one's life according to the Buddhist Diamond Sutra, and it is considered "fleet and ephemeral, yet beautiful and complete in itself. Coming and going empty-handed, our existence soon scatters with the breeze."[131] This description appears in the program of A Celebration of the Music and Artistry of Glenn Horiuchi & Friends concert that was organized to honor the pianist and shamisen player-composer at a time when his health was deteriorating.

Horiuchi's body of work encompasses a variety of compositional styles, including film music, which he studied at the University of California, Los Angeles, film scoring program from 1990 to 1991. Film scores he wrote for the TV pilot of *Lotusland* and TV drama *What Love* won prizes at the Houston International Film Fest in the early 1990s. Music to accompany the poetry of Mexican poets Juan Felipe Herrera and Margarita Luna Robles; theater music, "Langston Hughes: Good Morning Revolution" and "Up from the Soul"; and dance music, "Noh Bozos" and "Little Tokyo Suite" all display a mature musical output. Horiuchi's frequent collaborations with artists speak to the wide berth of his creativity, painting a picture of a robust artistic intellect. Performing as a guest or sideman on eight albums, including *Time to Discover* with the locally well-known Los Angeles jazz-fusion band Visions in 1993, is also part of his legacy. During his stint playing pop-oriented jazz fusion with Visions, Horiuchi discovered the pioneering Japanese American band Hiroshima. It is their music that revealed to Horiuchi the social and cultural potential open to Asian American musicians—a potential Horiuchi so passionately set out to realize, making his untimely departure devastating for those who knew him and for the community at large.

HIROSHIMA: ASIAN PERSUASION FROM SOUTHERN CALIFORNIA

We shift our attention to Hiroshima, a Japanese American jazz-pop ensemble from southern California known for captivating audiences across the United States. Birthed by Sansei brothers who grew up in East LA and the predominantly Black Crenshaw neighborhood, Hiroshima began its musical journey in 1974, becoming a major voice for the Japanese American and, more broadly, Asian American public. Original core members included Dan Kuramoto (bandleader, flute, sax), June Kuramoto (koto), Johnny Mori (*taiko* and percussion), Peter Hata (electric guitar), Dave Iwataki (keyboards), and Danny Yamamoto (drums.) Hiroshima's distinct sound reflects the diverse influences on band members' upbringing in the subcultural milieu of Blacks, Latinx, and whites in their neighborhoods, resulting in their preference for R&B, soul, rock, and Latinx dance music of the late 1960s and 1970s. The band cultivated a broad listenership with their brand of music, which synthesized traditional Japanese instruments, scales, and rhythms in an R&B-inflected, jazz-fusion style. Their music offered a blended sonic mix that resonated with Sansei audiences in their search for music they could call their own. With a foundation in R&B and soul music, Hiroshima's overall style projected a decidedly more commercial jazz-fusion feel. The intercultural blend of Hiroshima's signature sound showcases the multiplicity of voices within their musicking and a strong affinity for commercially successful African American music, which has attracted a fair percentage of African American audiences from outside the band's core community. One such event is the Playboy Jazz Festival, which draws large crowds (full capacity at 17,500 seats). Seeing them in this venue in the late 1980s, I was elated by the broad cross-cultural and cross-racial appeal of Hiroshima's music, drawing African Americans, Latinx, Asian Americans, and Euro-Americans. Attending this concert was one of the few occasions in my experience when I felt close to being "home" as a Japanese American.

The Kuramoto brothers formed Hiroshima in their desire to create a sound that represented not only Asian Americans but also other ethnic and racial groups in a style they called "cultural fusion." In the words of band leader Dan Kuramoto:

> We create musically a cross-commentary about a multitude of cultures that come from our backgrounds as Asian Americans growing up in a racially diverse America. The album title, "Between Black and White" grew from the idea that as people of Japanese heritage, we are ethnically

in the middle of black and white, drawing from the traditions of both races yet also creating an identity that is unique to our heritage.[132]

In reconfiguring racial triangulation deployed by dominant whites, Hiroshima's music bridged subordinated groups to counter competition and dissent through an intercultural sound that embodied the very essence of the band's musical credo. The band sought to connect diverse audiences, and in an early incarnation, Hiroshima revealed a strong Latinx alliance, inviting *conguero* Jess Acuña and drummer Carlos Vega to perform with the band. In 1974, the group collaborated with Latinx musician Daniel Valdez and his band America de los Indios in a concert held in San Jose, California.

The idea to form a band arose from the members' desire to explore their Japaneseness and coalesce Japanese musical elements with that of other cultural groups in forging their musical niche. The challenge was how to cross-fertilize musical elements from diverse sources to form an aesthetically balanced style. Early stylistic influences included Earth, Wind & Fire and Carlos Santana.

As an academic, Dan Kuramoto had a hand in forming Asian American Studies Central, an umbrella organization that supported the emergence of Asian American groups and activities, such as the film and media organization Visual Communications, the newspaper *Gidra*, and community picnics that brought people together. Kuramoto's stint as director of the first Asian American Studies program at California State University at Long Beach sensitized him to the need of Asians in America to forge their own identity in countering the negative stereotypes and representations of Asians in the public transcript and mass media. The band imparted to audiences what it is to be Asian American. While African Americans had a score of artists in rhythm and blues, jazz, and soul to identify with, and Chicanos and Latinx had Santana and Malo as their musical emblems of identity, Asian Americans had no musical icons to which they could aspire. Hiroshima sought to fill this void. Dan and John Kuramoto intentionally chose the name Hiroshima for its political reference: "it represented something that we should never forget because it was the single-most devastating act that man could commit upon man."[133] The attribution aimed not only to raise Asian Americans' consciousness of their Asian heritage but also to urge a sense of responsibility to never allow such destruction to be repeated. Thus, the very announcement of the band's existence embodied social activism.

For Japanese Americans, Hiroshima's music symbolizes a generation, who, in turning to their Japanese heritage as a source of inspiration, created a viable transculturated music, which made its mark in popular culture. The breadth of their popularity is evident into the 2000s, when a Hiroshima song could be heard nationwide in supermarket-canned music. The band's popularity among baby boomers remains intact as they continue to tour throughout the United States and occasionally in Mexico. Hiroshima's mainstream appeal points to the viability of creating a cultural space carved out by Japanese American artists. The band earned numerous awards at the end of the 1970s into the 1980s on the heels of the acclaim they received for their eponymous album *Hiroshima* recorded in 1979. Highlights of their awards include an Emmy for Best Music for a Children's Series, *Beansprouts* in 1978; Best New Jazz Group, Cash Box in 1979; Jazz Breakout Artist of the Year, Billboard in 1980; Grammy nomination for Best Rhythm and Blues Instrumental Performance in 1981 for "Winds of Change" on their second album, *Odori* (1980); Best Live Jazz Group, Cash Box in 1987; and the Soul Train Music Award for Best Jazz Album in 1988 for *Go*. Albums *Another Place* (1985) and *Go* (1987) received the coveted Gold Record, indicative of sales of more than five hundred thousand units domestically. In 1989, the band expanded their repertoire with a highly acclaimed musical drama, *Sansei*, starring members of Hiroshima. Compositions from their hit album *East* (1989) seeded the musical score for the drama. *Sansei* attracted large audiences, requiring an extended run at the Mark Taper Forum in Los Angeles, becoming one of the top-grossing plays in the history of that distinguished theater.[134] Notable among the accolades presented to Hiroshima from Asian American communities in Los Angeles is the 2012 Visionary Award from East West Players, the oldest Asian Pacific American theater company in the United States. More recently, the Asian Pacific American Center at the Smithsonian Institution conferred the 2019 Legend Award to Hiroshima in recognition of their enduring legacy and success nationally. Internationally, Japanese listeners' interest in their American diasporic relations led to the rerelease of the Hiroshima album *Departure* (2011) in Japan with liner notes and composition titles translated into Japanese by Minoru Kanda, an Asian American music aficionado and Asian Improv aRts liaison.

Incorporating Japanese instruments—koto, shamisen, shakuhachi, and *taiko*—imparts to the band's sound a decidedly Japanese sonic cast. It is the inclusion of these instruments in the music that gained the support of the Japanese American community early on. The idea of a popular music band with Asian American musicians drew the attention and backing of Chinese, Korean, and Filipino communities in Los Angeles. The group played for events and benefits for community organizations, such as Joint Communications,

Asian Drug Abuse Program (ADAP), Amerasia Bookstore, Little Tokyo Service Center, Japanese American Community Services (JACS), SCINCIP ("picnics" spelled backwards; sponsored by the newspaper *Gidra*), and the annual potlucks of the Asian American Studies Program at California State University at Long Beach. The community reciprocated by providing moral and financial support, making it possible for Hiroshima to record its debut album *Hiroshima*. Arista Records hazarded to produce the new band's first album; the company was impressed when one hundred and twenty thousand copies sold. Calling into the radio stations to request the music of Hiroshima and purchasing the album was all part of the community's lobbying efforts to promote the band. Great support also came from African American communities, who understood the band members' search for their own identity, giving them airtime on Black music stations. The radio program *Quiet Storm* along with mainstream jazz and pop radio stations contributed toward the success of the first Asian American band to receive radio play.

In a Hiroshima performance, June Kuramoto's florid display on Japanese koto is a main attraction. Her koto playing enacts a Japanese American identity as she weaves innovative musical ideas with traditionally idiomatic koto stylings into pop-inflected jazz fusion. Central to the impact of seeing and hearing Japanese Americans and traditional Japanese instruments live is exposing listeners to a rearticulation of Japanese musical elements in the band's oeuvre. Kuramoto's traditional training and masterful technique enable her to improvise in a popular-music setting with great flair. She retains the idiomatic sound of the koto by using various pentatonic modes heard in the traditional repertoire, superimposing them onto the band's harmonic structure. Using a pentatonic rather than a diatonic or chromatic scale allows her a wider range on the instrument and increased improvisational potential. Kuramoto prefers pentatonic scales since they form the basis of her musical training, which is Japanese, not Western. The challenge of fitting the idiomatic playing style of the koto into a contemporary music format by performing over the chord changes is well met by this artist; she is given free rein in the band to follow her musical impulse. Kuramoto, who also composes pieces for the band, is a pathfinder, who heralds a new direction for the koto while skillfully keeping alive idiomatic aspects of the instrument to preserve its Japanese sound. Hiroshima's music lends weight and legitimacy to Japanese American musicking.

The successful use of traditional Japanese instruments in Hiroshima's music sparked a trend among musicians who experimented with the idiomatic techniques and timbral colors of not only the koto and *taiko* but of the *biwa* (four-string plucked lute) and shakuhachi in jazz-fusion and American-pop music. Sweet Honey in the Rock approached Kuramoto to add koto stylings in one of their songs of the early 1980s. Continuing my study of the classical repertoire of the koto while enrolled in the ethnomusicology program at the University of California at Los Angeles, I experienced firsthand the influence of Hiroshima, whose music was an emblem of Japanese American culture. I became interested in the koto's stylistic niche in jazz-fusion and popular music and had an opportunity to contribute koto accompanimental parts and a solo in a jazz-fusion instrumental piece entitled "Salutations to the Sea," written by musician-composer George Candreva. (A recording of the piece was forwarded to Hiroshima for possible pick up by the famous group, although the prospect never materialized.) In 1982, Los Angeles singer-songwriter James Robert Poggensee invited me to compose a koto accompanimental part for his pop song "Friends and Lonely Lovers," recorded and marketed by the artist. Japanese musicians who emigrated to Los Angeles in the 1970s and 1980s also took part in the jazz-fusion trend: Kazu Matsui, a shakuhachi player and composer, whose album *Sign of the Snow Crane* (1989) was the first of a succession of fifteen; Osamu Kitajima, a *biwa* and koto player, whose albums *Masterless Samurai* and *Benzaiten* rode the wave of Japanese-infused music; and Yutaka Yokokura, a pianist commercially produced by Dave Grusin and Larry Rosen for his album *Love Light* in 1978 and *Yutaka* in 1988. These musicians formed a network and sometimes played on each other's albums.

Hiroshima's bold inclusion of traditional Japanese instruments in a popular-music idiom heralded music's capacity to represent Japanese Americans in American mainstream culture. The band reached many firsts in public: the first Japanese American group to receive radio play, earn Gold Record status in the music industry, and have their music be nationally distributed. The trail Hiroshima blazed within the commercial music world opened the possibility for other Japanese/Asian American musicians to consider success too. Most important is the band's interracial and intercultural musical mix could serve as a formula for future coalitions that could unite minoritarian communities in the struggle for equality and inclusion.

SOUTHERN CALIFORNIA ACTIVISM

The Hiroshima phenomenon was a product of the political activism of the Asian American movement in southern California and the coalitions of people of color brought together by Third World Liberation Front ideology and worldwide liberation struggles. Political activism in southern California flourished in tandem with direct action taken in the San Francisco Bay Area. Mo Nishida outlines two key themes of the Asian American movement that surfaced in southern California, identity and serving the people, concepts embraced by the broader Asian American movement. The themes were coupled in activists' minds: "We are people with no identity except the white man's and the only place and way you could find your identity was to serve the people in our respective communities."[135] Aligning with the Association for the Advancement of Creative Movement's community support model, college campuses and communities served as centers for the movement's activities in southern California. California State University, Long Beach, and UCLA led the fight for ethnic studies. Movement activists in San Francisco established links with southern California by setting up a branch of the Asian American Political Alliance at UCLA and, in 1968, sending organizers from TWLF to speak at California State University, Long Beach, to assist in developing organizational skills, strategies, and formulating political demands for instituting ethnic-studies curricula. At UCLA, the AAPA and Orientals Concerned organizations advanced Asian American students' political consciousness and community connections. The success of installing the Third World College at the University of California, San Diego, and the launching of the United Mexican American Students organization by Chicana/o students were part of TWLF coalition efforts.[136]

A handful of movement institutions were critical to political activism in southern California. *Gidra* was a monthly publication founded by UCLA Asian American students as a platform for discussing and sharing political ideas and strategies as well as analyzing the Asian American movement's objectives. Widespread community activism, a cornerstone of the movement, manifested in the creation of Yellow Brotherhood, Asian American Hardcore, and JACS to address the growing plight of drug abuse and gang membership among youth in Los Angeles. East Wind, a political league composed of local organization leaders involved in the Los Angeles Asian American movement, formed in 1972. It was a group of twenty-five to thirty members who linked campus and community activism, broadened community involvement beyond drug issues, and guided and directed coalition building. As a disciplined, Marxist-Leninist group, it worked on various fronts of the community: labor, redevelopment of Little Tokyo, *Gidra*, and the Pioneer Senior Center. True to their TWLF leftist ideology, East Wind supported other minority groups while activating Japanese American political consciousness and providing necessary community services and goals to effect social change.[137] Southern California activists may have taken their political cues from Bay

Area political workers, but they developed their own movement organizations and institutions in addressing local issues and community needs.

GEORGE ABE: MUSICIAN WITH DEEP ROOTS

George Abe, a performer of shakuhachi and Japanese court music, is a Sansei pioneer in the Los Angeles Japanese American music scene. Born in Manzanar concentration camp, Abe's musicking and life as a shakuhachi performer and *taiko* drummer in Los Angeles narrates an upbringing with strong connections to Japanese culture through music and Buddhist practice. He grew up around artists and musicians: his mother was a *tanka* (seventeen-syllable poetry) poet, and his father played and repaired *biwas*. Abe's parents exposed him to Japanese music at an early age, bringing him to recitals of *naniwa-bushi*, *rōei* (court-music songs), and *shigin*. Songs that became a part of his persona were the Japanese folk songs "Tanko-bushi," "Kuroda-bushi," and "Itsuki no komori uta," which he listened to at home in his formative years. After the war, when the Wakita family of musicians in Los Angeles hosted his family, Abe regularly heard live koto and shamisen music. His musical training also includes Western instruments; he studied clarinet in elementary school and subsequently switched to saxophone while attending Los Angeles High School. Abe's membership at the Senshin Buddhist Temple in Los Angeles, which commenced with Japanese-language instruction, is key to his identification as a Japanese American musician. Also integral is his training in *gagaku* for ten years with Suenobu Togi, preparing him to play for Buddhist ceremonies at Senshin. Cofounding Kinnara Buddhist Taiko with Rev. Masao Kodani further cemented his commitment and interest in Japanese music. Abe immersed himself in the Kinko school of shakuhachi playing for eight years, with some training in the Zen style. His overall experience imbues a strong spiritual aesthetic in the music he plays. Performing primarily on Japanese instruments, he identifies his musical sensibilities as *Japanese American*, citing the influence of Motown, rock, and jazz on his playing.[138]

Abe's response to the Third World Liberation Front and Asian American movement in the late 1960s to 1970s offers a glimpse into the local activism of the City of Angels. He was compelled to act when questions about identity—"Who are we in America?" and "What's been our history here?"—were raised by the Asian American student movement. Attempting to answer these questions intellectually with very few sources available compelled Abe and other activists to open Amerasia Bookstore in Japantown. The bookstore functioned as a retail store, gallery, meeting place, and concert venue for the community.¹³⁹ Abe's knowledge and interest in Japanese music coalesced with his active participation in the community as his identification as Japanese American further evolved.

Vital to the Asian American jazz scene in Los Angeles were the Jazz Fest series from 1982 to 1983, showcasing jazz makers from both the local area and San Francisco. Abe had a hand in forming the nonprofit wing of Amerasia Bookstore, which sponsored the jazz series as part of its programming of book-release parties, poetry readings, panel discussions, and concerts highlighting the music and poetry of women artists. San Francisco Bay Area's Russel Baba (soprano sax), Jeanne Mercer (*taiko*), Paul Yamazaki (bass clarinet), Mark Izu (bass), Randy Senzaki (tenor sax), and Glen Iwaoka (drums) exposed audiences to an array of innovative music. These artists demonstrated their free-jazz, experimental, and boundary-pushing approach to music.¹⁴⁰ An untitled piece opened the 1982 concert starring Baba, on *suona*, alto sax, and flute, Jeanne Baba, and Mark Izu. The performance explored new sonic territory with an introductory blast of a Chinese double-reed *suona*, intoning long-held notes of a pentatonic scale in a minimalistic melody supported by circular breathing. A rhythmic ostinato played on *taiko* and a repeated note motif plucked on string bass formed the backdrop for Baba's improvisations on *suona* and alto saxophone. The playful, short phrases sounded on saxophone contrasted with the sustained notes of the opening *suona* improvisatory passages. The sparse texture and unusual instrumental combination of acoustic bass, *taiko*, and *suona*, the interspersed saxophone stylings embodying the ensemble's spirit of adventure, and hints of a minimalist Japanese aesthetic, which some of the members internalized from their *gagaku* training, created an artful moment. The inventiveness and dynamism of the Bay Area's free-jazz musicians enlivened the jazz scene in Los Angeles, promoting improvisational and conceptual approaches to music. Prompted by these musical explorations, Abe, on shakuhachi, joined forces with local musicians Sharon Koga, on cello, and Danny Yamamoto, on *taiko*, percussion, and vibraphone in a 1982 performance of three pieces programmed as one of the Jazz Fest events. The trio, calling themselves Moonlight Orchestra, tested the intersection of shakuhachi, plucked cello, and vibraphone melodic stylings combined with *taiko* rhythms. In the group's performance, an untitled composition opened with the sound of a bronze meditation gong used in Buddhist rituals, followed by the entrance of a traditional shakuhachi melody accompanied by plucked chords and bassline on cello. The texture thickened with *taiko* playing a gradually accelerating drum roll, modeled on the *kakko* drum roll in *gagaku*, alternating with freely performed idiomatic rhythms. The *taiko* then set up a steady beat; Abe entered playing Japanese folk melodies on *takebue* (bamboo flute). From there, the music gradually unfolded into a series of free-form *taiko* solos and dialogues between *taiko* and hand-held brass *atarigane* gong, alternating with traditional folk melodies on *takebue* all supported by a second *taiko* keeping a steady beat. The composition shifts between traditional and new material; a venturing away from the traditional to a new musical landscape, returning to time-honored sounds.

The 1970s and 1980s, two fertile decades for Asian American musicians, ignited growing musical activity among numerous artists and bands in Los Angeles. Many formed dance bands, such as Winfield Summit, which played top-forty American popular music as well as original material for fraternity and sorority parties. Other musical currents included folk music, which Joanne (now named Nobuko) Miyamoto, Chris Iijima, and Charlie Chin popularized among Asian Americans with their politically charged songs. Budding artists and songwriters would gather and spend hours merely jamming and reveling in rock-and-jazz-fusion styles, forming a network of musicians. These informal sessions served as a training ground for many in honing their music writing and performing skills.

JAPANESE AMERICAN VISION

Visions, a jazz-pop fusion band, stands out in the Japanese/Asian American music scene in southern California. A husband-and-wife team—Alan and Marsha Furutani from Gardena, California—founded the group in the 1970s. The couple were active in a few bands prior to founding Visions. Music groups they initiated included Street Flower, a top-forty band with pianist Scott Nagatani, and a blues band, which often shared billing with Hiroshima at many Asian American events affiliated with the Asian American movement. One of the longest-lasting bands, Visions, performed locally in the Japanese American community from the middle of the 1970s until the early 1990s. Performing at a variety of events was their primary contribution to the community.

Asked whether music was an effective vehicle for expressing a Japanese American identity prompted cautious responses from the couple:

Alan: Yes, even though I am sure it comes out in my own playing, being Asian, putting your finger on it [musically identifying what is Asian] is not easy to do, but it's there with whatever kind of music you're playing.
Marsha: Well, I think it depends on how you approach the music too. If it [being Japanese American] is an expression of how you feel about things,

yes. But if you are trying to create a Japanese American sound, then I don't think it's [Vision's music] is necessarily that representative.¹⁴¹

The Furutanis considered the affective quality of their music paramount. They were less occupied with creating a Japanese American sound, choosing instead to write music from the heart and from their own experiences—music that had feeling and could connect with listeners. They spoke about their approach to musicking:

> I think it's hard for Asian Americans. I think Hiroshima developed a sound . . . a long time ago when Benny Yee was with them. His songs really got to your heart. The problem I feel now is that a lot of it [music written by Asian Americans] is more intellectual than sounds from your heart, which is what we wanted to do. We weren't that concerned with trying to create a sound but trying to do something that we felt—that we had feeling for. I think that's hard because it depends on what you grew up with, what's in your ear, and things like when you had your first girlfriend and such. We tried to write music on that basis: from our own experiences.¹⁴²

These insights reveal the Furutanis' preference for an organic, emotive creative process vis-á-vis a deliberately intellectual approach to musicking they felt characterizes the free-jazz stylings of some artists. Alan Furutani deemed his compositions as being typically American. He attributes this quality to his youth, when he listened to traditional jazz and top-forty popular music. The musical style of his songs contrasts greatly with the more experimental music of Russel Baba and Makoto Horiuchi, whom he thought successful in combining Japanese and American musical streams.

As producers, the Furutanis organized numerous music festivals highlighting Asian American musicians, including the folk trio Joanne, Chris, and Charlie and other local bands. One such festival held in Gardena, a predominantly Japanese American community, featured all Asian American dance bands in the area. Alan Furutani actively produced concerts for Yellow Brotherhood, showcasing musicians from the neighborhood, and, for a period of four years, the Jazz Fest at Amerasia Bookstore in downtown Los Angeles. One of the highlights of Amerasia Bookstore's programming was a women's performing series, featuring varied Asian American singers, poets, and other performers. Although Los Angeles and its environs' local culture and music continued to distinguish itself from that of the San Francisco Bay Area, political activism and cultural awakening spurred by the Asian American movement created a bond between the two locales in musically expressing a shared heritage.

The more commercial, pop- and R&B-influenced sounds coming out of Los Angeles–area bands easily drew audiences. In the early years, Asian American listeners filled audiences for Hiroshima and Visions, performing primarily for Japanese American community events. Many musician-composers and bands relied on community support for their success. The ascent in popularity of Hiroshima and their Asian and R&B-inflected jazz-fusion style soon attracted cross-racial and cross-cultural listeners, diversifying audiences for Asian American music.

SONGS OF STRUGGLE

We now turn to the artistry and politics of the folk-music group Joanne, Chris, and Charlie, activist musicians who advocated revolutionary socialism through their songs and performances throughout the United States.[143] From 1970 to 1974, they expressed their radical views, singing songs critical of capitalism, racism, and sexism and propagating socialist stances meant to liberate and empower people of color in the United States.[144] The group sang at protest demonstrations and rallies, college campuses, conferences, and community-based events across the country, prompting the rise of other Asian American songwriters and bands as well. Although this trio formed in New York City, their singular impact in raising the political consciousness of Asian American students and cultural workers in the United States merits their inclusion in this volume. Moreover, shaped by Black Panther ideology, Joanne Nobuko Miyamoto, the most emphatic of the three about Asian Americans taking a stand and addressing issues of racism and United States aggression in Vietnam, originally hails from Los Angeles (and currently has returned there to continue her work). Miyamoto's music, dance, and theater of the past forty years are synonymous with Asian American artistic activity in southern California.

The tale of this well-known trio active in the Asian American movement begins with the collaboration between Nobuko (formerly Joanne) Miyamoto and Chris Iijima. The two singer-songwriters initially met at an Asian Americans for Action meeting, organized by activist Nisei in New York City.[145] About a year later, singer-songwriter Charlie Chin joined, forming a trio. The trio wrote songs of struggle, fully believing that their lyrics could raise the political and social consciousness of Asian Americans throughout the East

Coast, Midwest, and West Coast. Miyamoto's and Iijima's songs, written in a folk/blues style, rang out as a call to action to Asian Americans in the 1970s. Their only album as a trio, *A Grain of Sand: Music for the Struggle by Asians in America* (1973), was politically driven as a means to build and promote alternative forms of media, art, and new methods of agitprop in forming a revolutionary culture—a culture that would bilaterally serve the Third World Liberation Front and Asian American movement.

The trio's Marxist ideological orientation aligned itself with the Third World Liberation Front in its view that the struggles of people of color in the United States were part of the global struggle against imperialism, capitalism, racism, and sexism. The liner notes to *A Grain of Sand* forcefully asserts the group's agency of deploying music in the revolutionary struggle to bring about social and political change. They preface a description of their songs through an historical lens: "We live in a society that has systematically, throughout its history, attempted to alienate us from each other, our people and ourselves. As Asians in America we know how the history of our people has been a constant battle to survive in the midst of a hostile environment and we know also that we are not unique in regard to that situation."[146] Their lyrics pointedly voice the group's belief in Third World unity and the support of global struggles against US imperialism. Joanne, Chris, and Charlie viewed music as a direct means to educate people about issues and expose them to new ideas and a revolutionary culture that could "talk back" to the forces that oppressed them. Marxist conceptions about the potential role of art as a tool for social change fueled their musicking and the notion that music held great promise:

> Music has the power to touch; at the same time it can move people collectively while striking some emotion deep within an individual. The struggle must recognize that power and utilize it! We are fighting the most sophisticated propaganda in the world. What we possess is truth—something real that people are searching for. We possess something that can really reach people and we must put thought, creativity and energy into our attempts to communicate our politics if we are to fully realize the potential of music and art as organizing tools and propaganda.[147]

Imbedded in their songs is the notion of collective struggle and a belief in the efficacy of coalitions. The power and appeal of the trio's music stem not only from the political force of their songs but also from a decided aesthetic expressed in the blues-inflected, sometimes rock-inflected, guitar stylings and soulful voice of Chris Iijima that could reach people on a deeper, more personal level.

The folk trio felt strongly about the political role of art and the artist's responsibility to use it as a weapon in their political struggles: "We have tried to integrate our music with our politics so that our music is an extension of our politics and not the other way around. To that end we believe artists should engage in political struggle outside the realm of 'Art' so that whatever is created is from a broad perspective and not from a limited aspect of the struggle."[148] The radical stance of this trio falls to the extreme Left within the spectrum of political positionings among Japanese/Asian American musicians. Their uncompromising politics empowered many Japanese/Asian American youth who heard the trio perform their songs at rallies, conferences, and college settings.

It is instructive to follow the evolution of the most politically militant member of the trio, Joanne Nobuko Miyamoto. Born in Los Angeles in 1939, Miyamoto grew up during the upheaval of the Japanese American internment during World War II. After the war, she and her family lived with her aunt and uncle in Los Angeles, communing closely with other Japanese American families for economic survival and moral support. As a youth, Miyamoto lived in a few locales in Los Angeles—Crenshaw, Boyle Heights, and Pico Union, neighborhoods where substantial numbers of Japanese Americans formed communities. It was "out of need,"[149] she recalls, that a sense of community existed among Japanese Americans. Directly experiencing wilting racial discrimination during the war years laid the foundation for her strong antiracist views.

Asian Americans for Action, founded in New York City by two Nisei women—Kazu Iijima (Chris Iijima's mother) and Minn Matsuda—bolstered Miyamoto's and Iijima's political motivations. Living in New York brought Miyamoto into contact with the Kochiyama and Iijima families, politically active Nisei and Sansei who were members of AAA. Miyamoto and Iijima began writing political-commentary music as AAA volunteers. "The People's Beat," the first song they wrote jointly at a week-long Japanese American Citizens League conference, pulled together Asian American political groups in Chicago. The duo introduced the song to the Black Panthers in Chicago, with lyrics based on a speech given by Fred Hampton, who had just been assassinated by Chicago police. Before performing the song, Miyamoto and Iijima showed two films: one about the atomic bombing of the city of Hiroshima and another of the Vietnam War. The films served to support their talk about the similar attitudes that mainstream Americans had toward people of both African and Asian descent. "The People's Beat" elicited a strong link between Asian and Black political agendas.

Miyamoto's and Iijima's musical partnership continued as they cowrote songs to perform for Asian American community organizations across California, such as Yellow Brotherhood in Los Angeles, Japanese Community Youth Council in San Francisco, Yellow Seed Youth Program in Stockton, and others. After Chin joined them in 1970, the trio toured around the United States, networking with Asian American political and community organizations.

The trio's political bent toward interracial solidarity spoke to their affiliation with the Third World Liberation Front.[150] They reached out to New York City's Latinx community by writing political commentary songs in Spanish for the Puerto Rican and Dominican squatters' movement. Their popularity within this segment of the population resulted in recording two songs followed by a year of singing engagements for Puerto Rican organizations and communities. Performing at the Puerto Rican Liberation Day celebration at Madison Square Garden in New York was evidence of their close ties to this community. Joining Nueva Canción singers and *cancionero* poets,[151] who accompanied them on *cuatro* (four-string plucked lute), at The Dot coffeehouse in New York City reinforced the relationship. Singing about the struggles for freedom and equality in Latin American and Caribbean nations with Latinx musicians and poets inspired the trio to merge Nueva Canción songs into their repertoire. They freely traversed Asian, Black, and Latinx communities as well as schools and colleges, spreading their political messages through song.

The impact of Joanne, Chris, and Charlie's music lies in its intent and clarity. Their music accompanied the journey many Asian Americans undertook in those times of possibility and change. Chris Iijima's grasp of the roots of Asian American identity, broadly conceived and moving beyond merely reclaiming one's heritage, expanded audiences' awareness of what could be achieved. Having been raised in an activist family in New York City, he had experience that led him to believe that Asian American identity "originally had less to do with who one was and more to do with for what one stood for."[152] Iijima describes Asian American identity as a composite of strategies and actions that one could envision as spokes of a wheel, representing both separate and shared social and political issues that interrelate and find common cause in the center. One spoke, he notes, signifies organizing and engaging Asian Americans in addressing specific political concerns. Reaching out to other racial groups around shared political issues and causes denotes a second spoke, while establishing ground with the larger public to address racism and institutionalized discrimination delineates a third spoke. The interracial coalition Iijima suggests foretells the political strategy needed to form relationships between communities to address the current racial reckoning in the sharply divided society we face today. Building Asian American representation within an international arena from which to fight governmental policies that impoverish people globally is the final spoke in Iijima's composite identity. He challenges Asian Americans, suggesting that one's identity is constructed through ethnic, national, and global coalitions in pursuing social and political change. Iijima laments the absence of a connection between racial identity and progressive politics today, with identity being narrowed to merely heritage, dismantling any coherent Asian American identity.[153]

Spurred by the songs and political ardor of Joanne, Chris, and Charlie, three San Jose musicians formed another Asian American movement band, Yokohama, California, coined from the title of an early Japanese American novel by Toshio Mori. Songs about social change on the album *A Grain of Sand* galvanized original band members, Peter Horikoshi (guitar, vocals), Sam Takimoto (vocals, recorder), and Michael Okagaki (guitar, vocals), to begin writing and performing original songs. Yokohama, California expanded to include songwriter Robert Kikuchi-Yngojo (vocals, keyboard, percussion) and Keith Inouye (guitar, vocals) for the band's eponymous album released in 1977. Live performances at community events in California in the late 1970s called for additional musicians: Ricky Takahashi (drums), José Alarcon (flute), Steve Yamaguma (bass), and Doug "Duke" Santos (congas). Songs on the album are commentaries about past and current struggles, individual experiences, and sentiments of Japanese Americans, all calls for unity and social change among oppressed people. Again, growing interest among Japanese of their diasporic counterparts in the United States resulted in the rerelease of the album *Yokohama, California* in Japan in 2012. Minoru Kanda, introduced earlier, translated the album's liner notes and song lyrics from English into Japanese. Yokohama, California's music is etched into the history of the Asian American movement's music.[154]

ICONIC TAIKO BEATS: MUSICAL PULSE OF JAPANESE AMERICA

The account of *taiko* drumming presented here traces its early development, commencing in the late 1960s into the 1970s, of a transculturated Japanese music embraced by Sansei as an expression of their Buddhist practice, their political activism impelled by the Asian American movement, or a recovery of their Japanese heritage; for some, drumming served at least two or perhaps all three purposes. Other scholars have written extensively about *taiko* practices and music.[155] It is the cultural and political value of *taiko* to Japanese Americans that is important to this study. I argue for this diasporic drumming tradition, initially fostered by Japanese Americans, as a music style they could own, enabling them to articulate a reconfigured identity that powered their self-confidence.

The sound of *taiko* resonates with me. I felt its visceral power at folk festivals I attended while living in Japan—a power undoubtedly permeating generations of musicians performing this music as an integral part of Japanese rituals and celebrations. When I returned to the United States, after completing field research on *nōmai* (folk, masked dance drama), I briefly joined Kinnara Taiko in Los Angeles as a participant observer. My reason for joining followed on the heels of documenting this pioneering *taiko* group at Senshin Buddhist Temple for a *hōraku* ceremony.[156] Playing *taiko* enriched my understanding of the training and meaning attached to *taiko* performance. I reacted enthusiastically to the assertive sound of the drum, its power exerting a positive force in claiming my identity as a Japanese American. Reading anthropologist Kimberly Powell's study of sound identity in *taiko* reinforced my affinity with the art. Powell details how the sound evokes an "acoustemological sense of knowing," a kind of instinctual connection felt by Japanese Americans upon hearing and performing *taiko*, claiming that aesthetic forms are important avenues for Asian Americans in socially constructing identities.[157]

Taiko drumming is the most celebrated and widely practiced music of Japanese/Asian America. As we head into the 2020s, drummers include a growing number of non-Asians as well. Amidst the rise of the Asian American movement, the thundering sound and force of *taiko* drumming established itself as a dynamic response to racial and ethnic marginalization and pejorative stereotypes of Japanese/Asian Americans in American mainstream culture and media. The *taiko*'s sound became an emblem of cultural pride and empowerment for Sansei. Third-generation drummers exercise their agency by performing *taiko* not merely as a form of cultural expression but, for many, as a musical statement of their political position, renouncing the assimilationist tendencies of Nisei parents. Originally a member of San Jose Taiko, Susan Hayase asserts: "The movement for justice and equality for all people against assimilation and racist violence, for pride and a new Nikkei (Japanese American) identity and culture are what give American *taiko* its strong appeal, its power to inspire."[158]

During its incipient stage, ensemble-style *taiko*—*kumi daiko*, a music practice that sprang up in Japan during the 1950s—served as the prototype for newly created groups. The practice evolved into a Japanese American performance tradition from the late 1960s on and further fashioned as broadly Asian American, beginning in the 1970s. Central to the US tradition of *taiko* is its connection to Japanese/Asian music and culture, but there is no expectation that performers be of Asian descent. As a result, members hail from a variety of racial and ethnic backgrounds, although most practitioners in the United States remain Asian American.

For Sansei, thunderous sounds powerfully performed with synchronized, choreographed movements create both a sonic and visual aesthetic that projects our ancestral ties to Japan. The sound and *sight* of *taiko* symbolizes and captures a tradition of drumming that has its roots in Japanese folk-festival music. *Taiko* is speculated to be two thousand years old, and it made its way to the United States with Japanese immigrants, who first arrived starting in the late 1800s. Its primary function is to provide rhythmic accompaniment to dance in religious rituals, festivals, folk songs, and Kabuki theater performances. In Japan, its ubiquitous use in festivals, court music and dance, Buddhist and Shinto rituals, folk and classical theater traditions, as well as folk music and dance imbues the *taiko* with a cultural significance that made it emblematic of a Japanese American ethnic identity. In the traditional contexts mentioned above, the drum was played singly or, in some instances, in pairs. The post–World War II phenomenon of *taiko* ensembles in Japan took place in the hands of Daihachi Oguchi, who, in 1951, assembled a group of *taiko* drummers to reinvent ancient rhythms of the Osuwa shrine. Oguchi, a jazz drummer, utilized a trap drum as his prototype, arranging different-sized *taiko* to play varying rhythmic layers, giving the drumming a more improvisatory feel. He scored the high-pitched *shime-daiko* to play the repetitive *ji* (backing rhythm); the *o-daiko*, a simple rhythm, serving as a base; and the *chū-daiko* for a variety of "propulsive riffs" that give the music rhythmic momentum. To this polyrhythmic texture, Oguchi added the small *atarigane* hand-held gong, sounding its own rhythmic line. Rev. Mas Kodani of Senshin Buddhist Temple and cofounder of the ensemble Kinnara Taiko relates how the first originally composed music for *taiko* was performed impromptu by groups at a hot spring (*onsen*) in Hokkaido, the northernmost island of Japan:

> The first groups existed before *taiko* ever arrived here [in the US]. So, the Hokkaido *onsen* groups started as entertainment for the guests. They came up with this idea of "let's get a whole bunch of *taiko*s and make some pieces; they created original pieces. They drew on whatever their sensibility was, but they were all brand-new pieces. . . . The earliest one I can trace is 1957, which is pretty early.[159]

Sukeroku Daiko, another pioneering *taiko* ensemble in Japan, based its playing style on drumming rhythms on the Edo-*bayashi* festival-music

Figure 5.5. Kinnara Taiko of Senshin Buddhist Temple, Los Angeles, n.d. Photo by Rev. Masao Kodani.

tradition in Tokyo. Formed under the patronage of Yushima Tenjin Shrine, Sukeroku Daiko developed a performing style that combined *hōgaku* (traditional Japanese drumming of the Edo period [1600–1868]) and *Edo-bayashi* (Tokyo festival music). They also initiated synchronized choreographic drumming movements, and their drumming features quick tempos, fluency, and flashy solos, contributing to the growing *taiko* movement in Japan.[160] These stylistic features, along with their repertoire and drum-stand designs, are pervasive in the practices of most North American *taiko* ensembles.

North American *taiko* traces its lineage to three groups in the United States: San Francisco Taiko Dojo established in 1968 by Seichi Tanaka;[161] Kinnara Buddhist Taiko formed in 1970 by Rev. Mas Kodani and George Abe (figure 5.5); and San Jose Taiko founded in 1973 by P. J. and Roy Hirabayashi.[162] The three ensembles formed the first wave of *taiko* groups to emerge in the United States, sharing repertoires, drills, forms, styles, and instrument building. I focus on the first wave of groups because they coincide with the rise of Asian American political activism and the search for an identity with a link to an Asian past. Participants in this first wave of groups were predominantly Japanese Americans who performed *taiko* as a religious practice, an artistic endeavor, or a political response to the mobilization of Asian Americans in the movement, in general, and to the injustice of the internment camps, in particular.

San Francisco Taiko Dojo's (SFTD) practice mirrors the *kumi daiko* performance style of Sukeroku Daiko in Japan. As a member of Sukeroku

Daiko, Seichi Tanaka learned their repertoire and drumming techniques. Before coming to the United States, he was given permission by the group to teach and disseminate their style of drumming to interested parties abroad. Tanaka's *taiko* training typifies a Japanese hierarchical structure that calls for martial-arts discipline and precision. His training method emphasizes "strict mental discipline, athleticism, and the idea of *rei*, respectful courtesy."[163] The martial approach to training, originally introduced by Sukeroku Daiko and further developed by Tanaka, introduced Japanese spiritual and philosophical concepts that fostered centering the mind and body, building musicianship and drumming techniques, and cultivating respect, courtesy, and unity within a group.[164] San Francisco Taiko Dojo has played a major role in the development of many *taiko* groups in North America; its rigorous martial and spiritual approach to drumming excites audiences and participants alike.

A look at Kinnara Buddhist Taiko (KBT) reveals a different approach and function. KBT is responsible for fashioning what founder Rev. Masao Kodani calls a truly Japanese American art form—a hybrid mixture of Japanese and American elements. KBT's style of drumming is a Japanese American rearticulation of *taiko* that has "no direct ancestor in Japan." Buddhist *taiko* is an innovation within the *hōraku* tradition of "Dharma entertainment," an event intended "to lead the performer as well as the viewer to a deeper awareness of the Dharma [meaning 'the teachings,' 'the law,' 'the way']."[165] Music in Buddhism expresses the joy of religious awakening and functions as a conduit to lead others on the path. In Buddhist *taiko*, two instruments are key: *taiko*, which serves as the *hōko* or dharma drum, and the conch shell, as the *hōra*. Both instruments represent the voice of Buddha or the universality of the Buddha's teachings that "signal one's movement along the path of religion—it is the beckoning and urging voice of the Buddha-Dharma."[166] Rev. Kodani and George Abe created KBT in their quest to attract youth to the Senshin Buddhist Temple and instruct them about Buddhist concepts and attitudes. The ensemble is part of *kinnara*, a Buddhist study group dedicated to the preservation and promotion of Buddhist culture in America. The objective of the study group includes maintaining Japanese court music and dance performance for *hōraku*[167]—an offering of entertainment following major Buddhist ceremonies. KBT members strive to play *taiko* in a Buddhist manner that teaches one to become "selfless." The ability to drum in unison is learned as practitioners endeavor to achieve "egolessness." Rehearsals involve no formal training of the fundamentals of playing *taiko*; in following a Buddhist approach, neophytes learn by emulating and memorizing what other members do. Learning *taiko* in this way cultivates a Japanese facet of one's identity that holds that learning through imitation leads to achieving selflessness, which, in turn, promotes self-discovery. Rev. Mas Kodani articulates the process this way:

> We very rarely talk about *taiko*. We just do it, and whatever you get out of it is your own personal discovery of it. Self-discovery is faster; the time it takes to break down your ego and the time it takes to teach you each theory and then take you to a lab and do it takes much longer. It's easier to take the time breaking down your ego to get you to a point of exasperation, and then when you get beyond that point, you're like a sponge. What seems to be at the heart of Japanese music to me is learning the subtleties [of the music] over the years, not having it be taught to you and verbalizing everything, like you do here. And the way you learn *taiko*, you are tested to see if you'll stick with it first of all. Then you go on to reach these levels, and it's mostly through self-discovery.[168]

KBT, furthermore, is unorthodox in the way the group is managed. It is a collective in which all members rotate tasks involved in running the ensemble.[169] As well, one of the group's great contributions to the *taiko* world is the innovation of building drums from oak wine barrels and stretching skin drumheads with car jacks, enabling groups to make their own drums in lieu of procuring them in Japan at considerable expense. Tanaka and KBT collaborated in developing the drum-making process. KBT shared this process with other groups, giving workshops and laying out the steps involved in a volume, *Hōraku*, written in 1979 by Rev. Kodani and published by the Senshin Buddhist Temple. *Hōraku* is a seminal guide for Buddhist *taiko* groups in articulating drumming as a practice to obtain a deeper knowledge of Buddhist dharma. A practice inaugurated at Senshin Buddhist Temple reinforces KBT's Buddhist-centered drumming as a Japanese American spiritual art form. KBT has both assisted and inspired the formation of dozens of other Buddhist *taiko* ensembles throughout the United States, stretching from California to Chicago, New Jersey, and Virginia, in addition to other non-Buddhist groups that have come into existence.

Third in the taiko lineage is San Jose Taiko (SJT), the first group to advance an approach to *taiko* involving "social action" as integral to their "community involvement, cultural preservation, and Asian American identity."[170] Many North American groups favor the activist intent of *taiko* as part of their mission. Political advocates P. J. and Roy Hirabayashi (wife and husband team) took their cues from the TWLF strike and the Asian American movement in linking *taiko* to Asian American studies at UC Berkeley and San Jose State University and to their communal work for Issei elders in San Jose's Japanese American community. The couple applied their community-organizing experience in structuring SJT into a collective, enabling them to build group consciousness. P. J. Hirabayashi shares:

> Coming from my community work, there was this collective atmosphere that I thrived on. Everything was like group consciousness. So, a lot of the beginning organization of the group kind of took that leaning where there was a collective approach. There was no sensei [teacher]. There was no one to tell us how to do it. But we had to have some semblance of unity and organization. So, our reflection and our experiences through working in the community, in Asian American studies, was taking that ball and letting it roll. There were a lot of processes there that we wanted to continue and bring into San Jose Taiko. So, that's what kind of set us apart in a way from other beginning groups.[171]

I feel privileged to have obtained, firsthand, a preview of *taiko*'s evolution in the hands of creative Sansei Rev. Kodani and P. J. Hirabayashi. Upon interviewing these individuals, I received insightful glimpses of how this drumming tradition evolved, becoming emblematic of a multidimensional Japanese American identity. The following quotes from my interview with P. J. Hirabayashi comprise a rich source of *taiko*'s creative process and ongoing development.

SJT's origins as a YBA group at the San Jose Buddhist temple, later evolving into a wider communal activity, validates its strong ties to the Japanese American community.

> We started in 1973. Roy was actually one of three founding members of the group beside Rev. Hiroshi Abiko, the reverend at that time, and another youth advisor. Both Roy and Dean Meikuso [sp.?] were YBA advisors, and they wanted to bring *taiko* as an activity to involve young people—bring them back to the church. It lasted for a while, but because they were so young and other people were invited from the community to come in, it actually became a community activity very quickly and not just Buddhist, completely.[172]

San Jose Taiko's drumming style evolved from a cross section of influences resulting from their work with both Kinnara Buddhist Taiko[173] and San Francisco Taiko Dojo. Kinnara Taiko, from whom they purchased their first drums, was the model and first influence for SJT because of their shared Buddhist orientation. Studying with Tanaka Sensei of the San Francisco Taiko Dojo for one year solidified their drumming techniques and method of training. He then encouraged SJT to create their own music and style based on the Sukeroku Daiko style.

SJT's fledgling artistry grew between 1977 to 1979, following their cultural exchange with members of the renowned Japanese *taiko* ensemble Ondeko-Za, then at the peak of its professional career. Members of SJT discovered that their experiences as Japanese Americans contrasted with those of Japanese drummers who had trained them, prompting them to launch an ensemble with the specific goal of allowing greater individual creativity and focusing on strengthening leadership skills. SJT found the North American style of *taiko* to be more upbeat compared to Japanese *taiko* styles. "Actually, I like to think that our style back then really influenced them [Ondeko-Za] to see another side of what they could do. I don't think that it would be saying, 'that came from San Jose,' but American *taiko* in general seems to have more of a joyful feeling." The Ondeko-Za leader, Den Tagayasu, was keen to pick up on this distinction, referring to SJT's brighter sound as the "California sunshine quality"[174] of drumming. While continuing to shape their sound, SJT elucidates how *taiko* was an expression of their Asian American reality and their need to forge an identity:

> It was fascinating to say we're Japanese Americans. We're creating music that reflects who we are. So, you're going to hear a lot more rock 'n' roll or some other jazz influence that we've grown up with through radio. So, our pieces were very reflective of who we were and not Japanese from Japan. It's the format of jazz to encourage self-expression, soloing. It's open and that's not really Japanese. [According to Japanese training] you do it this way. You can't go off on your own free expression. Do it this way. If anything, I've heard so many Japanese groups that just play the number, and it's all in sync and that; no, it's taboo to take off and do your solo. Most of our pieces are arranged so that people are highlighted and are able to individually express themselves.[175]

P. J. Hirabayashi pinpoints the influence of jazz as she speaks about individual expression manifested in *taiko* solos. Perhaps individuality promoted in American mainstream society in general also contributes to a freer style of drumming.

Early on, Japanese American *taiko* differentiated itself from its ancestral prototype with its approach to composing and introducing soloing. P. J. talks about the balance of individual and collective input to create new pieces. She gives us a glimpse of the composing process:

> Each composer has a different way of operating. Some of them already have it on paper and say, "this is the way I'd like you to play it, but I'm open to hearing opinions of how to make it better." There are other composers that are very technical. Anna is wonderful. She's so technical; she's a math major. She'll break it down to prime numbers. I would have to weigh that for myself. "Is this really *taiko*? Don't you play from inside and let it come out?" Yeah, this is *taiko*, this is part of what we're endorsing—the creative process.[176]

While there is allowance for varied methods of composing *taiko* repertoire, it appears that it is vital to play from one's interior energy/spirit. I imagine such intuitive performing follows extensive training.

SJT's opportunity to perform in Japan onstage with Ondeko-Za in the mid-1980s was a turning point for the group in accomplishing their mission as a professional performing ensemble keen to share the art of *taiko* with other enthusiasts. SJT continues to be Asian American–centric due to the inviolable relationship they have with the San Jose Japanese American community and their solid Japanese training. Still, non-Asian members of the group regularly participate, adopting the ethos P. J. and Roy Hirabayashi foster in the ensemble.

For Sansei, the art of *taiko* fulfills the desire to meld both the Japanese and American dimensions of themselves. The aesthetic appeal of *taiko* music lies in a number of its features: its timbre and sonic vibrations as it resonates through the body; the aesthetic concept of *ma*, which signifies silences between sounds; the elasticity of musical phrases as dictated by breath rhythms and length; the martial stance and choreographed movements (*kata*) in generating life-force energy (*ki*); the use of *kakegoe*—a shout used to channel *ki* or words of encouragement to other drummers; and the wearing of Japanese folk apparel—*happi* short jacket, *obi* belt or sash, *tabi* socks, and a *hachimaki* headband. In considering the mesmerizing sensation of shared energy and cumulative power of a group collectively performing in synchronization, one begins to fully grasp the singular magnetism of this uniquely Japanese American form of expression. These features amount to an enactment of a Japanese tradition. The American part of the equation in *taiko* performance is the sense of empowerment it engenders and the stretching of boundaries as imparted by P. J.: "It's a kind of personal empowerment, really maximizing what you've got to challenge ourselves individually, challenge ourselves as a group, and still stay knitted [together]. I think the Western view of knowing where it [*taiko* tradition] comes from, respecting it but then seeing how much you can explore and push the boundaries in order to find something new. Isn't that American, the New World premise, right?"[177] To my question of how she reconciles pushing the tradition perhaps too far and risking loss of the tradition's essence, P. J. reflects: "If you're going to be collaborating with people, how do you maintain that essence without getting very far off? That's a hard one. As long as you know as a group or as a person that you're still practicing those elements genuinely then you're not veering."[178]

A less hierarchical, individualized approach to playing *taiko* rearticulates the tradition, creating a hybrid Japanese American performing art. Central to a freer American approach is the open format borrowed from jazz and rock, allowing for improvised solos. Although Daihachi Oguchi was the first jazz drummer to introduce arranged parts for different drums in *taiko* repertoire, North American groups, such as SJT and Kinnara Buddhist Taiko, innovated the inclusion of improvised solos. To imbue individual expression in *taiko* pieces through soloing is a marker of Japanese American *taiko* performance.[179] American jazz artists of the 1970s and 1980s most likely were an influence, highlighting improvisation at a time when young people felt the urge to follow their creative impulse in expressing their changing self-identification. Moreover, absent from *taiko* repertoire in Japan prior to the 1970s are rhythmic influences from rock, soul, R&B, and other popular music present in original *taiko* compositions in North America, reflecting the contemporary musical tastes of Asian American youth. The nonhierarchical administration of some *taiko* groups and the collective approach to composing music surely are a mark of an American sensibility since these practices contrasted with those of earlier Japanese *taiko* groups. Empowerment through music enabled Sansei to perceive their Japaneseness through a positive lens.

Tracing how Japanese and American characteristics in North American *taiko* relate to Sansei cultural identity is a fascinating process when posed with the question, "*How* does *taiko* drumming express your Japanese American identity?" P. J. offers a nuanced response, intimating the dimensional quality inherent in such a line of inquiry:

> That's a question that I feel has to be addressed to the individual. Because even though an individual comes to play with San Jose Taiko, I cannot speak for them. For me, I feel that it reflects Japanese American culture because of my experiences, of what I've been through. Had I not been given the opportunity to go through the difficult times of Asian

American studies, doing community work, all my childhood dance experiences, I would not be here now. Plus, my family: there was something always inherently there because we were a Japanese American family. There was etiquette and a way of doing things that are distinctly of the Japanese culture.[180]

Aspects "distinctly of the Japanese culture," such as the sound of Japanese words uttered, expectations of a certain protocol, and consideration of the group before the individual—all emblematic of the *taiko* vis-à-vis experience—are inherently familiar to us Sansei.

A compelling feature of North American *taiko* is the predominance of women practitioners, setting it apart from performing groups in Japan in the 1970s, which were exclusively male. Sansei women launched many *taiko* groups, attracting others to join. Ethnomusicologist and *taiko* performer Mark Tusler highlights the primacy of gender in *taiko*: "The involvement of women in North American *taiko* drumming has played an important role in the development of identity for Japanese American women; gender has therefore been an important articulating factor for the continued success of *taiko* groups."[181] The strength and endurance required for *taiko* drumming particularly appeals to Sansei women interested in deconstructing stereotypes of Asian women as weak, demure, and subordinate. The liberating power and physicality of drumming energize Sansei activism in creating a positive and dynamic image of how women want to be perceived, and it functions as a counterpoint to the Asian stereotypes of women so pervasive in American society and promoted by American media. Deborah Wong, through her own experience of performing *taiko*, emphasizes women's assertiveness when she describes the Asian/Asian American woman's body in *taiko* performance: "*Taiko* is not a matter of Asian American women 'rediscovering' a certain kind of Asian body but is rather an intricate process of exploring a Japanese bodily aesthetic and refashioning/re-embodying its potential for Asian American women. For Asian American women, *taiko* is a true performative act, one so profoundly understood through the body that it is rarely channeled into other media like words."[182] Clearly, the demonstrative *act* of performing *taiko* is the allure for Sansei women to form and join ensembles. In doing so, they create an active site where they can affirm their political, social, emotional, and bodily selves through sound and movement. It is primarily in the hands of Sansei women that the Japanese American aesthetic and meaning of *taiko* were reinforced.

Collaborations between *taiko* performers and jazz artists point to the dynamic interplay among musicians in developing Asian American musicking and, by association, the coalition-building strategies promoted by activists. A few Bay Area musician-composers have incorporated *taiko* in their compositions. Experimental music of early pioneers utilized idiomatic practices of playing *taiko* from a variety of Japanese music genres: *gagaku*, *nō*, and folk-festival (*matsuri*) styles. Jon Jang composed a number of pieces incorporating the sound of *taiko*, such as "Tanko Bushi Celebration" and "Reparations Now!" (both on *Never Give Up*, 1989) and "Ikiru" (*Big Bands behind Barbed Wire*, 1988). *Taiko* sound is most prominent in his composition "Reparations Now!"—a four-movement concerto for a jazz and *taiko* ensemble, which he wrote in 1987 in collaboration with members of SJT and dedicated to Japanese American inmates of World War II. Another larger work featuring *taiko* motives is Anthony Brown's "E. O. 9066 (Truth Be Told)" and "Never Again! (Mo Shimasen!)," also commemorating Japanese Americans unjustly imprisoned during the war. In his multimovement piece *Last Dance*, Mark Izu composed *taiko* parts throughout the composition with particularly rousing effect in his celebratory Japanese festival music for the final movement, "Kiryoku." In all these pieces, the drum is emblematic of Japanese American resistance and resilience in its driving rhythmic display. Composers sought the participation of SJT members expressly for their musicianship, activist stance, and openness to new and innovative ways to integrate *taiko* in collaborative projects and compositions.

As elucidated by P. J., the collective spirit of San Jose Taiko enhances and broadens their audience appeal. The group has attracted audience members beyond the borders of Japanese/Asian American communities, expanding listeners to include a more diverse pool of followers.

> Of course, in the very beginning, it was largely Japanese Americans, Asian Americans. But because of the type of projects that we've pursued over the last ten years, our audience base has really diversified. And I would say that there's a lot of Euro-Americans that are coming through and coming to our performances. But we've chosen that path. It's not been accidental. A body of our work includes collaborations with other artistic disciplines, like theater, other dance companies, like Anthony's [Brown] group through jazz. So that what we try to gain from those experiences is really learning about another art form but through our interaction—what is there artistically or what is there organizationally that will help us become more solid as a group or create that diversity through our music. Working with a dance company might introduce us to how to become more mobile. So that's why we choose to do

collaborations: to learn from other people, to appreciate their art form, to also be inspired to receive and add to our repertoire.[183]

Celebrating interdisciplinary collaboration is yet another distinct feature of Japanese American *taiko* that differentiates it from this art form as practiced in the motherland.

That *taiko* performance played a decisive role in constructing a newly empowered Japanese American ethnic identity cannot be denied, yet the ever-growing numbers of non-Japanese American and non-Asian members begs the question, Is *taiko* still a Japanese American tradition? The question scrutinizes the emblematic role of this art form in representing a Japanese American identity. SJT's P. J. Hirabayashi admits that the meaning behind *taiko* can become convoluted, for example, when a Euro-American performer processes *taiko* through their own experience. She affirms that SJT welcomes diverse enthusiasts interested in performing and composing music for the ensemble. How then is the sound identity of *taiko* maintained? P. J. maintains that *taiko* remains a Japanese American tradition if the group consciously connects to the Japanese American community and if the group continues to instill the value of *taiko*—an art form rooted in Japanese ritual and folk tradition:

> Yes, [*taiko* remains a Japanese American tradition] if it's within the perspective of community, if you're conscious of connecting to the community—Japanese American community, physical community, mental community, also the *taiko* community. You see the difference between the Japanese *taiko* community and the American *taiko* community. It's a Japanese American thing if you're able to instill the values of what it is that you have as an art form and allow it to be shared. As Japanese Americans, we've selected the drum to express who we are.[184]

There is a desire among non-Asian members to partake in the aesthetic and cultural world of *taiko*; a world that cultivates discipline, humility, mindfulness, the link between body and mind, and respect for others in a dynamic and physical display. Japanese-style *taiko* training rooted in traditional folk-festival rhythms anchors *taiko* to its Japanese primal source. In addressing the growing diversity of *taiko* players and the concomitant changes in meaning, P. J. articulates *taiko*'s function:

> A traditional link to Japanese culture; a vehicle for how you can become the best person you are. Choosing the path to do *taiko* will allow you to

become open, to understand and get to know who you are as an individual, to understand your link with other people. The interdynamics of humanity, I guess; your dynamics as a person through your art form, touching people out there. That's the next level of consciousness that we strive to interject and cultivate for people within the group and in the larger community.[185]

This broader meaning embodies a spiritual essence of *taiko* as a Japanese tradition that has a strong ritualistic, ceremonial, and communal function, yet it allows for hybrid musical spaces inclusive of other cultures and art forms that *taiko* groups inhabit as the music continues to evolve. In its fifty-year-plus history, North American *taiko* has expanded to more than one thousand groups in the United States and Canada. Today, the popularity of this truly Japanese American phenomenon continues to rise, reaching across national borders, forming a *taiko* diaspora with ensembles in the Americas, Asia, Australia, Europe, and Africa.[186]

KENNY ENDO: BREAKING BOUNDARIES

One of the first musicians to propel *taiko* beyond the boundaries of the *kumi-daiko* style in the United States is Kenny Endo, a born and bred Los Angeleno. An innovative *taiko* performer-composer, Endo is a leader in contemporary *taiko* music both in Japan and the United States. He composes pieces from a mélange of influences. Ethnomusicological studies at UCLA and the University of Hawaii, where he participated in *gagaku* and African drumming ensembles and heard Indian sitar music, broadened Endo's sonic palette. He was further inspired by Brazilian, Hawaiian slack-key guitar, and Indonesian music, as well as Tahitian rhythms and other styles and genres that complement his background in American soul, funk, rock, and jazz. Yet the core of Endo's technique and compositions is the professional training he received in Japan for a decade from 1980 to 1990, enabling him to maintain a thread of continuity with the legacy and long history of Japanese drumming traditions. His Japanese training eclipsed his trap-drumming activities as part of the San Francisco creative-music scene when he performed with various musicians at the Jigoku Club and other venues.

It is often through others' eyes and perspectives that we set on a path toward discovering ourselves. It was *not* the political path forged by the Asian American movement and the rise of an empowered identity that led Kenny Endo in his quest to recover his Japanese heritage. It was the eloquent stories told by elderly Native Americans of the richness of their traditional ways and culture that galvanized him. It was the resistance and spirit of these Native Americans, whom he referred to as "warriors," that touched and motivated him to embark on a journey of self-discovery. In inquiring of Endo about his own culture, the "warriors" triggered the realization of how little he knew about his Japanese heritage. Endo came into contact with this community while interning as a social worker on the Colorado River Indian Reservation for the Health, Education, and Welfare Department, working with alcoholism and youth programs. He describes this life-changing experience:

> I was very idealistic, and I felt like I was going to help; I wanted to change the world. And what happened is that the American Indians ended up helping me. It was a really good experience for me, and, in fact, that experience is what is really important in terms of what my direction became. We don't hear enough about what a beautiful culture they have and what positive things they can have for American society, even today. That experience showed me how little I knew about my own culture and that I should be part of my own culture, and I needed to somehow get back in touch with that. After that experience, I went back to Los Angeles and, within six months, hooked up with Kinnara Taiko.[187]

Endo distinguishes himself by being one of few Japanese Americans who lived and trained in Japan, immersing himself in the traditional arts. Existing on the cusp between Nisei and Sansei—as a result of having an Issei father and Nisei mother along with many relatives in Japan—places him in closer proximity to his heritage than most Sansei. Studying Japanese *gagaku* with Suenobu Togi, first at UCLA and later at San Francisco's Buddhist Institute with fellow musicians and artists in the 1970s, immersed Endo in Japanese music. He feels strongly that learning traditions in Japan is essential for tracing one's roots:

> By limiting yourself to the experience of Asians in this country, you're cutting off a whole legacy that goes back centuries and thousands of years. And that's also part of your past where you choose to go back that far. It's not only in terms of technical knowledge or musical knowledge, but it also goes back to what one of my teachers told me: when you appear on stage, you cannot rely on your own power to perform. You have to tap into the energy and spirit of the people who have performed before you.[188]

In fulfilling this aspiration, in 1980, Endo traveled to Japan intending to further his drumming skills in a course lasting one or two years and instead remained in the country ten years, studying three major genres of folk and classical drumming. The training sessions with Seiichi Tanaka and the San Francisco Taiko Dojo for five years provided a foundation for Endo's intensive instruction in Japan. He achieved competency in *kumidaiko* (folk ensemble drumming), *Sukeroku daiko* (particularly Edo-*bayashi* festival music), and *hōgaku hayashi* (*nō* and Kabuki theater drumming). In 1982, his accomplishments gained him full-time professional work as a *kumidaiko* performer, and in 1987, he earned his *natori* (professional stage name) in *hōgaku hayashi*, being the first non-Japanese national to attain such excellence. Endo consummated a requirement that he prescribes himself: "for people to be proud of their culture and really keep its art alive, it has to be performed at a pretty high level."[189] "Endo's training in Japan informs how he approaches and teaches *taiko*: First, you have to study the tradition and know it. Next you must become a practitioner of the tradition. After that, you must be a bearer of the tradition. And finally, you have to break the tradition, meaning to innovate or expand on it."[190] As an emissary of Japanese drumming styles, the meaning and art of *taiko*, as taught to him in Japan, is central to how Endo transmits his knowledge to others. Beyond the spectacle and sound of *taiko*, to Endo, drumming bridges a spiritual connection between the instrument, performers, and the audience.

> The art of *taiko* is in putting your spirit into the drum, and getting the spirit of the drum into you, so that there is an energy that flows through you, the drum and the audience at the same time. Finally, you have to call on the energy of the spirit world. This is the first and last lesson in learning *taiko*. I tell my students they must understand this before they ever hit the drums.[191]

Endo's *hōgaku hayashi* drum teacher, Bokusei Mochizuki, introduced him to the process, emphasizing drummers' striving for "oneness" with audiences—the spiritual dimension that Endo refers to as "eternal energy."

The traditional training Endo received in Japan engenders a strong Japanese cast in his music combined with contemporary and eclectic sounds. Endo feels confined by what he regards as set parameters for drumming that characterize the musicking of most Japanese American *taiko* groups. In contrast to the widespread consideration of *taiko* drumming as an icon of Japanese American musicking, Endo describes his music as "contemporary music for *taiko*"[192] to differentiate his approach to composing. He understands that for someone not raised in Japan, capturing an authentic sound on a Japanese drum is futile. Instead, his study of a pastiche of musical styles drives his impulse to meld traditional sounds with familiar American popular genres and rhythms and music from across the globe. Endo continues to experiment with a variety of rhythmic meters and instrumental combinations, employing shamisen, shakuhachi, koto, bass, keyboards, guitar, vibraphone, and saxophone into his ensembles.

Suffused with influences from Japanese music, Endo's compositions incorporate certain timbral and aesthetic ideas associated with sounds in nature: "I try to achieve a real fusion—[for example] not just using the *taiko* as an ornament to jazz but bringing out the natural tone and rhythm of the drum to truly reflect traditional Japanese music."[193] At another point, he adds:

> I used to work in Kabuki theater, and a lot of my ideas come from sound effects for the stage. *Taiko* range from very small, sensitive hand drums to others seven feet high. For the sound of snow, we use a mallet with rounded padding at the end. The sound of snow, the sound of waves of wind and water and rain—all of these can be used to express much, much more. The sound of water can mean any kind of stream or body of water in the literal sense. But at the end of a play, you might have two lovers walking off into the distance, and to show that their love is eternal we play the sound of water to suggest that their love is like flowing water. We use the sounds of nature to convey emotions.[194]

Endo dissects his fusion compositional approach further by describing how he seeks to combine the musical sophistication of *hogaku hayashi* with the dynamic power of *kumi daiko*. One can discern a certain rhythmic swing in some compositions of this former jazz drummer, but as a whole, it is the rhythms and techniques Endo learned in *kumidaiko*, Sukeroku Daiko, and *hōgaku hayashi* that anchor his work. To add variety to his arrangements, Endo uses traditional instruments in innovative ways and employs improvisation. Collaborations with the Japanese drummer Eitetsu Hayashi[195]—founding member of the internationally famous *taiko* group Ondekoza, who later left to form the equally renowned group Kodo—broadened Endo's artistic vision as they experimented with modern sounds and instruments. Together the two worked with a number of jazz, rock, ethnic-folk, contemporary, classical, and *butoh* (Japanese avant-garde dance) artists. Their goal was "to break down musical boundaries and bring *taiko* drumming out of a purely traditional framework."[196] Endo and Hayashi experimented with nontraditional ensembles that incorporated electric guitars, synthesizers, and Latin instruments in pushing the boundaries of their eclectic work.[197] Formation of the Kenny Endo Taiko Ensemble, featured on his 1994 album, *Eternal Energy*, is a manifestation of his collaborations with Japanese musicians.

Having permanently settled in Honolulu, Hawaii, Endo actively promotes traditional and contemporary Japanese drumming through the Taiko Center of the Pacific (TCP), a school he established in 1994. He trains drummers of all ages who participate in TCP's performing adult and youth groups, learning not only basic form and technique of *kumidaiko* but also cultural customs that accompany the art form. Endo is responsible for spreading *taiko* in Hawaii to a wide demographic through workshops he conducts in continuing-education classes for the University of Hawaii and by demonstrating this style of drumming in libraries, schools, hospitals, prisons, and senior-citizen centers for the Statewide Cultural Extension Program. Immersed in the US *taiko* community, Endo has headed ensembles based in Los Angeles, Honolulu, and Tokyo and is in demand throughout the country by *taiko* ensembles conducting workshops that advance the technique of their members. As tradition bearer, Endo's disciplined and honed approach toward *taiko* drumming upholds the spirit of the art in aspiring to promote a high level of performance among groups not only in Hawaii but throughout the United States. Kenny Endo identifies as Japanese American, but he regards his performance as contemporary *taiko* music, a music that bridges Japan and the United States, joining musicians from both sides of the Pacific as they bring *taiko* into the intercultural twenty-first century.

Kenny Endo's story is a patch in the rich tapestry of Sansei musicking, which, rather than negotiating its ethnic boundaries in a racist society, raises an account of personal histories through 'critical awareness,' urging the construction of creative spaces that promote interracial and intercultural collaborations and the prospect of a multicultural national identity. To avoid essentializing Sansei musicking, I endeavored to explore Japanese musical influences and elements in our work and gain deeper insight into the complex yet fascinating interplay between social, political, and emotional intent in evoking Japanese sensibilities in music that stamp our cultural heritage and our American core. The groundbreaking twenty-year period from the 1960s to the 1980s was an extraordinary time for Asian American artists as we sought to link aesthetic ventures with our newfound sociopolitical leanings in spawning a subculture in which we could thrive. Social and political movements during this time—civil rights, Black liberation, women's, American Indian,

Asian American, Chicano, gay rights, the anti–Vietnam War movement, and environmental justice—jettisoned new self-awareness and robust cultural and musical production that crossed racial and cultural borders, opening creative frontiers. Bold innovations in art and music must continue to "sound our way home" for an increasingly diverse population. Sansei artistic production is an inspiring contribution toward social progress and cultural enrichment of the United States meant to advance an antiracist national ethos.

EPILOGUE

The Promise of Interracial Music Coalitions

Social and political divisiveness destabilizing the US nation-state today necessitates forming musico-political alliances that spotlight antiracist goals and coalition building. The interracial musical accord between Asian American and African American musicians fostered by the coalitional politics of the Third World Liberation Front movement demonstrates intercultural partnerships that, through community building, could reframe and reassemble dominant structures.

The joining of creative forces between artists of various subaltern groups may be the answer to forging coalitions that unify rather than divide us in the ideological struggle to gain political power and effective political representation. In her book *Resounding Afro Asia: Interracial Music and the Politics of Collaboration*, ethnomusicologist Tamara Roberts presses for sustained engagements between racial and cultural groups in her analyses of the interracial and intercultural collaborations between Asian American and African American musicians. Her study of Afro Asian music ensembles reveals, "Through mixing of racialized sounds, and, sometimes, explicit extra-musical politics, Afro Asian artists increase the opportunities for people of color to establish counterdominant formations."[1]

Interdisciplinary artist Coco Fusco insists that artists' cultural border crossings and participation in multiple communities reflect contemporary American life in all its cultural variety. She contends that artists are moving beyond solely reconstructing their own cultural past and are traversing other worlds, crosscutting different languages, aesthetic ideas, genres, and images into their work.[2] Recontextualizing dominant cultural tropes promoted by the mainstream media and governmental institutions is a way for artists to resist and reshape them.

Affecting change depends on bold, creative visionaries such as multifaceted artist Nobuko Miyamoto. Originally an activist singer-songwriter, Miyamoto diversified her socially and politically conscious art over the years, combining music with dance, movement, and spectacle. Her cross-cultural and interdisciplinary work conjoins the Japanese American community with other racial and cultural communities in Los Angeles in an array of pursuits that extend to educational programming about gardening and recycling waste intended to raise awareness of environmental stewardship.

In 1978, Miyamoto founded the Los Angeles–based Great Leap; it stands as a model arts and political advocacy community organization. Great Leap sets the standard for how to effectively structure such partnerships. Miyamoto's educational approach to community projects along with the success of her intercommunity programs garner strong funding from local, state, and federal sources. Local Los Angeles partners include the Japanese American Cultural and Community Center, Los Angeles County Arts & Culture, East LA Community Corporation, Arts District Little Tokyo, Artivist Entertainment, New Generation Fund (housing), and the Department of Cultural Affairs, City of Los Angeles. Great Leap has received state-sponsored support from California Cultural District, Little Tokyo, Alliance for California Traditional Arts, and the California Endowment. Financial backing from national organizations, such as the Mellon Foundation and the Kresge Foundation, has also been crucial. Great Leap's local and national assistance points to a certain logic in building alliances and coalitions: the more communities involved in events and projects, the broader the base for financial support and advocacy.

Miyamoto remains politically vigilant. Her response to the Los Angeles riots in 1992 and the 9/11 attacks prompted a broadening of Great Leap's repertoire to include cultures and faiths outside Asian America. Fighting for racial and cultural equity has become central to the work of Great Leap. The group's vision of art's potential to advance intercultural relationships and promote dialogue between diverse communities is more critical than ever. Forming a creative workshop—Art of Weaving Faiths—in an effort to bring about healing, Miyamoto envisions using art as both performative and creative practice to deepen relations among people of diverse cultures. Concerned about the demonization of Muslims in the United States, Miyamoto reached within her own family to incorporate Sufi practices into the 2020 virtual FandangObon festival. In preparation for the festival that took place on November 15, 2020, the workshop Praise Songs and Presence: The Art of Qasidah and Hadrah was broadcast live on YouTube and Facebook on October 3, 2020. Featuring father and daughter duo Kamau Ayubbi and Asiyah Ayubbi (Miyamoto's son and granddaughter), the workshop introduced participants "to the realm of Heart and Soul through shared Sufi practices of song, breath, and simple intentional movement."[3] The duo demonstrates the role of singing and movement in the mind-body connection: "Sufi songs that celebrate movements from oppression to light and liberation. The movements and chants align body, mind, and spirit in natural rhythms of contraction and expansion, and the balanced spin within the Cosmos."[4] The Sufi songs (*qasidah*) and movement are a natural outgrowth of the ever-wider circle of inclusion celebrated at FandangObon, an event that initially wove together Japanese and Mexican festival songs and dances. Sharing a similar function, Bon odori songs and dances presented at Japanese Obon festivals to commemorate ancestors, and Spanish-origin *fandango son jarocho* of Veracruz, Mexico, performed for Day of the Dead celebrations form a unique cross-cultural fusion.

Miyamoto's creative impulse extends not only to music, dance, and movement but storytelling and theater as well. *To All Relations* (1997), Miyamoto's second solo album, and *A Slice of Rice, Frijoles and Greens*, a touring theater production, blend music and poetry to address social issues as told by artists from a variety of cultures. Cross community work, also part of Great Leap's mission, found form in a series of community residencies with the theme "To All Relations." One such residency entailed working with Mexican, Jewish, and Japanese community members to perform stories about the Los Angeles's Boyle Heights neighborhood where these communities reside. In a second residency, Miyamoto codirected a poetic musical, *Sacred Moon Songs*, knitted with stories from Muslim, Mexican, and Japanese communities.

Yet another Great Leap creative endeavor is Eco-Arts, a progressive community arts program that educates diverse communities about the relationship between culture and the environment. The aim of this community enterprise is to produce entertaining music videos of environmental theme music mixed with humor and concrete information to raise people's awareness about being stewards of the environment.[5] Eco-Arts uses media technology for their public offering of videos on YouTube; the so-called Eco-vids "Cycles of Change," "Mottai-nai," and "BYO Chopstix" have engaged people of all ages and cultures.[6]

What sets Great Leap's activities and Miyamoto's artistry apart are the lectures, workshops, and seminars that engage artists, teachers, community organizers, corporate administrators, and cultural and faith-based groups, providing them with the tools to organize short- and long-term projects that promote increased interracial and cross-cultural understanding. In these interactive sessions, Miyamoto builds people's collaborative possibilities through breath, movement, and the sharing of stories with hopes of developing individual creativity and positive group dynamics. One such project is Collaboratory, an artist mentorship program that guides emerging artists and community members in the process of creating theater works of their personal stories. Embedded in the philosophy of Great Leap is a sense of passing on cultural and spiritual practices and merging or juxtaposing them in cross-culturally inventive ways that build community and, in the process, broaden audiences for progressive creative work.[7]

As a prototype for interracial and intercultural projects, FandangObon launched, in 2013, a remarkable intercommunity initiative. Great Leap company collaborated with Quetzal, the Chicano rock band from East Los Angeles, in creating cross-cultural music for this event.[8] Mixing "rhythmic footwork, the strumming of *jaranas* [plucked lutes], and *fandango son jarocho* folk song verses"[9] with Bon odori music and dance is a fresh example of bridging musical cultures. Bon odori folk songs, traditionally, accompany dancing for Obon festivals. A composer of Japanese American Bon odori songs, Miyamoto has a repertoire that includes: "Yuiyo,"[10] "Tampopo Ondo," "Gardener's Song," "Ichigo Ichie," "Mottai-nai," "Bambutsu no Tsunagari," "Sembazuru,"[11] and "Camp Bushi,"[12] all with lyrics in English. Her recent Bon odori songs "Mottai-nai" (Don't Waste) and "Bambutsu no Tsunagari" (Ten Thousand Things All Connected) are delightful examples of diasporic Japanese music with a purpose: the former, an environmental song, and the latter, a call meant to unite communities.[13] From the intertwining of Bon odori and *fandango* songs emerges infectious music to accompany dancing and to celebrate the building of communities through the fusion of cultures.[14]

As a former activist of the Black liberation and Asian American movements, Miyamoto's political orientation remains inviolable. She expressly composed "Bambutsu no Tsunagari" to express Great Leap's support of the national Japanese American political organization, Tsuru for Solidarity, and their efforts to close incarceration centers where predominantly Latin American refugees are being held. In weaving together Bon odori and Mexican fandango song styles, the song nurtures Japanese American and Mexican solidarity around immigration issues. FandangObon has a definitive political slant that enables participants to exercise their agency. Bandleader, Quetzal Flores shares,

> FandangObon is a critical piece in today's political climate. These spaces need to be based on love, caring, and hope. And our hope is not predicated on those people marching on the streets and saying hateful stuff.

It's not predicated on ignorance. It's predicated on a deep understanding of humanity through our traditional cultures, through our traditional practices. When we engage in these practices, we are automatically resisting, and we are simultaneously building.[15]

Striking is the notion of deploying traditional cultural practices to foster "love, caring, and hope" in promoting relationships rather than inviting confrontation between cultural groups.

Miyamoto celebrates the blossoming of FandangObon over the years, and reflects on its essence:

FandangObon is coming into its eighth season, bringing people into a circle from the Mexican, Japanese, African American, and Muslim communities. We share our participatory arts, music, and dance traditions; the ways that people have been gathering through time to keep their communities connected. It's been a powerful way to deepen understanding and build relationships between people of different cultures. . . . We also focus on environmental knowledge because this is the way that our people have thrived and sustained through time every day with Earth Day. . . . We are about bringing people together into the same space. . . . This is a big experiment for us. From ancient times, humans have been gathering in circles to give thanks, ask for rain, good crops, safety, healing. We need that now; just the same, we are gathering around our computers. This has been an unprecedented time, and it's pretty radical; I haven't seen anything like it in my time to literally stop the world and see that we are all connected. This has brought out some heroic and human actions by people, but it has also brought out ignorance, racism, and divisions. This is why we have to continue doing what we are doing and try to spread it. Now, you might think that dancing in a circle is sort of a quaint idea, but actually there is science behind it—that when we grieve and move together, we are tuning our energies together. As Johanna of Dembaya Ballet will tell you that when people drum and dance together, their hearts actually synchronize. So, this is an old-new way, a kind of recycling. . . . Let's just start with a little breath to tune us in.[16]

Pausing to recognize that we are all connected through the ritual of forming a circle in which to attune to one another enables us to imagine cooperation and a way forward. It is Miyamoto's uplifting way to bring people together.

Ever expanding, the festival held in 2017 was advertised as FandangObon Environmental ENCUENTRO, an arts and culture eco fest: "Rooted in culturally based sustainability practices, FandangObon honors the balance between Mother Earth and humanity by bringing together Japanese, Mexican, and African American communities into one circle through participatory music, dance, and gardening practices."[17] The eco fest evolved as an extension of Miyamoto's Eco-Arts community arts program. FandangObon Environmental ENCUENTRO offered cross-cultural works of music, song, dance, and movement performed by Le Ballet Dembaya and accompanying drummers, Mottainai Band, Quetzal and Fandangueros, and Francis & Omowale Awe, all representing communities involved in the event; each troupe presented their particular repertoire of music and dance. Truly wondrous, however, was the shared musicking among the groups, resulting in a dynamic blending of sounds that shifted the stereotypical sonic features that might be associated with each ensemble. Miyamoto's projects reveal ways to be both creative and awareness raising—an inspirational direction for others to follow.

In the year of COVID-19, Great Leap celebrated the eighth FandangObon virtually on Sunday, November 15, 2020. Five workshops, scheduled throughout September and October, prepared participants for the culminating festival, serving as a time for instruction and rehearsal of various music and dance steps as well as learning how to construct a retablo, or altar. Such training is key, ensuring the participation and success of FandangObon every year. The poster in figure 6.1 provides a menu outlining the cultural ingredients that go into assembling a FandangObon festival, a truly gourmet multicultural feast.

The Black Lives Matter movement is very personal for Miyamoto, whose African American husband and biracial son are at risk in a climate of ongoing racial injustices and police brutality faced by African Americans in the United States today. The murder of George Floyd on May 25, 2020, became the tipping point for many, igniting nation-wide protests that came to be known as the Black Lives Matter movement. Miyamoto composed and produced the protest song "Black Lives Matter," adding her cry to the voice of millions in the United States and across the globe. The somber jazz-inflected composition builds momentum with a weighty piano ostinato bassline and lyrics, outlining the history of injustice for Black lives, the sanctity of these lives, and, by association, all lives. The song climaxes with a chorus of "Black lives matter!" and ends quietly with a simple, repeated pentatonic melodic motif. Miyamoto affirms her commitment to the ongoing struggle: "Fighting for racial and cultural equity is nothing new for Great Leap. The ways in which we use the

Figure 6.1. Poster advertising five workshops in preparation for the 2020 virtual FandangObon 8 festival in Los Angeles.

power of art to deepen understanding, to challenge, inspire and engage conversation is more critical than ever now."[18]

Musico-political alliances facilitate critical conversations between racially and culturally diverse communities born from a sense of urgency and arising out of artists' agency. It is an effective way to chart a course toward forming relationships that lead to a multicultural society. We must draw inspiration and strength from the arts to stimulate dialogue, bring about healing, and restore justice in overcoming racial, ethnic, and class differences. It is my hope that cross-cultural musical synergies bolster coalitions needed to unite disparate racial and cultural groups on the journey to expand US national culture and reframe our democracy, aspiring to create a just future for all.

GLOSSARY

AACM—Association for the Advancement of Creative Musicians, a collective of musicians and composers based in Chicago and dedicated to the performance of original creative music and the training of new generations of performers, artists, and teachers.
AAPA—Asian American Political Alliance.
AIA—Asian Improv aRts.
AIR—Asian Improv Records.
amae—roughly meaning "dependency" (a Japanese value).
Asian American movement—a sociopolitical movement of Americans of Asian descent that formed in the late 1960s and early 1970s.
assimilationism—a practice or policy that encourages people of all ethnicities and cultural origins to conform to the cultural practices and customs of mainstream society of a particular country.
BAG—Black Artists Group, a multidisciplinary arts collective in St. Louis, Missouri, that lasted from 1968 to 1972.
biwa—a short-necked, fretted plucked lute used to accompany narrative singing.
Black Arts movement—the cultural arm of the Black Power movement formed in the first half of the 1960s by Black artists in their endeavor to create artistic forms that expressed the African American cultural and historical experience.
bon-kei—miniature landscape on a tray.
Bon odori—dance performed at Obon.
Buddhahead—slang referring to Japanese Americans from Hawaii.
Bunraku—classical Japanese puppet theater.
bushi—folk-song genre derived from Buddhist chants.
butoh—avant-garde Japanese theater.
buyō—classical Japanese dance.
Chikuzen *biwa*—*biwa* tradition influenced by narrative shamisen music.
chū-daiko—a mid-size *taiko* drum that performs a variety of "propulsive riffs" that give the music rhythmic momentum.
cuatro—Latin American four-string lute.
Dekaseginin—sojourner.
dongo taiko—rhythm.
Engeibu— dramatic society.
engei-kai—variety performances of music and drama; talent shows.
enka—a particular style of Japanese popular song that stylistically emulates traditional Japanese singing.
erhu—Chinese two-stringed bowed lute.
fukuinkai—Japanese gospel societies.

gagaku—Japanese court music.
Gaimenteki dōka—assimilation involving only outward appearances, such as clothing, furnishings, observing a host culture's customs and holidays, and avoiding the use of items that are conspicuously Japanese.
Gentlemen's Agreement—an informal agreement between the United States and Japan intended to stop the flow of Japanese immigrants in an attempt to ease the tension between the two competing Pacific countries.
gidayū—narrative *biwa* music popularized by its use in Bunraku, or puppet theater.
gidayū-bushi—see *gidayū*.
Gila River Relocation Center—concentration camp located in Arizona.
Gosei—fifth generation Japanese American.
hachimaki—headband; Japanese folk apparel.
hakujin—Caucasian.
hapa—Hawaiian term for someone of mixed ethnic heritage.
happi—short jacket; Japanese folk apparel.
Heian period—Japanese historical period from 794 to 1190.
hibakusha—atomic bomb survivors.
hichiriki—short double-reed pipe used in Japanese court music.
Hina Matsuri—Girl's Day, a Japanese celebration.
hōko—dharma drum that represents the voice of the Buddha.
hōra—conch shell that represents the voice of the Buddha.
hōraku—Buddhist term that has two meanings: joy in the dharma (teachings) or dharma entertainment; more generally refers to Buddhist performing arts in Japan.
Hōshō *yōkyoku*—school of nō drama singing.
iemoto—Japanese music and dance instruction traditionally organized into schools or clubs.
ikebana—art of Japanese flower arranging.
Ikuta—one of the two major koto schools in Japan.
Issei—first generation to emigrate and settle in a country outside of Japan.
JACL—Japanese American Citizens League, which emerged in 1929 as an umbrella organization of existing Nisei political organizations in California and Washington that included the American Loyalty League, the Seattle Progressive Citizens League, and the San Francisco–based New American Citizens League.
jarana—fretted plucked lute from Mexico.
ji—backing rhythm played on *shime-daiko*.
jo-ha-kyū—tripartite compositional form heard in traditional Japanese music.
jōruri— narrative shamisen music.
jūshokubun—associate professional; for lay people, it is the highest level of achievement in singing *yōkyoku*.
Kabuki—Japanese classical drama.
kagura—sacred Shinto music and dance.
kakegoe—a shout used to channel *ki*.
kakko—hourglass-shaped drum used in Japanese court music.
Kanze *yōkyoku*—singing style of the Kanze school of *nō* in Japan.
Karuk (also Karok)—one of the largest Indigenous populations of California, residing mostly in northern California into southern Oregon.
karuta—Japanese card game.
Kashū Mainichi (Japan-California Daily News)—name of a Japanese American newspaper in Los Angeles.
kata—form; choreographed movement.

kenbu—sword dance.
kenkyū-kai—study or research club.
ki—life-force energy.
Kibei—Nisei born in the United States but sent to Japan by their families for three or more years of education before returning home.
"Kimigayo"—the Japanese anthem.
Kinko—school of shakuhachi playing.
Kinnara Taiko (also KT)—pioneering Buddhist *taiko* ensemble in Los Angeles affiliated with the Senshin Buddhist Temple.
Kinshin—new school of Satsuma *biwa*.
Kita *yōkyoku*—singing style of the Kita school of *nō* in Japan.
kiyomoto—a genre that borders between the lyric and the narrative styles of shamisen music used in Kabuki theater.
kobu—gnarled cypress tree roots and trunks.
"Kōjō no Tsuki" (Moon Over the Ruined Castle)—one of the most famous Japanese songs ever written, composed by Rentarō Taki in 1901; the lyrics were written by Bansui Doi from Sendai, Tōhoku.
koto—thirteen- to twenty-five-string board zither.
ko-tsuzumi—small shoulder drum.
Kūkai—founder of Shingon Buddhism.
kumi daiko—ensemble-style *taiko* playing.
kumoi-joshi—traditional Japanese pentatonic scale.
kyōgen—comic plays performed between *nō* plays.
LRS—League of Revolutionary Struggle was an organization that represented Marxist-Leninist unity in the United States, formed from the merging of the August Twenty-Ninth Movement and I Wor Kuen in 1978.
ma—aesthetic concept, translated as "space" or "interval"; in Japanese performing arts, *ma* refers to a natural sense of effective timing and the use of pauses to heighten the effect
manong—bachelor Filipino worker.
manzai—comic dialogue.
Meiji period—Japanese historical period that lasted from 1868 to 1912.
minyō—Japanese folk song.
nagauta shamisen—narrative shamisen genre performed as both accompaniment to Kabuki theater and as chamber music.
naniwa-bushi—popular narrative singing style that is a mixture of storytelling and singing accompanied by shamisen.
nativism—policy of protecting the interests of native inhabitants against those of immigrants.
natori—professional status indicated by the bestowing of a professional name.
NCRR—National Coalition for Redress and Reparations, a Japanese American organization that pushed for redress and reparations for West Coast Japanese Americans who were incarcerated during World War II.
neh (also *ney*)—Persian end-blown flute.
Nichibei Mainichi (Japanese American Daily News)—Japanese American newspaper in San Francisco.
Nichi Bei Shimbun (Japanese American News)—former Japanese American newspaper in San Francisco that was one of the most prominent ethnic newspapers on the US mainland.
Nihonmachi—literally, "Japantown."
Nikkei—person of Japanese descent.
Nippon seishin—Japanese mind, spirit, soul.

Nisei—second-generation Japanese American; first generation born in a country outside of Japan.
nō—medieval Japanese drama.
nōkan—accented, high-pitched transverse flute performed in nō plays.
Nueva Canción—sociopolitical song movement throughout Latin America and the Caribbean.
Obon—Buddhist celebration to commemorate the dead.
obi—belt or sash; Japanese folk apparel.
o-cha—Japanese tea; art of tea ceremony.
o-daiko—large taiko that plays a simple rhythm, serving as a base in a taiko ensemble.
o-hana—art of flower arrangement.
Oliver Club—youth organization.
o-mochi—rice cake.
ondo—generic term for various kinds of folk songs.
origami—art of paper folding.
o-Shōgatsu—New Year's.
o-tsuzumi—large hand drum.
Poston, Arizona—one of ten concentration camps where Japanese Americans were held during World War II.
Rafu Shimpo—Los Angeles newspaper.
rei—respectful courtesy.
rōei—ancient vocal genre with Chinese poetic texts.
Rohwer, Arkansas—one of ten concentration camps where Japanese Americans were held during World War II.
ryūkōka—commercial popular music from Japan, which could also be heard on local radio programs and in Japanese films shown in urban-community theaters.
saibara—folk songs arranged for Japanese court-music repertoire.
Sansei—third-generation Japanese American; second generation born in a country outside of Japan.
Satsuma biwa—a genre of lute music and its instrument.
senryū—a humorous or witty seventeen-syllable poem, usually in colloquial language.
SFTD—San Francisco Taiko Dojo.
shakuhachi—bamboo end-blown flute.
shamisen—three-string plucked lute.
sheng—Chinese mouth organ.
shibai—a play or drama.
shigin—Chinese classical poems set to ancient classical melodies.
shimai—nō drama form of dancing.
shime-daiko—high-pitched, shallow drum that plays a repetitive ji (backing rhythm) in a taiko ensemble.
shin Issei—literally, "new Issei"; second wave of Japanese immigrants to the United States, starting in 1965.
Shingon—a Buddhism sect.
shinpa—modern dramatic play.
shō—mouth organ used in Japanese court music.
shodō—calligraphy.
shōmyō—Buddhist chanting.
shushin—moral education.
SJT—San Jose Taiko.
Sukeroku Daiko (also Oedo Sukeroku Daiko)—considered the first professional taiko group in Japan, based in Tokyo.

suona—Chinese double-reed wind instrument.
tabi—Japanese style socks.
taiko—drum.
takebue—bamboo transverse flute.
tanka—seventeen-syllable poem.
Third World Liberation Front—a coalition of African American, Asian American, Chicano, and Native American students that formed in 1968 to 1969 at San Francisco State University and University of California, Berkeley, to fight institutionalized racism and hold strikes to force the creation of ethnic studies programs at universities.
Tokugawa period—historical period that lasted from 1603 to 1867.
Tozan—school of shakuhachi playing that developed around 1904 in Japan.
TWLF—Third World Liberation Front.
TWLF strike—the student strikes organized by the Third World Liberation Front at San Francisco State University and the University of California, Berkeley, to protest institutionalized racism and demand the creation of ethnic studies programs.
Ujikoma-kai—one of the first *gidayū* groups in San Francisco.
undōkai—picnics that included exercises and games.
utai—intoning of classical poetry in *nō*-drama-style singing.
wa—social harmony (a Japanese value).
wasan— Buddhist hymn.
WRA—War Relocation Authority; US government agency created to manage the illegal removal and incarceration of Japanese Americans during World War II.
Yamada—one of the two major koto schools.
yamato damashii—the spirit of the Japanese.
YBA—Young Buddhist Association; young people's group organized at Buddhist temples in the United States.
YMBA—Young Men's Buddhist Association; Buddhist young men's organization modeled after the Christian YMCA.
yōkyoku—singing style performed in *nō* theater.
Yonsei—fourth generation; third generation to be born in a country outside of Japan.
zaibei doho—meaning "Japanese in America"; transculturated Issei identity.

NOTES

CHAPTER 1: THE NEXUS OF MUSIC, IDENTITY, AND POLITICS

1. Cat Zhang, "What Is Asian American Music Really?" *Pitchfork*, May 31, 2021, https://pitchfork.com/features/asian-american-music-history/?fbclid=.
2. Jerry Adler, "'Sweet Land of Liberties': If Everyone Has His Own Niche, What Do We Have in Common Anymore?" *Newsweek*, July 10, 1995, https://www.newsweek.com/sweet-land-liberties-184578.
3. Adler, "Sweet Land."
4. The majority-minority myth spread by media headlines exacerbates the sociopolitical polarization in the United States. In the year 2000, the US Census forecast a growing majority-minority demographic. This data is inaccurate in that it does not reflect the complexity of multiracial identities. The misleading information stems from the Census Bureau categorizing ethno-racially mixed Americans as non-white. This arbitrarily skews the public data since a majority of multiracial individuals have a white parent. Richard Alba, Morris Levy, and Dowell Myers, "The Myth of a Majority-Minority America," *The Atlantic*, June 13, 2021, https://www.theatlantic.com/ideas/archive/2021/06/myth-majority-minority-America/619190.
5. Viet Thanh Nguyen, "American Like Me: What It Means to Love My Country, No Matter How It Feels about Me," *Time* 192, no. 22–23 (November 26, 2018): 30.
6. Alba, Levy, and Myers, "The Myth of a Majority-Minority America."
7. Christopher Small, "Whose Music Do We Teach Anyway?" *Muse Letter* 2 (March 1990): 5–6.
8. Deborah Wong made a call to action for music studies to interrogate the intersection of musicking and politics at the preconference symposium of the Society for Ethnomusicology national meeting in 2005. The President's Roundtable on "Music and Politics" at the 57th Annual Meeting of the Society for Ethnomusicology, November 1–4, 2012, in New Orleans also focused on this important topic.
9. Pioneering books utilizing such frameworks are *Dangerous Crossroads: Popular Music, Postmodernism, and the Poetics of Place* (1994) by George Lipsitz, Philip V. Bohlman and Ronald Radano's *Music and the Racial Imagination* (2000), Deborah Wong's *Speak It Louder: Asian Americans Making Music* (2004), Timothy D. Taylor's *Beyond Exoticism: Western Music and the World* (2007), and Su Zheng's *Claiming Diaspora: Music, Transnationalism, and Cultural Politics in Asian/Chinese America* (2010).
10. Lisa Lowe, *Immigrant Acts: On Asian American Cultural Politics* (Durham, NC: Duke University Press), 4.
11. Lowe, *Immigrant Acts*, 1–3.

12. Quoted in Grace Lee, director, *American Revolutionary: The Evolution of Grace Lee Boggs*, San Francisco, CA: Center for Asian American Media, 2013. Grace Lee Boggs was an American writer, social activist, philosopher, and feminist known for her work in the civil rights, Black Power, labor, Asian American, environmental justice, and feminist movements for seven decades. As a community organizer and activist in Detroit for many decades, she was a guiding light for contemporary activists with her final book, *The Next American Revolution: Sustainable Activism for the Twenty-First Century*. The documentary film *American Revolutionary* chronicles her intellectual and activist life.

13. Dale A. Olsen, *The Chrysanthemum and the Song: Music, Memory, and Identity in the South American Diaspora* (Gainsville: University of Florida Press, 2004), xviii.

14. Avtar Brah, *Cartographies of Diaspora: Contesting Identities* (London: Routledge, 1996), 1.

15. Brah, *Cartographies of Diaspora*, 1.

16. Lowe, *Immigrant Acts*, 2–3.

17. Jeff Chang, *We Gon' Be Alright: Notes on Race and Resegregation* (New York: Picador, 2016), 57.

18. Lowe, *Immigrant Acts*, 7.

19. Y. Scott Matsumoto, "Okinawa Migrants to Hawaii," *Hawaiian Journal of History* 16 (1982): 125–33, eVols.

20. Hokubei Okinawa Kurabu, *History of the Okinawans in North America*, trans. Ben Kobashigawa (Los Angeles, CA: Okinawan Club of America, 1989); James E. Roberson, "Singing Diaspora: Okinawan Songs of Home, Departure and Return," *Identities* 17, no. 4 (2010): 430–53.

21. Lowe, *Immigrant Acts*, ix, x, 6, 24.

22. Chang, *We Gon' Be Alright*, 56, 57.

23. Chang, *We Gon' Be Alright*, 56.

24. Chang, *We Gon' Be Alright*, 9, 12.

25. Coco Fusco, "Passionate Irreverence: The Cultural Politics of Identity," in *Art Matters: How the Culture Wars Changed America*, eds. Brian Wallis, Marianne Weems, and Philip Yenawine (New York: New York University Press, 1999), 64.

26. Dorinne Kondo, *About Face: Performing Race in Fashion and Theater* (New York: Routledge, 1997), 4.

27. Ketu H. Katrak, review of *Immigrant Acts: On Asian American Cultural Politics*, by Lisa Lowe, *Journal of Asian American Studies* 3, no. 3 (October 2000): 373.

28. Su Zheng, *Claiming Diaspora: Music, Transnationalism, and Cultural Politics in Asian/Chinese America* (Oxford: Oxford University Press, 2010), 18.

29. Zheng, *Claiming Diaspora*, 19.

30. David Rosenberg, "Discerning Diaspora: Roots and Routes," *SEM Student News* 10 (Spring–Summer 2015): 10.

31. Glenn Mimura, *Ghostlife of Third Cinema* (Minneapolis: University of Minnesota Press, 2009), 14.

32. Fusco, "Passionate Irreverence," 71.

33. Zheng, *Claiming Diaspora*, 12.

34. Zheng, *Claiming Diaspora*, 49.

35. Daryl J. Maeda, *Chains of Babylon: The Rise of Asian America* (London: University of Minnesota Press, 2009), 70, 75.

36. Deborah Wong, *Speak It Louder: Asian Americans Making Music* (New York: Routledge, 2004), 4.

37. D. Wong, *Speak It Louder*, 8.

38. Kondo, *About Face*, 7.

39. Lowe raises this question for the broader population of Asian Americans. I modified this question to address Japanese American cultural representation within the US polity, but it is applicable to other immigrant populations who come to the United States in search of "home." See Lowe, *Immigrant Acts*, 1–36.

40. Quoted in Marcus Banks, *Ethnicity: Anthropological Considerations* (London: Routledge, 1996), 44.

41. Claire Jean Kim, "The Racial Triangulation of Asian Americans," in *Asian Americans and Politics: Perspectives, Experiences, and Prospects*, ed. Gordon H. Chang (Stanford, CA: Stanford University Press, 2001), 39.

42. Kim, "The Racial Triangulation," 41. Potentially, more axes of racial domination could be added to the field of racial positions as scholars test this model with other subordinate populations.

43. Maeda, *Chains of Babylon*, 10–11.

44. Francis Fukuyama asserts that the first major expression of modern identity politics was nineteenth-century European nationalism. It was a time when cultural groups first demanded state recognition. See Francis Fukuyama, "Against Identity Politics: The New Tribalism and the Crisis of Democracy," *Foreign Affairs* 97, no. 5 (September–October 2018): 169.

45. Mimura, *Ghostlife of Third Cinema*, 20.

46. Stuart Hall, "The Local and the Global: Globalization and Ethnicity," in *Culture, Globalization, and the World-System: Contemporary Conditions for the Representation of Identity*, ed. Anthony D. King (Minneapolis: University of Minnesota Press, 1997), 36.

47. Stuart Hall, "Old and New Identities, Old and New Ethnicities," in *Culture, Globalization, and the World-System: Contemporary Conditions for the Representation of Identity*, ed. Anthony D. King (Minneapolis: University of Minnesota Press, 1997), 52.

48. Martin Stokes, "Introduction: Ethnicity, Identity and Music," in *Ethnicity, Identity and Music: The Musical Construction of Place*, ed. Martin Stokes (Oxford: Berg, 1994), 7.

49. Lisa Wangsness, "Strangers in Their Own Land, as They Came of Age," *Boston (MA) Globe*, September 8, 2011, 1.

CHAPTER 2: DUAL IDENTITIES: JAPANESE IMMIGRANT COMMUNITY, IDENTITY, AND MUSIC

1. Masao Kodani, interview with author, July 12, 1996.

2. Eiichiro Azuma, *Between Two Empires: Race, History, and Transnationalism in Japanese America* (New York: Oxford University Press, 2005), 61.

3. Yamato Ichihashi, *Japanese in the United States: A Critical Study of the Problems of the Japanese Immigrants and Their Children* (Stanford: Stanford University Press, 1932), 114.

4. In the summer of 1904, my maternal grandfather moved to St. Louis, Missouri, to see the World's Fair called the Louisiana Purchase International Exposition and Olympic Games. From St. Louis, Kichitaro Taki went to Chicago and then settled in New York City, where he started his family.

5. Valerie Matsumoto, *Farming the Home Place: A Japanese American Community in California, 1919–1982* (Ithaca, NY: Cornell University Press, 1993), 21.

6. The predominance of males in the early settlements throughout the American West made prostitution a viable trade for women. See Yuji Ichioka, *The Issei: The World of the First Generation Japanese Immigrants, 1885–1924* (New York: Free Press, 1988), 9.

7. Roger Daniels, *Asian America: Chinese and Japanese in the United States since 1850* (Seattle: University of Washington Press, 1988), 107.

8. Ichiro Mike Murase, *Little Tokyo: One Hundred Years in Pictures* (Los Angeles, CA: Visual Communications; Asian American Studies Central, 1983), 7.

9. Azuma, *Between Two Empires*, 65.

10. Azuma, *Between Two Empires*, 4. A more detailed discussion of the racist discourse of American Orientalism appears in a subsequent section of this chapter.

11. Ichioka, *The Issei*, 69, 71.

12. I commend my paternal grandfather for having the vision to college educate his four daughters as well as his five sons. He was a progressive man who realized the importance of educating his daughters to ensure their success.

13. Daniels, *Asian America*, 151.

14. Yuji Ichioka, *Before Internment: Essays in Prewar Japanese American History*, eds. Gordon H. Chang and Eiichiro Azuma (Stanford, CA: Stanford University Press, 2006), 118.

15. Carey McWilliams, *Prejudice: Japanese Americans; Symbol of Racial Intolerance* (Boston, MA: Little, Brown & Co., 1944), 44.

16. There is a growing body of research about the Asian American body and the impact it has had and continues to have on how Asian Americans are viewed and received on a visceral level. Elena Tajima Creef's book *Imaging Japanese America* is an insightful study of the "distinct visual rhetoric in the symbolic and cultural representation of Japanese Americans in the mid-to-late twentieth century, when the racist hysteria of World War II unjustly framed this ethnic community as disloyal citizens of the nation." See Elena Tajima Creef, *Imaging Japanese America: The Visual Construction of Citizenship, Nation, and the Body* (New York: New York University, 2004), 9.

17. Minako K. Maykovich, *Japanese American Identity Dilemma* (Tokyo: Waseda University Press, 1972), 29. "Field," in this context, refers to a complex of forces that serve as causative agents in human behavior.

18. Ryusaku Tsunoda, Wm. Theodore de Bary, and Donald Keene, comps., *Sources of Japanese Tradition* (New York: Columbia University Press, 1958), 1:138.

19. Kodani, interview.

20. Minako Waseda, "Japanese American Musical Culture in Southern California: Its Formation and Transformation" (PhD diss., University of California, 2000). The *Zaibei Nihonjinshi* is a 1,300-page history of Issei written and edited by educated members of this generation. See Zaibei Nihonjinshi Editorial Staff, *Zaibei Nihonjinshi* (San Francisco, CA: Zaibei Nihonjinkai, 1940). It was a collaboration of many Japanese immigrants and community leaders, who contributed information and their stories and raised funds for the volume's publication. See Azuma, *Between Two Empires*, 90. I have relied heavily on Minako Waseda's data for Issei musical activity in Los Angeles. The in-depth research completed for her dissertation is invaluable and fills in gaps in my information. As a native Japanese, Waseda was able to glean important information from Issei sources available only in the Japanese language. Issei newspapers, early on, were all published in Japanese. The Los Angeles *Rafu Shimpo*, for example, did not start publishing any English sections of the paper until 1915. Japanese community directories and yearbooks were printed in Japanese up until the 1940s.

21. Waseda, "Japanese American Musical Culture."

22. Waseda, "Japanese American Musical Culture."

23. Waseda, "Japanese American Musical Culture," 518–19.

24. This is a professional name given to Mm. Ishikawa by the Kineya school when she mastered a certain number of *nagauta* compositions and gained her license, or *natori*, to teach. The Kineya school dominates the world of *nagauta*. It evolved from the Kineya clan of musicians dating back to the eighteenth century. Head shamisen performers in the major Kabuki theaters belong to the Kineya school.

25. Waseda, "Japanese American Musical Culture," 529.

26. Waseda, "Japanese American Musical Culture," 79–80.

27. Seizo Oka, interview by author, August 15, 1994.
28. Nichibei Shimbun Editorial Staff, *Japanese American Yearbook* (San Francisco, CA: Nichibei Shimbun, 1914), 20–21.
29. Shin Sekai, *New World Directory* (San Francisco, CA: Shin Sekai, 1922), 62.
30. Waseda, "Japanese American Musical Culture," 56–57.
31. Nichibei Shimbun Editorial Staff, *Japanese American Directory* (San Francisco, CA: Nichibei Shimbun, 1941), 11.
32. Komiya Toyotaka, "The Late Meiji Era," in *Japanese Music and Drama in the Meiji Era*, ed. Komiya Toyotaka, trans. and adapted by Donald Keene (Tokyo: Ōbunsha, 1956), 408–9.
33. The Kinshin school came to dominate the Satsuma school in Japan in the late Meiji and Taishō eras (the latter, 1912–1926) because of its more melodic style of singing, replacing the recitational style of the older tradition.
34. Waseda, "Japanese American Musical Culture," 55.
35. Nichibei Shimbun Editorial Staff, *Japanese American Yearbook*, 20.
36. Waseda, "Japanese American Musical Culture," 60–63.
37. Oka, as mentioned earlier, was an important Nisei historian of the Japanese American community in northern California. He held the position of executive director of the Japanese American History Archives at the Japanese American Cultural and Community Center of Northern California for many years.
38. National Japanese American Historical Society, *Nikkei Music Makers: The Swing Era*, 1995, calendar, San Francisco, CA.
39. In the late 1920s, "*kayōkyoku*" replaced the term "*ryūkōka*" ("songs that are popular") when the Nippon Hōsō Kyōkai (NHK) broadcasting system decided on this designation. Both terms are still in use, although *kayōkyoku* is heard more often. *Kayōkyoku* referred to the lied, or art song, of Western classical music during the Meiji and Taisho periods, so it is curious why such a term was chosen to identify popular music. It may have been one way to elevate the stature of *ryūkōka*.
40. Joanne Combs, "Ondo! Japanese Street Dancing in Los Angeles," lecture at the joint meeting of the Congress on Research and Dance, Dance History Scholars, and the American Dance Guild, University of California, Los Angeles, CA, June 23, 1981.
41. As I note elsewhere:
> Hole hole bushi are work songs sung by Japanese workers in Hawaii from 1885 and 1900. The extemporized lyrics of the songs expressed the difficult life and dashed hopes of women workers who were responsible for *hole hole*—work stripping sugar cane leaves from stalks. It is believed that the basic tune of the songs is most directly related to Hiroshima prefecture work songs, especially a rice-threshing melody. [This connection is supported by the fact that women normally did the threshing and hulling of rice in villages.] The popularity of these songs endured and gradually made their way from plantation camps to teahouses in Hilo and Honolulu and were popular in the 1910s in Hawaii as drinking songs.

See Susan Asai, "The Cultural Politics of *Issei* Identity and Music Making: 1894–1941," *Journal of the Society for American Music* 10, no. 3 (August 2016): 321n52, https://doi.org/10.1017/S1752196316000225. See also Harry Minoru Urata and Franklin S. Odo, "Hole Hole Bushi: Song of Hawaii's Japanese Immigrants," *Mana: A South Pacific Journal of Language and Literature* 6, no.1 (1981): 70. Many of the plantation workers transmigrated to the continental United States, so it is possible such folk songs were also sung here.
42. Garrett Hongo, "Introduction," in *Songs My Mother Taught Me: Stories, Plays, and Memoir*, by Wakako Yamauchi, ed. Garrett Hongo (New York: Feminist Press at the City University of New York, 1994), 9.

43. Mari Yoshihara, *Musicians from a Different Shore: Asians and Asian Americans in Classical Music* (Philadelphia, PA: Temple University Press, 2007), 17. This book is invaluable for its detailed history of the spread and influence of Western music in Japan and other parts of Asia.

44. Waseda, "Japanese American Musical Culture," 97–98.

45. *Los Angeles Rafu Shimpo*, "Students' Benefit Concert Program Meets Success," March 14, 1927, 3.

46. Shotaro Frank Miyamoto, "Social Solidarity among the Japanese in Seattle," *University of Washington Publications in the Social Sciences* 11, no. 2 (December 1939): 68.

47. Waseda, "Japanese American Musical Culture," 89–91.

48. *Nikkei Music Makers*.

49. *Los Angeles Rafu Shimpo*, "'Japan Night' Program Seen by Many at USC," January 13, 1930, 3.

50. Sondra Wieland Howe, "American Music in Meiji Era Japan," *Ritsumeikan gengo bunka kenkyū* [Ritsumeikan Language and Cultural Studies] 26, no. 1 (2014): 63–70, https://www.ritsumei.ac.jp/acd/re/k-rsc/lcs/kiyou/pdf_26-1/RitsIILCS_26.1pp.63-70HOWE.pdf.

51. *Los Angeles Rafu Shimpo*, "Trans-Pacific Radio Dial, Station JZJ," May 18, 1937.

52. Azuma, *Between Two Empires*, 171.

53. Azuma, *Between Two Empires*, 178.

54. Patriotic songs are a subset of a Japanese genre called *gunka*—war songs or military music. The *gunka* repertoire includes patriotic songs, the national anthem, and war-time propaganda music—Japanese national music of the period between 1868 and 1945. See "Gunka—Japanese War Songs," Nihon no gunka, accessed June 20, 2023, http://gunka.sakura.ne.jp/en/index.html.

55. Azuma, *Between Two Empires*, 187.

56. In the 1880s, Western imperialism shifted to controlling overseas colonies. In Southeast Asia, France colonized Cambodia, and Great Britain intervened in Burma; then in the 1885 Conference of Berlin, European countries divided the continent of Africa and colonized it.

57. Azuma, *Between Two Empires*, 18.

58. McWilliams, *Prejudice*, 18.

59. Azuma, *Between Two Empires*, 20.

60. Azuma, *Between Two Empires*, 10.

61. David Palumbo-Liu, *Asian American Historical Crossings of a Racial Frontier* (Stanford: Stanford University Press, 1999), 17.

62. Palumbo-Liu, *Asian American Historical Crossings*, 20.

63. Philip Gleason, "American Identity and Americanization," in *Concepts of Ethnicity*, eds. Philip Gleason, Michael Novak, and William Petersen, Dimensions of Ethnicity: A Series of Selections from the Harvard Encyclopedia of Ethnic Groups (Cambridge, MA: Belknap Press, 1982), 62–63.

64. Gleason, "American Identity," 79, 85.

65. Palumbo-Liu, *Asian American Historical Crossings*, 17, 26.

66. Kim, "The Racial Triangulation of Asian Americans," 48, 50.

67. John Kuo Wei Tchen, "Believing Is Seeing: Transforming Orientalism and the Occidental Gaze," in *Asia/America: Identities in Contemporary Asian American Art*, curated by Margo Machida (New York: Asia Society Galleries; New Press, 1994), 15.

68. John Kuo Wei Tchen discusses how Westerners have been enculturated to view the Asian body and other physical features from the perspective of the "Orientalist socialization" of nineteenth-century American commercial culture. Within this context, he introduces the social construction of "yellowface," describing it as a means for Asians to assimilate into mainstream society. See Tchen, "Believing Is Seeing."

69. Palumbo-Liu, *Asian American Historical Crossings*, 17, 26.

70. Roger Daniels, *The Politics of Prejudice: The Anti-Japanese Movement in California and the Struggle for Japanese Exclusion*, University of California Publications in History 71 (New York: Atheneum, 1973), 66–67.

71. Gleason, "American Identity," 94.

72. Lowe, *Immigrant Acts*, 20.

73. Daniels, *The Politics of Prejudice*, 65.

74. Azuma, *Between Two Empires*, 6.

75. Azuma, *Between Two Empires*, 6.

76. Cultural assimilation is specifically stated here to distinguish it from structural assimilation, which is a process in which minority groups gain entrance into the institutions of the majority group, especially on a primary-group level. Structural assimilation was not possible for Issei due to racial exclusionism, nor was it desirable by a majority Issei whose ethos and loyalties remained rooted in Japan.

77. Azuma, *Between Two Empires*, 50.

78. Gleason, "American Identity," 85.

79. Azuma, *Between Two Empires*, 59.

80. Azuma, *Between Two Empires*, 187.

81. Azuma, *Between Two Empires*, 57, 60.

82. Azuma, *Between Two Empires*, 52.

83. Azuma, *Between Two Empires*, 14.

84. Azuma, *Between Two Empires*, 59.

85. Azuma, *Between Two Empires*, 61.

86. Ronald Takaki, *Strangers from a Different Shore: A History of Asian Americans* (Boston: Little, Brown and Co., 1989), 180.

87. Harry H. L. Kitano, *Japanese Americans: The Evolution of a Subculture* (Englewood Cliffs: Prentice-Hall, 1969), 54.

88. The nature of Issei patriotism complicated their position. Issei patriotism was not extremist; it differed from the more militaristic views of their compatriots in Japan. Instead, it was the fulfillment of their social obligation to assist Japanese soldiers enduring the harsh winter in Manchuria as news reports of the soldiers' hardships reached immigrant communities. Patriotism was couched in the context of Japanese ethics and the Issei duty to aid their countrymen and nation. Psychologically, Japanese patriotism filled the void for immigrants who were denied political participation in the United States. Patriotism in immigrant communities reflected internal struggles surrounding the legitimacy of nationalistic campaigns to assist Japan in its imperialistic intentions in China and enabling it to achieve a position of power. The level of a community member's donation toward Japan's war effort became a measure of their authenticity as a Japanese. See Azuma, *Between Two Empires*, 167. A renewal of the Issei's Japaneseness served as a reference point and a position of strength as they sought to move forward.

89. Seizo Oka, interview by author, July 23, 1996.

90. Azuma, *Between Two Empires*, 184.

CHAPTER 3: CAUGHT ON THE CULTURAL CUSP: NISEI POLITICS OF IDENTITY AND MUSIC

1. Quoted in George Yoshida, *Reminiscing in Swingtime: Japanese Americans in American Popular Music, 1925–1960* (San Francisco, CA: National Japanese American Historical Society, 1997), 4.

2. Daniels, *Asian America*, 156.

3. John Modell, *The Economics and Politics of Racial Accommodation: The Japanese of Los Angeles, 1900–1942* (Urbana: University of Illinois Press, 1977), 166.

4. Opposition to nonconformist tendencies is rather entrenched in Japanese culture, favoring collective identities over individual ones. The idea of "hammering down the nail that sticks up" is equivalent to the familiar saying "Don't rock the boat."

5. Lon Kurashige, *Japanese American Celebration and Conflict: A History of Ethnic Identity and Festival in Los Angeles, 1934–1990* (Berkeley: University of California Press, 2002), 7. Kurashige's book is a thorough and insightful look at the role of Nisei Week from economic, political, and social perspectives. It is an in-depth work that exposes the complex negotiations that were involved in balancing a Japanese American identity within the contexts of the years before, during, and following World War II.

6. Creef, *Imaging Japanese America*. Creef analyzes a broad range of visual and "textual" material making it very useful for delving into the visceral aspects of difference.

7. David Yoo, *Growing Up Nisei: Race, Generation, and Culture among Japanese Americans of California, 1924–49* (Urbana: University of Illinois Press, 2000), 4.

8. Daniel I. Okimoto, *American in Disguise* (New York: Walker; Weatherhill, 1971), 5.

9. Yoo, *Growing Up Nisei*, 8.

10. Quoted in Kurashige, *Japanese American*, 4.

11. Paul R. Spickard, *Japanese Americans: The Formation and Transformations of an Ethnic Group* (New York: Twayne Publishers; London, Prentice-Hall International, 1996), 89.

12. Azuma, *Between Two Empires*, 118–19.

13. Azuma, *Between Two Empires*, 164.

14. Jerrold Takahashi, "Japanese American Responses to Race Relations: The Formation of Nisei Perspectives," *Amerasia Journal* 9, no. 1 (1982): 50.

15. Kurashige, *Japanese American*, 29.

16. Yoo, *Growing Up Nisei*, 7.

17. Susan Asai, "Transformations of Tradition: Three Generations of Japanese American Music Making," *Musical Quarterly* 79, no. 3 (Fall 1995): 432.

18. The Oliver Club was Little Tokyo's first youth organization, formed by Nellie Oliver in 1917. Nisei children learned Robert's Rules of parliamentary procedure, participated in community sing-alongs, and learned correct grammar and how to dance. The club organized fundraising events and sports competitions and offered meals and snacks. See Kurashige, *Japanese American*, 39.

19. Yoo, *Growing Up Nisei*, 38.

20. Bill Hosokawa, *The Nisei: The Quiet Americans* (New York: William Morrow and Co., 1969), 171.

21. Takahashi, "Japanese American Responses," 42.

22. Yoo, *Growing Up Nisei*, 73.

23. Yoo, *Growing Up Nisei*, 73, 76.

24. Waseda, "Japanese American Musical Culture," 84–85.

25. Waseda, "Japanese American Musical Culture," 86. The names of both artists mentioned here are their professional names given to them when they received their professional certification (*natori*).

26. Waseda, "Japanese American Musical Culture," 87.

27. Waseda, "Japanese American Musical Culture," 89.

28. Waseda, "Japanese American Musical Culture," 90.

29. *Los Angeles Rafu Shimpo*, "Famous Singer Pleases Many Admirers Here," November 29, 1926, 3.

30. *Los Angeles Rafu Shimpo*, "Central Junior High Invites Public to 'Japanese Night,'" February 27, 1941, n.p.

31. *Los Angeles Rafu Shimpo*, New Year's broadcast program, December 29, 1941, n.p.

32. *Los Angeles Rafu Shimpo*, Imperial County Fair program, February 27, 1941, n.p.

33. *Los Angeles Kashū Mainichi Shimbun*, "Gakuen Graduates Given Diplomas at San Fernando," July 30, 1928, 7.

34. Kats Kunitsugu, ed., *Teachers of Japanese Cultural Arts in Southern California Directory* (Los Angeles, CA: Japanese American Cultural and Community Center, 1994), 2–4, 21, 22, and 26.

35. *Kiyomoto* is a genre that borders between the lyric and the narrative styles of shamisen music used in Kabuki theater. It is sung in a high tessitura with falsetto-like tones. The shamisen used to accompany *kiyomoto* is made thinner to accommodate the higher pitched tunings. See William Malm, *Japanese Music and Musical Instruments* (Rutland, VT: Charles E. Tuttle Co., [1959] 1974), 199.

36. Kineya Jyorokusho, interview by author, August 30, 1994.

37. Rei Kasama, interview by author, August 25, 1994.

38. Large numbers of Japanese workers first settled in Hawaii during the 1880s and 1990s to work on sugarcane plantations. Significant numbers of Japanese migrated to the US mainland during the 1900s and 1910s. As a result, Japanese in Hawaii are a generation ahead. So Lillian Nakano, although considered a Sansei in Hawaii, was socialized on the mainland as a Nisei since her cohort group were Nisei.

39. Lillian Nakano, interview by author, August 25, 1994.

40. Nakano, interview.

41. The NCRR is one of two grassroots organizations in the Japanese American community responsible for the success of obtaining restitution for losses and injuries suffered by Nikkei (people of Japanese ancestry) and others who were unjustly evacuated and incarcerated by the US government during World War II. See "About NCRR," Nikkei for Civil Rights and Redress, last modified January 24, 2003, https://ncrr-la.org/about. Legislation passed and signed into law by Ronald Reagan on August 10, 1988, acknowledged the federal government's wrongdoings against Japanese Americans during World War II through a formal apology. The legislation, named the Civil Liberties Act of 1988, also appropriated over a billion dollars in compensation to be paid to each surviving internee ($20,000 per individual) as well as an educational trust fund to promote awareness of the World War II internment and prevent similar injustices from recurring in the future. See Sharon Yamato, "Civil Liberties Act of 1988," Densho Encyclopedia, accessed June 5, 2023, https://encyclopedia.densho.org/Civil%20Liberties%20Act%20of%201988.

42. The town of Florin no longer exists. It never recovered following the imprisonment of *all* its inhabitants during World War II, but the spirit of the community lives on in the hearts and memories of those who once had ties to this town. See Florin Japanese American Citizens League Oral History Project and the Mary Tsukamoto Japanese American Collection, University Library Special Collections and University Archives, California State University, Sacramento, https://csu-csus.primo.exlibrisgroup.com/discovery/fulldisplay?docid=alma99182726050101671&context=L&vid=01CALS_USL:01CALS_USL&lang=en&search_scope=Everything&adaptor=Local%20Search%20Engine&tab=Everything&query=creator,exact,California%20State%20University,%20Sacramento.%20Oral%20History%20Program.,AND&mode=advanced&offset=0.

43. Molly Miyako Kimura, interview by Hiroko Tsuda, Florin Japanese American Citizens League Oral History Project and Mary Tsukamoto Japanese American Collection, University Library Special Collections and University Archives, California State University, Sacramento, https://csu-csus.primo.exlibrisgroup.com/discovery/fulldisplay?docid=alma99182726050101671&context=L&vid=01CALS_USL:01CALS_USL&lang=en&search_scope=Everything&adaptor=Local%20Search%20Engine&tab=Everything&query=creator,exact,California%20State%20University,%20Sacramento.%20Oral%20History%20Program.,AND&mode=advanced&offset=0.

44. Kurashige, *Japanese American*, 43.

45. Kurashige, *Japanese American*, 51.

46. *Los Angeles Kashū Mainichi Shimbun*, "Nisei Week Featured on Radio Friday," August 8, 1935, 5.

47. *Los Angeles Rafu Shimpo*, "Young Soprano from North to Make Debut Here Soon," April 2, 1928, 8.

48. Buddhist temples came to be called Buddhist churches as the temples gradually adopted the activities and organizational structure of Christian churches in an attempt to Westernize and attract the younger generation. Today, many Buddhist churches have switched back to using the term "temple" in response to Japanese Americans retracing their heritage.

49. *Los Angeles Rafu Shimpo*, "Emperor's Birthday Celebration, Plan of Japanese People," April 9, 1928, 11.

50. Waseda, "Japanese American Musical Culture," 103.

51. Waseda, "Japanese American Musical Culture," 10.

52. *Los Angeles Rafu Shimpo*, Yoshie Fujiwara's KHJ radio-broadcast performance, November 29, 1928, 3.

53. *Los Angeles Rafu Shimpo*, "Central Junior High Invites Public to 'Japanese Night,'" February 27, 1941, 5.

54. *Los Angeles Rafu Shimpo*, Los Angeles Japanese Orchestra fifth annual spring concert, March 5, 1928, 1.

55. *Los Angeles Rafu Shimpo*, "2 Nisei to Appear in Opera Reading Club Presentation," January 5, 1941, 6.

56. *Los Angeles Rafu Shimpo*, "Nisei Sings Operatic Role," May 8, 1941, 11.

57. Along with Dmitri Tiomkin, he was considered one of Hollywood's top composers. But Cadman first and foremost was a serious composer who wrote for nearly every genre. His chamber-music works are generally considered among his best. There, he tried to introduce elements of ragtime music into the classical-music format, thus anticipating George Gershwin, Igor Fyodorovich Stravinsky, and Darius Milhaud, among others. It was his "Piano Trio," op. 56, composed in 1913, that drew the critics' attention and praise.

58. *Los Angeles Kashū Mainichi Shimbun*, "Program Arranged for Concert Given by Miss Miyakawa," April 23, 1928, 8.

59. *Los Angeles Kashū Mainichi Shimbun*, "Nisei Artists to Appear on Union Church Program," September 9, 1935, 5.

60. *Los Angeles Rafu Shimpo*, "Troop 379 Drum and Bugle Corps Wins Legion Award," May 6, 1941, 1.

61. *Los Angeles Rafu Shimpo*, "Frisco Harmonica Band Broadcast Over NBC System," January 27, 1930, n.p.

62. *Los Angeles Rafu Shimpo*, "Boys to Organize Harmonica Band," February 14, 1930, n.p.

63. *Los Angeles Rafu Shimpo*, "Musical Numbers Please Audience of Young People," August 6, 1928, 6.

64. *Los Angeles Rafu Shimpo*, "Big Annual Carnival Held by Combined Oliver Clubs," January 1, 1928, 11.

65. *Nichibei Shimbun*, "200 Attend Silver Echo Club Dance," January 15, 1929, 1.

66. *Los Angeles Rafu Shimpo*, "Club Social Activities—Nisei Rug-cutters," February 12, 1941, 7.

67. *Los Angeles Kashū Mainichi Shimbun*, "Nipponettes to Hold Dance," May 18, 1937, 11.

68. *Pacific Citizen*, "Santa Barbara to Give Dance for Season's Grads," 13, no. 154 (June 1941): 12.

69. Stylistically, the music of swing bands stands between Tin Pan Alley and jazz. These bands often featured: one or more singers (Frank Sinatra, Jo Stafford, Doris Day, Perry Como, Billie Holiday, Dick Hames, Bob Eberle, Helen Ward, Helen Forrest, and Bing Crosby); instrumental pieces that were usually fast; a rhythm section that kept a steady beat; brass and reed instruments performing syncopated rhythms; and improvising soloists for half or full choruses. These were all features of Black jazz bands, giving their musical styling some recognition

among white audiences. See Charles Hamm, "Popular Music, III, 4: Tin Pan Alley," in *The New Grove Dictionary of American Music*, eds. H. Wiley Hitchcock and Stanley Sadie (London: Macmillan, 1986), 3:600–1. "Big bands" and "dance bands" are both terms used in this article to refer to swing bands.

70. George Yoshida, interview by author, March 30, 2006.

71. James Lincoln Collier, "Jazz, IV, 3: The Big Band Boom," in *The New Grove Dictionary of American Music*, eds. H. Wiley Hitchcock and Stanley Sadie (London: Macmillan, 1986), 2:548.

72. Rita H. Mead and Ned Sublette, "Broadcasting 2: Commercial Development to 1940," in *The New Grove Dictionary of American Music*, eds. H. Wiley Hitchcock and Stanley Sadie (London: Macmillan, 1986), 2:297.

73. Taxi dances involved men buying individual tickets to be able to dance with the women present. It was surmised that this gave the social clubs a chance to raise some revenue.

74. Yoshida, *Reminiscing in Swingtime*, 7–9.

75. Yoshida, *Reminiscing in Swingtime*, 10, 12, 14.

76. The instrumentation of Nisei bands, in general, featured a number of saxophones, trumpets, a trombone, and a rhythm section. Some ensembles included banjo, tuba, clarinet, and a singer.

77. This band was one of the first white swing bands to imitate a Black big-band sound and to promote this sound to a wide audience. The ensemble's sophisticated musical arrangements and the high-level musicianship of its members set the standard for many swing bands later on. See Ronald Radano, "Casa Loma Orchestra," in *The New Grove Dictionary of American Music*, eds. H. Wiley Hitchcock and Stanley Sadie (London: Macmillan, 1986), 1:375.

78. Yoshida, *Reminiscing in Swingtime*, 19–21.

79. It was said that the well-known blues singer Sophie Tucker befriended and nurtured Kono Takeuchi as she built her career. See Yoshida, *Reminiscing in Swingtime*, 17.

80. Yoshida, *Reminiscing in Swingtime*, 126.

81. Yoshida, interview, March 30, 2006.

82. Dorothy Bryant, "George Yoshida: Still Swingin'," *Berkeley (CA) Daily Planet*, July 30, 2009, 1.

83. Race records were a seventy-eight-rpm recording series of mostly vocal jazz music produced for Black consumers between 1921 and 1942. Record companies such as Okeh, Paramount, Columbia, Vocalion, and Victor sold a race series. Many smaller companies also had race series, so by 1927, 500 race records were sold annually. "Classic" blues singers and spiritual and gospel quartets released race records between 1921 and 1925. Throughout the 1930s, self-accompanied blues singers, preachers (either solo or accompanied by their congregations), blues vocal duets, quartets, and small groups were all recorded and sold in race series. Following World War II, the phrase "race records" was substituted with "rhythm and blues," before this term came to designate a specific musical style. See Paul Oliver, "Race Record," in *The New Grove Dictionary of American Music*, eds. H. Wiley Hitchcock and Stanley Sadie (London: Macmillan, 1986), 4:1–2.

84. Yoshida, interview, March 30, 2006.

85. Yoshida, interview, March 30, 2006.

86. Japan America Theatre, Music to Remember: A Tribute to Japanese American Musicians and Singers of the '40s, program booklet, concert at Japanese American Cultural and Community Center in association with Mas Fukai and Friends, Los Angeles, CA, February 18–19, 1995.

87. May Takayanagi and Taka Takayanagi, interview by author, March 7, 2006.

88. Kathryn Grayson was a coloratura soprano featured on radio programs until she was recruited by MGM talent scouts to be groomed as one of their top musical stars of the 1940s. Her two most memorable roles were in productions of the early 1950s: *Showboat* and *Kiss Me Kate*. Her performing career included singing in nightclubs and on stage. See IMDB, "Kathryn Grayson: Biography," accessed May 8, 2023, http://www.imdb.com/name/nm0337113/bio.

89. Yutaka Kobayashi, interview by author, June 13, 2006.

90. I recommend Valerie J. Matsumoto's *City Girls: The Nisei Social World in Los Angeles, 1920–1950*. This 2014 publication captures, in detail, the social world of Nisei women in the city of angels.

91. Kiku Uno, interview by author, June 18, 2006.

92. Hisayo Asai, interview by author, August 31, 2006.

93. Walter Moriya, interview by author, June 5, 2009.

94. Donald Shirachi, ed., *Reunion Booklet of YBA Orchestra* (Watsonville: YBA, 2005), 1.

95. Haruko Akamatsu, interview by author, May 28, 2007.

96. Sue Okabe, interview by author, July 28, 1995.

97. Her performing stories are narrated in the next chapter on musicking in the concentration camps.

98. Robert Naka, interview by author, March 8, 2006.

99. For a detailed analysis of one Nisei's exploration of the "racial borderlands of 1940s America," see Matthew M. Briones, *Jim and Jap Crow: A Cultural History of 1940s Interracial America* (Princeton, NJ: Princeton University Press, 2012). Briones's study follows Charles Kikuchi, a socially conscious Nisei trained as a sociologist, whose direct experience of discrimination during and following World War II leads him to envision an America that moves beyond exclusion and racial segregation. *Jim and Jap Crow* is a case study that sheds light on what it was to be a Japanese American in the mid-twentieth century, and his writings provide an "indispensable historical link in the overlapping network of intellectuals—immigrant, Black, Nisei, and others—that would dominate the landscape of democratic and ideological discourse throughout the 1940s." Briones, *Jim and Jap Crow*, 3.

100. Tchen, "Believing Is Seeing," 17.

101. For a comprehensive and detailed study of the role of music in shaping American perceptions of the Japanese, the influence of Japanese music on American composers, and the place of Japanese Americans in American musical life, see W. Anthony Sheppard, *Extreme Exoticism: Japan in the American Musical Imagination* (New York: Oxford University Press, 2019). The view of Japanese/Asian Americans as exotic is a stereotype that continues to promote Asians as unassimilable and perpetually foreign in some social spheres and regions of the United States.

102. Sheppard, *Extreme Exoticism*, 17–18.

103. Quoted in Ichihashi, *Japanese in the United States*, 353.

104. Jere Takahashi, *Nisei/Sansei: Shifting Japanese American Identities and Politics* (Philadelphia, PA: Temple University Press, 1997), 48.

105. Abiko Kyūtaro was a highly esteemed Issei leader and publisher of the daily newspaper *Nichibei Shimbun*, a publication that was the most influential Japanese daily, reaching a peak distribution of twenty-five thousand subscribers in the 1920s throughout California, the Pacific Northwest, and the Rocky Mountain region. Abiko disseminated the cultural-bridge concept to his readers; he felt Nisei had the potential to educate Americans about Japan in their role as liaisons between the two countries. In order for the Nisei to serve as bridges of understanding, however, they needed to learn about Japanese history and political affairs. From 1924 into the 1930s, the *Nichibei Shimbun* and other immigrant newspapers and organizations sponsored study tours to Japan, sending Nisei who exhibited leadership potential. Nisei were also encouraged to live and study in Japan, and by 1935, fifty-thousand Nisei resided in the country of their ancestors. The occupation of Manchuria by junior Japanese officers in 1931, the Sino-Japanese War in 1937, and the abrogation in 1940 of the 1911 United States-Japanese Treaty of Commerce and Navigation inevitably politicized the bridge-of-understanding concept, and it became a liability rather than a benefit. See Ichioka, *Before Internment*, 25, 26, 35, 46.

106. Takahashi, "Japanese American Responses," 33–34.

107. Modell, *The Economics*, 165.
108. Modell, *The Economics*, 35.
109. Modell, *The Economics*, 36.
110. Hosokawa, *The Nisei*, 199.
111. Takahashi, "Japanese American Responses," 57.
112. Takahashi, "Japanese American Responses," 62.
113. Takahashi, "Japanese American Responses," 42.
114. Glenn Omatsu, "Always a Rebel: An Interview with Kazu Iijima," *Amerasia Journal* 13, no. 2 (1986–1987): 89.
115. Omatsu, "Always a Rebel," 46–47.
116. Omatsu, "Always a Rebel," 48.
117. Azuma, *Between Two Empires*, 129.
118. Azuma, *Between Two Empires*, 130.
119. Some Nisei leaders, however, did benefit from the Issei eclectic reading of Nippon *seishin*. James Y. Sakamoto, publisher of the *Japanese American Courier* in Seattle and leader of the Japanese American Citizens League, for example, drew strength from Bushido principles by emphasizing loyalty and good character as an American.
120. Kurashige, *Japanese American*, 37.
121. Daisuke Kitagawa, *Issei and Nisei: The Internment Years* (New York: Seabury Press, 1967), 27.
122. Yoo, *Growing Up Nisei*, 52.
123. Sandra C. Taylor, *Jewel of the Desert* (Berkeley: University of California Press, 1993), 13.

CHAPTER 4: "BUDDHAHEAD BLUES": MUSICAL COMMUNITIES IN THE US CONCENTRATION CAMPS OF WORLD WAR II

1. Yoshida, *Reminiscing in Swingtime*, 120–21.
2. It has recently come to light that there were thirteen confinement sites in Hawaii, four of which are introduced in a short documentary film entitled *The Untold Story*, written and produced by Hawaii-born Yonsei (fourth-generation) filmmaker Ryan Kawamoto. See Ryan Kuwamoto, "Stepping into the Past: Behind the Scenes of *The Untold Story*: Internment of Japanese Americans in Hawai'i," Discover Nikkei, October 11, 2013, http://www.discovernikkei.org/en/journal/2013/10/11/internment-hawaii/.
3. The War Relocation Authority deprived Japanese Americans of their liberty by unconstitutionally incarcerating them and placing them in heavily guarded concentration camps. Consequently, this population found they had lost much of their property and lands when they returned home after the camps.
4. Yoshida, *Reminiscing in Swingtime*, 122.
5. Yoshida, *Reminiscing in Swingtime*, 125.
6. Yasutaro Soga, *Life behind Barbed Wire: The World War II Concentration Memoirs of a Hawaiian Issei*, trans. Kihei Hirae (Honolulu: University of Hawaii Press, 2008), 37.
7. Ronald Radano and Philip V. Bohlman, "Introduction: Music and Race, Their Past, Their Presence," in *Music and the Racial Imagination*, eds. Ronald Radano and Philip V. Bohlman (Chicago: University of Chicago Press, 2000), 6.
8. Fusco, "Passionate Irreverence," 64.
9. Arthur A. Hansen, "Cultural Politics in the Gila River Relocation Center, 1942–1943," *Arizona and the West* 27, no. 4 (Winter 1985): 330.
10. Resistance historiography is reviewed in Gary Y. Okihiro, "Tule Lake under Martial Law: A Study in Japanese Resistance," *Journal of Ethnic Studies* 5, no. 3 (Fall 1977): 71–72; and Gene Wise, *American Historical Explanations: A Strategy for Grounded Inquiry* (Homewood,

IL: Dorsey Press, 1973), 86–89, 97–100. For other works that employ resistance historiography, see Gary Y. Okihiro, *The Columbia Guide to Asian American History* (New York: Columbia University Press, 2005), 164–74; Gary Y. Okihiro, "Japanese American Resistance in America's Concentration Camps: A Re-Evaluation," *Amerasia Journal* 2, no. 1 (1973).

11. Mentioned earlier in the chapter were the Issei feelings of frustration and loss of power when Nisei were appointed by the WRA administration to fill decision-making positions in the camps. Issei viewed this generation as lacking in experience and ability for responsible positions. Nisei empowerment disrupted the Issei's hegemonic hold on the Japanese community.

12. Hansen, "Cultural Politics," 344.

13. Hansen, "Cultural Politics," 359.

14. No details of the performance were given. It is possible that the entertainment was a Kabuki production since the drama society Engeibu was in attendance at the banquet. Otherwise, either *shigin* songs or a shakuhachi performance comes to mind as the most likely to have been offered considering the club attendees and their Japanese nationalist stance.

15. The Engeibu demonstrated their nationalistic tendencies not only in restoring pure Japanese dramatic art but also by plying their dramatic performances in service of their pro-Japanese political agenda. The Sumo Club, considered the most menacing pro-Japanese club by the Canal administration, often included the shouting of loud "*banzais*" and the singing of Japanese nationalistic songs at their tournaments and meetings. The lower-class membership of the Sumo Club and their association with gambling activities reflect their unrefined treatment toward those who opposed them.

16. Hansen, "Cultural Politics," 342.

17. Hansen, "Cultural Politics," 342.

18. Emily Roxworthy, *The Spectacle of Japanese American Trauma: Racial Performativity in World War II* (Honolulu: University of Hawaii Press, 2008), 123–24.

19. Roxworthy, *The Spectacle*, 13.

20. Andy Noguchi, "Camp Art: Strength, Dignity and Culture in the Concentration Camps," *East Wind Magazine* 2, no.2 (Fall–Winter 1983): 54.

21. Allen H. Eaton, *Beauty behind Barbed Wire: The Arts of the Japanese in Our War Relocation Camps* (New York: Harper and Brothers, 1952), 11, 13, 15, 17, 21, 25, 29, 43, 45, 47, 59, 67, 71, 75, 79, 121, 145, 147, 157. This book is invaluable for its numerous photographs of the various mediums of art that blossomed in the camps.

22. Eaton, *Beauty behind Barbed Wire*, 42, 61, 155. An event affecting 450 artifacts created in the camps was the planned auction on April 17, 2015, of a collection, encompassing art pieces and functional items, for profit. Announcement of the auction raised a firestorm of protest by Japanese Americans. The owner planned to auction Allen H. Eaton's collection, which Eaton had received from inmates in appreciation of his efforts to write about their suffering and provide exposure for their works of beauty. Eaton's collection includes decorative items, paintings, arts and crafts pieces, calligraphy, furniture, and household articles. Black and white photographs of these artifacts appear in *Beauty behind Barbed Wire*, which Eaton authored. The owner rescinded his plans to auction off the works through a New Jersey–based auction house days after the announcement in response to national petitions and protests launched on websites. See Lorna Fong, "Negotiate in Good Faith with the Japanese American Community to Preserve American Concentration Camp Artifacts," Change.org, last updated May 1, 2015, www.change.org/p/rago-negotiate-with-japanese-american-families-to-preserve-american-concentration-camp-artifacts (with 7,909 supporters); and Tsuru for Solidarity, "Japanese American History: NOT for Sale," Facebook, accessed on June 18, 2015, www.facebook.com/japaneseamericanhistorynotforsale?fref=ts (with 7,183 likes). The Japanese American History Consortium coalesced for the express purpose of deciding on the future of the collection.

Institutions participating on the consortium include Japanese American National Museum, Smithsonian Asian Pacific American Center, the Wing Luke Museum in Seattle, the Japanese American Citizens League, Heart Mountain Wyoming Foundation, the Ad Hoc Committee to Oppose the Sale of Japanese American Historical Artifacts, and others. In response to the Japanese American National Museum's (JANM) acquisition of the collection, the consortium submitted a letter to JANM board members and President Greg Kimura, expressing their concern: "How will the many issues associated with these cultural properties, including provenance and treatment be determined and how will the community be heard in the process?" See Japanese American History: NOT for Sale, "Letter to the Board of Trustees of JANM and President Greg Kimura," Facebook, June 12, 2015, https://www.facebook.com/japaneseamericanhistorynot forsale/posts/letter-to-the-board-of-trustees-of-janm-and-president-greg-kimurathe-artifacts -f/1571833183079575/.

23. Rihoko Ueno, "One Spot of Normalcy: Chiura Obata's Art Schools," Archives of American Art, Smithsonian Institution, September 10, 2019, https://www.aaa.si.edu/blog/2019/09 /one-spot-of-normalcy-chiura-obatas-art-schools.

24. Quoted in Ueno, "One Spot of Normalcy."

25. Shirli Gilbert, *Music in the Holocaust: Confronting Life in the Nazi Ghettos and Camps* (New York: Oxford University Press, 2006), 2–3.

26. Shelemay's "Musical Communities" is a thoughtful exposé of the idea of "community" and how it has been defined and used over time since its application in the work of the German sociologist Ferdinand Tönnies (1855–1936). In this article, she lays out a history of the changes in the meaning and usage of this concept in the fields of sociology, historical musicology, ethnomusicology, anthropology, and cultural studies. After evaluating alternative terms used for "community" that have had parlance since the 1980s—subculture, musical pathways, the music scene—she forwards her own expanded scheme of thinking about community based on her work of Ethiopian society and music, of musical communities formed from social and musical processes that she labels as descent, dissent, and affinity. See Kay Shelemay, "Musical Communities: Rethinking the Collective in Music," *Journal of the American Musicological Society* 64, no. 2 (Summer 2011): 349–90.

27. Shelemay, "Musical Communities," 349.

28. Shelemay, "Musical Communities," 364–65.

29. A special thanks to Prof. Adelaide Reyes, who graciously agreed to read this chapter and provide invaluable comments. She directed me toward a more in-depth analysis of the "musical-communities" model by posing questions shaped by the local circumstances and conditions of the camps.

30. Schelemay, "Musical Communities," 376.

31. Schelemay, "Musical Communities," 367–68.

32. Shirley Muramoto Wong, *Hidden Legacy: Tribute to Teachers of Japanese Traditional Arts in the War Relocation Authority Camps*, program booklet, concert at Koyasan Buddhist Temple, Resource Development and Publications, Asian American Studies Center, University of California, Japanese American Cultural and Community Center, Los Angeles, CA, 2010, 10–11; Kayoko Wakita, interview by author, July 30, 1996.

33. Edward Spicer et al., *Impounded People: Japanese-Americans in the Relocation Centers* (Tucson: University of Arizona Press, 1969), 219.

34. Minako Waseda, "Extraordinary Circumstances, Exceptional Practices: Music in Japanese American Concentration Camps," *Journal of Asian American Studies* 8, no. 2 (June 2005): 182–83.

35. Shirley Muramoto Wong joined by Lane Ryo Hirabayashi (chair, Asian American Studies Department, University of California, Los Angeles), Japanese American Cultural and

Community Center, and Koyasan Buddhist Temple, Los Angeles, presented Hidden Legacy, an event that honored seven elderly Nisei teachers and performers who taught Japanese traditional arts in the various detention camps. Hidden Legacy took place on April 24, 2010, at the Koyasan Buddhist Temple in Little Tokyo, Los Angeles, and it included a recital of Japanese music and dance performed by the honorees and a panel discussion about artists in the camps. In 2014, Muramoto Wong successfully produced and distributed a film of the Nisei teachers and performers featured in the 2010 concert. It is available on DVD. See Shirley Kazuyo Muramoto Wong, director, *Hidden Legacy: Japanese Traditional Performing Arts in the World War II Internment Camps* (Oakland, CA: Murasaki Productions, 2014), DVD. The film is available at "Hidden Legacy: Japanese Traditional Performing Arts in the World War II Internment Camps (DVD)," Japanese American National Museum, accessed June 20, 2023, https://janmstore.com/search?type=product&q=%22Hidden+Legacy%22. Also see the review I was invited to write of the film: Susan Asai, review of *Hidden Legacy: Japanese Traditional Performing Arts in the World War II Internment Camps*, directed by Shirley Kazuyo Muramoto Wong, *International Journal of Asian Studies* 14, no. 1 (January 2017).

36. *Manzanar Free Press*, "Japanese Music Policy Explained," September 19, 1942, 1.
37. Waseda, "Japanese American Musical Culture," 140.
38. Renato Rosaldo, "Cultural Citizenship and Educational Democracy," *Cultural Anthropology* 9, no. 3 (1994): 402.
39. Shirley Nagatomi Okabe, interview by Alisa Lynch, January 30, 2013, Manzanar National Historic Site Collection, Densho Digital Repository, accessed May 14, 2023, https://ddr.densho.org.
40. Muramoto Wong, *Hidden Legacy*, 12.
41. Jyorokusho, interview.
42. Muramoto Wong, *Hidden Legacy*, 13.
43. The photos are not accessible at the moment but will hopefully become part of the collection at the Asian American Studies Center at the University of California, Los Angeles.
44. Asai, review of *Hidden Legacy*, 2.
45. *Gila News Courier*, "Butte Festival Program," November 25, 1942, 4.
46. Quoted in Waseda, "Japanese American Musical Culture," 188.
47. Jiro Nakano and Kay Nakano, eds. and trans., *Poets behind Barbed Wire*, illustrated by George Hoshida (Honolulu: Bamboo Ridge Press, 1984), 59.
48. Kurashige, *Japanese American*, 88.
49. University of Denver, "Loyalty Questions," Behind Barbed Wire: The Story of the Japanese-American Internment during World War II, accessed June 22, 2023, https://www.du.edu/behindbarbedwire/loyalty_questions.html.
50. Michi Weglyn, *Years of Infamy: The Untold Story of America's Concentration Camps* (New York: Morrow Quill Paperbacks, 1976), 145. This was particularly true of Issei in camps located closer to California, where they were exposed to a constant bombardment of "racially slanted" news and reports.
51. Spicer et al., *Impounded People*, 156.
52. Weglyn, *Years of Infamy*, 233.
53. George Yoshida, interview by author, August 2, 2012.
54. *Newell (CA) Star*, "Center-wide Program to Be at Auditorium," March 16, 1944, 3.
55. *Poston Chronicle*, "Symphony Set for Music Lovers," July 14, 1943, n.p.
56. Yo Shibuya, interview by Richard Potashin, June 2, 2010, Manzanar Historical Site Collection, Densho Digital Repository, accessed May 14, 2023, https://ddr.densho.org.
57. Mary Kageyama Nomura, interview by Tom Ikeda, July 9, 2009, Manzanar National Historic Site Collection, Densho Digital Repository, accessed May 14, 2023, https://ddr.densho.org.
58. Nomura, interview.

59. Bruce T. Kaji and Sharon Yamato, *Jive Bomber: A Sentimental Journey* (Gardena, CA: Kaji and Associates, 2010), 41.

60. Kaji and Yamato, *Jive Bomber*, 41, 42.

61. Alecia D. Barbour, "'For the Good of Our Country': Ruth Watanabe and the 'Good that Is in Music' at the Santa Anita Detention Center," *Notes* 74, no. 2 (December 2017): 228.

62. Barbour, "'For the Good of Our Country,'" 225.

63. Mamie Noda, interview by author, March 22, 2002.

64. *Tulean Dispatch*, June 14, 1943, based in the Tule Lake detention camp. Quoted in Yoshida, *Reminiscing in Swingtime*, 122.

65. Joel Millman, "From Barbed Wire to Boogie-Woogie," *Wall Street Journal*, March 25, 2010, https://www.wsj.com/video/from-barbed-wire-to-boogie-woogie/18EA555C-7CB0-4B05-B331-F4912904AFD9.html.

66. Amy Uyeki, director, *Searchlight Serenade: Big Bands in the WWII Japanese American Incarceration Camps* (Eureka, CA: KEET-TV, 2012), DVD.

67. Uyeki, *Searchlight Serenade*.

68. Uyeki, *Searchlight Serenade*.

69. Uyeki, *Searchlight Serenade*.

70. Yoneichi Fukui, interview by author, August 16, 1994.

71. Uyeki, *Searchlight Serenade*.

72. Uyeki, *Searchlight Serenade*.

73. Uyeki, *Searchlight Serenade*.

74. Uyeki, *Searchlight Serenade*.

75. Uyeki, *Searchlight Serenade*.

76. George Yoshida, interview by author, July 25, 1996. "Jap," freely used by individuals, public officials, and print media throughout WWII, embodies the vitriolic hate and animosity Americans expressed toward Japanese Americans during the war. The word is viscerally used by Yoshida to describe the anguish and bitterness of an American citizen whose civil rights were violated. Use of the word "Jap" in this context importantly conveys the injustice experienced by Japanese Americans.

77. Howard Reich, "'It Took Our Minds off the Bad Things': Japanese Concentration Survivors Remember the Swing Music that Helped Them Endure," *Chicago Tribune*, October 10, 2001, 11.

78. Koichi Art Hayashi, *Minidoka Stories* (Washington, DC: National Park Service, 2003).

79. Yoshida, interview, August 2, 2012.

80. Yoshida, interview.

81. Kaji and Yamato, *Jive Bomber*, 41.

82. *Oakland (CA) Tribune*, "From Stark World War II Internment Camps—Music," February 17, 1998, 6.

83. Reich, "'It Took Our Minds,'" 11.

84. Millman, "From Barbed Wire."

85. Japan America Theatre, Music to Remember, 1.

86. Cole Porter, "Don't Fence Me In," In *Hollywood Canteen*, directed by Delmer Daves. Burbank, CA: Warner Bros., 1944. Film. Lyrics by Robert Fletcher. Alfred Music, 1202554, [1934] 1944, audio. Used with permission, January 4, 2023.

87. Charles Kikuchi, *The Kikuchi Diary: Chronicle from an American Concentration Camp; The Tanforan Journals of Charles Kikuchi*, ed. John Modell (Urbana: University of Illinois Press, 1993), 187.

88. Marta Robertson, "Ballad for Incarcerated Americans: Second Generation Japanese American Musicking in World War II Camps," *Journal of the Society for American Music* 11, no. 3 (2017): 300. Both composers were members of the Popular Front in the US.

89. Robertson, "Ballad for Incarcerated Americans."

90. Robertson discusses the multiple meanings that, over time, became associated with the cantata. In the expressive performance of "Ballad for Americans" by singer-activist Paul Robeson in the 1940 Victor recording, the cantata became emblematic of the Double V struggle for African American civil rights. Robertson suggests that Japanese Americans, in their exposure to Blackness, may have noted an equivalence of their unlawful imprisonment to that of African American slavery and civil rights issues. A third, anomalous meaning appended to "Ballad for Americans" was the Euro-American cultural mainstream's appropriation of it as a patriotic anthem used to build support for the US as it became more embroiled in World War II. Robertson, "Ballad for Incarcerated Americans," 303.

91. George Nakata, interview by Masako Hinatsu, August 23, 2004, Oregon Nikkei Endowment Collection, Densho Digital Repository, accessed May 14, 2023, https://ddr.densho.org.

92. Takahashi, *Nisei/Sansei*, 86.

93. Kikuchi, *The Kikuchi Diary*, 204. Kikuchi was twenty-six years old and a graduate student in social welfare at the University of California at the time he was incarcerated with his family. He was one of the founding editors of the Tanforan Assembly Center's newspaper, the *Tanforan Totalizer*. Recruited by Berkeley sociologist Dorothy Swaine Thomas for the Japanese Evacuation and Relocation Study (JERS), Kikuchi began to keep a diary and completed field surveys at the Tanforan Assembly Center in northern California and at the Gila River Relocation Center in Arizona where he was incarcerated. In 1943, he chronicled Nisei who left the camps and settled in Chicago. Just before the bombing of Hiroshima, he was drafted into the US Army. Kikuchi's diaries include correspondence and related printed material about Japanese Americans and their relocation during World War II.

94. Kurashige, *Japanese American*, 7–8.

95. The Immigration Act of 1924 denied these Issei men the right to bring wives from Japan. Not having a wife made it difficult to financially become successful as an independent farmer or storeowner. In not having children, they did not have much contact with mainstream society and, as a result, were not well integrated.

96. James M. Sakoda, "Reminiscences of a Participant Observer," in *Views from Within: The Japanese American Evacuation and Resettlement Study*, ed. Yuji Ichioka (Los Angeles: Resource Development and Publications, Asian American Center, University of California, 1989), 249.

97. This was an unfair qualification considering that the Issei were racially barred from obtaining citizenship. Some Issei were quite nationalistic both politically and culturally, but these inclinations were in part due to being denied citizen status in the first place!

98. Takahashi, *Nisei/Sansei*, 108.

99. Spicer et al., *Impounded People*, 100–101.

100. Block Councils served generally to decide on questions of space usage of the block area, for example, for food growing or for children's recreation, or in what proportion it should be allocated for the various uses proposed by internees.

101. Sakoda, *Reminiscences of a Participant Observer*, 253.

102. Art Sakamoto, "Art, Culture, and Identity," lecture at the Japanese American National Museum, Los Angeles, CA, July 28, 2010. Sakamoto references Japanese *aikido* in explaining how Japanese defeat opponents (oppressors) in a maneuver in which the opponent's force is redirected and employed against them rather than meeting an attack head-on. In this way, the JACL, by cooperating with the US government, hoped to redirect the hate and discrimination directed at Japanese Americans and eventually gain entrée into American society. Other examples that I think illustrate "shaming the enemy" is the dedication of the 442nd Infantry Regimental Combat Team of the US Army, composed almost entirely of Japanese American soldiers. The 442nd combat team received the most medals of a unit of its size in the history

of the US military. See "442nd Regimental Combat Team," Go for Broke: National Education Center, accessed June 4, 2012, https://goforbroke.org/history/unit-history/442nd-regimental-combat-team/.

103. Takahashi, *Nisei/Sansei*, 85–86.

104. Spencer et al., *Impounded People*, 165.

105. Sakoda, *Reminiscences of a Participant Observer*, 222.

106. The Japanese American Evacuation and Resettlement Study (JERS) was a special wartime research project, which studied the mass concentration of Japanese Americans. JERS researchers included three separate groups of social scientists and anthropologists. One group was officially employed by the WRA, the federal agency, which administered the camps. The Bureau of Sociological Research was specifically created to hire a second group of social scientists whose responsibility was to conduct research at Poston, Arizona, under the sponsorship of the Office of Indian Affairs. Dorothy Swaine Thomas, a scholar from the University of California at Berkeley specializing in social demography, directed a third research team. Three post-war publications based on JERS findings point to the importance of this project in establishing the initial academic framework of studies of the wartime incarceration of Japanese Americans. The first book, published in 1946, was *The Spoilage* written by Thomas and Richard S. Nishimoto about internees who were classified as disloyal and were segregated at Tule Lake. Published in 1952, a second volume, *The Salvage*, written by Thomas, concerns the Japanese Americans who were allowed to leave the camps and resettle predominantly in the Midwest for work. *Prejudice, War, and the Constitution*, published in 1954 and written by Jacobus TenBroek et al., provides the historical backdrop of the racial hostility endured by Asians in the western region of the United States, factors that gave rise to the concentration camps and the constitutional issues surrounding the internal migration. See Yuji Ichioka, "JERS Revisited: Introduction," in *Views from Within: The Japanese Evacuation and Resettlement Study*, ed. Yuji Ichioka (Los Angeles: Resource Development and Publications, Asian American Studies Center, University of California, 1989), 3–4.

107. University presidents in California initially urged Governor Culbert Olson of California to undertake the needs of Nisei college students who had been incarcerated. Upon writing to President Roosevelt for assistance, it was Mrs. Eleanor Roosevelt who took an interest and is credited with playing a crucial role in the formation of the National Japanese American Student Relocation Council (NJASRC) in the spring of 1942. Mrs. Roosevelt conferred with Clarence Pickett, a close Quaker friend, who suggested to John McCoy, assistant secretary of war, and to Milton Eisenhower, the first national director of the WRA, that interned college students in camps be relocated. McCoy solicited the Quakers to assume the leadership of NJASRC. The council successfully enrolled 3,613 Nisei in 680 colleges and universities across the United States over a four-year period. All the necessary clearances, securing of scholarship funds, and college-entrance paperwork were completed by the council. This is an unheralded effort on the part of volunteers to continue the education of Nisei during World War II. NJASRC continues to receive donations and award student scholarships. See Nisei Student Relocation Commemorative Fund, "Our Origins: The National Japanese American Student Relocation Council (NJASRC)," accessed May 10, 2023, http://www.nsrcfund.org/our-history-our-stories/our-origins.

108. Following the bombing of Pearl Harbor, the army discharged Nisei, and local boards deferred others. Suspicion was cast on Nisei because of their race and the supposed potential for sabotage or spying. My father experienced this firsthand when he was discharged from the US Army after serving as a second lieutenant in the Artillery Division. Being willing to risk his life for the United States and then be rejected left him bitter and disappointed.

109. Spicer et al., *Impounded People*, 122.

110. Spicer et al., *Impounded People*, 121.
111. Spicer et al., *Impounded People*, 198.
112. Kurashige, *Japanese American*, 79.
113. Kurashige, *Japanese American*, 79.
114. Takahashi, *Nisei/Sansei*, 105.
115. Takahashi, *Nisei/Sansei*, 106–7.
116. Diane Fujino, "Race, Place, Space, and Political Development: Japanese-American Radicalism in the 'Pre-Movement' 1960s," *Social Justice* 35, no. 2 (2008): 61–62.
117. Quoted in Fujino, "Race, Place, Space," 62.

CHAPTER 5: SANSEI: THE POLITICAL ADVOCACY OF MUSIC AND A TURN TOWARD THE EAST

1. Excerpt of a poem by Quincy Troupe, quoted in Heidi R. Moore, "The Aesthetics of Place and the Comedy of Discomfort: Six Humorists" (PhD diss., Union Institute and University, 2007), 144.
2. This is a body of work recognized as a legitimate musical style within the national and international jazz press in the 1990s, resulting from successive Asian American jazz festivals, the ongoing activity of Asian Improv aRts, and musician-composers' achievements and careers. See Michael Dessen, "Asian Americans and Creative Music Legacies," *Critical Studies in Improvisation* 1, no. 3 (2006): 11, criticalimprov.com/index.php/csieci/article/view/56/89.
3. I define "Japanese/Asian American music" as that which reflects and expresses the experiences of Asians in America and the concomitant sensibilities, emotions, and nuances of being that it entails.
4. Mat Callahan, *The Explosion of Deferred Dreams: Musical Renaissance and Social Revolution in San Francisco, 1965–1975* (Oakland, CA: PM Press, 2017), 10.
5. Kondo, *About Face*, 4.
6. Quoted in Dessen, "Asian Americans," 1.
7. Dessen, "Asian Americans," 1.
8. Dessen, "Asian Americans," 2.
9. Maeda, *Chains of Babylon*, 77.
10. Maeda, *Chains of Babylon*, 75.
11. William Wei, *The Asian American Movement* (Philadelphia, PA: Temple University Press, 1993), 45–47.
12. A majority of Sansei in other parts of the United States did not directly participate in the vision and Progressive politics of the group responsible for the social and political transformation described in this chapter, but the reverberation of the changes that took place ultimately reached Sansei in a ripple effect as the struggle to gain full acceptance as Americans continues.
13. Fujino, "Race, Place, Space."
14. Fujino, "Race, Place, Space," 2.
15. Fujino, "Race, Place, Space," 13.
16. Fujino, "Race, Place, Space," 11.
17. Fusco, "Passionate Irreverence," 70.
18. Fusco, "Passionate Irreverence," 72.
19. Fusco, "Passionate Irreverence," 71.
20. Dessen, "Asian Americans," 5.
21. Dessen, "Asian Americans," 4.
22. Joanne Nobuko Miyamoto, Chris Iijima, and Charlie Chin, "We Are the Children," lyrics by Chris Iijima and Nobuko Miyamoto, on *A Grain of Sand*, Paredon Records, PARE 1020, [1973] 1992, CD.

23. Wei, *The Asian American Movement*, 20.
24. Maeda, *Chains of Babylon*, 75.
25. Maeda, *Chains of Babylon*, 2.
26. Takahashi, *Nisei/Sansei*, 9.
27. Maeda, *Chains of Babylon*, 10.
28. Maeda, *Chains of Babylon*, 11.
29. "Racial triangulation" as a concept must be analyzed and modified for it does not account for the intercultural exchanges between Asian Americans and Latinx artists. Folk musicians and *taiko* drummers, discussed later, demonstrate strong musical ties to Latinx communities.
30. Maeda, *Chains of Babylon*, 90.
31. Lucia Enriquez, "Ghost Like Us: The Gift of Then Pioneer Asian American Artists," in *They Painted from Their Hearts: Pioneer Asian American Artists*, ed. Mayumi Tsutakawa (Seattle: Wing Luke Museum, 1994), 62. This work was for Wing Luke Asian Museum and the Asian American Artists Directory, compiled by Alan Lau and Kazuko Nakane for the Archives of American Art and the Smithsonian Institution. The catalog was published in conjunction with an exhibition organized by the Wing Luke Museum, September 9, 1994, through January 15, 1995.
32. Emmett Price III, "Free Jazz and the Black Arts Movement, 1958–1967" (PhD diss., University of Pittsburgh, 2000), 45.
33. Fred Ho, "Fred Ho's Tribute to the Black Arts Movement: Personal and Political Impact and Analysis," unpublished manuscript, 2004, 14. Fred Ho, deceased in April 2014, was a saxophonist, composer, bandleader, activist/agitator, intellectual, writer, producer, and visionary who lived his life with great political purpose and determination. To learn about this revolutionary artist, I recommend reading two edited volumes: Diane Fujino, ed., *Wicked Theory, Naked Practice: A Fred Ho Reader* (Minneapolis: University of Minnesota Press, 2009); and Roger N. Buckley, ed., *Yellow Power, Yellow Soul: The Radical Art of Fred Ho* (Urbana: University of Illinois Press, 2013).
34. Ho, "Fred Ho's Tribute," 24.
35. "Oriental" is a Eurocentric, outdated term used to categorize people of Asian descent, and it carries a pejorative designation of being exotic or "Other."
36. It is ironic that the Japanese Canadian president of San Francisco State University S. I. Hayakawa bitterly opposed and disrupted the Third World Liberation Front strikers. Hayakawa ultimately relented and established the first university ethnic studies college in the country.
37. Karen Umemoto, "'On Strike!' San Francisco State College Strike, 1968–69," *Amerasia Journal* 15, no. 1 (1989): 19, 22.
38. Fred Ho, "Beyond Asian American Jazz: My Musical and Political Changes in the Asian American Movement," in *Wicked Theory, Naked Practice: A Fred Ho Reader*, ed. Diane C. Fujino (Minneapolis: University of Minnesota Press, 2009), 48.
39. Vijay Iyer, "Monk's Japanese Folk Song: Performative Strategies on Asian American Jazz," lecture at the Society for Ethnomusicology National Meeting, Toronto, Canada, November 3, 2000.
40. Quoted in Lisa Chen, "Disorienting Gender: Representations of Asian American Women," in *Persistence of Vision: Perspective, Process and Possibilities*, eds. Francis Wong et al. (San Francisco, CA: Asian Improv aRts, 1994), 28.
41. Fred Ho, "An Asian American Tribute to the Black Arts Movement," in *Wicked Theory, Naked Practice: A Fred Ho Reader*, ed. Diane C. Fujino (Minneapolis: University of Minnesota Press, 2009), 180.
42. Paul Yamazaki, interview by author, July 30, 2003.
43. Yamazaki, interview.
44. Dessen, "Asian Americans," 3.

45. Dessen, "Asian Americans," 5.

46. Francis Wong, "Asian Improv Records," *East Wind Magazine* 7, no. 1 (Spring–Summer 1989): 55.

47. This is a take on Malcolm X's maxim "The Ballot or the Bullet."

48. F. Wong, "Asian Improv Records," 56.

49. Other designations of this subgenre—improvised music, avant-garde jazz, modal jazz, or just Black music—circulate among musicians.

50. Joachim Berendt, *The Jazz Book: From New Orleans to Rock and Free Jazz*, trans. Dan Morgenstern, Helmut Bredigkeit, and Barbara Bredigkeit (New York: Lawrence Hill & Company, [1953] 1975), 24.

51. Samuel Floyd, *The Power of Black Music: Interpreting Its History from Africa to the United States* (New York: Oxford University Press, 1995), 186–89.

52. Ho, "Fred Ho's Tribute," 25.

53. Ho, "Fred Ho's Tribute," 25.

54. A basic definition describes harmolodics as a performance practice in which rhythm, melody, and harmony receive equal treatment in a musical composition.

55. Ian Carr, Digby Fairweather, and Brian Priestley, *Jazz: The Essential Companion* (New York: Prentice Hall Press, 1987), 174.

56. Anthony Brown, interview by author, July 22, 2003.

57. Brian Auerbach, "Asian American Jazz: An Oral History with Paul Yamazaki," *Options* 3–4 (March–April 1985): 37.

58. Francis Wong, interview by author, July 29, 2003.

59. Yamazaki, interview.

60. Miya Masaoka, interview by author, July 30, 2003.

61. Hafez Modirzadeh, interview by author, July 28, 2003.

62. Hafez Modirzadeh, *In Chromodal Discourse*, liner notes, Asian Improv Records, AIR 0012, 1993, CD.

63. Modirzadeh, interview.

64. Modirzadeh, interview.

65. F. Wong, interview.

66. San Francisco's urban-renewal efforts to demolish the International Hotel and transform sections of Japantown became part of student struggles to support their communities. In the fight to save the Japanese community, groups such as the J-Town Art and Media generated cultural and artistic activities in their efforts to sustain the neighborhood in the face of urban renewal.

67. Suenobu Togi taught *gagaku* in the Ethnomusicology Program at UCLA from 1961 to 1993. In 1976, Rev. Mas Kodani made arrangements for Mr. Togi to teach *gagaku* at the Institute of Buddhist Studies in Berkeley. In Los Angeles, the Tenrikyo Church (Shinto sect) also engaged Togi Sensei in forming a *gagaku* ensemble for their services.

68. Auerbach, "Asian American Jazz," 38.

69. Richard Oyama, "Profile: Gerald Oshita," *East Wind Magazine* 2, no. 1 (Spring–Summer 1983): 71.

70. Auerbach, "Asian American Jazz," 71.

71. Oyama, "Profile," 71.

72. Oyama, "Profile," 71.

73. Oyama, "Profile," 71.

74. BAG musicians included saxophonists Julius Hemphill, Oliver Lake, J. D. Parran, Hamiet Bluiett, and Luther Thomas. Other instrumentalists who were members included trumpeters

Baikida Carroll and Floyd LeFlore, trombonists Joseph Bowie, Bensid Thigpen, and Charles "Bobo" Shaw, bassists Bobby Reed and Arzinia Richardson, and others.

75. Yamazaki, interview.

76. Oyama, "Profile," 72.

77. Russel Baba, interview by author, August 1, 2003.

78. Auerbach, "Asian American Jazz," 23.

79. Baba, interview.

80. Baba, interview.

81. Baba, interview.

82. Baba, interview.

83. Yamazaki, interview.

84. Baba, interview.

85. In the 1940s and 1950s, there were more than two dozen nightclubs in the "the Harlem of the West," where Ella Fitzgerald, Billie Holiday, Duke Ellington, and Louis Armstrong performed.

86. Quincy Troupe quoted in Moore, "The Aesthetics of Place," 144.

87. Scott Yanow, "Enthusiasm," *Jazziz* 11, no. 2 (February–March 1994): 28–34.

88. Anthony Brown, "Asian American Jazz," lecture at the Asian American Center, Northeastern University, Boston, MA, September 16, 2010.

89. *ImprovisAsians!*, "A Conversation with Mark Izu," 4, no. 1 (February 1995): 4.

90. A Japanese court dancer, musician, and teacher, Suenobu Togi resigned as a member of Japan's Imperial Household in 1961 before resettling in Los Angeles. He joined the ethnomusicology faculty at the University of California, Los Angeles in 1968. Togi had also studied European classical music, at the Tokyo University of Fine Arts, specializing on cello.

91. Mark Izu, *Circle of Fire*, liner notes by Dan Ouellette, Asian Improv Records, AIR 0009, 1992, CD.

92. Izu, *Circle of Fire*.

93. Mark Izu, "Threading Time," liner notes, 2000, demo CD.

94. Calvin Ahlgren, "Izu: 'Circle' Ready to Get Off Square One," *San Francisco (CA) Chronicle*, February 23, 1992, n.p.

95. Mark Izu, interview by author, April 30, 2005.

96. The Ghost Festival, also known as the Hungry Ghost Festival, Zhongyuan, and Yulanpen, is a traditional Buddhist and Daoist festival practiced in Asian countries. It is an occasion when deceased ancestors are believed to visit the living.

97. Mark Izu, *Last Dance*, liner notes, Bindu Records, BIN 0205-2, 1998, CD.

98. "Thousand cranes" refers to the children's historical novel written by Canadian American author Eleanor Coerr, published in 1977. *Sadako and the Thousand Paper Cranes* details the story of a young girl exposed to atomic-bomb radiation in Hiroshima during World War II. Inspired by the Japanese legend about creating a thousand origami cranes to be granted a wish, Sadako set out to fold the required number. Sadly, she only folds 644 cranes before succumbing; family members and friends complete the task. The cranes are buried with Sadako.

99. Mark Izu, interview by author, July 18, 1996.

100. Karuk (also Karok) means "upstream people." The Karuk are one of the largest Indigenous populations of California, residing mostly in northern California into southern Oregon. The mission of the Karuk tribal council is to establish equality and justice for the tribe, restore and preserve tribal traditions, customs, language, and ancestral rights, and to secure the inherent rights of self-governance for the Karuk people and their descendants. Karuk Tribe, accessed May 11, 2023, www.karuk.us.

101. First Voice, "About First Voice," accessed May 11, 2023, http://www.firstvoice.org/about-first-voice.

102. Brown, interview, July 22, 2003.

103. Anthony Brown, *Family*, liner notes, Asian Improv Records, AIR 0027, 1997, CD.

104. Brown, *Family*.

105. Brown, *Family*.

106. The film also detailed political factions that lobbied to have Japanese Americans removed from their verdant Central Valley farmlands in California in an effort to eliminate economic competition for white farmers.

107. Fifth Stream Music, "Mission," accessed May 12, 2023, http://www.fifthstreammusic.org/mission.

108. Ron Jacobs, "Day of Remembrance and the Music of Anthony Brown," CounterPunch, February 19, 2019, https://www.counterpunch.org/2019/02/19/day-of-remembrance-and-the-music-of-anthony-brown/.

109. Anthony Brown, interview by author, August 17, 1998.

110. Brown, interview.

111. *Tozai Times*, "Glenn Horiuchi: Sansei Musician Takes the Next Step," 4, no. 45 (July 1988): 108.

112. Glenn Horiuchi, interview by author, August 28, 1994.

113. Glenn Horiuchi, "Glenn Horiuchi, Pianist and Composer," artist statement, n.d.

114. Jon Jang, *Next Step*, liner notes, Asian Improv Records, AIR-0002, 1988, CD.

115. *ImprovisAsians!*, "What's That Sound?," 3, no. 1 (February 1994): 6.

116. Dean Takehara, "Jazz Pianist Combines Music with Politics," *Los Angeles Pacific Citizen*, March 1, 1988, 1.

117. Takehara, "Jazz Pianist," 4.

118. Loren Kajikawa, "The Sound of Struggle: Black Revolutionary Nationalism and Asian American Jazz," in *Jazz/Not Jazz: The Music and Its Boundaries*, eds. David Garrett Ake, Charles Hiroshi, and Daniel Goldmark (Berkeley: University of California Press, 2012), 202.

119. Kevin Whitehead and Glenn Horiuchi, *Oxnard Beet*, liner notes, Soul Note, 121228, 1992, CD.

120. *Hirajoshi* is a Japanese koto tuning borrowed from shamisen music (e.g., C-D-Eb-G-Ab-C).

121. Whitehead and Horiuchi, *Oxnard Beet*.

122. The Civil Liberties Act of 1988 is a US federal law requiring reparations be granted to Japanese Americans who were unjustly incarcerated by the US government during World War II. California's Democratic Congressman Norman Mineta, an inmate as a child, and Wyoming's Republican Senator Alan K. Simpson, who had met Mineta while visiting an incarceration camp, jointly sponsored the legislation.

123. Takehara, "Jazz Pianist," 1.

124. *Tozai Times*, "Glenn Horiuchi," 108.

125. Kajikawa, "The Sound of Struggle," 206.

126. The *nagauta* shamisen is a three-stringed plucked lute used to perform lyrical songs that accompany dance in Kabuki theater.

127. A *dongo taiko* rhythm is one of three underlying *taiko* rhythms that form a rhythmic foundation for all rhythms played within an ensemble. It is described as two alternating beats: a strong first beat followed by a second weaker beat played with a sense of swing.

128. Jon Jang, "88 Keys to Revolution," *East Wind Magazine* 4, no. 1 (Winter–Spring 1985): 34–35.

129. *International Examiner*, "Glenn Horiuchi, Francis Wong, and Lillian Nakano—Nov. 3 at the Seattle Asian Art Museum," October 18, 1994, 11.

130. Brian Phillips, "Glenn Horiuchi: Atonal Energy Music," Perfect Sound Forever, May 2001, https://www.furious.com/perfect/glennhoriuchi.html.

131. Japan America Theatre, A Celebration of the Music and Artistry of Glenn Horiuchi & Friends, program booklet, concert at Japan America Theatre, Los Angeles, CA, January 22, 2000.

132. Jonathan Widran, "Hiroshima Web Bio," Hiroshima, accessed June 9, 2023, https://www.hiroshimamusic.com/bios.html.

133. Henry Ong, "Dan Kuramoto: The Leader of a Band Named Hiroshima Aims to Discover His Asianness," *AsiAm* (July 1987): 30.

134. USAsians.net, "Hiroshima: Historic Asian American Band!," accessed June 11, 2023, http://us_asians.tripod.com/features-hiroshima.html.

135. Quoted in Laura Pulido, *Black, Brown, Yellow, and Left: Radical Activism in Los Angeles* (Berkeley: University of California Press, 2006), 108.

136. Mo Nishida, "Where Do We Go From Here?," *Gidra* (April 1974): 21–22.

137. Nishida, "Where Do We Go From Here?"

138. George Abe, interview by author, July 13, 1996.

139. Abe, interview.

140. Abe, interview.

141. Alan Furutani and Marsha Furutani, interview by author, July 10, 1996.

142. Furutani and Furutani, interview.

143. For a detailed study of these three artists whose songs and activism inspired many Asian American youth, see chapter 5 of Maeda, *Chains of Babylon*.

144. Joanne Miyamoto, Chris Iijima, and Charlie Chin, *A Grain of Sand*, liner notes, Paredon Records, PARE 1020, [1973] 1992, CD.

145. AAA was a political organization in New York City formed in 1969 by Kazu Iijima and Minn Matsuda, two Nisei who had been politically active since the 1930s. The Black Power movement was the inspiration for the formation of AAA. Both women wanted their children to be politically aware and know something about their Japanese heritage.

146. Miyamoto, Iijima, and Chin, *A Grain of Sand*.

147. Miyamoto, Iijima, and Chin, *A Grain of Sand*.

148. Miyamoto, Iijima, and Chin, *A Grain of Sand*.

149. Nobuko Miyamoto, interview by author, July 25, 1995.

150. Maeda, *Chains of Babylon*, 141.

151. In the 1970s, many countries in Latin America were experiencing great political and social upheavals in which folk and traditional music served as a form of resistance against capitalist domination, social inequalities, and dictatorial governments. The sung resistance gave rise to the Nueva Canción movement, which continues to symbolize the current struggles of many people in this part of the world.

152. Amy Ling, *Yellow Light: The Flowering of Asian American Arts* (Philadelphia, PA: Temple University Press, 1999), 320.

153. Ling, *Yellow Light*, 320.

154. Yokohama, California, *Yokohama, California*, liner notes, Peter Horikoshi-YokohamaCa.com, 2016, CD.

155. Other *taiko* sources provide background, trends, and updated information within the tradition. See Mark Tusler, "Taiko Drumming in California: Issues of Articulation and the Construction of Ethnic Identity," lecture at the meeting of Society for Ethnomusicology Southern California Chapter, University of California, Riverside, CA, February 23–24, 1999; Paul Jong-Chul Yoon, "'She's Really Become Japanese Now!': Taiko Drumming and Asian American Identification," *American Music* 19, no. 4 (Winter 2001): 417–38; D. Wong, *Speak It Louder*, 195–231; Deborah Wong, *Louder and Faster: Pain, Joy, and the Body Politic in Asian American Taiko* (Oakland: University of California Press, 2020); Masami Izumi, "Big Drum: Taiko in the United States DVD," *Journal of American History* 93, no. 1 (June 2006): 158–61; Shawn Morgan Bender, *Taiko Boom: Japanese Drumming in Place and Motion* (Berkeley: University of California Press,

2012); Kimberly Anne Powell, "Composing Sound Identity in Taiko Drumming," *Anthropology and Education Quarterly* 43, no. 1 (2012): 101–19; Kimberly Anne Powell, "Drumming against the Quiet: The Sounds of Asian American Identity in an Amorphous Landscape," *Qualitative Inquiry* 14, no. 6 (September 2008): 901–25, https://doi.org/10.1177/1077800408318308; Heidi Varian, *The Way of Taiko* (Berkeley, CA: Stone Bridge Press); Ahlgren, "Izu." There are many more updated publications too long to list here.

156. My documentation of *taiko* performance in *hōraku* (a Buddhist ceremony) resulted in an article. See Susan Asai, "Hōraku: Buddhist Performing Arts and the Development of Taiko Drumming in the United States," in *Selected Reports in Ethnomusicology*, eds. Nazir Jairazbhoy and Sue Carole DeVale (Los Angeles: University of California Press, 1985), 6:163–72.

157. Powell, "Composing Sound Identity," 102. This study is part of growing scholarship that regards "senses as cultural systems" in the field of sensory studies and anthropology of the senses. As a participant observer, Powell seeks to comprehend "seeing, feeling, and touching" involved in performance as well as listening in order to comprehend how people discern cultural and social values as expressed in musical performance. Powell applies Steven Feld's notion of "acoustemology" to *taiko* to address its sonic meaning in a broader world of sound that includes ambient and incidental sounds and noises and the bodily experience of *taiko* drumming itself. Powell, "Composing Sound Identity," 103.

158. Susan Hayase, "Taiko!" *East Wind Magazine* 4, no. 1 (Winter–Spring 1985): 47.

159. Kodani, interview.

160. Taiko Source, "The Sukeroku Style Moves Forward," accessed June 10, 2023, https://taikosource.com/tag/sukeroku-taiko/.

161. The National Endowment for the Arts recognized Seiichi Tanaka as a master artist, awarding him with an NEA National Heritage Fellowship in 2001.

162. The National Endowment for the Arts also recognized Roy and P. J. Hirabayashi, awarding them as NEA National Heritage Fellows in 2011.

163. Peter Stack, "Pounding a New Path/Local Taiko Master Brought Japanese Drumming to the US," *San Francisco (CA) Chronicle*, November 8, 2001, SFGATE, accessed June 10, 2023, https://www.sfgate.com/entertainment/article/Pounding-a-new-path-Local-taiko-master-brought-2859766.php.

164. Heidi Varian, *The Way of Taiko* (Berkeley, CA: Stone Bridge Press, 2005), 84–91.

165. Rev. Masao Kodani, *Hōraku* (Los Angeles, CA: Senshin Buddhist Church, 1979), 1.

166. Kodani, *Hōraku*, 1.

167. *Hōraku* has two meanings. The first is interpreted as religious joy experienced as a result of what Rev. Mas Kodani calls "awakening or awareness of oneself and of Amida Buddha." An individual may be moved to express this religious joy through ritual offering or through music, dance, and poetry. Such expression relates to a second meaning that is translated as "dharma entertainment," referring to music, songs, plays, and dances. Such entertainment emphasizes the Buddhist concept of sharing, and it is designed to direct the viewer as well as the performer toward an increased awareness of the dharma or Buddhist teachings and values. See Kodani, *Hōraku*, 1.

168. Kodani, interview.

169. Chris Komai, "Kinnara Taiko Celebrates 20th Anniversary," *Los Angeles Rafu Shimpo*, February 16, 1990, 1.

170. Powell, "Composing Sound Identity in Taiko," 106.

171. P. J. Hirabayashi, interview by author, July 22, 1996.

172. Hirabayashi, interview.

173. San Jose Taiko's connection with Kinnara Buddhist Taiko is strong. SJT initially began as a Buddhist *taiko* group assembled by Roy Hirabayashi. Also, most *taiko* groups, including

SJT, gained their start from Kinnara's innovations in drum making, making it possible to have a set of drums without the exorbitant expense of buying them from Japan.

174. Hirabayashi, interview.
175. Hirabayashi, interview.
176. Hirabayashi, interview.
177. Hirabayashi, interview.
178. Hirabayashi, interview.
179. Powell, "Drumming against the Quiet," 918.
180. Hirabayashi, interview.
181. Tusler, "Taiko Drumming in California."
182. D. Wong, *Speak It Louder*, 219.
183. Hirabayashi, interview.
184. Hirabayashi, interview.
185. Hirabayashi, interview.
186. The North American Taiko Conference (NATC) is a major *taiko* biennial event organized by the Taiko Community Alliance (TCA), founded in 1997 to support the growth of *taiko* in North America. In August 2017, the NATC convened at University of California, San Diego, to host *taiko* ensembles within the United States, Canada, and from abroad. Hands-on workshops, discussion sessions, jam sessions, *taiko* battles, and a final Taiko Ten: Celebration concert marked NATC's twentieth anniversary, featuring many *taiko* groups sharing the stage. In November 2020, the World Taiko Conference (WTC) in Tokyo live streamed a two-day event with a series of panel discussions about *taiko* as performance and *taiko* and community (Kaminari UK Taiko Drummers announced the 2020 WTC on their Facebook page and through Twitter accounts, with the hashtags #WTC and #WorldTaikoConference). A second diasporic *taiko* project is the Wake Up Drums organization that sponsored taiko gatherings at the Esplanade du Sacré-Coeur Paris in 2013, 2014, 2016, 2017, and 2018, creating a worldwide *taiko* chain and spreading its message of world unity. In 2013, thirteen groups from Argentina, Belgium, France, Germany, Italy, Japan, the Netherlands, Singapore, Spain, South Africa, and the United States participated by performing for one another from their homelands via satellite. Another important *taiko* enterprise is the documenting and archiving of information on *taiko* performers, ensembles, and activities uploaded to the Taiko Source online database. The database is the brainchild of Ben Pachter, an educator, ethnomusicologist, and musician and *taiko* performer, and Wendy Jedlicka, a packaging designer, sustainable-design and business educator, and enthusiastic *taiko* drummer. Taiko Source has compiled and uploaded a song database, written articles, collected *taiko* clipart, a map of *taiko* groups globally, interviews, and references, and includes a multimedia database. It is invaluable for researchers, performers, and aficionados. Such global interest is a true testament to how Japanese American *taiko*'s cultural and political dynamism have engendered a sense of unity to which people around the world have responded.
187. Kenny Endo, interview by author, July 30, 1996.
188. Endo, interview.
189. Mark Doyle, "The Beat Goes On: Kenny Endo's Blend of Ancient Taiko Drumming and Modern Jazz Has Given Him Fans around the World," *Mid Week* 12, no. 38 (1996): 4.
190. Doyle, "The Beat Goes On," 4.
191. Doyle, "The Beat Goes On," 1.
192. Endo, interview.
193. Michael Hatamiya, "Kenny Endo: Following the Beat of a Different Drum," *Mainichi Daily News*, November 21, 1988, 1.
194. Benjamin Epstein, "Tapping into Taiko Sources—to Dramatic Effect," *Los Angeles (CA) Times*, August 13, 1994, 203.

195. Eitetsu Hayashi's collaborations with the Berlin Philharmonic orchestra, traditional Korean drummers, Guinean *djembe* drummers, and avant-garde jazz artists cross-culturally expanded use of the *taiko*.

196. Yuri Kageyama, "Following the Drumbeat: Percussionist Pursues His Ancestral Heritage," *Japan Times Weekly*, June 21, 1986, 16.

197. Kageyama, "Following the Drumbeat," 16.

EPILOGUE: THE PROMISE OF INTERRACIAL MUSIC COALITIONS

1. Tamara Roberts, *Resounding Afro Asia: Interracial Music and the Politics of Collaboration* (New York: Oxford University Press, 2016), 176.

2. Fusco, "Passionate Irreverence," 70–71

3. Great Leap, FandangObon e-mail announcement to author, October 1, 2020. See Great Leap/Noboku Miyamoto, "Praise Songs and Presence: The Art of Qasidah and Hadrah," October 3, 2020, YouTube video, 1:25:15, https://www.youtube.com/watch?v=sODe1CIljQk.

4. Great Leap/Nobuko Miyamoto, "Praise Songs and Presence."

5. See Great Leap/Noboku Miyamoto, "Little Tokyo Virtual Earth Day (2020)," June 25, 2020, YouTube video, 1:22:50, https://www.youtube.com/watch?v=QsxoDTIlkfI&feature=youtube. This was sponsored by Great Leap, Japanese American Cultural & Community Center, and Sustainable Little Tokyo, Los Angeles.

6. See Great Leap/Noboku Miyamoto, "Great Leap's ECO-VIDS Sampler," March 2, 2015, YouTube video, 3:17, https://www.youtube.com/watch?v=hauqdkYT4Ag.

7. Great Leap, Inc., "Lectures, Seminars, Workshops, Performances," video, 8:23, accessed June 10, 2023, https://greatleap.org/community-engagement/.

8. Great Leap/Noboku Miyamoto, "Great Leap—FandangObon Short Documentary," February 6, 2014, YouTube video, 5:15, https://www.youtube.com/watch?v=bPwaYvXH_gw; and Great Leap/Noboku Miyamoto, "Great Leap | FandangObon Full Performance with Quetzal," January 23, 2014, YouTube video, 7:24, https://www.youtube.com/watch?v=ooNnphMIu6g.

9. Great Leap, Inc., "FandangObon—A Festival of Music, Dance, and Environmental Consciousness," video, 5:30, accessed June 10, 2023, https://greatleap.org/fandangobon/.

10. "Yuiyo" was a Bon odori song commissioned by the Senshin Buddhist Temple in Los Angeles in 1984 and danced by two thousand people from eighteen temples throughout southern California. A performance of it also appeared in a scene in the popular film *The Karate Kid Part II*. See Franklin Odo, *The Columbia Documentary History of the Asian American Experience* (New York: Columbia University Press, 2002), 432.

11. "Sembazuru" is a song geared toward children that narrates the story of the atomic-bomb-victim Sadako Sasaki, the protagonist in the popular children's book *Sadako and the Thousand Cranes*.

12. "Camp Bushi" is a song impelled by the resiliency of Japanese Americans wrongfully incarcerated in concentration camps.

13. Great Leap/Noboku Miyamoto, "Bambutsu for Tsuru for Solidarity," June 23, 2020, YouTube video, 5:45, https://www.youtube.com/watch?v=24FEYJYTknQ.

14. See Great Leap/Noboku Miyamoto, "FandangObon 2017," March 8, 2018, YouTube video, 4:37, https://www.youtube.com/watch?v=xJb7ET7yyOY.

15. Great Leap/Noboku Miyamoto, "FandangObon 2017."

16. Great Leap/Noboku Miyamoto, "FandangObon 2017."

17. Ray Fukumoto, "Senshin Obon 2014—Fandango Live!" July 6, 2014, YouTube video, 8:58, http://www.youtube.com/watch?v=p9xj4xGlju8.

18. Great Leap, "Mid-Year Update: Our Initiatives to Support Social Change," e-mail to author, July 13, 2020.

BIBLIOGRAPHY

Abe, George. Interview by author. July 13, 1996.
Adler, Jerry. "'Sweet Land of Liberties': If Everyone Has His Own Niche, What Do We Have in Common Anymore?" *Newsweek*, July 10, 1995. https://www.newsweek.com/sweet-land-liberties-184578. https://www.newsweek.com/sweet-land-liberties-184578.
Ahlgren, Calvin. "Izu: 'Circle' Ready to Get Off Square One." *San Francisco (CA) Chronicle*, February 23, 1992.
Akamatsu, Haruko. Interview by author. May 28, 2007.
Alba, Richard, Morris Levy, and Dowell Myers. "The Myth of a Majority-Minority America." *The Atlantic*, June 13, 2021. https://www.theatlantic.com/ideas/archive/2021/06/myth-majority-minority-america/619190/.
Asai, Hisayo. Interview by author. August 31, 2006.
Asai, Susan. "The Cultural Politics of *Issei* Identity and Music Making: 1893–1941." *Journal of the Society for American Music* 10, no. 3 (August 2016): 304–30. https://doi.org/10.1017/S1752196316000225.
Asai, Susan. "Hōraku: Buddhist Performing Arts and the Development of Taiko Drumming in the United States." In *Asian Music in North America*, edited by Nazir Jairazbhoy and Sue Carole DeVale, 163–72. Vol. 6 of *Selected Reports in Ethnomusicology*. Los Angeles: University of California Press, 1985.
Asai, Susan. Review of *Hidden Legacy: Japanese Traditional Performing Arts in the World War II Internment Camps*, directed by Shirley Kazuyo Muramoto Wong. *International Journal of Asian Studies* 14, no. 1 (January 2017): 107–9.
Asai, Susan. "Transformations of Tradition: Three Generations of Japanese American Music Making." *Musical Quarterly* 79, no. 3 (Fall 1995): 429–53.
Asian Improv. "Remember Glenn." November 29, 2000. https://www.asianimprov.com/glenns tribute.htm.
Auerbach, Brian. "Asian American Jazz: An Oral History with Paul Yamazaki." *Options* 3–4 (March–April 1985): 37–39.
Azuma, Eiichiro. *Between Two Empires: Race, History, and Transnationalism in Japanese America*. New York: Oxford University Press, 2005.
Baba, Russell. Interview by author. August 1, 2003.
Banks, Marcus. *Ethnicity: Anthropological Considerations*. London: Routledge, 1996.
Barbour, Alecia D. "'For the Good of Our Country': Ruth Watanabe and the 'Good that Is in Music' at the Santa Anita Detention Center." *Notes* 74, no. 2 (December 2017): 221–34.
Bender, Shawn Morgan. *Taiko Boom: Japanese Drumming in Place and Motion*. Berkeley: University of California Press, 2012.

Berendt, Joachim. *The Jazz Book: From New Orleans to Rock and Free Jazz*. Translated by Dan Morgenstern, Helmut Bredigkeit, and Barbara Bredigkeit. New York: Lawrence Hill & Company, [1953] 1975.
Brah, Avtar. *Cartographies of Diaspora: Contesting Identities*. London: Routledge, 1996.
Briones, Matthew M. *Jim and Jap Crow: A Cultural History of 1940s Interracial America*. Princeton, NJ: Princeton University Press, 2012.
Brown, Anthony. "Asian American Jazz." Lecture at the Asian American Center, Northeastern University, Boston, MA, September 16, 2010.
Brown, Anthony. *Family*. Liner notes. Asian Improv Records, AIR 0027, 1997, CD.
Brown, Anthony. Interview by author. August 17, 1998.
Brown, Anthony. Interview by author. July 22, 2003.
Bryant, Dorothy. "George Yoshida: Still Swingin'." *Berkeley (CA) Daily Planet*, July 30, 2009.
Buckley, Roger N., ed. *Yellow Power, Yellow Soul: The Radical Art of Fred Ho*. Urbana: University of Illinois Press, 2013.
Callahan, Mat. *The Explosion of Deferred Dreams: Musical Renaissance and Social Revolution in San Francisco, 1965–1975*. Oakland, CA: PM Press, 2017.
Carr, Ian, Digby Fairweather, and Brian Priestly. *Jazz: The Essential Companion*. New York: Prentice Hall Press, 1987.
Chang, Jeff. *We Gon' Be Alright: Notes on Race and Resegregation*. New York: Picador, 2016.
Chen, Lisa. "Disorienting Gender: Representations of Asian American Women." In *Persistence of Vision: Perspective, Process and Possibilities*, edited by Francis Wong, Mark Izu, Alleluia Panis, Marle Chen, and Ken Yamada, 28–29. San Francisco, CA: Asian Improv aRts, 1994.
Collier, James Lincoln. "Jazz, IV, 3: The Big Band Boom." In *The New Grove Dictionary of American Music*, edited by H. Wiley Hitchcock and Stanley Sadie, 547–48. Vol. 2 of 4 vols. London: Macmillan Publishers.
Combs, Joanne. "Ondo! Japanese Street Dancing in Los Angeles." Lecture at the joint meeting of the Congress on Research and Dance, Dance History Scholars, and the American Dance Guild, University of California, Los Angeles, CA, June 23, 1981.
Creef, Elena Tajima. *Imaging Japanese America: The Visual Construction of Citizenship, Nation, and the Body*. New York: New York University, 2004.
Daniels, Roger. *Asian America: Chinese and Japanese in the US since 1850*. Seattle: University of Washington Press, 1988.
Daniels, Roger. *The Politics of Prejudice: The Anti-Japanese Movement in California and the Struggle for Japanese Exclusion*. University of California Publications in History 71. New York: Atheneum, 1973.
Dessen, Michael. "Asian Americans and Creative Music Legacies." *Critical Studies in Improvisation* 1, no. 3 (2006). https://www.criticalimprov.com/index.php/csieci/article/view/56.
Doyle, Mark. "The Beat Goes On: Kenny Endo's Blend of Ancient Taiko Drumming and Modern Jazz Has Given Him Fans around the World." *Mid Week* 12, no. 38 (1996): 4.
Eaton, Allen H. *Beauty behind Barbed Wire: The Arts of the Japanese in Our War Relocation Camps*. New York: Harper and Brothers, 1952.
Endo, Kenny. Interview by author. July 30, 1996.
Enriquez, Lucia. "Ghost Like Us: The Gift of Then Pioneer Asian American Artists." In *They Painted from Their Hearts: Pioneer Asian American Artists*, edited by Mayumi Tsutakawa, 62–66. Seattle: Wing Luke Museum, 1994.
Epstein, Benjamin. "Tapping into Taiko Sources—to Dramatic Effect." *Los Angeles (CA) Times*, August 13, 1994.
Fifth Stream Music. "Mission." Accessed May 12, 2023. http://www.fifthstreammusic.org/mission.
First Voice. "About First Voice." Accessed May 11, 2023. http://www.firstvoice.org/about-first-voice.

Florin Japanese American Citizens League Oral History Project and Mary Tsukamoto Japanese American Collection. University Library Special Collections and University Archives. California State University, Sacramento. https://csu-csus.primo.exlibrisgroup.com/discovery/fulldisplay?docid=alma99182726050101671&context=L&vid=01CALS_USL:01CALS_USL&lang=en&search_scope=Everything&adaptor=Local%20Search%20Engine&tab=Everything&query=creator,exact,California%20State%20University,%20Sacramento.%20Oral%20History%20Program.,AND&mode=advanced&offset=0.

Floyd, Samuel. *The Power of Black Music: Interpreting Its History from Africa to the United States*. New York: Oxford University Press, 1995.

Fong, Lorna. "Negotiate in Good Faith with the Japanese American Community to Preserve American Concentration Artifacts." Change.org. Last updated May 1, 2015. www.change.org/p/rago-negotiate-with-japanese-american-families-to-preserve-american-concentration-artifacts.

Fujino, Diane. "Race, Place, Space, and Political Development: Japanese-American Radicalism in the 'Pre-Movement' 1960s." *Social Justice* 35, no. 2 (2008): 57–79.

Fujino, Diane, ed. *Wicked Theory, Naked Practice: A Fred Ho Reader*. Minneapolis: University of Minnesota Press, 2009.

Fukui, Yoneichi. Interview by author. August 16, 1994.

Fukuyama, Francis. "Against Identity Politics: The New Tribalism and the Crisis of Democracy." *Foreign Affairs* 97, no. 5 (September–October 2018): 90–112.

Furutani, Alan, and Marsha Furutani. Interview by author. July 10, 1996.

Fusco, Coco. "Passionate Irreverence: The Cultural Politics of Identity." In *Art Matters: How the Culture Wars Changed America*, edited by Brian Wallis, Marianne Weems, and Philip Yenawine, 63–73. New York: New York University Press, 1999.

Gila News Courier. "Butte Festival Program." November 25, 1942.

Gilbert, Shirli. *Music in the Holocaust: Confronting Life in the Nazi Ghettos and Camps*. New York: Oxford University Press, 2006.

Gleason, Philip. "American Identity and Americanization." In *Concepts of Ethnicity*, edited by Philip Gleason, Michael Novak, and William Petersen, 57–143. Dimensions of Ethnicity: A Series of Selections from the Harvard Encyclopedia of Ethnic Groups. Cambridge, MA: Belknap Press, 1982.

Go for Broke: National Education Center. "442nd Regimental Combat Team." Accessed June 4, 2012. https://goforbroke.org/history/unit-history/442nd-regimental-combat-team/.

Great Leap, Inc. "FandangObon." Video, 5:30. Accessed June 10, 2023. https://greatleap.org/fandangobon/.

Great Leap, Inc. "Lectures, Seminars, Workshops, Performances." Video, 8:23. Accessed June 10, 2023. https://greatleap.org/community-engagement/.

Great Leap/Noboku Miyamoto. "Bambutsu for Tsuru for Solidarity." June 23, 2020. YouTube video, 5:45. https://www.youtube.com/watch?v=24FEYJYTknQ.

Great Leap/Noboku Miyamoto. "FandangObon 2017." March 8, 2018. YouTube video, 4:37. https://www.youtube.com/watch?v=xJb7ET7yyOY.

Great Leap/Noboku Miyamoto. "Great Leap | FandangObon Full Performance with Quetzal." January 23, 2014. YouTube video, 7:24. https://www.youtube.com/watch?v=ooNnphMIu6g.

Great Leap/Noboku Miyamoto. "Great Leap—FandangObon Short Documentary." February 6, 2014. YouTube video, 5:15. https://www.youtube.com/watch?v=bPwaYvXH_gw.

Great Leap/Noboku Miyamoto. "Great Leap's ECO-VIDS Sampler." March 2, 2015. YouTube video, 3:17. https://www.youtube.com/watch?v=hauqdkYT4Ag.

Great Leap/Noboku Miyamoto. "Little Tokyo Virtual Earth Day (2020)." June 25, 2020. YouTube video, 1:22:50. https://www.youtube.com/watch?v=QsxoDTIlkfI&feature=youtube.

Great Leap/Noboku Miyamoto. "Praise Songs and Presence: The Art of Qasidah and Hadrah." October 3, 2020. YouTube video, 1:25:15. https://www.youtube.com/watch?v=sODe1CIljQk.

Hall, Stuart. "The Local and the Global: Globalization and Ethnicity." In *Culture, Globalization, and the World System: Contemporary Conditions for the Representation of Identity*, edited by Anthony D. King, 19–39. Minneapolis: University of Minnesota Press, 1997.

Hall, Stuart. "Old and New Identities, Old and New Ethnicities." In *Culture, Globalization, and the World System: Contemporary Conditions for the Representation of Identity*, edited by Anthony D. King, 41–68. Minneapolis: University of Minnesota Press, 1997.

Hamm, Charles. "Popular Music, III, 4: Tin Pan Alley." In *The New Grove Dictionary of American Music*, edited by H. Wiley Hitchcock and Stanley Sadie, 600–601. Vol. 3 of 4 vols. London: Macmillan Publishers, 1986.

Hansen, Arthur A. "Cultural Politics in the Gila River Relocation Center, 1942–1943." *Arizona and the West* 27, no. 4 (Winter 1985): 327–62.

Hatamiya, Michael. "Kenny Endo: Following the Beat of a Different Drum." *Mainichi Daily News*, November 2, 1988.

Hayase, Susan. "Taiko!" *East Wind Magazine* 4, no. 1 (Winter-Spring 1985): 46–48.

Hayashi, Koichi Art. *Minidoka Stories*. Washington, DC: National Park Service, 2003.

Hirabayashi, P. J. Interview by author. July 22, 1996.

Ho, Fred. "An Asian American Tribute to the Black Arts Movement." In *Wicked Theory, Naked Practice: A Fred Ho Reader*, edited by Diane C. Fujino, 161–210. Minneapolis: University of Minnesota Press, 2009.

Ho, Fred. "Beyond Asian American Jazz: My Musical and Political Changes in the Asian American Movement." In *Wicked Theory, Naked Practice: A Fred Ho Reader*, edited by Diane C. Fujino, 46–62. Minneapolis: University of Minnesota Press, 2009.

Ho, Fred. "Fred Ho's Tribute to the Black Arts Movement: Personal and Political Impact and Analysis." Unpublished manuscript, 2004.

Hongo, Garrett. "Introduction." In *Songs My Mother Taught Me: Stories, Plays, and Memoir*, by Wakako Yamauchi, edited by Garrett Hongo, 1–16. New York: Feminist Press, 1994.

Horiuchi, Glenn. "Glenn Horiuchi, Pianist and Composer." Artist statement. n.d.

Horiuchi, Glenn. Interview by author. August 28, 1994.

Hosokawa, Bill. *The Nisei: The Quiet Americans*. New York: William Morrow and Co., 1969.

Howe, Sondra Wieland. "American Music in Meiji Era Japan." *Ritsumeikan gengo bunka kenkyū* 26, no. 1 (2014): 63–70. https://www.ritsumei.ac.jp/acd/re/k-rsc/lcs/kiyou/pdf_26-1/RitsIILCS_26.1pp.63-70HOWE.pdf.

Ichihashi, Yamato. *Japanese in the United States: A Critical Study of the Problems of the Japanese Immigrants and Their Children*. Stanford, CA: Stanford University Press, 1932.

Ichioka, Yuji. *Before Internment: Essays in Prewar Japanese American History*. Edited by Gordon H. Chang and Eiichiro Azuma. Stanford, CA: Stanford University Press, 2006.

Ichioka, Yuji. *The Issei: The World of the First Generation Japanese Immigrants, 1885–1924*. New York: Free Press, 1988.

Ichioka, Yuji. "JERS Revisited: Introduction." In *Views from Within: The Japanese Evacuation and Resettlement Study*, edited by Yuji Ichioka, 3–27. Los Angeles: Resource Development and Publications, Asian American Studies Center, University of California, 1989.

IMDB. "Kathryn Grayson: Biography." Accessed May 8, 2023. http://www.imdb.com/name/nmo337113/bio.

ImprovisAsians! "A Conversation with Mark Izu." 4, no. 1. (February 1995): 4–5.

ImprovisAsians! "What's That Sound?" 3, no. 1 (February 1994): 6.

International Examiner. "Glenn Horiuchi, Francis Wong, and Lillian Nakano—Nov. 3 at the Seattle Asian Art Museum." October 18, 1994.

Iyer, Vijay. "Monk's Japanese Folk Song: Performative Strategies on Asian American Jazz." Lecture at the Society for Ethnomusicology National Meeting, Toronto, Canada, November 3, 2000.
Izu, Mark. *Circle of Fire*. Liner notes by Dan Ouellette. Asian Improv Records, AIR 0009, 1992, CD.
Izu, Mark. Interview by author. April 30, 2005.
Izu, Mark. Interview by author. July 18, 1996.
Izu, Mark. *Last Dance*. Liner notes. Bindu Records, BIN 0205-2, 1998, CD.
Izu, Mark. "Threading Time." Liner notes. 2000, demo CD.
Izumi, Masami. "Big Drum: Taiko in the United States DVD." *Journal of American History* 93, no. 1 (June 2006): 158–61.
Jacobs, Ron. "Day of Remembrance and the Music of Anthony Brown." CounterPunch. February 19, 2019. https://www.counterpunch.org/2019/02/19/day-of-remembrance-and-the-music-of-anthony-brown/.
Jang, Jon. "88 Keys to Revolution." *East Wind Magazine* 4, no. 1 (Winter–Spring 1985): 34–35.
Jang, Jon. *Next Step*. Liner notes. Asian Improv Records, AIR-0002, 1988, CD.
Japanese American History: NOT for Sale. "Letter to the Board of Trustees of JANM and President Greg Kimura." Facebook, June 12, 2015. https://www.facebook.com/japaneseamericanhistorynotforsale/posts/letter-to-the-board-of-trustees-of-janm-and-president-greg-kimurathe-artifacts-f/1571833183079575/.
Japanese American National Museum. "Hidden Legacy: Japanese Traditional Performing Arts in the World War II Internment Camps (DVD)." Accessed June 20, 2023. https://janmstore.com/search?type=product&q=%22Hidden+Legacy%22.
Japan America Theatre. *A Celebration of the Music and Artistry of Glenn Horiuchi & Friends*. Program booklet. Concert at Japan America Theatre, Los Angeles, CA, January 22, 2000.
Japan America Theatre. *Music to Remember: A Tribute to Japanese American Musicians and Singers of the '40s*. Program booklet. Concert at Japanese American Cultural and Community Center in association with Mas Fukai and Friends, Los Angeles, CA, February 18–19, 1995.
Jyorokusho, Kineya. Interview by author. August 30, 1994.
Kageyama, Yuri. "Following the Drumbeat: Percussionist Pursues His Ancestral Heritage." *Japan Times Weekly*, June 21, 1986.
Kaji, Bruce T., and Sharon Yamato. *Jive Bomber: A Sentimental Journey*. Gardena, CA: Kaji and Associates, 2010.
Kajikawa, Loren. "The Sound of Struggle: Black Revolutionary Nationalism and Asian American Jazz." In *Jazz/Not Jazz: The Music and Its Boundaries*, edited by David Garrett Ake, Charles Hiroshi, and Daniel Goldmark, 190–216. Berkeley: University of California Press, 2012.
Karuk Tribe. Accessed May 11, 2023. www.karuk.us.
Kasama, Rei. Interview by author. August 25, 1994.
Katrak, Ketu H. Review of *Immigrant Acts: On Asian American Cultural Politics*, by Lisa Lowe. *Journal of Asian American Studies* 3, no. 3 (October 2000): 371–75.
Kikuchi, Charles. *The Kikuchi Diary: Chronicle from an American Concentration Camp; The Tanforan Journals of Charles Kikuchi*. Edited by John Modell. Urbana: University of Illinois Press, 1993.
Kim, Claire Jean. "The Racial Triangulation of Asian American." In *Asian Americans and Politics: Perspectives, Experiences, and Prospects*, edited by Gordon H. Chang, 39–78. Stanford, CA: Stanford University Press, 2001.
Kimura, Molly Miyako. Interview by Hiroko Tsuda. Florin Japanese American Citizens League Oral History Project and Mary Tsukamoto Japanese American Collection. University

Library Special Collections and University Archives. California State University, Sacramento. https://csu-csus.primo.exlibrisgroup.com/discovery/fulldisplay?docid=alma 99182726050101671&context=L&vid=01CALS_USL:01CALS_USL&lang=en&search_scope =Everything&adaptor=Local%20Search%20Engine&tab=Everything&query=creator,exact ,California%20State%20University,%20Sacramento.%20Oral%20History%20Program.,AND &mode=advanced&offset=0.

Kitagawa, Daisuke. *Issei and Nisei: The Internment Years*. New York: Seabury Press, 1967.

Kitano, Harry H. L. *Japanese Americans: The Evolution of a Subculture*. Englewood Cliffs: Prentice-Hall, 1969.

Kobayashi, Yutaka. Interview by author. June 13, 2006.

Kodani, Masao. *Hōraku*. Los Angeles, CA: Senshin Buddhist Church, 1979.

Kodani, Masao. Interview by author. July 12, 1996.

Komai, Chris. "Kinnara Taiko Celebrates 20th Anniversary." *Los Angeles Rafu Shimpo*, February 16, 1990.

Komiya, Toyotaka, ed. *Japanese Music and Drama in the Meiji Era*. Translated and adapted by Donald Keene. Tokyo: Toyo Bunko, [1956] 1969.

Kondo, Dorinne. *About Face: Performing Race in Fashion and Theater*. New York: Routledge, 1997.

Kunitsugu, Kats, ed. *Teachers of Japanese Cultural Arts in Southern California Directory*. Los Angeles, CA: Japanese American Cultural and Community Center, 1994.

Kurabu, Hokubei Okinawa. *History of the Okinawans in North America*. Translated by Ben Kobashigawa. Los Angeles, CA: Okinawan Club of America, 1989.

Kuramoto, June. Interview by author. July 19, 1995.

Kurashige, Lon. *Japanese American Celebration and Conflict: A History of Ethnic Identity and Festival in Los Angeles, 1934–1990*. Berkeley: University of California Press, 2002.

Kuwamoto, Ryan. "Stepping into the Past: Behind the Scenes of *The Untold Story*; Internment of Japanese Americans in Hawai'i." Discover Nikkei. October 11, 2013. http://www.discover nikkei.org/en/journal/2013/10/11/internment-hawaii/.

Lee, Grace, director. *American Revolutionary: The Evolution of Grace Lee Boggs*. San Francisco, CA: Center for Asian American Media, 2013.

Ling, Amy. *Yellow Light: The Flowering of Asian American Arts*. Philadelphia, PA: Temple University Press, 1999.

Los Angeles Kashū Mainichi Shimbun [Japan-California Daily News]. "Gakuen Graduates Given Diplomas at San Fernando." July 30, 1928.

Los Angeles Kashū Mainichi Shimbun. "Nipponettes to Hold Dance." May 18, 1937.

Los Angeles Kashū Mainichi Shimbun. "Nisei Artists to Appear on Union Church Program." September 9, 1935.

Los Angeles Kashū Mainichi Shimbun. "Nisei Week Featured on Radio Friday." August 8, 1935.

Los Angeles Kashū Mainichi Shimbun. "Program Arranged for Concert Given by Miss Miyakawa." April 23, 1928.

Los Angeles Rafu Shimpo. "Big Annual Carnival Held by Combined Oliver Clubs." January 1, 1928.

Los Angeles Rafu Shimpo. "Boys to Organize Harmonica Band." February 14, 1930.

Los Angeles Rafu Shimpo. "Central Junior High Invites Public to 'Japanese Night.'" February 27, 1941.

Los Angeles Rafu Shimpo. "Club Social Activities—Nisei Rug-cutters." February 12, 1941.

Los Angeles Rafu Shimpo. "Emperor's Birthday Celebration, Plan of Japanese People." April 9, 1928.

Los Angeles Rafu Shimpo. "Famous Singer Pleases Many Admirers Here." November 29, 1926.

Los Angeles Rafu Shimpo. "Frisco Harmonica Band Broadcast Over NBC System." January 27, 1930.
Los Angeles Rafu Shimpo. Imperial County Fair program. February 27, 1941.
Los Angeles Rafu Shimpo. "'Japan Night' Program Seen by Many at USC." January 13, 1930.
Los Angeles Rafu Shimpo. Los Angeles Japanese Orchestra fifth annual spring concert. March 5, 1928.
Los Angeles Rafu Shimpo. "Musical Numbers Please Audience of Young People." August 6, 1928.
Los Angeles Rafu Shimpo. New Year's broadcast program. December 29, 1941.
Los Angeles Rafu Shimpo. "Nisei Sings Operatic Role." May 8, 1941.
Los Angeles Rafu Shimpo. "Students' Benefit Concert Program Meets Success." March 14, 1927.
Los Angeles Rafu Shimpo. "Trans-Pacific Radio Dial, Station JZJ." May 18, 1937.
Los Angeles Rafu Shimpo. "Troop 379 Drum and Bugle Corps Wins Legion Award." May 6, 1941.
Los Angeles Rafu Shimpo. "2 Nisei to Appear in Opera Reading Club Presentation." January 5, 1941.
Los Angeles Rafu Shimpo. Yoshie Fujiwara's KHJ radio-broadcast performance. November 29, 1928.
Los Angeles Rafu Shimpo. "Young Soprano from North to Make Debut Here Soon." April 2, 1928.
Lowe, Lisa. *Immigrant Acts: On Asian American Cultural Politics.* Durham, NC: Duke University Press, 1996.
Maeda, Daryl J. *Chains of Babylon: The Rise of Asian America.* Minneapolis: University of Minnesota Press, 2009.
Malm, William. *Japanese Music and Musical Instruments.* Rutland, VT: Charles E. Tuttle Co., [1959] 1974.
Manzanar Free Press. "Japanese Music Policy Explained." September 19, 1942.
Masaoka, Miya. Interview by author. July 30, 2003.
Matsumoto, Valerie. *Farming the Home Place: A Japanese American Community in California, 1919–1982.* Ithaca, NY: Cornell University Press, 1993.
Matsumoto, Y. Scott. "Okinawan Migrants to Hawaii." *Hawaiian Journal of History* 16 (1982): 125–33. eVols.
Maykovich, Minako K. *Japanese American Identity Dilemma.* Tokyo: Waseda University Press, 1972.
McWilliams, Carey. *Prejudice: Japanese Americans; Symbol of Racial Intolerance.* Boston, MA: Little, Brown and Co., 1944.
Mead, Rita H., and Ned Sublette. "Broadcasting 2: Commercial Development to 1940." In *The New Grove Dictionary of American Music,* edited by H. Wiley Hitchcock and Stanley Sadie, 296–98. Vol. 2 of 4 vols. London: Macmillan, 1986.
Millman, Joel. "From Barbed Wire to Boogie-Woogie." *Wall Street Journal,* March 25, 2010. https://www.wsj.com/video/from-barbed-wire-to-boogie-woogie/18EA555C-7CB0-4B05-B331-F4912904AFD9.html.
Mimura, Glenn M. *Ghostlife of Third Cinema.* Minneapolis: University of Minnesota Press, 2009.
Miyamoto, Joanne Nobuko, Chris Kando Iijima, and Charlie Chin. "We Are the Children." Lyrics by Chris Iijima and Nobuko Miyamoto. On *A Grain of Sand.* Smithsonian Paredon Records, PARE 1020, [1973] 1992, CD.
Miyamoto, Joanne Nobuko, Chris Kando Iijima, and Charlie Chin. *A Grain of Sand.* Liner notes. Smithsonian Paredon Records, PARE 1020, [1973] 1992, CD.
Miyamoto, Nobuko. Interview by author. July 25, 1995.
Miyamoto, Shotaro Frank. "Social Solidarity among the Japanese in Seattle." *University of Washington Publications in the Social Sciences* 11, no. 2 (December 1939): 57–130.
Miyauchi, John. Interview by author. August 18, 1994.

Modell, John. *The Economics and Politics of Racial Accommodation: The Japanese of Los Angeles, 1900–1942*. Urbana: University of Illinois Press, 1977.
Modirzadeh, Hafez. *In Chromodal Discourse*. Liner notes. Asian Improv Records, AIR 0012, 1993, CD.
Modirzadeh, Hafez. Interview by author. July 28, 2003.
Moore, Heidi. "The Aesthetics of Place and the Comedy of Discomfort: Six Humorists." PhD diss., Union Institute and University, 2007.
Moriya, Walter. Interview by author. June 5, 2009.
Muhammad Speaks. "Third World Students Want MS to Tell Their Story First." February 7, 1969.
Muramoto Wong, Shirley, director. *Hidden Legacy: Japanese Traditional Performing Arts in the World War II Internment Camps*. Oakland, CA: Murasaki Productions, 2014. DVD.
Muramoto Wong, Shirley. *Hidden Legacy: Tribute to Teachers of Japanese Traditional Arts in the War Relocation Authority Camps*. Program booklet. Concert at Koyasan Buddhist Temple, Resource Development and Publications, Asian American Studies Center, University of California, Japanese American Cultural and Community Center, Los Angeles, CA, April 24, 2010.
Murase, Ichiro Mike. *Little Tokyo: One Hundred Years in Pictures*. Los Angeles, CA: Visual Communications; Asian American Studies Central, 1983.
Naka, Robert. Interview by author. March 8, 2006.
Nakano, Jiro, and Kay Nakano, eds. and trans. *Poets behind Barbed Wire*. Illustrated by George Hoshida. Honolulu: Bamboo Ridge Press, [1983] 1984.
Nakano, Lillian. Interview by author. August 25, 1994.
Nakata, George. Interview by Masako Hinatsu. August 23, 2004. Oregon Nikkei Endowment Collection, Densho Digital Repository. Accessed May 14, 2023. https://ddr.densho.org.
National Japanese American Historical Society. *Nikkei Music Makers: The Swing Era*. 1995. Calendar. San Francisco, CA.
Newell (CA) Star. "Center-wide Program to Be at Auditorium." March 16, 1944.
Nguyen, Viet Thanh. "American Like Me: What It Means to Love My Country, No Matter How It Feels about Me." *Time* 192, no. 22–23 (November 26, 2018): 28–34.
Nichibei Shimbun [Japanese American Newspaper]. "200 Attend Silver Echo Club Dance." January 15, 1929.
Nichibei Shimbun Editorial Staff. *Japanese American Directory*. San Francisco, CA: Nichibei Shimbun, 1941.
Nichibei Shimbun Editorial Staff. *Japanese American Yearbook*. San Francisco, CA: Nichibei Shimbun, 1914.
Nihon no Gunka. "*Gunka*—Japanese War Songs." Accessed June 20, 2023. http://gunka.sakura.ne.jp/en/index.html.
Nikkei for Civil Rights and Redress. "About NCRR." Last modified January 24, 2003. https://ncrr-la.org/about.
Nisei Student Relocation Commemorative Fund. "Our Origins: The National Japanese American Student Relocation Council (NJASRC)." Accessed May 10, 2023. http://www.nsrcfund.org/our-history-our-stories/our-origins.
Nishida, Mo. "Where Do We Go From Here?" *Gidra* (April 1974): 21–22.
Noda, Mamie. Interview by author. March 22, 2002.
Noguchi, Andy. "Camp Art: Strength, Dignity, and Culture in the Concentration Camps." *East Wind Magazine* 2, no. 2 (Fall–Winter 1983): 54–56.
Nomura, Mary Kageyama. Interview by Tom Ikeda. July 9, 2009. Manzanar National Historic Site Collection, Densho Digital Repository. Accessed May 14, 2023. https://ddr.densho.org.
Oakland (CA) Tribune. "From Stark World War II Internment Camps—Music." February 17, 1998.

Odo, Franklin. *The Columbia Documentary History of the Asian American Experience*. New York: Columbia University Press, 2002.

Oka, Seizo. Interview by author. August 15, 1994.

Oka, Seizo. Interview by author. July 23, 1996.

Okabe, Shirley Nagatomi. Interview by Alisa Lynch. January 30, 2013. Manzanar National Historic Site Collection, Densho Digital Repository. Accessed May 14, 2023. https://ddr.densho.org.

Okabe, Sue. Interview by author. July 28, 1995.

Okihiro, Gary Y. *The Columbia Guide to Asian American History*. New York: Columbia University Press, 2005.

Okihiro, Gary Y. "Japanese American Resistance in America's Concentration Camps: A Re-Evaluation." *Amerasia Journal* 2, no. 1 (1973): 20–34.

Okihiro, Gary Y. "Tule Lake under Martial Law: A Study in Japanese Resistance." *Journal of Ethnic Studies* 5, no. 3 (Fall 1977): 71–85.

Okimoto, Daniel I. *American in Disguise*. New York: Walker; Weatherhill, 1971.

Oliver, Paul. "Race Record." In *The New Grove Dictionary of American Music*, edited by H. Wiley Hitchcock and Stanley Sadie, 1–2. Vol. 4 of 4 vols. London: Macmillan Press, 1986.

Olsen, Dale A. *The Chrysanthemum and the Song: Music, Memory, and Identity in the South American Japanese Diaspora*. Gainesville: University Press of Florida, 2004.

Omatsu, Glenn. "Always a Rebel: An Interview with Kazu Iijima." *Amerasia Journal* 13, no. 2 (1986–1987): 83–98.

Ong, Henry. "Dan Kuramoto: The Leader of a Band Named Hiroshima Aims to Discover His Asianness." *AsiAm* (July 1987): 30.

Oyama, Richard. "Profile: Gerald Oshita." *East Wind Magazine* 2, no. 1 (Spring–Summer 1983): 70–71.

Pacific Citizen. "Santa Barbara to Give Dance for Season's Grads." 13, no. 154 (June 1941): 12.

Palumbo-Liu, David. *Asian American Historical Crossings of a Racial Frontier*. Stanford, CA: Stanford University Press, 1999.

Phillips, Brian. "Glenn Horiuchi: Atonal Energy Music." Perfect Sound Forever. May 2001. furious.com/perfect/glennhoriuchi.html.

Porter, Cole. "Don't Fence Me In." In *Hollywood Canteen*, directed by Delmer Daves. Burbank, CA: Warner Bros., 1944. Film. Lyrics by Robert Fletcher. Alfred Music, 1202554, [1934] 1944, audio.

Poston Chronicle. "Symphony Set for Music Lovers." July 14, 1943.

Powell, Kimberly Anne. "Composing Sound Identity in Taiko Drumming." *Anthropology and Education Quarterly* 43, no. 1 (2012): 101–19.

Powell, Kimberly Anne. "Drumming against the Quiet: The Sounds of Asian American Identity in an Amorphous Landscape." *Qualitative Inquiry* 14, no. 6 (September 2008): 901–25. https://doi.org/10.1177/1077800408318308.

Price, Emmett, III. "Free Jazz and the Black Arts Movement, 1958–1967." PhD diss., University of Pittsburgh, 2000.

Pulido, Laura. *Black, Brown, Yellow, and Left: Radical Activism in Los Angeles*. Berkeley: University of California Press, 2006.

Radano, Ronald, and Philip V. Bohlman. "Introduction: Music and Race, Their Past, Their Presence." In *Music and the Racial Imagination*, edited by Ronald Radano and Philip V. Bohlman, 1–56. Chicago: University of Chicago Press, 2000.

Ray Fukumoto. "Senshin Obon 2014—Fandango Live!" July 6, 2014. YouTube video, 8:58. http://www.youtube.com/watch?v=p9xj4xGlju8.

Reich, Howard. "It Took Our Minds off the Bad Things: Japanese Internment Survivors Remember the Swing Music that Helped Them Endure." *Chicago Tribune*, October 10, 2001.

Roberson, James E. "Singing Diaspora: Okinawan Songs of Home, Departure and Return." *Identities* 17, no. 4 (2010): 430–53.

Roberts, Tamara. *Resounding Afro Asia: Interracial Music and the Politics of Collaboration.* New York: Oxford University Press, 2016.

Robertson, Marta. "Ballad for Incarcerated Americans: Second Generation Japanese American Musicking in World War II Camps." *Journal of the Society for American Music* 11, no. 3 (2017): 284–312.

Rosaldo, Renato. "Cultural Citizenship and Educational Democracy." *Cultural Anthropology* 9, no. 3 (1994): 402–11.

Rosenberg, David. "Discerning Diaspora: Roots and Routes." *SEM Student News* 10 (Spring-Summer 2015): 9–10.

Roxworthy, Emily. *The Spectacle of Japanese American Trauma: Racial Performativity in World War II.* Honolulu: University of Hawaii Press, 2008.

Sakamoto, Art. "Art, Culture, and Identity." Lecture at the Japanese American National Museum, Los Angeles, CA, July 28, 2010.

Sakoda, James M. "Reminiscences of a Participant Observer." In *View from Within: The Japanese American Evacuation and Resettlement Study*, edited by Yuji Ichioka, 219–45. Los Angeles: Resource Development and Publications, Asian American Studies Center, University of California, 1989.

Shelemay, Kay. "Musical Communities: Rethinking the Collective in Music." *Journal of the American Musicological Society* 64, no. 2 (Summer 2011): 349–90.

Sheppard, W. Anthony. *Extreme Exoticism: Japan in the American Musical Imagination.* New York: Oxford University Press, 2019.

Shibuya, Yo. Interview by Richard Potashin. June 2, 2010. Manzanar Historical Site Collection, Densho Digital Repository. Accessed May 14, 2023. https://ddr.densho.org.

Shin Sekai [New World]. *New World Directory.* San Francisco, CA: Shin Sekai, 1922.

Shirachi, Donald, ed. *Reunion Booklet of YBA Orchestra.* Watsonville: YBA, 2005.

Small, Christopher. "Whose Music Do We Teach Anyway?" *Muse Letter* 2 (March 1990): 87–94.

Soga, Yasutaro. *Life behind Barbed Wire: The World War II Internment Memoirs of a Hawaiian Issei.* Translated by Kihei Hirae. Honolulu: University of Hawaii Press, 2008.

Spicer, Edward, Asael T. Hansen, Katherine Luomala, and Marvin K. Opler. *Impounded People: Japanese-Americans in the Relocation Centers.* Tucson: University of Arizona Press, 1969.

Spickard, Paul R. *Japanese Americans: The Formation and Transformation of an Ethnic Group.* New York: Twayne Publishers; London: Prentice-Hall International, 1996.

Stack, Peter. "Pounding a New Path/Local Taiko Master Brought Japanese Drumming to the US." *San Francisco (CA) Chronicle*, November 8, 2001. SFGATE. Accessed June 10, 2023. https://www.sfgate.com/entertainment/article/Pounding-a-new-path-Local-taiko-master-brought-2859766.php.

Stokes, Martin. "Introduction: Ethnicity, Identity and Music." In *Ethnicity, Identity, and Music: The Musical Construction of Place*, edited by Martin Stokes, 1–27. Oxford: Berg, 1994.

Taiko Source. "The Sukeroku Style Moves Forward." Accessed June 10, 2023. https://taikosource.com/tag/sukeroku-taiko/.

Takahashi, Jerrold. "Japanese American Responses to Race Relations: The Formation of Nisei Perspectives." *Amerasia Journal* 9, no. 1 (1982): 29–57.

Takahashi, Jerrold. *Nisei/Sansei: Shifting Japanese American Identities and Politics.* Philadelphia, PA: Temple University Press, 1997.

Takaki, Ronald. *Strangers from a Different Shore: A History of Asian Americans.* Boston, MA: Little, Brown and Co., 1989.

Takayanagi, May, and Taka Takayanagi. Interview by author. March 7, 2006.

Takehara, Dean. "Jazz Pianist Combines Music with Politics." *Los Angeles Pacific Citizen*, March 1, 1988.
Taylor, Sandra C. *Jewel of the Desert*. Berkeley: University of California Press, 1993.
Tchen, John Kuo Wei. "Believing Is Seeing: Transforming Orientalism and the Occidental Gaze." In *Asia/America: Identities in Contemporary Asian American Art*, curated by Margo Machida, 12–25. New York: Asia Society Galleries; New Press, 1994.
Toyotaka, Komiya. "The Late Meiji Era." In *Japanese Music and Drama in the Meiji Era*, edited by Komiya Toyotaka, translated and adapted by Donald Keene, 387–458. Tokyo: Ōbunsha, 1956.
Tozai Times. "Glenn Horiuchi: Sansei Musician Takes the Next Step." 4, no. 45 (July 1988): 108.
Tsunoda, Ryusaku, Wm. Theodore de Bary, and Donald Keene, comps. *Sources of Japanese Tradition*. New York: Columbia University Press, 1958.
Tsuru for Solidarity. "Japanese American History: NOT for Sale." Facebook. Accessed June 18, 2015. www.facebook.com/japaneseamericanhistorynotforsale?fref=ts.
Tusler, Mark. "Taiko Drumming in California: Issues of Articulation and the Construction of Ethnic Identity." Lecture at the meeting of Society for Ethnomusicology Southern California Chapter, University of California, Riverside, CA, February 23–24, 1999.
Ueno, Rihoko. "One Spot of Normalcy: Chiura Obata's Art Schools." Archives of American Art. Smithsonian Institution. September 19, 2019. https://www.aaa.si.edu/blog/2019/09/one-spot-of-normalcy-chiura-obatas-art-schools.
Umemoto, Karen. "'On Strike!' San Francisco State College Strike, 1968–69." *Amerasia Journal* 15, no. 1 (1989): 3–41.
University of Denver. "Loyalty Questions." Behind Barbed Wire: The Story of the Japanese-American Internment during World War II. Accessed June 22, 2023. https://www.du.edu/behindbarbedwire/loyalty_questions.html.
Uno, Kiku. Interview by author. June 18, 2006.
Urata, Harry Minoru, and Franklin S. Odo. "Hole Hole Bushi: Song of Hawaii's Japanese Immigrants." *Mana: A South Pacific Journal of Language and Literature* 6, no. 1 (1981): 70.
USAsians.net. "Hiroshima: Historic Asian American Band!" Accessed June 11, 2023. http://us_asians.tripod.com/features-hiroshima.html.
Uyeki, Amy, director. *Searchlight Serenade: Big Bands in the WWII Japanese American Incarceration Camps*. Eureka, CA: KEET-TV, 2012. DVD.
Varian, Heidi. *The Way of Taiko*. Berkeley, CA: Stone Bridge Press, 2005.
Wakita, Kayoko. Interview by author. July 30, 1996.
Wangsness, Lisa. "Strangers in Their Own Land, as They Came of Age." *Boston (MA) Globe*, September 8, 2011.
Waseda, Minako. "Extraordinary Circumstances, Exceptional Practices: Music in Japanese American Concentration Camps." *Journal of Asian American Studies* 8, no. 2 (June 2005): 171–209.
Waseda, Minako. "Japanese American Musical Culture in Southern California: Its Formation and Transformation." PhD diss., University of California, 2000.
Weglyn, Michi. *Years of Infamy: The Untold Story of America's Concentration Camps*. New York: Morrow Quill Paperbacks, 1976.
Wei, William. *The Asian American Movement*. Philadelphia, PA: Temple University Press, 1993.
Whitehead, Kevin, and Glenn Horiuchi. *Oxnard Beat*. Liner notes. Soul Note, 121228, 1992, CD.
Widran, Jonathan. "Hiroshima Web Bio." Hiroshima. Accessed on June 10, 2023. https://www.hiroshimamusic.com/bios.html.
Wise, Gene. *American Historical Explanations: A Strategy for Grounded Inquiry*. Homewood, IL: Dorsey Press, 1973.

Wong, Deborah. *Louder and Faster: Pain, Joy, and the Body Politic in Asian American Taiko*. Oakland: University of California Press, 2020.
Wong, Deborah. *Speak It Louder: Asian Americans Making Music*. New York: Routledge, 2004.
Wong, Francis. "Asian Improv Records." *East Wind* 7, no. 1 (Spring–Summer 1989): 55–56.
Wong, Francis. Interview by author. July 29, 2003.
Yamato, Sharon. "Civil Liberties Act of 1988." Densho Encyclopedia. Accessed June 5, 2023. https://encyclopedia.densho.org/Civil%20Liberties%20Act%20of%201988.
Yamazaki, Paul. Interview by author. July 30, 2003.
Yanow, Scott. "Enthusiasm." *Jazziz* 11, no. 2 (February–March 1994): 28–34.
Yinger, J. Milton. "Ethnicity." *Annual Review of Sociology* 11 (1985): 151–80.
Yokohama, California. *Yokohama, California*. Liner notes. Translated into Japanese by Minoru Kanda. Peter Horikoshi-YokohamaCa.com, 2016, CD.
Yoo, David. *Growing Up Nisei: Race, Generation, and Culture among Japanese Americans of California, 1924–49*. Urbana: University of Illinois Press, 2000.
Yoon, Paul Jong-Chul. "'She's Really Become Japanese Now!': Taiko Drumming and Asian American Identification." *American Music* 19, no. 4 (Winter 2001): 417–38.
Yoshida, George. Interview by author. July 25, 1996.
Yoshida, George. Interview by author. March 30, 2006.
Yoshida, George. Interview by author. August 2, 2012.
Yoshida, George. *Reminiscing in Swingtime: Japanese Americans in American Popular Music, 1925–1960*. San Francisco, CA: National Japanese American Historical Society, 1997.
Yoshihara, Mari. *Musicians from a Different Shore: Asians and Asian Americans in Classical Music*. Philadelphia, PA: Temple University Press, 2007.
Zaibei Nihonjinshi Editorial Staff. *Zaibei Nihonjinshi*. San Francisco, CA: Zaibei Nihonjinkai, 1940.
Zhang, Cat. "What Is Asian American Music Really?" Pitchfork. May 31, 2021. https://pitchfork.com/features/asian-american-music-history/?fbclid=IwAR1RcJNHxl.
Zheng, Su. *Claiming Diaspora: Music, Transnationalism, and Cultural Politics in Asian/Chinese America*. Oxford: Oxford University Press, 2010.

INDEX

References to figures are in **bold**.

Abe, George, 233–35, 245
Abiko, Hiroshi, 247
abstraction, 188, 222, 224
acculturation, 22, 37–39
Acuña, Jess, 228
African American music: avant-garde, 188; Black aesthetic, 185; blues as expression of disenfranchisement, 121; breadth of music to identify with, 228; collective aspect of, 189–90; improvisation, 175, 183, 185, 188, 189–90, 194; influence on Hiroshima (band), 227; jazz as vehicle of protest, 189; way to express humanity, 191
African American musicians: affinity with Sansei, 171, 173, 174, 175; as inspiration for Japanese American musician-composers, 174–75, 184–85; intercultural collaborations, 172, 177, 203–5, 258; music-collectives, 174–75, 186; segregation of, 89
Afro-Asian collaborations, 203–5
Aion (journal), 184, 185
Akamatsu, Haruko, 102–3, 107
Alternative Facts (Osaki), 218
Americanism: avenues for promotion of, 166; JACL's stance on, 163; *Nippon seishin*, 115–16, 132; Nisei Progressives, 114; Nisei's pull to, 56, 112–13; Popular Front, 159; whiteness as standard, 110
Americanization movement, 44, 48–49. *See also* assimilation; JACL (Japanese American Citizens League); Nisei, Americanization of
Anglo-Saxon nationalism, 43, 44

Anthony Brown's Asian American Orchestra (AAO), 210, 218, 219. *See also* Asian American Jazz Orchestra (AAJO); Brown, Anthony
anti-imperialism, 178. *See also* imperialism
anti-Japanese sentiments: beginnings, 24–25; campaign-for-education promoting Japan-US relations, 40–42; hampered political change in favor of Nisei, 57; performing arts and, 67; in rural areas, 99, 113; used by white supremacy groups, 28
antiwar movement, 174, 177–78, 181
Aoki, Brenda Wong, 205, 209, 212–13
Aoki, Richard, **177**, 178
Aoki, Tatsu, 187
Art Ensemble of Chicago, 188, 189, 197, 208, 215
Asai, Hisayo, 85, 97–100, **98**, 108, 109
Asai, Matsujiro, 26
Asian American identity: aesthetics and, 167–68, 174–76; the Asian body, 28, 110–11; "between two empires," 21–22; Issei's dual identities, 47–53; Japanese music as cultural rearticulation, 75; *Music and the Racial Imagination*, 123; music as means to express one's, 123, 235–36, 248–49; political representation, 179; racial triangulation, 17, 182, 228; shifts during incarceration due to WRA policies, 122; terminology, 176–77, 183; wheel spokes to represent issues, 240–41. *See also* Asian American movement; Issei identity; Nisei identity; transculturation
Asian American identity politics, 176–82, 240–41

Asian American jazz: Asian American Jazz Festival, 205–6, 210, 212, 215; chromodal discourse, 193–94; harmolodics, 188, 192; Moonlight Orchestra, 234–35; origins, 172–74; relationship to Black music, 183–86, 188–91; San Francisco, 186–88; Sansei musicking, 174–76. *See also* Asian American music; Hiroshima (band)

Asian American Jazz Orchestra (AAJO), 210, 217. *See also* Anthony Brown's Asian American Orchestra (AAO)

Asian American movement: Asian American Political Alliance, 181, 185, 232; community of media organizations, 184; embracing Black Americans, 110; formation of, 177–81; identity as key theme, 231; Joanne, Chris, and Charlie, 237–38; Kearny Street Workshop, 212; multiethnic racial formation, 181–82; reframed Sansei citizenship, 172–73; response to Otherness, 19; serving one's country as key theme, 232; "We Are the Children," 179–81. *See also* Asian American identity; Asian Improv Records; Joanne, Chris, and Charlie (trio); Mirikitani, Janice

Asian American music: context for rise of, 194–95; FandangObon festival, 262, 263, 264–66, **267**. *See also* Asian American jazz

Asian American Political Alliance (AAPA), 181, 185, 232

Asian Americans for Action (AAA), 114, 237, 239

Asian Improv aRts, 210, 229

Asian Improv Records: Asian American movement, 172; expansion to Asian Improve aRts, 210; founding of, 186–87; releases, 224; Yoshida, 215. *See also* Wong, Francis

Asian musical systems, 192, 193

assembly centers, 120–21, **121**, 123, 152. *See also* concentration camps; *and individual names*

assimilation: Asians as unassimilable, 17, 45, 53, 110, 286n101; Christianity, 49; class, 50, 109; cultural, 48; doubt regarding assimilability, 124; *gaimenteki dōka*, 49; of Issei bachelors, 162; Issei resistance to, 41, 112; policy of "coerced," 138; relationship to *taiko*, 242. *See also* Americanism;

Americanization movement; Nisei, Americanization of; War Relocation Authority (WRA)

Association for the Advancement of Creative Musicians (AACM), 184–85, 222, 232; Abrams, 190; Lewis, 184, 190, 197; Oshita and, 175, 198. *See also* Art Ensemble of Chicago

atomic bombs, 210–11

atonality, 188, 212, 222, 226

audiences: American, 49; of Asian American Jazz Festival, 212; attraction tactics, 35, 37; boundary between white and Black bands, 110; broadened through collective spirit, 252–53; connection with performer and instrument, 256; cross-cultural appeal of Hiroshima (band), 227; diversification of, 237; for *engeikai* (talent shows), 65, 137; mainstream, 67; musicking and, 5; for Nisei Week, 75; San Francisco, 219–20; *Sansei* (Hiroshima [band]), 229; segregation, 46, 75, 89; at war bond rallies, 104–5; white, 41–42

avant garde jazz. *See* free jazz

Ayler, Albert, 208, 215

Azuma, Eiichiro, 21, 42, 47, 48

Baba, Russel Hisashi, **199**; Brown and, 215, 216; expressing one's message, 199–200; *gagaku*, 196, 199, 202; jazz and, 198, 234; Space Shuttle Omnibus, 186, 203; style of, 236; *suona*, 234; *taiko* and, 198–200

Barbour, Alecia D., 145–46

Bay Area, 214–15; artists of, 214–15; free jazz, 188, 234; importance to Japanese American musicking, 186; Jazz Fest 1982, 234–35; Togi's *gagaku* class, 196

Between Two Empires (Azuma), 42

big band music. *See* swing band music (big band)

biological racism, 44

biwa (lute), 135; Abe, 233; in concentration camps, 132; Hiroshima (band), 230–31; Issei musicking, 32, 33, 134; Nisei musicking, 64–65. *See also* Chikuzen *biwa*

Black Artists Group (BAG), 175, 198, 204

Black Arts Movement (BAM), 173, 177, 183, 222

Black Lives Matter movement, 266

Black music. *See* African American music

Blackness, 110, 175, 182, 184
Black Panther Party (BPP), 178, 222, 237, 239
Black Power movement, 188
blues, 120–21, 180–81, 197, 214, 220, 235. *See also* African American music; rhythm and blues (R&B)
Bohlman, Philip V., 124
Bon odori, 132, 263, 264
Boy Scouts, 81, 88, 106, 143, 147
Braxton, Anthony, 197, 223
Brown, Anthony, 213–20; Asian Improv Records, 187; *Big Bands behind Barbed Wire*, 11, 217, 252; *Don't Lose Your Soul*, 215; "E. O. 9066 (Truth Be Told)," 216–18, 252; *Family*, 215, 216; on free jazz's connection to politics, 188–89; *Go for Broke! A Salute to Nisei Veterans* (Mirikitani), 218; "Never Again! (Mo, Shimasen!)," 216–17, 252; *1945: A Year of Infamy*, 219; *We Insist! Freedom Now Suite*, 219. *See also* Anthony Brown's Asian American Orchestra (AAO)
Brown, Charles, 177
"Buddhahead Blues" (Masunaga), 119–20, 152
Buddhism: Abe, 122; Cage and Harrison, 193; in camps, 72; conservative Nisei, 163; gongs, 206, 234; *hōraku* ceremony, 242; importance of aesthetics, 29; *kinnara* (study group), 245; role of church in Nisei identity development, 60–61; *shōmyō* (chanting), 195; *taiko* and, 137, 241, 243, 245; Zen, 226. *See also* Kinnara Buddhist Taiko (KBT); Obon festivals
Buddhist churches: Nisei and, 39, 75–77, 103, 117; sponsoring concerts, 63; Young Men's Buddhist Association, 39, 77, 85, 116, 247; Young Women's Buddhist Association, 39, 85. *See also* Senshin Buddhist Temple
butoh. *See* dance
buyō (classical Japanese dance), 64, 131, 132, 133, 135–36

Cadman, Charles Wakefield, 80
California: Alien Land Law (1913 and 1920), 26, 46, 112; American Loyalty League, 113; Asian American movement in, 231–33; Boy Scout drum and bugle corps, 81; "California-Japanese War (1900–1941)," 28–29; Florin, 71; Hiroshima (band), 172; Japanese agricultural workers, 24, 25–27, 34; propaganda about the "disloyals," 141; *taiko* ensembles in, 172; Visions (band), 235–37. *See also individual names*
California State University, Long Beach, 232
Callahan, Mat, 173–74
Canal Camp, 124–25. *See also* Gila River Relocation Center (Arizona)
capitalism, 46, 177, 188, 237, 238
Casa Loma Orchestra, 84
Chicago Association for the Advancement of Creative Musicians (AACM), 175
Chicanos, music to identify with, 228
Chihoko, Nakajima, 33
Chikuzen *biwa*, 33, 67, 72. *See also biwa* (lute)
Chin, Charlie, 172, **180**, 235, 237. *See also* Joanne, Chris, and Charlie (trio)
Chinese Exclusion Act, 24–25
Chinese music, 208, 216–17. *See also sheng*
Christianity: assimilation and, 49; churches as community centers, 93; church-sponsored concerts, 63; church support for Nisei musicking, 75–76; hymn singing, 37, 38, 39, 40, 77, 88, 91, 108, 146; Nisei members, 117; role in Americanization, 88; role of church in Nisei identity development, 60–61; role of church in Nisei socialization, 93
chromodal discourse, 193–94
circular breathing, 197–98
citizenship: Blacks and Indians excluded, 44; classes in camps, 166; denied to Nisei women, 113; eligibility for, 26, 28, 45, 46, 112; and Issei's relationship to United States, 41, 161–62; myth of performative citizenship, 126; nationality tied to ethnicity, 44; naturalization and, 25, 28, 45, 46–47, 50; needed for WRA's Community Councils, 162; Nisei's dual (Japan/US), 112–13, 131; permanent residency, 26–27; questionnaire to recruit interned Japanese Americans, 139–40; racial politics of, 43–47; Sansei's reframed in Asian American movement, 172–73. *See also* Issei
civic ostracism, 17, 18, 168, 178
Civil Liberties Act (1988), 223, 283n41
civil rights, 133, 139, 222
civil rights movement, 174, 176, 189
class: Americanization into middle class, 88; antagonism within Japanese community,

116; assimilation, 49, 50; biculturalism, 37–39; binary view of race, 17; in camps, 161–62; European classical music, 78; Japanese musical genres, 136–37; middle class, 7, 38–39, 61, 90, 91, 92, 97, 109, 141; musicking and, 30; Nisei and, 7, 57, 58–59, 61, 92; tension over Japanese imperialist intentions, 52

classical Japanese music, 163

Coleman, Ornette, 189; harmolodics, 188, 192–93; influence on G. Horiuchi, 222

Collins, Ray, 186

colonialism, 184; Japan's mercantilism, 42–43

Coltrane, John, 189; Brown and, 214; *Love Supreme* (album), 222; musical reaction to political upheavals, 117, 222; quartal harmonies, 192–93

communism, 114

concentration camps: art in, 126–28; Buddhism in, 72; compensation to internees, 283n41; conditions, 120, 121–22; cultural politics of music in, 122–26; Department of Justice camp, 98; effect on musical careers, 73; finding an instrument, 148, 150, 160; Girl Scout drum and bugle corps, 142, **143**; *Hidden Legacy*, 136; Kabuki performances in, 31; *kenkyû-kai* (a study society), 124, 125; Latin American refugees, 264; locations of, 123; map of, **121**; music about, 11, 209–12, 216–17, 218, 224, 252; music education in, 132–34, 143, 144–45, 156; musicking in, 129; numbers of interned, 152; oppositional consciousness, 167, 178; religious institutions in, 146; role of musicking in, 121–22, 128–30; segregation in, 140–41, 178; size of, 126; sociopolitical dynamics in, 161–66; *wa* (social harmony), 139

Concert of a Thousand Cranes Festival, 210. *See also* Executive Order 9066; Gila River Relocation Center (Arizona); Granada Relocation Centre (Amache); Heart Mountain Relocation Center; JACL (Japanese American Citizens League); Jerome Camp (Arkansas); Manzanar Relocation Center; Minidoka Relocation Center (Idaho); musical communities; Poston War Relocation Center (Arizona); Rohwer Camp (Arkansas); Topaz Prison Camp; Tule Lake Relocation Center

Confucianism, 21, 29

Consul of Japan, 66, 67

Creative Music Studio (CMS), 175

cuatro (four-string plucked lute), 240

cultural citizenship, 133, 134, 138, 159

cultural fusion style of music, 227–28

cultural nationalism, 14, 175, 177, 178, 183–84, 189. *See also* nationalism, Japanese

dance: Akamatsu, 103; Bon, 35, 137–38; *butoh* (dance theatre), 197, 257; *buyō* (classical Japanese dance), 64, 131, 132, 133, 135; in camps, 135–36, 147–49, 153; in circles, 265; Issei musicking, 35; jitterbug, 91, 93–94, 107, 147–48, 153, 156; Kabuki, 38–39; *kenbu* (sword dance), 64–65, 96; *kouta* (short lyrical songs), 137; *natori* (certificates of accredited mastery), 105, 136; Nisei and, 63, 83, 94, 96; *nōmai* (folk, masked dance drama), 242; Obon, 35, 137, 210, 262; Obon odori, 132, 263, 264; *ondo*, 74, 75; *shimai* (dancing), 69, 70, 103; taxi dances, 83; Winfield Summit, 235. *See also* swing band music (big band)

dance band music. *See* swing band music (big band)

Daoism, 194

dekaseginin (sojourners), 23

Delgado, Manuel, 177

Dessen, Michael, 175

Detroit, 175, 276n12

dimensionality, 223

discrimination: affect on assimilation, 41; effect in rural areas, 117; of farmers, 109; Japan's ban of labor emigration to US, 26; naturalization, 46–47; through the law, 28. *See also* racism

Dolphy, Eric, 189, 201

East Wind, 184, 232

education of Asian children: attending Japanese-language school, 88, 92, 95, 99, 104, 109, 114–15, 116, 141; public schools, 46, 51, 61, 63; *shushi* (moral education), 115. *See also* music education

Ellington, Duke, *Far East Suite* (with Strayhorn), 218

emigration, to United States. *See* Issei

Endo, Kenny, 187, 196, 203, 254–59

engeikai (talent shows), 64–65, 137. *See also* Minidoka Relocation Center (Idaho)
Enriquez, Lucia, 182–83
"E. O. 9066 (Truth Be Told)" (Brown), 216–17
erhu (two-stringed bowed lute), 208
espionage, 143, 218, 293n108
eugenics, 44, 45, 110
European classical music: in camps, 143–44; education, 99–100, 103; entry into mainstream America, 107, 109; opera, 78, 79, 80, 81, 91, 104; staple in Japanese American homes, 108; popular with Issei and Nisei, 90–91
Executive Order 9066, 123, 163, 210, 216–17
exoticism, 75, 110. *See also* Orientalism; Otherness
experimental music, 174, 193, 252

FandangObon festival, 262, 263, 264–66, **267**
fandango son jarocho, 263, 264
farmworkers movement, 174
fascism, 114
Filipinos, 123, 195, 201, 202, 229
First Voice, 205, 213
Flores, Quetzal, 264–65
folk music, as music as means to educate, 238. *See also* Joanne, Chris, and Charlie (trio)
Foster, Stephen, 70, 88, 97, 108
free jazz: affinity shared between Asian Americans and African Americans, 175; approaches to, 236; Bay Area, 188, 234; G. Horiuchi, 220, 222; resistance strategies as inspirational, 184; United Front, 204; as vehicle of expression, 188–91
Frizzell, Louis, 144, 145, 159
fue (Japanese transverse flute), 217
Fujii, Sei, 115
Fujino, Diane, 178
Fujiwara, Yoshie, 78–79, 80
Fukui, Yoneichi, 148
Furutani, Alan, 235–36. *See also* Visions (band)
Furutani, Marsha, 235–36. *See also* Visions (band)
Fusco, Coco, 179, 185, 207, 261

gagaku (ancient court music): Abe, 233; Baba, 198, 199, 202; Brown, 215, 216; *hichiriki* (double-reed pipe), 200, 207, 208, 211; Ichikotsu-cho, 216–17; Izu and, 206, 207–8; Jazz Fest 1982, 234–35; *shō* (Japanese mouth organ), 208; *taiko*, 208, 252; Togi, 196, 255
gaimenteki dōka, 49
gender: attracting Nisei men to performances, 68; Buddhism adoption of the YMCA model, 39; in camps, 127; citizenship denied to Nisei women, 113; *engeikai* (talent shows), 64; girls' clubs, 75; identity politics, 18; instrument preferences, 79; Issei bachelors, 162; in Issei entertainment, 34; in Issei musicking, 35; Japanese musical genres, 136–37; Kabuki, 71; language classes, 166; music as career, 81; in Old Japan culture, 41; permanent residency and marriage, 26–27, **27**; in *taiko*, 251; teenage socialization, 94, 96
George Igawa Orchestra, 148, 151. *See also* Igawa, George
Ghost Festival, 209
gidayū, 30, 132
Gidra, 184, 228, 230, 232
Gila River Relocation Center (Arizona), **121**; banquet in honor of Hirokane, 124, 125; disunity between classes, 161–62; Issei Night, 137; music education, 69; teaching Japanese arts, 135–36; two camps at, 154
gongs, 35, 197, 206, 234, 235, 243
Granada Relocation Center (Amache), 136, 146, 151, 156
Grant, Madison, 45
Grayson, Kathryn, 92
Gregory, Sarita, 174–75

Hanayagi, Michiya, 136
Hansen, Arthur A., 124
hapa (mixed-race), 213
happi, 249
Harmonaires, 147, 149–50, 151, 153–54. *See also* Mikados of Swing
harmonica bands, 81, **160**, 160–61
Harrison, Lou, 193
Hawaii: buddhahead, 120; folk songs, 220–21; internment population, 157; Japanese contract laborers in, 24, 35; Japanese emigration, 26; *Life behind Barbed Wire* (Soga), 123; music considered American vernacular, 143; Nisei and Kibei, 164;

number of confinement sites, 121; slack-key guitar, 254; Taiko Center of the Pacific (TCP), 258
Hawaiian-string bands, 157
Hayase, Susan, 242
Hayashi, Art, 104, 149–50
Hayashi, Eitetsu, 257–58
Heart Mountain Relocation Center, 148, 151, 154, 220, 224
hichiriki (double-reed pipe), 200, 207, 208, 211
Higaki, Paul, 152
Hirabayashi, P. J., 246–47, 248–51, 253
Hirabayashi, Roy, 246–47, 249
Hirano, George, 149
Hirashiki, Teruko, 79
Hirokane, Chota, 124
Hiroshima (band), 172, 195, 226–31, 235, 236, 237. See also Kuramoto, Dan; Kuramoto, June
Hiroshima, Japan: bombing of, 210–11, 217, 219, 239; immigrants from, 24, 35; inspiration for Hiroshima (band), 228
Ho, Fred, 179
hōgaku hayashi (nō and Kabuki theater drumming), 256, 257
hole hole bushi song, 35, 220–21
Hongo, Garrett, 36
Horiuchi, Glenn, 71, 187, 220–26
Horiuchi, Makoto, 195, 196, 201, 203, 236
Houn, Fred, 187, 188, 207
Hussain, Zakir, 207

ie, 51
Igawa, George, 152, 154. See also George Igawa Orchestra
Iijima, Chris, 114, 172, 179–81, **180**, 235, 237–38, 239–41. See also Joanne, Chris, and Charlie (trio)
Iijima, Kazu, 114, 239
imperialism, 42–43, 47–48, 77, 115, 182, 238. See also anti-imperialism
improvisation: African American music, 175, 183, 185, 188, 189–90, 194; Baba and, 202; Brown and, 215–16, 219; cross-cultural communication, 179; importance of, 190–94; Izu and, 208; *Ohm: Unit of Resistance* (United Front), 204; pentatonic scale and, 230. See also free jazz
Inouye, Keith, 241

Inouye, Kyo, 37, 79
internationalism, 159. See also nationalism
Issei: acculturation encouraged through Western music lessons, 37–39; and the aesthetic self, 29; "aliens ineligible for citizenship," 26, 46, 112; apoliticism of, 90, 109; collectivism in camps, 125, 139; communities of descent, 131–32; denial of citizenship based on race, 46–47; denial strengthened ties to Japan, 161–62; doubt regarding assimilability of Japanese, 124; effect of legal discriminatory laws, 51; emigration to United States, 23–29, 24, **24**, 25, **25**; *engeikai* (talent shows), 64–65, 137; European music-appreciation as cultural acclimation, 146; farmers, 24, 25, **25**, 27–28, 50; *fukuinkai*, 37; and Kibei power relations, 59–60; *Life behind Barbed Wire* (Soga), 123; patriotism, 51, 52; power in camps, 161–62; protection of rights as enemy aliens, 164–65; resistance to assimilation, 41, 112; responses to questionnaire to recruit Nisei, 139, 140; returning to Japan, 47, 59, 60; role in Japanese expansion, 47–48; sojourners (*dekaseginin*), 23, 59; surge of artistic activity in camps, 126–27. See also Horiuchi, Glenn
Issei identity: biculturalism, 37–39; binational identity, 21–23; choice of religion, 39; dual identities, 47–53; identity strengthened through music, 22–23; nurturing *Nippon seishin* (Japanese spirit), 63; *zaibei dōhō*, 22, 50, 53, 165
Issei musicking: *biwa*, 32, 33, 134; *bushi*, 35; collective identity, 168; engagement with Western musicking, 36–39, **38**, 108; *engeikai*, 37; identity strengthened through music, 22–23; Japanese folk music, 34–36; Kabuki performances, 30, **31**; *kayokyōku*, 53; *kenjinkai*, 35; radio programming, 40; *shigin*, 32, 134; singing, 33, 35–37, 41; studying Japanese music, 30, 32–35; view of performance, 21, 29–30; *yōkyoku*, 31–32
Iwanaga, Helen, 100, 109–10, 153
Iyer, Vijay, 187
Izu, Mark, **205**, 205–13; accomplishments and awards, 206, 213; Asian American Jazz Festival, 212; Asian Improv Records,

187; audience, 220; Brown and, 214–15, 216; *gagaku* and, 196; Japanese musical aesthetics, 206–7; *Last Dance*, 217–18, 252; Marron, 186; United Front, 204–5

JACL (Japanese American Citizens League): "constructive cooperation," 163; dance sponsor, 82, 83; founding, 113; Iijima and Miyamoto, 239–40; Kibei Nisei, 115; Nisei formed civic organization, 61; Nisei political activities, 57; Nisei Week, 73; promotion of Americanization, 113–14, 165–66, 168; recruiting Nisei, 63; scapegoat for camp problems, 164
Jang, Jon, 179, 187, 215, 216, 222, 225, 252
Japan: competition for dominance of Pacific region, 42–43; relations with United States, 111–12, 114
Japanese American Cultural and Community Center (JACCC). *See* Los Angeles
Japanese court music, 199, 200, 211, 212, 233. See also *gagaku* (ancient court music); *shō* (Japanese mouth organ)
Japanese folk music: agricultural laborers, 34–36; frequently heard in California, 195–96; *kumidaiko* (folk ensemble drumming), 256; *matsuri*, 252; *minyō* (folk songs), 195; *nōmai* (folk, masked dance drama), 242; *ondo*, 35, 74, 137; *taiko* and, 220–21, 235, 243. See also *taiko* (barrel drum)
Japanese militarism, 22, 51, 114, 115
Japanese supremacy, effect of, 28
jazz: Asian American Jazz Festival, 205–6, 210, 212, 215; Asian American Jazz Orchestra (AAJO), 210, 217; Baba and, 198, 234; experimental music and, 193; Fifth Stream Music, 218–19; influence on Abe, 233; Jigoku (club), 171, 201, 203, 220; melding cultural identities, 213–20; race records, 89, 110; Sansei musicking, 174. See also Aoki, Brenda Wong; Brown, Anthony; chromodal discourse; free jazz; improvisation; Izu, Mark; San Francisco; swing band music (big band)
jazz fusion, 174, 226, 230–31
jazz pop, 172
Jerome Camp (Arkansas), **121**, 127, 151, 154, 224
ji (backing rhythm), 243

Joanne, Chris, and Charlie (trio), 236, 237–40
jo-ha-kyū, 196, 202, 207
Jordan, Lewis, 186, 204–5, 220
jōruri (shamisen music of the puppet theater), 65
Jyorokusho, Kineya, 64, 68–69, 73, 136

Kabuki: enjoyed by Nisei families, 104; *hōgaku hayashi* (drumming), 256, 257; performances in camps, 31, 127, **136**, 136–37; performing, 71; Sansei exposure to, 195; *taiko* and, 243
kagura (Shinto ceremonial music), 207
Kaji, Bruce T., 145, 150–51
kakegoe, 249
kakko (hour-glass-shaped drum), 202, 234–35
Kamayatsu, Tib, 82
Kanazawa, Tomi, 79
Kanda, Minoru, 229, 241
Kāne, Kai (K. K.), 213
Kansuma, Fujima, 64
Karuk healing chant, 211, 212
Kasama, Rei, 69–70, 73
Kawahatsu, Masato, 209
Kawano, Hideo, 153
kayōkyoku (Western-inspired Japanese popular music), 53, 104, 279n39. See also *ryūkōka*
kenbu (sword dance), 64–65, 96
Kibei Nisei: assault accusation in camp, 124; communities of dissent, 159; and Issei power relations, 59–60; language skills, 69, 163–64; Norakuro Harmonica Band, 160; political stance of, 114; reasons for going to Japan, 56, 59; role in the family farm economy, 60; singing *shigin*, 59, 76–77. See also Nisei; Nisei, Americanization of; Nisei identity
Kikuchi, Charles, 157–58, 161
Kikuchi-Yngojo, Robert, 196, 241
Kim, Clare Jean, 17, 182
"Kimigayo" (His Imperial Majesty's Reign)/ Japanese national anthem, 66, 67, 68
Kimiyo, Kineya, 31
Kimura, Molly Miyako, 71–72, **72**, 73, 134–35
Kineya, Yasuyo, 66
Kinnara Buddhist Taiko (KBT), 233, 242, 243, 244, **244**, 245–46, 247–48, 250, 255

Kitano, Harry H., 51
Kitashima, "Sox," 149
kiyomoto (singing style), 69
Kobayashi, Yutaka, 92–99, 110
Kochiyama, Yuri, 167, 178, 239
Kodani, Masao, 21, 29–30, 233, 243, 245, 246
Kondo, Dorinne, 12, 174
koto (zither): author's relationship to, 173; Brown and, 215; in concentration camps, 131–32, 135; "Friends and Lonely Lovers" (Poggensee), 231; in *HIBAKUSHA! (Survivors)* (Izu), 211; Hiroshima (band), 229; Issei musicking, 32–33; J. Kuramoto, 227, 230; Jyorokusho, 64, 68, 69; Nisei's relationship with, 33, 90, 96, 102; Sansei's relationship to, 195, 196; transnationalism, 175–76
kumidaiko, 242, 244, 254, 256, 257
Kuramoto, Dan, 227, 228
Kuramoto, John, **228**
Kuramoto, June, 227, 230–31

Latinx: identifying with music, 227, 228; intercultural collaborations, 18, 172, 177, 180, 240
Lazarus, Emma, 52
Le Ballet Dembaya, 266
Leninism, 178, 232. *See also* Marxism
Lewis, George, 190, 197
Los Angeles: Amerasia Bookstore, 229–30, 233–34, 236; Boyle Heights, 95, 96, 106, 239, 263; Great Leap, 262, 263–64; important Japanese American city, 25–26; Japanese American Cultural and Community Center (JACCC), 173; Japanese Chamber of Commerce underwriting performances, 68; the Japanese Sandmen, 84–85; jazz fusion and Japanese émigrés, 231; Kabuki performances, 31; Little Tokyo redevelopment, 70–71, 73, 232; *Little Tokyo Suite* (G. Horiuchi), 223; "Little Tokyo Suite" (G. Horiuchi), 225, 226; local Nisei characteristics, 60; Los Angeles Japanese Orchestra, 79; "The Mikado Band," 37; "Music to Remember: A Tribute to Japanese American Musicians and Singers of the '40s" (performance), 151–52; Union of God's Musicians and Artists Ascension (UGMAA), 175. *See also* Senshin Buddhist Temple
Lydian chromatic concepts, 192

ma (aesthetic concept of silences), 196, 207, 248, 249
Maeda, Daryl J., 175, 182
manongs (bachelor Filipino workers), 187, 195
Manzanar Relocation Center: Abe and, 233; "Ballad for Americans" (Robinson), 159; Jive Bombers, 144, 150–51, 154–56; *Manzanar Voices* (G. Horiuchi), 224; music education at, 131–34; music facilities at, 144; Sierra Stars, 157; subversive performances at, 126
Maoism, 178
Marxism, 121, 178, 232, 238. *See also* Leninism
Masaoka, Miya, 184–85, 187, 191–92, 196, 215
Masunaga, Ernest Michio, 120, 152
Matsuda, Minn, 239
Matsui, Kazu, 231
McWilliams, Carey, 28
Merced Assembly Center, 152
Mercer, Jeanne, 200
Miharu, Bando, 136
mijuku, 21, 30
"Mikado Band, The," 37
Mikados of Swing, 83–84, 104, 147. *See also* Harmonaires
Miller, Glenn, 100, 107, 128, 150–51, 152
Minidoka Relocation Center (Idaho), 104, **121**, 147, 150, 151, 153–54, **160**, 160–61
Mirikitani, Janice, 184, 185, 217, 218
Mitchell, Roscoe, 184, 197
Miura, Tamaki, 78
Miyakawa, Agnes, 79–80
Miyamoto, Nobuko (Joanne), **180**; Black Lives Matter movement, 266–67; collaboration, 263–64; early life, 239; FandangObon, 262, 265; and Iijima, 237–38, 239–40; "We Are the Children" (with Iijima), 179–81
Miyauchi, John, 77
Mochizuki, Bokusei, 256
modal jazz. *See* free jazz
Modirzadeh, Hafez, 187, 190, 192, 207
Moore, Eddie, 186, 203
Mori, Johnny, 227
Moriya, Walter, 100–102, 108, 109–10
Muramoto, George, 116

Muramoto Wong, Shirley, 132, 133, 135
musical communities, 129–30, 167; of affinity, 130, 141–46, 158, 159–60, 167; of descent, 130–38, 167; of dissent, 130, 138–41, 159–60, 167
music education: in concentration camps, 132–34, 143, 144–45, 156; of European classical music, 99–100, 103; *Hidden Legacy*, 136; *natori* (certificates of accredited mastery), 31, 64–65, 69, 70, 256; of Nisei, 99–100, 105, 109; teacher-sponsored recitals, 65

Nagano, Chiye, 74
Nagasaki, Japan, 216–17, 219
Nagatomi Okabe, Shirley, 133–34
nagauta shamisen: G. Horiuchi, 223, 224; Kineya Jyorokusho, 68–69; Kabuki, 132; L. Nakano, 70, 224; teaching in camps, 132, 135–36; Y. Kineya, 31, 66. *See also* shamisen
naimenteki dōka, 49
Naka, Bob, **106**, 106–10
Nakamura, Noboru, 148
Nakamura, Sachiko, 198
Nakano, Lillian, 70–71, 73, 224, 226
Nako, Seiichi, 37
naniwa-bushi (popular narrative shamisen), 66, 74, 96, 132, 220
National Coalition for Redress and Reparations (NCRR), 71, 283n41. *See also* Redress/Reparations Committee (San Diego)
nationalism: Anglo-Saxon, 43, 44; Black, 188, 222; United States, 14. *See also* cultural nationalism; internationalism; transnationalism
nationalism, Japanese: *gunka* as propaganda tool, 41; Issei, 29, 41, 48, 162; Japanese militarism and, 51, 114, 115; in Japan Night concerts, 67–68; Kibei Nisei, 76–77, 115, 125; radio programming, 66; *shigin*, 32, 135; ultranationalism, 138
National Japanese American Student Relocation Council, 164
nation building, 16, 42, 43, 53
Native Americans, 17, 180, 211, 212, 254–55
New Year's (o-Shōgatsu), 66–67, 69, 86, 99, 102, 117
Nielson, Alex, 132–33

Nippon seishin (Japanese spirit), 63, 115–16, 132, 141, 165
Nisei: apoliticism of, 57, 90, 109, 115; challenges to unity, 163–64; employment, 60–61; family as stability, 157; farmers, 46, 209; food at home, 87, 95, 98–99, 102; importance of music to, 62–68; leasing of land, 27; life in rural areas, 97–102, 108, 109; life in suburbia, 102–3; movies, 92, 109, 110–11, 115; opposition to militarism in Japan, 114; population statistics, 55, 59, 62; shifting politics, 182; social and athletic clubs, 61, 77, 81–82, 96, 99; socializing, 103, 113; speaking English, 64, 115, 116; speaking Japanese, 99, 102, 115, 117, 141. *See also* Kibei Nisei; Nisei Week
Nisei, Americanization of: dancing, 94; doubt regarding assimilability of Japanese, 124; education about Japanese culture, 41, 49; food, 87; link with American popular music, 82, 87–90, 97, 102; into middle class, 109; promoted by JACL (Japanese American Citizens League), 113–14, 165–66, 168; proving their ability, 115; vision of Issei leaders, 48. *See also* assimilation
Nisei identity: as American, 99–100, 109, 116; American popular music and, 82–85, 87–90, 96, 102, 107, 158; bicultural, 133; Blackness and, 110; choice to be bridge between Asia and the United States, 102–3; difficulty in forming, 55–58; effect of incarceration on, 142; hybrid, 159; interview questions, 86; loyalty and, 112–13, 116, 122, 164; moving towards whiteness, 6, 18, 59, 110, 111; music performance to express political beliefs, 70–71, 73; not tied to interest in music, 105; politics of, 110–18; proving Americanness, 122; pull to Americanism, 56, 112–13; reconciling two contrasting cultures, 58–60; recruited for combat, 89, 139–40, 164, 168; shifting, 182; turn to Americanism, 116; unassimilability, 110
Nisei Melodians, 83, 84
Nisei musicking: aesthetic interest vs. identity based, 105, 107, 108–9; *biwa*, 64–65; dancing, 82, 93–94; *engeikai* (talent shows), 64–65; gender in music and art deemed

of "real worth," 41; harmonica, 81, 88; instrument preferences, 79; Japanese dance, **64**; Japan Night concerts, 67–68; learning to play *koto*, 9, 33, 120; music education, 99–100, 105, 109, 133–34, 144–45, 147; music performance to express political beliefs, 70–71, 73; music played at home, 88; and national belonging, 56; *Reminiscing in Swingtime* (Yoshida), 82–83; swing music (big band), 82, 83, 122, 151–52; traditional Japanese music, 63, 64, 68–69, 132, 133–34; *utai* (*nō* drama singing), 64–65; Western music, 37, 40, 78–86, 105

Nisei Progressives, 114

Nisei Week, 73–75, 221, 223

Nishida, Mo, 178

Nishijima Isamu, 30

Nobori, Larry, 151

Noda, Mamie, 146

nōkan (transverse flute), 202

Nomura, Mary Kageyama, 144–45

nō music: *hōgaku hayashi* (classical Japanese drumming), 256, 257; Okabe, 104; past, present, and future in, 207; *shimai* (dancing), 69, 70, 103; *utai* (singing), 64–65, 103, 132, 141; *yōkyoku* (singing), 31–32, 69–70, 132

Norakuro Harmonica Band, **160**, 160–61

Nozaki, Kiyoshi, 41

Nueva Canción, 240

Obata, Chiura, 127–28

Obon festivals, 35, 64, 137, 195, 220, 225, 263

o-daiko, 243

Oguchi, Daihachi, 243, 250

Oka, Francis, 184, 185

Oka, Seizo, 32, 34

Okabe, Sue, 56, 103–5, 108

Okagaki, Michael, 241

Okimoto, Daniel I., 58

Okinawa, Japan, 213–14

Oliver Club, 61, 77, 82

oppositional consciousness, 167, 178

oral histories. *See* Akamatsu, Haruko; Asai, Hisayo; Kobayashi, Yutaka; Moriya, Walter; Naka, Bob; Okabe, Sue; Takayanagi, May; Takayanagi, Taka; Uno, Kiku; Yoshida, George

Orientalism: and American identity, 43, 183; and American nationality, 45; the Asian body, 28, 110–11; Asians as unassimilable, 45; challenging the discourse on, 173; context for studying Japanese American musicking, 16. *See also* exoticism

Oshita, Gerald (G), 175, 186, 190–91, 196–98, 215, 216

o-Shōgatsu. *See* New Year's (o-Shōgatsu)

ostinatos, 188, 234, 266

Otherness, 19, 28–29, 50. *See also* exoticism

Ozaki, Otokichi Muin, 138

Palumbo-Liu, David, 43, 45

Park, Robert, 58

patriarchy, 23, 188

pentatonic scale (*kumoi-joshi*), 36, 196, 222–23, 225, 230, 234, 266

Persian (Iranian) music, 192, 193–94, 207, 218

Phillips, Brian, 225

Pomona Assembly Center, 152

Poston War Relocation Center (Arizona), **121**; importance of music at, 89; Kabuki in, 31; Music Makers, 89, 147, 149, 150, 151, 153, **153**; Nisei shared social affinity, 142; *Poston Sonata* (G. Horiuchi), 71, 224, 225; Rhythmaires, 148, 153; singing in, 36; size of, 153

Powell, Kimberly, 242

Puyallup Assembly Center, 147

Ra, Sun, 188, 189

race records, 89, 110

racism: binational identity thwarted by, 22; factor in musicking in camps, 129; FandangObon, 265; and farmers, 50, 99; identity and aesthetics, 174; Japanese media's response to, 62; Joanne, Chris, and Charlie (trio), 237, 238; multiethnic racially based alliances, 182; Nisei Progressives, 114; *The Passing of the Great Race* (Grant), 45; reason for wanting Japanese removed, 123; relationship to Anglo-Saxon nationalism, 44; replacement theory, 4; in rural areas, 99, 100; scope of effect on West Coast Japanese, 28. *See also* discrimination; Japanese supremacy, effect of; Orientalism; white supremacy

radio programming: affect on Brown, 214; Americanization through, 97; bicultural programming (KFWO), 40; big band music, 83, 88, 100–101; combining Japanese and European music, 73; Glenn Miller, 100, 107, 128; Hawaiian, 220; Hiroshima (band), 230, 231; The Japanese Sandmen band (KGER), 84–85; *Music Listening Hour*, 128; "Nisei Week Special" (KRKD), 74–75; purveyor of latest hits, 94; singing, 65–68
Rakuko, Nakamura, 32–33
Redress/Reparations Committee (San Diego), 223–24. *See also* National Coalition for Redress and Reparations (NCRR)
Reimichi, Hanayagi, 136
relative valorization, 17
repatriation to Japan, 167
rhythm and blues (R&B), 227, 229, 285n83. *See also* blues
Richard, Muhal, 190
Roach, Max, 219
Roberts, Tamara, 261
Robertson, Earl, 159
rock music, 105, 174, 214, 233, 250
Rohwer Camp (Arkansas), **121**, 127, 151, 154
rōkyoku. *See naniwa-bushi* (popular narrative shamisen)
Roosevelt, Theodore, 26
Rosaldo, Renato, 133
Roxworthy, Emily, 126
Russell, George, 192–93
ryūkōka, 34. *See also kayōkyoku* (Western-inspired Japanese popular music)

Sacramento, 31, 46, 51, 72, **72**, 85
Sakamoto, Art, 163
salsa, 208
Sams, George, 186
San Francisco: *1945: A Year of Infamy*, 219; Afro-Asian collaborations, 203–5; American Loyalty League (ALL), 113; cultural capital of Japanese American, 25; education of Asian children, 46; Fifth Stream Music, 218–19; Fillmore District, 171, 203–4, 220; free jazz, 188; importance to artists, 173–74; International Hotel (I-Hotel), 91, 184, 195, 296n66; Ito, 85; Japanese community in 1890, 23; jazz clubs in, 196; Jigoku (club), 171, 201, 203, 220, 254; Kearny Street Workshop, 184, 185, 195, 205–6, 212; local Nisei characteristics, 60; *nagauta* shamisen, 31; San Francisco J-Town Jazz Ensemble, 89; San Francisco Taiko Dojo, 200, 244, 247–48, 256; studying music, 63–64; Takeuchi, 85. *See also* Baba, Russel Hisashi; First Voice; Masaoka, Miya; Modirzadeh, Hafez; Oshita, Gerald (G)
San Francisco State University, 172, 177, 178
San Jose: importance in Japanese American musicking, 186; San Jose Taiko, 186, 210, 216, 217, 242, 244, 246–47, 250, 252; Yokohama, California (band), 241
Sansei: Asian American identity politics, 176–82; intercultural collaborations, 172, 177; learning Japanese music, 195–96; musical affinity with African American musicians, 171, 173, 174, 175, 184–85; shifting politics, 182. *See also* Asian American identity; Asian American movement
Santa Anita Assembly Center, 119–20, 145–46, 152
Santana, Carlos, 228
Santos, Duke, 204, 241
Sasaki, Lily Oyama, 55
saung (arched harp), 192
scientific racism, 45
Seattle: dance bands, 83–84, **84**, 147; JACL (Japanese American Citizens League), 113; numbers of Japanese in, 104; Progressive Citizens League, 113
segregation: in camps, 140–41, 178; effect on Nisei, 89, 111; of Japanese school children, 51, 63; relationship to Issei music preferences, 110; residential, 178; in Yakima Valley, 98
Seno, George, 79, **80**
Senshin Buddhist Temple, 233, 242, 243, 244, **244**, 245, 246
sexism, 237, 238
shakuhachi (bamboo flute): Abe, 233, 234; Akamatsu, 102; Brown and, 215; in concentration camps, 131, 132; Hiroshima (band), 229, 230–31; Issei musicking, 32, 33–34; Kinko, 34, 233; radio programming, 220; Sansei's relationship to, 195, 196, 197; transnationalism, 175–76

shamisen: G. Horiuchi, 220, 224–25; in *HIBAKUSHA! (Survivors)* (Izu), 211; Hiroshima (band), 229; *jōruri* (shamisen music of the puppet theater), 65; *naniwa-bushi* (popular narrative shamisen), 66, 74, 96, 132, 220; *Poston Sonata* (G. Horiuchi), 71; Sansei and, 195, 196. See also *nagauta* shamisen
Shelemay, Kay, 129–30, 167
sheng, **205**, 208, 211, 212, 216
shibai (play), 104, 132
Shibuya, Yoshindo, 144, 145
shigin (singing), 288n14; Issei, 134, 135; *kenbu* and, 96; Kibei Nisei, 59, 76–77; nationalism, 32, 135; Sansei, 195, 233. See also singing
shimai (nō drama dancing), 69, 70, 103
shime-daiko (a tunable shallow drum), 202, 243
Shin'ei, Wakita, 33
Shinto, 34, 146, 207, 243
Shiro, Joe, 147–48
shō (Japanese mouth organ), 206, 207, 208, 211, 212
Sho Tokyans, 82, 84, 154
Shōzō, Takaie, 31
Shunzō, Mitani, 78
shushi (moral education), 115
singing: arias, 104; *biwa* accompaniment, 33; of Christian hymns, 37, 38, 39, 40, 77, 88, 91, 108, 146; *enka* (Japanese popular music vocal style), 105; *fukuinkai*, 37; *hole hole bushi* song, 35; Issei farmers, 35–37; Issei musicking, 41; *kayokyoku*, 104; *kiyomoto* (singing style), 69; *kouta* (short lyrical songs), 137; Nisei Choir Festival, 77; radio programming, 65–68; *Songs My Mother Taught Me* (Yamauchi), 36; *utai* (nō-style) singing, 64–65, 103, 132, 141; *yōkyoku* (nō drama singing), 31–32, 132. See also *shigin* (singing)
social segregation: audiences for performances, 46, 75, 89; effect on Nisei, 61, 108; marriage, 46; residence, 28
Soga, Yasutaro, 123
Song, Jeff, 187
Space Shuttle Omnibus, 186, 203
Spencer, Robert F., 161
Spicer, Edward H., 165

Strayhorn, Billy, 218
structural racism, 50
Sufism, 194, 262–63
suona (double-reed wind instrument), 211, 216, 231, 234
Suto, Nobuko, 79
swing band music (big band): attending live performances, 89, 92, 94, 96, 107; bands in camps, 83, 144, 151, 156–57; *Big Bands behind Barbed Wire* (Brown), 11, 217, 252; Brown and, 214; camp bands playing outside of camps, 151, 154; "Don't Fence Me In," 154–55; Down Beats, 146; link with American popular music, 82, 87–90, 102; Nisei dancing to, 91, 92; radio programming of, 83, 88, 100–101; *Reminiscing in Swingtime* (Yoshida), 82–83, 89–90; role with urbanites, 108. See also dance; *specific bands*; *specific relocation centers*

tabla (S. Asian drum), 207, 215
Tada, Takao, 124
taiko (barrel drum), 241–54; Abe, 233; *atarigane*, 235, 243; Baba and, 198–200; Bon dances, 35; building drums, 246; composing process, 249; *dongo*, 221, 225; Edo-*bayashi*, 243–44, 256; Endo and, 255, 256–57; expression of Sansei's Buddhist practice, 241; *gagaku*, 208, 252; Hiroshima (band), 229, 230–31; *hōgaku*, 244; Horiushi's style compared to, 222; Japanese American identity and, 172, 200, 243; jazz and, 248–49, 250, 251–52, 256, 257; Jazz Fest 1982, 234–35; Kenny Endo Taiko Ensemble, 257–58; *kumi-daiko*, 242, 244, 254, 257; Mori, 227; Mount Shasta Taiko, 200; *nō*, 252; Obon, 137–38; Ondeko-Za, 248, 249, 257; *ostinato*, 234; popularity of, 176, 242, 246, 254; *Poston Sonata* (G. Horiuchi), 224; racial and ethnic backgrounds of practitioners, 242–43, 249, 253; San Francisco Taiko Dojo, 200, 244, 247–48, 256; San Jose Taiko, 186, 210, 216, 217, 242, 244, 246–47, 250, 252; Sansei's relationship to, 196, 242, 249, 250–51; *shime-daiko*, 202, 243; social action and, 246–47; the solo as marker of Japanese American *taiko*, 248–49, 250; Sukeroku Daiko, 243–45, 248, 256, 257; training, 245–46, 248, 258. See also Buddhism; Hawaii; Kinnara Buddhist Taiko (KBT);

ma (aesthetic concept of silences); San Francisco; Senshin Buddhist Temple
Takahashi, Helen, 82
Takahashi, Jere, 112, 182
Takaki, Ronald, 50
Takayanagi, May, 90–92, 107
Takayanagi, Taka, 90–92, 109
takebue (bamboo flute), 233–34
Takemitsu, Toru, 216
Taki, Kichitaro, 23
Takimoto, Sam, 241
Tamai, Shig, 143
Tanaka, Eddie, 157, **158**
Tanaka, Seiichi, 200, 256
Tanforan Assembly Center, 127, 153–54, 156, 157–58, 292n93
Tani, Kiyoshi, 125
Tapscott, Horace, 175, 222, 225
Taylor, Cecil, 192, 221–22, 223
Teraoka, Joy Takeshita, 148
Third World Liberation Front (TWLF), **177**; Abe's response to, 233–34; aftereffects of, 209; coalition politics, 177; context for rise in Asian American music, 194–95; cultural nationalism, 183–84; Joanne, Chris, and Charlie (trio), 238, 240; link to improvisation, 191; speaking at California State University, 232; student strike, 172, 173, 177–78, 181
Thomas, Dorothy Swaine, 164, 292n93
Tibetan drum, 202, 203
Togi, Suenobu, 200, 206, 233, 255–56
Topaz Prison Camp, 127, 128, 149, 151, 156–57
transculturation, 22, 53, 56–57, 206, 228–29
transnationalism, 5, 12–13, 14, 56–57, 175–76. See also *Between Two Empires* (Azuma); nationalism, Japanese
Troupe, Quincy, 171, 203–4
Tsuchiya, Eiji, 203
Tsuji, Tom, 152–53
Tule Lake Relocation Center, **121**; arts for direct purposes, 138; "Back to Japan" mission, 141; *biwa*, 134–35; Down Beats, 146, 151, 156; housing the "disloyals," 140–41; Issei planning Board, 162; payment to Japanese dance teacher, 133; Sierra Stars, 157; Starlighters, 151, 156; subjects studied in, 71; variety show in, 142–43
Tusler, Mark, 251

undōkai (picnics), 88
United States: anti-immigration sentiments, 168; Civil Liberties Act (1988), 223, 283n41; competition for dominance of Pacific region, 42–43; discourse of race, 17; fear of Japan's military prowess, 22; *hibakusha* (survivors), 211; Immigration Act of 1924, 25, 28, 112, 292n95; immigration policy, 44–45; majority-minority myth, 3–4; national identity preservation concerns, 43; Naturalization Act of 1790, 25; relations with Japan, 111–12, 114; response to Japan joining European Axis, 51–52. See also Bay Area; California; Executive Order 9066; *specific cities*
United States army: 442nd Battalion, 211, 218, 292n102; military base in Okinawa, 214; Nisei recruited for combat, 89, 139–40, 164, 168
Uno, Kiku, 95–97, 109
utai (*nō*-style singing), 64–65, 103, 132, 141

Valdez, Daniel, 228
Visions (band), 235–37

wa (social harmony), 125
Wakita, Kayoko, 131
Wanifuchi, Kenshu, 81
War Relocation Authority (WRA): Americanization of inmates, 136, 159, 163, 166, 168; Americanization program, 166; at Canal Camp, 125; encouraged musicking as pacifier, 123; financial support for bands, 150; policies caused identity shifts of inmates, 122; policy of "coerced assimilation," 138; position on Japanese cultural activities, 132–33; prisoners to govern themselves, 162, 163; questionnaire for combat recruitment, 139–40; resettlement program promoted by, 164; role in concentration camps, 122; treatment of inmates by, 129; volunteering band to play for outside events, 154
Waseda, Minako, 132
Watanabe, Gordon, 195, 196
Watanabe, Ruth, 145–46
Watanabe, Sadao, 197
Watanuki, H., 81
Watsonville YBA Orchestra, 100

White, Chickie, 147, 149
whiteness, 6, 18, 59, 110, 111, 182
white supremacy, 28, 50, 113, 188. *See also* racism
Williams, Brackette, 16
Wong, Deborah, 251, 275n8
Wong, Francis, 179, 187, 190, 194–95, 215, 216, 225

xenophobia, 22, 45, 53

Yamamato, Danny, 227–28, 234
Yamamoto, Kyokuso, **72**
Yamamoto, Todd, 151
yamato damashii. See *Nippon seishin* (Japanese spirit)
Yamauchi, Wakako, 36
Yamazaki, Paul: on African American improvisational music as inspirational, 189; on the Asian American Political Alliance (AAPA), 185; Brown and, 215; expressing one's message, 199–200; *gagaku* and, 196; on improvisation, 190–91; on Oshita's inventiveness, 198
Yasokiyo, Kineya, 31
Yasoyo, Kineya, 31, 69
Yellow Brotherhood, 232, 236, 240
YMCA (Young Men's Christian Association), 61, 93, 99
Yokokura, Yutaka, 231
yōkyoku (*nō* drama singing), 31–32, 69–70, 132
Yonsei, 105
Yoshida, George, 77, 82–83, **87**, 108, 109; Asian American Jazz Festival, 215; on dance bands, 147; importance of music for teenagers, 122; in *Last Dance* (Izu), 210; on link between American popular music and Americanization of Nisei, 87–90; music as healing, 149, 150; on playing swing as assertion of Americanness, 151; race records, 89, 110; on social affinity among Nisei, 142; using "Jap" self-referentially, 149
YWCA (Young Women's Christian Association), 61, 96, 99, 114

zaibei dōhō identity, 22, 50, 53, 165
Zaibei Nihonjinshi (The History of Japanese in America), 30

ABOUT THE AUTHOR

Susan Miyo Asai is professor emerita in the Music Department at Northeastern University in Boston, Massachusetts, and a third-generation Japanese American. Her primary research and writing focus is on the musicking of Japanese/Asian Americans and how it relates to their cultural identity. Asai's publications span Japanese folk performing arts, jazz-based music of Asian Americans, cultural politics of Japanese American musicking, and music as an effective medium in the struggle for social justice and agency among marginalized populations. Other scholarly interests include music of the African diaspora in Latin America and global popular music.

Asai's initial research in traditional Japanese music informed her understanding of the structure and aesthetics of this art form so important for analyzing and writing about the music of diasporic Japanese. Her book on Japanese folk performing arts—*Nōmai Dance Drama of Northern Japan: A Surviving Spirit of Medieval Japan*—was selected by Questia librarians as one of the fourteen best books on folk drama in 1999.

The article "Hōraku: Buddhist Performing Arts and the Development of *Taiko* Drumming in the United States," together with other articles and encyclopedic entries on Japanese American music, place Asai in the vanguard of research on the music making of this demographic. Her interest in the Asian American juncture with jazz culminated in authoring "Cultural Politics: The African American Connection in Asian American Jazz-Based Music" published in the journal *Asian Music*. Asai's other publications comprise "The Cultural Politics of *Issei* Identity and Music Making in California, 1893–1941," published in the *Journal of the Society for American Music*, and her film review of *Hidden Legacy: Japanese Traditional Performing Arts in the World War II Internment Camps* featured in the *International Journal of Asian Studies*. The most current articles penned by Asai are "The Sonic Politics of Interracial Coalitions" and "Raising the Imperative of Direct Action" as part of an anthology entitled *At the Crossroads of Music and Social Justice*. She coedited this volume with Brenda M. Romero, Katelyn E. Best, David A. McDonald, and Andrew G. Snyder for Indiana University Press's Activist Encounters in Ethnomusicology and Folklore Series.

www.ingramcontent.com/pod-product-compliance
Lightning Source LLC
Chambersburg PA
CBHW030605230426
43661CB00053B/1855